# INSTANT JAVASERVER PAGES™

# Instant JavaServer Pages™

*Paul Tremblett*

**McGraw-Hill**
New York   San Francisco   Washington, D.C.
Auckland   Bogotá   Caracas   Lisbon   London
Madrid   Mexico City   Milan   Montreal   New Delhi
San Juan   Singapore   Sydney   Tokyo   Toronto

**Library of Congress Cataloging-in-Publication Data**

Tremblett, Paul.
    Instant JavaServer pages / Paul Tremblett.
        p.   cm.
    ISBN 0-07-212601-9
    1. JavaServer pages.   2. Web sites—Design.   I. Title.
TK5105.8885.J38 T74   2000
005.7'2—dc21                        00-036827

*McGraw-Hill*

*A Division of The McGraw-Hill Companies*

1 2 3 4 5 6 7 8 9 0  AGM/AGM  0 5 4 3 2 1 0

P/N 0-07-212599-3   PART OF ISBN 0-07-212601-9

*JavaServer Pages ™ is a trademark of Sun Microsystems, Inc.*

*The sponsoring editor for this book was Rebekah Young, the editing supervisor was Curt Berkowitz, and the production manager was Clare Stanley. It was set in Century Schoolbook by Victoria Khavkina of McGraw-Hill's desktop composition unit in cooperation with Spring Point Publishing Services.*

*Printed and bound by Quebecor/Martinsburg.*

To my beloved wife, Eleanor, who started me on a wonderful journey I would have had neither the self-confidence nor courage to embark upon myself, and who encouraged and supported my every step along the way.

# CONTENTS

# PREFACE

In just a few short years, Java has become the language of choice for Web-based applications. JavaServer Pages technology fills the gap between the power of Java on the server and the flexibility of HTML on the browser. It does so by allowing separation of content and presentation. This separation permits Web designers and programmers to work together to achieve a common goal without getting in each others way and without forming a hurtful dependency on each other.

In recognition of the fact that the world is not defined by Web servers and browsers, JSP does not limit itself to HTML. It can be used equally well to deliver XML between components of enterprise applications or to deliver WML (the Wireless Markup Language) to wireless devices.

This book is designed to introduce you to JavaServer Pages technology and to help you start using it as quickly as possible.

## How the Book Is Organized

The first chapter introduces JavaServer Pages technology and presents some simple examples. The elements of JSP are presented in the second chapter. The remainder of the book shows how you can use JSP to solve a variety of common real-world problems. If you install, execute, and study each of the sample applications, you will use all of the elements presented in Version 1.0 of the JSP specification.

Appendices A and B help you create an environment in which the sample code can be run. Appendix C presents the JSP API, and, since the sample code uses some of the Servlet API, relevant portions of this API are presented in Appendix D. Appendix E presents the contents of the CD.

## Who Should Read This Book

This book is designed for those programmers who learn best by doing. The syntax of the JSP elements and what each element does, is presented in the first two chapters. The remainder of the book is devoted to what programmers work with every day—code.

## About the Sample Code

Isolated code "snippets" may serve to illustrate syntax, but they are not as valuable as complete applications and so the latter were chosen for use in the book. Admittedly, the sample applications are not models of good design; their purpose is to illustrate some ways in which JSP can be used. If, after running the sample code, you are stimulated into thinking "OK, I see how that was done, but I can take it way beyond that" then the sample code will have served its intended purpose.

One definition of bug-free code is code for which the conditions that cause failure have not yet been identified. There is little doubt that bugs will be found. The code that you find on the CD is also available for download from www.instantjsp.com. The code from this site will reflect any changes that have been made to correct bugs as they are found.

## A Look to the Future

For any technology to be successful, it must grow. The JavaServer Pages technology is doing just that. The book was written using version 1.0 of the JSP Specification. The specification for version 1.1 has been published and JSP has a new role as an integral part of Java 2 Enterprise Edition. If you examine this spec, which is available from java.sun.com/products/jsp/download.html, you will see that JSP can now support complex Web sites that are fully integrated with enterprise class applications.

# ACKNOWLEDGMENTS

I would like to thank my parents, who are responsible for my love of reading. That alphabet quilt has opened more doors than you ever could have imagined.

I must also thank my wife for tolerating the temporary widowhood thrust upon her as I wrote this book. There just aren't enough words in the dictionary, Ellie; so let me just say thanks.

Finally, I would like to offer a very special thank you to Adrian Colyer, whose transatlantic tips, pointers, code corrections, and constructive criticisms made such an important contribution to this book.

—PAUL TREMBLETT

# INSTANT JAVASERVER PAGES™

# An Introduction to JavaServer Pages

- Date and Time Displays
- Checkboxes and Radio Buttons
- Listboxes

In this chapter, we learn what JavaServer Pages (JSP)™ are and how they work. We see the benefits of using JavaServer Pages and compare JSP to ASP (Active Server Pages). By examining several code samples and the output they generate, we can learn some of the simpler elements of JSP.

# What Are JavaServer Pages?

In the early days of the Web, the pages you viewed when you visited a typical site could best be described as electronic brochures. The content was static and once you had seen what a site had to offer, you had little incentive to revisit the site.

So what kind of a Web site might you want to visit more than once? If a stock you are following wasn't performing well yesterday and you want to see how it's doing today, a site that delivers near-real-time stock quotes is a site you'd want to revisit. If your upcoming Caribbean vacation looks like it might be threatened by a hurricane, a site that shows the current and projected position of the storm is a site you'd want to check a few times before you packed. If you've had your eye on a new printer that was priced just beyond your budget, a site that offers frequent sales is a site you'd want to check at least once a week. What do these sites have in common that brings you back? The answer is *dynamic content that reflects real-world conditions.*

The earliest attempt at generating dynamic content was the Common Gateway Interface (CGI), which relied on Perl scripts or C programs that ran on the server. The write statements of these languages—`print` in Perl and `printf` in C—made dynamic generation of HTML possible but did not necessarily make the Web designer's job easier. Web designers were not likely to be programmers. One solution to this problem was to let the Web designer create HTML templates containing special tags indicating where dynamic content should be inserted. The Perl or C code would then read and parse the template files, performing substitutions where indicated before sending the HTML to a browser. The problem with this was the performance penalty associated with reading the template files, which contributed to the performance degradation resulting from loading the Perl interpreter or C program each time a request was received. Another problem with CGI was that it is stateless. The equivalent of a session was usually implemented by keeping track of the contents of hidden fields that were passed back and forth between the client and server. The burden of session management was placed on the programmer and there were almost as many solutions to the session management problem as there were programmers. The third and possibly the most serious problem with CGI was that business logic was contained in the same code that was responsible for the presentation layer. A change in one could possibly affect the other.

Java servlets solve two of the problems associated with CGI. The first is *performance*. A servlet is loaded once, either when the server starts or when the first request for the servlet is received by the server or, in some cases, when a new version of the servlet is made available. The second is *session management*. The servlet container automatically generates a unique identifier for each user. It also provides a means of associating this identifier with a session object in which application-specific data can be stored and keeping track of these identifiers and associations. The servlet programmer can concentrate on business logic and presentation and use a well-defined API to access session services. Dynamic generation of HTML is accomplished by servlets in exactly the same manner as by CGI code—using write statements. It's all done using the `print()` and `println()` methods. The presentation layer is embedded in the program code.

Separation of the presentation layer is addressed by JavaServer Pages. A JSP page is a text-based document that describes how to process a request to create a response. The description intermixes fixed template data with some dynamic actions. The JavaServer Pages Specification builds on the framework provided by the Java Servlet Specification. The semantic model underlying JavaServer Pages is that of a servlet. The most common implementation involves a translation phase that is performed only once and a request processing phase that is executed once per request. The translation phase usually uses the contents of the text document to create a class that implements the `javax.servlet.Servlet` interface and has the same life cycle as a servlet. A JSP container, which is a component installed on a Web server or Web-enabled application server delivers a request received from a client to the `_jspService()` method of the class derived from the JSP page. This method, which is the compiled form of the dynamic actions specified in the source JSP document, prepares a response that is delivered to the client via the JSP container.

As examples we will be studying make clear, JavaServer Pages are most often used to generate HTML. However, you should not infer from this that JavaServer Pages are limited to generating HTML. They can be used to generate any textual output. For example, in the world of business-to-business e-commerce JavaServer Pages can be used to generate

XML documents. With wireless connectivity to the Internet becoming more common, we could even use JavaServer Pages to generate Wireless Markup Language (WML) to communicate with handheld devices like mobile phones.

# How Are JavaServer Pages Accessed?

We already know how to access static HTML pages. We type a Uniform Resource Locator (URL) such as http://dormouse.instantjsp.com/SimplePage.html. The browser uses the Hypertext Transport Protocol (HTTP) to send a request for the contents of `SimplePage.html` to a Web Server running on host dormouse in the domain instantjsp.com. The Web Server retrieves the file and transmits it back to the browser, which uses the HTML tags in the file to visually render the page.

A client requests a JavaServer page in a similar manner specifying a file extension of `.jsp` instead of `.html`. The URL we mentioned before would thus become http://dormouse.instantjsp.com/SimplePage.jsp. The request is delivered to a JSP-capable Web Server or Web-enabled Application Server, which recognizes the `.jsp` extension and forwards the request to a JSP container, which invokes the `_jspService()` method of the compiled JSP page. The response from the `_jspService()` method is sent back to the JSP container, which sends it back to the client. Notice that we did not say that the request for the JavaServer Page originated from a browser. Most often it does, but it can also originate from a servlet or another JSP page.

*NOTE:* *Although the term "JSP page" is redundant, it is widely used by developers and so is used throughout this book.*

# The Benefits of Using JSP Technology

The most important benefit JSP pages offer is the ability to separate program logic from look and feel. A major problem that plagued Web sites in the early days of the Web and, to a large extent, even today was that pages produced by artists were attractive but lacked functionality. On the other hand, pages produced by programmers were functional but lacked the visual appeal necessary to attract visitors. Pages produced as the result of a collaborative effort between programmers and graphic designers solved this problem but proved to be problematic when it came to maintenance. A graphic designer often found it impossible to change the look and feel of a site without involving a programmer. Similarly, the programmer sometimes discovered that changing program logic affected the look and feel. Using JSP, both parties can truly work independently of each other.

Another important benefit is to be found in the phrase that so succinctly states Java's claim to fame—Write Once, Run Anywhere™. By virtue of their ultimate translation to Java byte code, JSP pages are *platform independent,* which means that they can be developed on any platform and deployed on any server.

JSP pages also make it easy to embed reusable components. Components such as JavaBeans and Enterprise JavaBeans that perform specialized tasks can be developed once and incorporated into any number of JavaServer Pages. Just imagine for a moment that you are assigned the task of developing a Web application whose primary purpose is to provide a modern user interface for a legacy system. You might spend a significant amount of time evaluating commercial Enterprise JavaBeans to enable your JSP pages to communicate with CICS or to perform 3270 terminal emulation or you might decide to develop your own. If your next assignment is to do the same for another legacy system, you simply include in your JSP pages those directives necessary to use the Enterprise JavaBeans you purchased or developed. In addition to reusable components, JSP pages can statically or dynamically include other JSP code.

JavaServer Pages technology is now an integral part of the Java 2 Enterprise Edition (J2EE), which brings Java technology to enterprise computing. By using JSP pages to construct your Web site, you can create a front-end component of the type of powerful N-tier applications made possible by J2EE.

Another benefit is the extensibility made possible by custom tag libraries. In addition to action types that are standard and must be implemented by all conforming JSP containers, Version 1.0 of the JSP specification provides a `taglib` directive that can be used to introduce new action types. This approach simplifies the efforts of the JSP container developer and shortens the learning time of the JSP author. The specification further states that future versions of the JSP specification will contain a tag extension mechanism to be used to describe the semantics of all nonstandard actions. Version 1.1 of the JavaServer Pages Specification provides more detail on how the taglib directive will be implemented. Taglib support is guaranteed to work across all JSP containers—it can be loaded dynamically and does not rely on preprovided support from the vendor who supplied the JSP container.

JSP elements defined in a tag library can be exposed at design time as controls in page composition tools. Tag libraries can also be used by JSP authoring tools.

# When Is It Appropriate to Use JavaServer Pages?

We have already said that JSP pages facilitate separation of business logic from look and feel. It is wise to consider this each time you are deciding whether to write a servlet or use a JSP page. After you see the power of JavaServer Pages, you may well be tempted to subscribe to the idea that, since the JSP pages are translated and compiled into a class that implements javax.servlet.Servlet anyway, why not use JSP for everything. By doing so, you'll come full circle back to the point where business logic and look and feel are implemented in the same code. If you remember that servlets are appropriate for business logic and JSP pages for presentation, you'll make the proper design decisions.

# JSP and ASP—A Comparison

JavaServer Pages was not the first and is certainly not the only server-side scripting technology. One of the more widely used scripting technologies is Active Server Pages (ASP) from Microsoft. JSP and ASP are both viable alternatives to CGI and are similar in that the end product of each is dynamically generated HTML; however, there are significant differences between the two. Table 1-1 shows a comparison between JSP and ASP.

**TABLE 1-1**

Comparing JSP
and ASP

|  | JSP | ASP |
|---|---|---|
| Platforms | Any platform to which Java has been ported (Solaris, Linux, Windows NT, Mac OS, AIX, HP-UX and a variety of other UNIX variants) | Microsoft Windows (third-party porting products are available for some other platforms) |
| Web Server | Any (more popular examples include Apache, Netscape, IIS) | Microsoft IIS or Personal Web Server |
| Scripting Language | Java | VBScript, JavaScript |
| Reusable, Cross-Platform Components | JavaBeans, Enterprise JavaBeans | NO |
| Memory Leak Protection | YES | NO |
| Customizable Tags | YES | NO |
| Database Integration | Any database that supports JDBC or ODBC technology | Any ODBC-compliant database |
| Components | JavaBeans, Enterprise JavaBeans, extensible JSP tags | COM |

## Some Simple Examples

Sample code is an effective leaning tool and is used extensively through-out this book. Each of the samples consists of one or more JSP pages and, in some cases, HTML. Source codes for Java classes are also shown where appropriate. The page(s) displayed in a browser when each sample is run is also shown.

All of the samples were written to conform to Version 1.0 of the JavaServer Pages Specification. Appendix A shows you how to load and configure the server software required to run the sample code; any browser may be used.

### The Obligatory Hello World

The study of almost every modern computer language begins with the ubiquitous "Hello World." Here is a JavaServer Page that displays that famous message:

```
<html>
<head>
<title>Hello World</title>
</head>
<body bgcolor="#FFFFFF">
<font face = "Arial, Helvetica"><font size="+2">
<br>
<br>
<br>
<center>
<b>
Hello World!
<p>
I'm ready for some Instant JSP!!!!
</b>
</center>
</font>
</body>
</html>
```

Figure 1-1 shows how you would request this JSP page using a browser. When the page executes, it produces the output shown in Figure 1-2. Now, if you are looking for differences in the contents of Hello.jsp and the HelloWorld.html you wrote when you first learned HTML, you will find none. That's because all text in a JSP page that is not a JSP ele-

**Figure 1-1**

Requesting a JSP Page

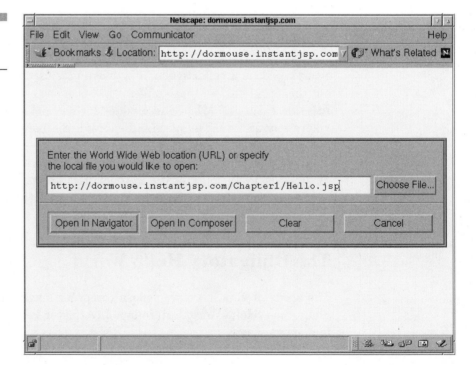

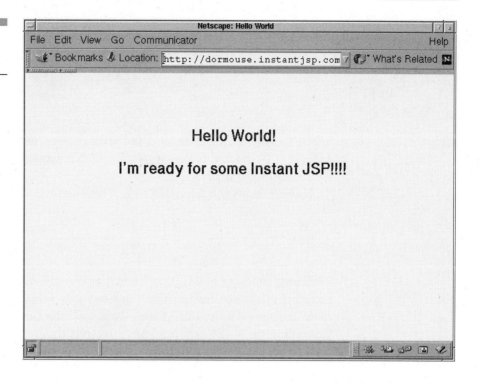

ment is treated by the JSP container as fixed template data and is passed verbatim back to the client.

## Does Anybody Really Know What Time It Is?

Now we take a look at a sample that goes beyond simple HTML and, more important, produces dynamic output. This sample displays the date and time at the moment you requested the page. Here is the code:

```
<html>
<head>
<title>What Time Is It?</title>
</head>
<body bgcolor="#FFFFFF">
<font face = "Arial, Helvetica"><font size="+2">
<center>
<br>
<br>
<br>
<br>
<b>
You requested this page on
```

```
<%=
new java.util.Date()
%>
</b>
</center>
</font>
</body>
</html>
```

When you store this code in a file with a .jsp extension (we'll choose DateTime.jsp) and access it using a Web browser, it produces the page displayed in Figure 1-3.

Take a look at the following code from the preceding sample:

```
<%=
new java.util.Date()
%>
```

This code block is a scripting element. We will encounter a variety of scripting elements but for now you need only know that a scripting element begins with the tag <% and ends with the tag %>. The = character that follows the <% start tag indicates that this scripting element is an

**Figure 1-3**
Output from
DateTime.jsp

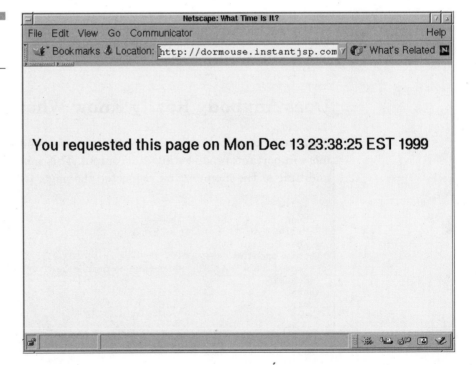

*expression.* You will notice that the code in the expression is the Java code required to create an instance of Date that represents the date and time at which it was created. The result returned from the evaluation of this expression is coerced into a string and becomes what you view in Figure 1-3.

To further understand what's happening, take a look at Figure 1-4, which contains the HTML source that was delivered to and rendered by the browser. As you can see, all of the text in DateTime.jsp was, as we mentioned when we looked at Hello.jsp, treated as fixed template data and passed along unchanged. A string containing the current date/time has replaced the scripting element.

## And Now Let's Hear from You

The samples we have examined so far have dealt with data from the server side. What about data originating from the client? Look at the following HTML code contained in the file EchoName.html:

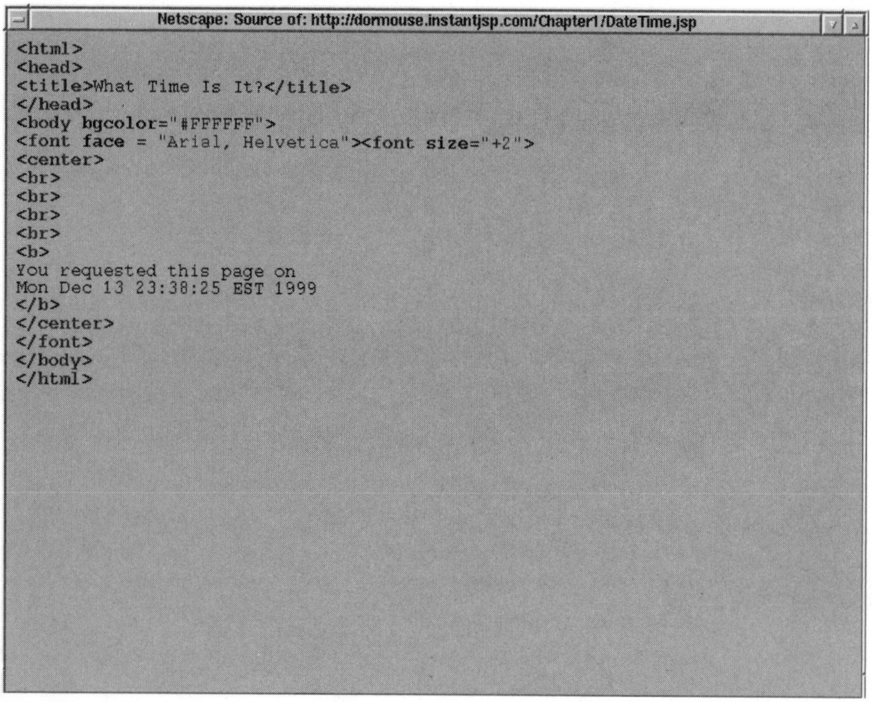

**Figure 1-4**
HTML Generated by
DateTime.jsp

```
Netscape: Source of: http://dormouse.instantjsp.com/Chapter1/DateTime.jsp
<html>
<head>
<title>What Time Is It?</title>
</head>
<body bgcolor="#FFFFFF">
<font face = "Arial, Helvetica"><font size="+2">
<center>
<br>
<br>
<br>
<br>
<b>
You requested this page on
Mon Dec 13 23:38:25 EST 1999
</b>
</center>
</font>
</body>
</html>
```

```
<html>
<head>
<title>Echo Name</title>
</head>
<body bgcolor="#FFFFFF">
<form method="post" action="EchoName.jsp">
<br>
<br>
<br>
<center>
<b>
Enter your name here:
<input name="userName" type="text">
<br>
<br>
<br>
<input type="submit" name="submit" value="ENTER">
</b>
</center>
</form>
</center>
</body>
</html>
```

This HTML code produces the page shown in Figure 1-5. The only element in the code that might not look familiar to you is the value of the

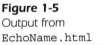

**Figure 1-5**
Output from
EchoName.html

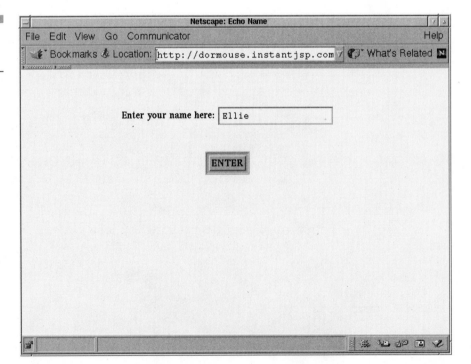

action attribute of the <form> tag. This action indicates that the form is to be processed by the JSP page in file EchoName.jsp. This JSP page is shown next.

```
<html>
<head>
<title>Echo My Name</title>
</head>
<body bgcolor="#FFFFFF">
<font face = "Arial, Helvetica"><font size="+2">
<br>
<br>
<br>
<center>
<b>
Well hello there,
<%= request.getParameter("userName")%>
!!!
</b>
</center>
</body>
</html>
```

Let's look at the line that reads:

```
<%= request.getParameter("userName")%>
```

By now you know that the characters <%= identify this line as an expression. The expression is the result returned by the getParameter() method of request. But what exactly is this request object? The only object we've encountered up to now is an instance of Date. We can account for that object quite easily because we instantiated it. So where did request come from? The answer is that every JavaServer Page has access to a number of objects called implicit objects and the request object is one such object. Table 1-2 contains a list of the implicit objects available to a JSP page. We discuss the column labeled "Scope" later.

The request object is an instance of HttpServletRequest and the getParameter() method we are invoking is inherited from ServletRequest. According to the JSDK documentation, this method returns a string containing the lone value of the specified parameter (userName). The value "userName" represents the name assigned to the text entry field defined by the following tag in the HTML form in EchoName.html:

```
<input name="userName" type="text">
```

The value the user enters is passed as a request parameter to the Web

**TABLE 1-2**

Implicit Objects

| Implicit Variable | Of Type | What It Represents | Scope |
|---|---|---|---|
| request | protocol-dependent subtype of javax.servlet.ServletRequest (e.g., javax.servlet.HttpServlet-Request) | The request triggering the service invocation | request |
| response | protocol-dependent subtype of javax.servlet.ServletResponse (e.g., javax.servlet.HttpServlet-Response) | The response to the request | response |
| pageContext | javax.servlet.jsp.PageContext | The page context for this JSP | page |
| session | javax.servlet.http.HttpSession | The session object created for the requesting client (if any) | session |
| application | javax.servlet.ServletContext | The servlet context obtained from the servlet configuration object [as in the call getServletConfig(). getContext()] | application |
| out | javax.servlet.jsp.JspWriter | An object that writes into the output stream | page |
| config | javax.servlet.ServletConfig | The ServletConfig for this JSP | page |
| page | java.lang.Object | The instance of this page's implementation class processing the current request | page |

server as part of the HTTP POST. The servlet API, and hence JSP, makes this available via the getParameter() method.

Figure 1-6 shows what is displayed after you enter your name and click on the ENTER button. As you saw before, the HTML is simply passed along and the result of evaluating the expression is converted to a string, which is inserted in the position that was occupied by the expression.

### Dealing with Missing Data

The sample we just examined works, except if we forget to type something into the text field before we click on the ENTER button. So now let's look at code that handles this situation.

**Figure 1-6**
Output from
EchoName.jsp

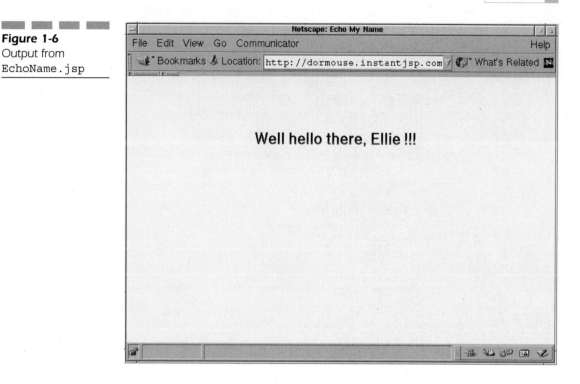

```
<html>
<head>
<title>Echo My Name</title>
</head>
<body bgcolor="#FFFFFF">
<center>
<b>
<font face = "Arial, Helvetica"><font size="+2">
<br>
<br>
<br>
<%
 String name = request.getParameter("userName");
 if (name.length() == 0) {
%>
Error - No name entered!
<%
}
else {
%>
<%= "Well hello there, " + name + "!!!" %>
<%}
%>
</b>
</center>
</body>
</html>
```

This code, which we will save in a file called `EchoName2.jsp`, introduces us to yet another JSP element—the *scriptlet,* which is a code fragment that is executed at request-processing time. You can recognize a scriptlet by the presence of the `<%` start tag and the `%>` end tag with no special character following the start tag.

The first scriptlet in the preceding code is:

```
<%
 String name = request.getParameter("userName");
 if (name.length() == 0) {
%>
```

The second scriptlet is:

```
<%
}
else {
%>
<%= "Well hello there, " + name + "!!!" %>
<%}
%>
```

It is important that you understand that a scriptlet is not necessarily a full block of code; it can be (and most often is) a fragment. The specification requires that the concatenation of all scriptlets in a JavaServer Page in the order in which they appear must yield a Java statement or series of statements considered syntactically valid by a Java compiler.

Unlike expressions, which are always evaluated and coerced into a string that is inserted into the HTML stream, scriptlets may or may not produce output. Scriptlets can create and modify objects; they can determine which portions of a page are included in the HTML that is sent to the requester; or, they can iteratively generate output (such as the rows of a table).

Although it is indeed possible to perform complex tasks using scriptlets, you should avoid doing so. Remember that one of the goals of JSP is separating business logic from the presentation. You should place business logic inside embedded components and use scriptlets sparingly to aid the presentation. You should treat scriptlets as the JSP programmer's glue.

Now let's look at just what takes place when our two scriptlets are compiled and executed. The `getParameter()` method of the implicit object `request` returns a string that is stored in the variable name. Next, the value returned by the `length()` method of the String object name is tested for a value of zero in an `if` statement. Now comes something that may seem strange and even confusing at first but will make sense shortly—we add an end tag and terminate the scriptlet. Why? To answer that, we must refine what we said earlier about the HTML elements of a JSP page simply being "passed along." In actual truth, such elements are translated into Java statements that look like:

```
out.println("HTML element");
```

Such a statement sends the HTML element to `out`, which we have already seen was described in Table 1-2 as an instance of javax.servlet.jsp. JspWriter that writes into the output stream.

As we already stated, an expression is evaluated and coerced into a string but rather than simply being passed along, it too appears in a Java statement that looks like:

```
out.println(expression);
```

When we terminate one scriptlet, insert an HTML element consisting of a simple string, and then code another scriptlet containing a nested expression, the translator produces the following code to the Java compiler:

```
String name = request.getParameter("userName");
if (name.length() == 0) {
out.println("Error - No name entered");
}
else {
  out.println(name);
}
```

This code compiles properly. If we had not terminated the first scriptlet, we would have passed the following to the compiler:

```
String name = request.getParameter("userName");
if (name.length() == 0) {
Error—No name entered!
```

The compiler would have complained about the line following the `if` statement and execution of the JSP page would have resulted in an error.

Now let's modify `EchoName.html` so that the form is processed by `EchoName2.jsp`. Here is the modified HTML, which we will store in the file `EchoName2.html`.

```
<html>
<head>
<title>Echo My Name</title>
</head>
<body bgcolor="#FFFFFF">
<form method="post" action="EchoName2.jsp">
<br>
<br>
<br>
<center>
<b>
<input name="userName" type="text">
<br>
<br>
<br>
<input type="submit" name="submit" value="ENTER">
</b>
</center>
</form>
</body>
</html>
```

Now when you access EchoName2.html and click on the ENTER button
without entering a name, instead of seeing a blank page you see the page
shown in Figure 1-7.

**Figure 1-7**
Output from
EchoName2.jsp

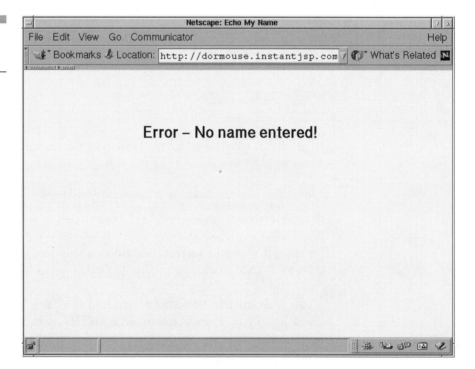

### Dealing with Missing Data—An Alternate Approach

The error screen displayed by EchoName2.jsp when required data are missing is only a small improvement over the blank screen displayed by EchoName.jsp. We next examine an alternate approach to handling missing data, an approach that provides the user with a way to go back and enter the missing data. Examine the following JSP page, which we will save in file EchoName3.jsp:

```
<html>
<head>
<title>Echo My Name</title>
</head>
<body bgcolor="#FFFFFF">
<center>
<b>
<%
 String name = request.getParameter("userName");
 if (name.length() == 0) {
%>
<%@ include file = "NoData.jsp" %>
<%
}
else {
%>
<br>
<br>
<br>
<font face = "Arial, Helvetica"><font size="+2">
<%= "Well hello there, " + name + "!!!"%>
<%}
%>
</b>
</center>
</body>
</html>
```

The new code introduced in this sample is:

```
<%@ include file = "NoData.jsp" %>
```

The presence of the start tag <% tells you that this is a scripting element. The @ character following the start tag identifies this particular scripting element as a directive, the purpose of which is to send a message to the JSP container. The message in this case is to insert the text found in the file NoData.jsp into the current JSP page at translation time. The include directive is analogous to the #include so familiar to C programmers.

One advantage provided by the include directive is that of *code reusability*. If you have a number of JSP pages that require code to handle missing data, instead of including the error-handling code in each JSP page, you can write the code once and use the `include` directive to instruct the JSP container to insert it at translation time.

**NOTE**: *Although code reusability is good, component reusability is more desirable. Later, when we discuss Beans, we see that there is a better approach to handling missing data.*

Another advantage is that of simplification of code maintenance. Suppose a user requested that you change the wording of an error message. If the code that generates this error message appears in multiple places, you are faced with the task of identifying every file containing such code and modifying it. One problem with this approach is that there exists a very real possibility that you will miss at least one file, which will be found by the user at the worst possible moment. Another problem is that the more code you change, the greater the likelihood you will introduce an error into code that had been working. Using the `include` directive enables you to make the required change in a single file.

The contents of the file `NoData.jsp` are shown next:

```
<br>
<br>
<br>
<h1>Missing Data</h1>
<br>
<b>
Click on the button below to retry your request.
</b>
<form method=get action="EchoName3.html">
<input type=submit name="submit" value="OK">
</form>
```

To use the JSP page containing the `include` directive, we modify our HTML file to look like:

```
<html>
<head>
<title>Echo My Name</title>
</head>
<body bgcolor="#FFFFFF">
<form method="post" action="EchoName3.jsp">
<br>
<br>
<br>
<center>
<b>
<input name="userName" type="text">
```

```
<br>
<br>
<br>
<input type="submit" name="submit" value="ENTER">
</b>
</center>
</form>
</body>
</html>
```

When we store this HTML code in a file named EchoName3.html, access it using a browser, and click on the ENTER button without entering data, we see the page shown in Figure 1-8. Notice that this page provides clear directions as to how the user should reenter the missing data. In our prior two versions, we assumed the user would guess that he or she should use the browser's BACK button.

**NOTE**: NoData.jsp *contains a hard-coded URL and so is not reusable. We address this issue later.*

**Figure 1-8**
Output from
NoData.jsp

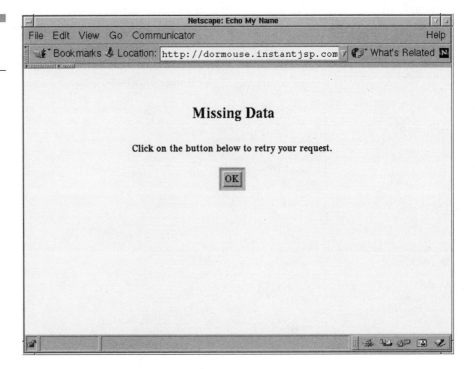

## Handling Multiple Data Elements

The data we processed from an HTML form in the cases we just studied consisted of a single item—the contents of a text entry field. Not all forms are that simple. Look at the HTML file named RadioButtons.html shown next. When requested from a browser, it displays the page shown in Figure 1-9.

```
<html>
<head>
<title>Radio Buttons</title>
</head>
<body bgcolor="#ffffff">
<form method="post" action="ExtractSingleValue.jsp">
<br>
<center>
<b>
<font face = "Arial, Helvetica"><font size="+1">
Click one of the radio buttons below:
</b>
</center>
<br>
<input name="singleValue" type="radio" value="red" checked>Red
<br>
```

**Figure 1-9**
Output from
RadioButtons.
html

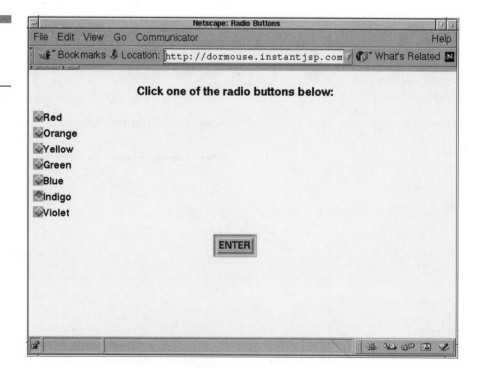

```
<input name="singleValue" type="radio" value="orange">Orange
<br>
<input name="singleValue" type="radio" value="yellow">Yellow
<br>
<input name="singleValue" type="radio" value="green">Green
<br>
<input name="singleValue" type="radio" value="blue">Blue
<br>
<input name="singleValue" type="radio" value="indigo">Indigo
<br>
<input name="singleValue" type="radio" value="violet">Violet
<br>
<br>
<center>
<input type="submit" name="submit" value="ENTER">
</b>
</center>
</form>
</center>
</body>
</html>
```

You can see that the page contains three radio buttons with the same name. Here is a JSP page that uses the name assigned to the radio buttons to determine which one is selected:

```
<html>
<head>
<title>Radio Buttons</title>
</head>
<body bgcolor="#FFFFFF">
<center>
<b>
<font face = "Arial, Helvetica"><font size="+2">
<br>
<br>
The color you selected is
<%=
 request.getParameter("singleValue");
%>
</b>
</center>
</body>
</html>
```

Since, by definition, only one of a group of radio buttons with the same name can be selected at a time, the expression request.getParameter ("singleValue") displays this value. When this JSP page is executed as the result of clicking on the ENTER button in Figure 1-9, the page shown in Figure 1-10 is displayed.

Here's another HTML file named Checkboxes.html that generates the page shown in Figure 1-11. It is similar to Figure 1-9 but contains checkboxes. Unlike radio buttons, for which only one may be selected

**Figure 1-10**
Output from
`ExtractSingle-
Value.jsp`

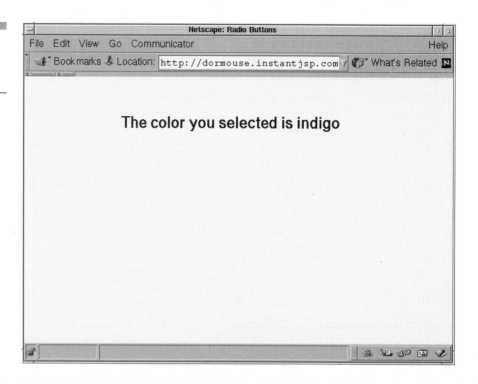

**Figure 1-11**
Output from
`Checkboxes.html`

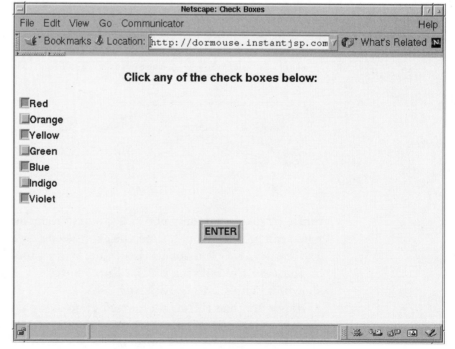

from a group of buttons bearing identical names, any number of check-boxes in a group of identically named boxes can be checked.

```html
<html>
<head>
<title>Check Boxes</title>
</head>
<body bgcolor="#ffffff">
<form method="post" action="ExtractMultipleValues.jsp">
<br>
<center>
<b>
<font face = "Arial, Helvetica"><font size="+1">
Click any of the check boxes below:
</b>
</center>
<br>
<input name="multipleValues" type="checkbox" value="red" checked>Red
<br>
<input name="multipleValues" type="checkbox" value="orange">Orange
<br>
<input name="multipleValues" type="checkbox" value="yellow">Yellow
<br>
<input name="multipleValues" type="checkbox" value="green">Green
<br>
<input name="multipleValues" type="checkbox" value="blue">Blue
<br>
<input name="multipleValues" type="checkbox" value="indigo">Indigo
<br>
<input name="multipleValues" type="checkbox" value="violet">Violet
<br>
<br>
<center>
<input type="submit" name="submit" value="ENTER">
</b>
</center>
</form>
</center>
</body>
</html>
```

Here is the JSP page invoked by `Checkboxes.html`. Because multiple values are possible, we use a `for` loop to iterate across the array `names` in which such values are returned by the `getParameterValues()` method. The length of the array is the number of checked boxes.

```html
<html>
<head>
<title>Check Boxes</title>
</head>
<body bgcolor="#FFFFFF">
<center>
<b>
<font face = "Arial, Helvetica"><font size="+2">
<br>
```

```
<br>
You selected the following color(s):
<br>
<br>
</b>
</center>
<%
 String[] names = request.getParameterValues("multipleValues");
  for (int i = 0; i < names.length; ++i) {
%>
<%= names[i] %>
<br><br>
<%
  }
%>
</b>
</body>
</html>
```

When this JSP page executes, it produces the output shown in Figure 1-12.

Another way to provide a way to select multiple choice is the Multiple Select listbox. The HTML that presents such a listbox is shown in Figure 1-13.

**Figure 1-12**
Output from
Checkboxes.html
(from checkboxes)

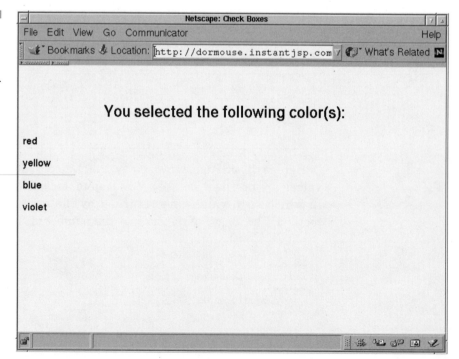

**Figure 1-13**
Output from
ExtractMultiple-
Values.html (from
Multiple Select listbox)

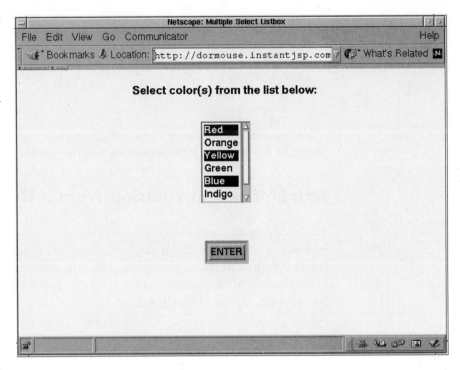

```
<html>
<head>
<title>Multiple Select Listbox</title>
</head>
<body bgcolor="#ffffff">
<form method="post" action="ExtractMultipleValues.jsp">
<br>
<center>
<b>
<font face = "Arial, Helvetica"><font size="+1">
Select color(s) from the list below:
</b>
<br>
<br>
<br>
<select name="multipleValues" size=6 multiple>
<option value="red" selected>Red
<option value="orange">Orange
<option value="yellow">Yellow
<option value="green">Green
<option value="blue">Blue
<option value="indigo">Indigo
<option value="violet">Violet
</select>
<br>
<br>
<br>
```

```
<br>
<input type="submit" name="submit" value="ENTER">
</b>
</center>
</form>
</center>
</body>
</html>
```

Notice that the action `ExtractMultipleValues` of the `<form>` tag points to the same JSP page used to handle checkboxes.

## Extracting Information from a Request

We have already seen that `request` is an implicit object that is an instance of the ServletRequest class, which contains a number of methods that return useful information about the request. The following code invokes several of these methods and produces the output shown in Figure 1-14. You might be thinking that this looks suspiciously like the output from the SnoopServlet you wrote when you first learned servlet programming. In fact, this is the JSP equivalent.

**Figure 1-14**
Output from
`RequestInfo.jsp`

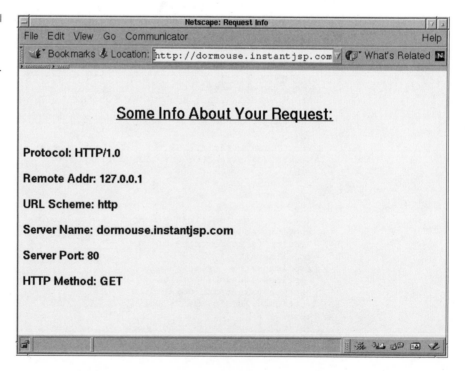

```
<html>
<head>
<title>Request Info</title>
</head>
<body bgcolor="#ffffff">
<br>
<br>
<font face="Arial, Helvetica"><b><font size="+2">
<center>
<br>
<b><u>Some Info About Your Request:</u></b>
</font></font>
</center>
<font face="Arial, Helvetica"><b><font size="+1">
<br>
<br>
Protocol:
<%= request.getProtocol() %>
<br>
<br>
Remote Addr:
<%= request.getRemoteAddr() %>
<br>
<br>
URL Scheme:
<%= request.getScheme() %>
<br>
<br>
Server Name:
<%= request.getServerName() %>
<br>
<br>
Server Port:
<%= request.getServerPort() %>
<br>
<br>
HTTP Method:
<%= request.getMethod() %>
</font>
</body>
</html>
```

# JSP—A More Detailed Look

- Page Directives
- Establishing Sessions
- Error Pages
- User Input
- Greetings

In this chapter, we explore JSP in greater depth. We discuss directives, actions, declarations, scriptlets, and expressions. We look at `request` and `response` objects as well as objects available to all JSP pages and the use of objects we create ourselves. We also see how to manage page resources using `jspInit` and `jspDestroy`.

# Directives

We have already seen that *directives* are messages to the JSP container. Directives, which do not produce any output to the current out stream, have the general syntax:

```
<%@ directive attributeList %>
```

The `attributeList` can be one or more occurrences of an attribute/value pair, which has the syntax `attribute="value"`.

## The page Directive

The `page` directive defines a number of page-dependent attributes and communicates them to the JSP container. The syntax of the page directive is:

```
<%@ page pageDirectiveAttributeList %>
```

The `pageDirectiveAttributeList` can contain either a single attribute/value pair or a number of such pairs. Table 2-1 lists the full set of page attributes and their allowable values. You have the choice of coding all your attribute/value pairs in a single `page` directive or distributing the attribute/value pairs among multiple `page` directives; however, you should be aware of one restriction. The JSP container creates a cumulative list of the attribute/value pairs contained in all of the page directives in a *translation unit*, which is a JSP source file and the source contained in files included via the `include` directive. If the cumulative list of attribute/value pairs contains multiple occurrences of any single attribute, a fatal error will occur. An important exception is the `import` attribute—you may use as many `import` attributes as you find necessary. We discuss the `import` attribute shortly.

**TABLE 2-1**

Page Attributes

| Attribute | Allowable Values |
|---|---|
| language | "Java" |
| extends | "className" |
| import | "importList" |
| session | "true \| false" |
| buffer | "none \| sizeKB" |
| autoFlush | "true \| false" |
| isThreadSafe | "true \| false" |
| info | "info_text" |
| errorPage | "error_url" |
| isErrorPage | "true \| false" |
| contentType | "ctinfo" |

### The `info` Attribute

Now it's time to see some uses of the page directive. Let's do a simple one first by creating a modified version of the famous Hello.jsp and saving it in Hello2.jsp. Here is the code.

```
<%@ page info="A JSP Page to Greet the World" %>
<html>
<head>
<title>Hello World</title>
</head>
<body bgcolor="#FFFFFF">
<font face = "Arial, Helvetica"><font size="+2">
<br>
<br>
<br>
<center>
<b>
Hello World!
<p>
I'm ready for some Instant JSP!!!!
</b>
</center>
</font>
</body>
</html>
```

When you access Hello2.jsp using a browser, you see the page displayed in Figure 2-1, which is identical to what you saw when you first

**Figure 2-1**
Output from
`Hello2.jsp`

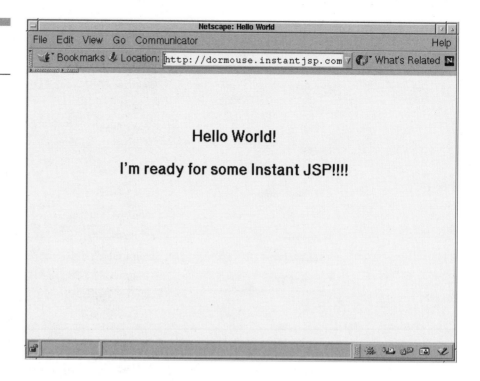

ran `Hello.jsp` in Chapter 1 (Figure 1-2). This reinforces the earlier statement that directives do not produce any output to the current `out` stream. This might cause you to question whether the `info` attribute of the `page` directive really serves any purpose. After all, couldn't a simple HTML comment have been used to document what the page is and what it does? To answer that question, we have to risk beating our simple `HelloWorld.jsp` to death by creating `Hello3.jsp`, which looks like this:

```
<%@ page info="A JSP Page to Greet the World" %>
<html>
<head>
<title>Hello World</title>
</head>
<body bgcolor="#FFFFFF">
<font face = "Arial, Helvetica"><font size="+2">
<br>
<br>
<br>
<center>
<b>
Hello World!
```

```
<p>
I'm ready for some Instant JSP!!!!
</b>
</font></font>
<br>
<br>
<br>
<font face = "Arial, Helvetica"><font size="+1">
The page that produced this greeting is described as:
<br>
<br>
<%= getServletInfo() %>
</font></font>
</center>
</font>
</body>
</html>
```

When you access this JSP page, you see the output shown in Figure 2-2. It differs from Figure 2-1 in that it contains the text specified as the value of the info attribute. The code that causes this text to be displayed in the browser is the expression:

```
<%= getServletInfo() %>
```

**Figure 2-2**
Output from
Hello3.jsp

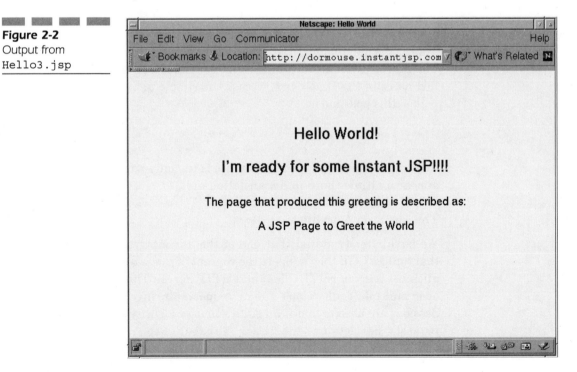

In a real-world application, you probably would not include such information in a Web page. However, you might want to write the information to a log. If you encounter an error, this is one way you could associate that error with a particular page.

### The `import` Attribute

To demonstrate use of the `import` attribute of the `page` directive, we will modify yet another of the JSP pages we created in Chapter 1. `DateTime2.jsp` looks like this:

```
<%@ page import="java.util.*" %>
<html>
<head>
<title>What Time Is It?</title>
</head>
<body bgcolor="#FFFFFF">
<br>
<br>
<font face = "Arial, Helvetica"><font size="+1">
It is now
<%=
new Date()
%>
</font>
</body>
</html>
```

This JSP page produces the same output as `DateTime.jsp` (Figure 1-3). The difference is that in this JSP page, instead of using the fully qualified name of the Date class, we use the simple name. The directive that makes this possible is:

```
<%@ page import="java.util.*" %>
```

Remember that the `import` attribute is the only page attribute that can appear multiple times in a translation unit.

### The `session` Attribute

We have already stated that one of the advantages of using servlets is that, unlike CGI, they support the concept of a *session*, which is an association between an HTTP Client and HTTP Server. This association persists over multiple connections and/or requests during a given time period. Sessions are used to maintain state and user identity across multiple page requests. Servlets use the `javax.servlet.http.HttpSession` interface to provide session services. Since the semantic model underlying a

JSP page is that of a servlet, a JSP page can participate in an HTTP session. The session data are maintained in the implicit object `session`, which is available to every JSP page by default; so, code in a JSP page can invoke any of the `session` object's methods. Here's a JSP page that invokes some of these methods:

```
<html>
<head>
<title>Session Info</title>
</head>
<body bgcolor="#FFFFFF">
<font face = "Arial, Helvetica"><font size="+2">
<br>
<br>
<br>
Session ID:
<%= session.getId() %>
<br>
<br>
Created:
<%= session.getCreationTime() %>
<br>
<br>
Last Accessed:
<%= session.getLastAccessedTime() %>
<br>
<br>
New:
<%= session.isNew() %>
</font></font>
<center>
<form method=get action="SessionInfo.jsp">
<input type=submit name="submit" value="REPEAT">
</form>
</center>
</body>
</html>
```

If we save this code as `SessionInfo.jsp` and make this the very first page we access after we start the JSP container, we see the output shown in Figure 2-3. Reloading the page results in Figure 2-4.

A JSP page's participation in session management is optional. If you do not want a JSP page to participate in an HTTP session, add the following directive to your code:

```
<%@ page session="false" %>
```

When this directive is present in a JSP page, the implicit `session` object is not available to the page and an attempt to use any of the methods of that object will result in an error. You can prove this by adding the direc-

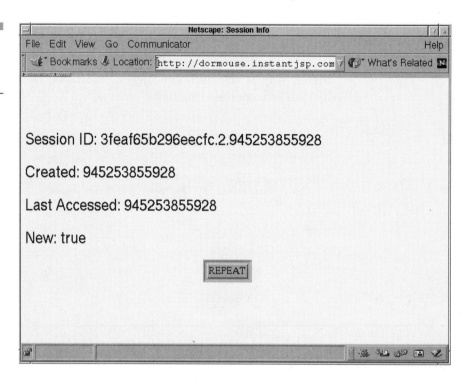

**Figure 2-3**
Output from First
Access of
SessionInfo.jsp

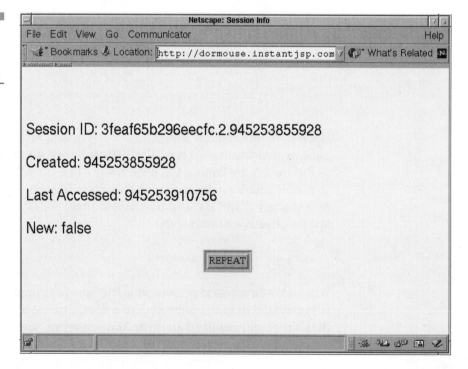

**Figure 2-4**
Output from Second
Access of
SessionInfo.jsp

tive to the preceding code and trying to run it. The default value of the
`session` attribute of the `page` directive is "true".

### The `buffer` Attribute

The `buffer` attribute specifies how the initial `out` JspWriter object handles content output from the page. The simplest value this attribute can
have is "none", in which case no buffering is performed and all output is
written directly through to the ServletResponse PrintWriter. The `page`
directive would read:

```
<%@ page buffer="none" %>
```

The other possible value for this attribute is a buffer size measured in
kilobytes. When a buffer size is specified, output from the page is written
first to a buffer of the specified size. The default value of the `buffer`
attribute is the attribute/value pair `buffer="8kb"`. What happens
when the buffer becomes full depends on the value of the `autoFlush`
attribute.

### The `autoFlush` Attribute

As we mentioned earlier, the `autoFlush` attribute controls what happens when output from a page is buffered and the buffer becomes full. If
the attribute has a value of "true", the buffer is flushed each time it
becomes full. If the attribute has a value of "false", an exception is raised
when buffer overflow occurs. The default value for the `autoFlush` attribute is "true". If you set `buffer="none"` and `autoFlush="false"`, you
will generate an error condition.

### The `isThreadSafe` Attribute

The `isThreadSafe` attribute lets the JSP container know how it should
dispatch requests to the page. Setting this attribute to "false" instructs
the container to dispatch only one request at a time to the page in the
order in which requests are received. Setting the attribute to "true"
informs the container that it may safely dispatch multiple outstanding
requests to the page simultaneously. It is very important that you understand that the value you assign to the `isThreadSafe` attribute is nothing more than your statement about the ability of your code to handle
multiple threads. Merely assigning a value of "true" does not cause code
that was never designed to handle multiple threads to undergo some
magical transformation. As a matter of good programming practice, you
should try to write all your code as if it will run in a threaded environ-

ment. If you are faced with a situation in which a class you are using is documented as not suitable for use in a threaded environment, then you should use isThreadSafe="false". The default value is "true".

The JavaServer Pages Specification makes the following important statement about isThreadSafe="false":

> If isThreadSafe="false", the JSP page implementation shall implement javax.servlet.SingleThreadModel, thus indicating that all requests dispatched to that instance shall be delivered serially to the service() method of the page implementation class.
>
> However, some implementation(s) may additionally use a pool consisting of multiple page implementation class instances to do load balancing. Therefore, even when indicating that the page is not thread safe, a page author cannot assume that all requests mapped to a particular JSP shall be delivered to the same instance of that page's implementation class. The consequence of this is that an author must assume that any mutable resources not private/unique to a particular page's instance may be accessed/updated simultaneously by two or more instances; thus any static field values, objects with session or application scope, or objects shared through some other (unspecified mechanism) by such instances must be accessed appropriately synchronized to avoid nondeterministic behaviors.

### The isErrorPage Attribute

The isErrorPage attribute works in conjunction with the errorPage attribute. It indicates that this page is intended to be the URL target of another page's errorPage attribute. If the value of errorPage is "true", then the implicit scripting language variable "exception" is defined and its value is a reference to the offending Throwable from the source JSP page in error. If the value of isErrorPage is "false" then the "exception" implicit variable is unavailable, and a fatal translation error will occur if you attempt to reference it within the body of the JSP. The default value is "false".

Here is SimpleErrorPage.jsp, which is an example of an errorPage attribute:

```
<%@ page isErrorPage="true" %>
<html>
<head>
<title>ERROR</title>
</head>
```

```
<body bgcolor="#ffffff">
<center>
<br>
<br>
<h1>ERROR!!!</h1>
<br>
<b>
<h2>
<%= exception.getMessage() %>
</h2>
</b>
</center>
</body>
</html>
```

### The `errorPage` Attribute

Exceptions that are thrown during the processing of a JSP page but not caught can be handled by another JSP page that has been designated as an `errorPage` (i.e., has `isErrorPage="true"`). An exception is passed to the page designated by the value of the `errorPage` attribute by saving a reference to the `Throwable` object in the common `ServletRequest` object by invoking the `setAttribute()` method using a name of "javax.servlet.jsp.ServletException".

Here is an example of a JSP page containing the `errorPage` attribute:

```
<%@ page info="Deliberately Bad Page" %>
<%@ page errorPage="SimpleErrorPage.jsp" %>
<html>
<head>
<title>Page With Deliberate Error</title>
</head>
<body bgcolor="#ffffff">
<%
  boolean tf = true;
  if (tf) {
    String info = getServletInfo();
    throw new Exception("Exception in " + info);
  }
%>
</body>
</html>
```

As you can see, the scriptlet throws an `Exception`. Since no `catch` statement is present, the `Exception` is passed to `SimpleErrorPage.jsp`, which has been designated as the `errorPage`. When this code is stored in file `PageWithDeliberateError.jsp` and accessed from a browser, it produces the output shown in Figure 2-5.

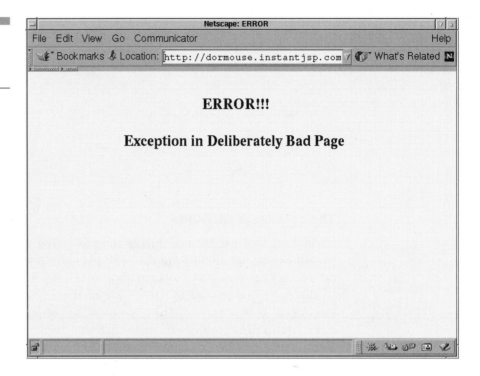

### The `contentType` Attribute

The `contentType` attribute defines the character encoding for the JSP page and for the response of the JSP page and the MIME type for the response of the JSP page. Values are either of the form "TYPE" or "TYPE; charset=CHARSET" with an optional white space after the ";". The value of CHARSET, if present, and TYPE, which is a MIME type, must be a permissible value as defined by the Internet Assigned Numbers Authority (IANA).

At the present time, most JSP pages generate HTML and, since the default value for TYPE is "text/html" and default value for the character encoding is ISO-8859-1, you usually will not see the `contentType` attribute. As use of JSP Technology for business-to-business e-commerce becomes more widespread, you can expect to encounter TYPE = "text/xml".

## The `include` Directive

We have already used the `include` directive in Chapter 1. It is used to insert text and/or code at translation time. The syntax is:

```
<%@ include file="relativeURLspec" %>
```

If you have stored your company's logo and code to retrieve and display a message of the day in a file named `banner.jsp`, you can incorporate the graphics and code in any page using the directive:

```
<%@ include file="banner.jsp" %>
```

An `include` file can contain any JSP elements and can even contain other `include` directives. The sum of a JSP source plus all of its `include` files is called a *translation unit*. You should keep in mind the restriction that multiple appearances of any `page` attribute except `import` in a translation unit results in an error.

**NOTE:** *A JSP container will detect changes made to a "root" JSP document and will automatically retranslate it. However, you should not rely on detection of changes to an* `include` *file, since this is implementation dependent.*

## The `taglib` Directive

Most providers of existing implementations of the JavaServer Pages Specification are still working on delivering an implementation of the `taglib` directive. IBM's WebSphere Application Server does include taglibs for database access and connection management. Version 1.1 of the specification makes the following statements about the `taglib` directive:

The set of significant tags a JSP container interprets can be extended to include custom tags with their own semantics. Such a collection is called a "tag library".

The `taglib` directive declares that the page uses custom tags, uniquely names the tag library defining them, and associates a tag prefix that will distinguish usage of those tags. The Uniform Resource Identifier (URI) identifying the tag library is associated with a tag library description.

A JSP container may "know of" some specific URIs and may provide alternate implementations for the tag libraries described by these URIs, but the user must see the same behavior as that described by the required, portable tag library description described by the URI.

If a JSP container implementation cannot find a tag library description for a given URI, a fatal translation error shall result.

It is a fatal translation error for the `taglib` directive to appear after actions using the prefix introduced by the `taglib` directive.

*Examples*: In the following example, a tag library is introduced and made available to this page using the super prefix; no other tag libraries should be introduced in this page using this prefix. In this particular case, we assume the tag library includes a doMagic element type, which is used within the page.

```
<%@ taglib uri="http://www.mycorp/supertags" prefix="super" %>
...
<super:doMagic>
...
</super:doMagic>
```

# Actions

As their name implies, *actions* cause something to happen. You will find two types of actions in the JSP specification. The first is the *standard* action, which is defined as an action that is always available regardless of the version of the JSP container or Web server. The second type of action is the *custom* action, which is implemented using the `taglib` directive. We now discuss the standard actions.

## <jsp:useBean>

The combination of fixed template data and scripting elements contained in JSP pages is rich in functionality. However, if you attempted to develop a complex system using only these elements, you'd quickly discover that such a solution would not be the best one. Complex systems usually involve databases and back-end systems with which you must communicate. Such communication is best handled by objects that transport data with no knowledge of the visual representation of the data. The useBean action provides you with a way to make an instance of such an object available to your JSP page as a scripting variable.

The syntax of the useBean action depends on whether the action has a body or not. First, let's look at the case when the action has no body. The syntax is:

```
<jsp:useBean id="name" scope="page|request|session|application"
typespec />
```

If the useBean action has a body, the syntax becomes:

```
<jsp:useBean id="name" scope="page|request|session|application"
typespec >

    body

</jsp:useBean>
```

The id="name" attribute/value pair has a special meaning to the JSP container. It is, in effect, an entry in a namespace table and, as such, it must be unique within a translation unit. The name that is the value assigned to id becomes a variable that is available for use by scripting elements.

The scope="page|request|session|application" attribute modifies the behavior of the id attribute. It determines the visibility of the object named by the id attribute. Table 2-2 shows the meaning of

**TABLE 2-2**

Scope Attributes

| Scope | Meaning |
|---|---|
| page | Objects with page scope are accessible only within the page where they are created. All references to such an object shall be released after the response is sent back to the client from the JSP page or the request is forwarded somewhere else. References to objects with page scope are stored in the pageContext implicit object. |
| request | Objects with request scope are accessible from pages processing the same request where they were created. All references to the object shall be released after the request is processed; in particular, if the request is forwarded to a resource in the same runtime, the object is still reachable. References to objects with request scope are stored in the request implicit object. |
| session | Objects with session scope are accessible from pages processing requests that are in the same session as the one in which they were created. It is not legal to define an object with session scope from within a page that is not session. All references to the object shall be released after the associated session ends. References to objects with session scope are stored in the session object associated with the page activation. |
| application | Objects with application scope are accessible from pages processing requests that are in the same application as the one in which they were created. All references to the object shall be released when the runtime environment reclaims the ServletContext. Objects with application scope can be defined (and reached) from pages that are not session aware. References to objects with application scope are stored in the application object associated with a page activation. |

each of the possible values of the scope attribute as described in the JavaServer Pages Specification. The default value is "page".

Possible values of typespec are:

class = "className"

class = "className" type = "typeName"

type = "typeName" class = "className"

beanName = "beanName" type = "typeName"

type = "typeName" beanName = "beanname"

type = "typeName"

The value of the class attribute specified by "className" is a fully qualified name of the class that implements the object.

The value of the beanName attribute specified by "beanName" is the name of a Bean as expected by the instantiate() method of the java.beans.Beans class. The value of "beanName" does not have to be hard-coded but can be a request-time attribute expression; in which case, instead of coding the value component of the attribute/value pair as value="hard-coded-value", you code "value="<%= scriptlet_expression %>. The value becomes the value of the scriptlet expression.

The type of attribute defines the type of the scripting variable. By default, the type of the scripting variable is the same as that of the class attribute. Other allowable choices are a superclass of the class or an interface implemented by the class. If you attempt to specify a choice other than these two, a ClassCastException will be thrown at request time.

Now let's see how the <jsp:useBean> action works. The steps taken by the JSP container to process the action, as defined by the JavaServer Pages Specification, are:

1. Attempt to locate an object based on the attribute values (id, scope). The inspection is done appropriately synchronized per scope namespace to avoid nondeterministic behavior.

2. Define a scripting language variable with the given id in the current lexical scope of the scripting language of the specified type (if given) or class (if type is not given).

3. If the object is found, the variable's value is initialized with a reference to the located object, cast to the specified type. If the cast fails, a java.lang.ClassCastException shall occur. This completes the processing of this useBean action.

4. If the jsp:useBean element had a nonempty body it is ignored. This completes the processing of this useBean action.

5. If the object is not found in the specified scope and neither class nor beanName is given, a `java.lang.InstantiationException` shall occur. This completes the processing of this `useBean` action.

6. If the object is not found in the specified scope; and the `class` specified names a nonabstract class that defines a public no-args constructor, then that class is instantiated, and the new object reference is associated with the scripting variable and with the specified name in the specified scope using the appropriate scope-dependent association mechanism (see `PageContext`). After this, step 7 is performed. If the object is not found, and the class is either abstract, an `interface`, or no public no-args constructor is defined therein, then a `java.lang.InstantiationException` shall occur. This completes the processing of this `useBean` action.

7. If the object is not found in the specified scope, and `beanName` is given, then the method `instantiate()` of `java.beans.Beans` will be invoked with the ClassLoader of the Servlet object and the beanName as arguments. If the method succeeds, the new object reference is associated the with the scripting variable and with the specified name in the specified scope using the appropriate scope-dependent association mechanism (see `PageContext`). After this, step 8 is performed.

8. If the `jsp:useBean` element has a nonempty body, the body is processed. The variable is initialized and available within the scope of the body. The text of the body is treated as elsewhere; if there is template text, it will be passed through to the out stream; scriptlets and action tags will be evaluated.

9. A common use of a nonempty body is to complete initializing the created instance; in that case, the body will likely contain `jsp:setProperty` actions and scriptlets. This completes the processing of this `useBean` action.

We will see sample code that uses the `<jsp:useBean>` action shortly but first we need to cover one more action, the `<jsp:getProperty>` action.

## `<jsp:getProperty>`

The `<jsp:getProperty>` sends a string representing the value of a property of a Bean instance to the current `out` object. The syntax is:

```
<jsp:getProperty name="beanName" property="propertyName" />
```

The beanName in the `name="beanName"` attribute/value pair is the name of an existing instance of a Bean; in other words, it is the value of name in the `id="name"` attribute/value pair of a `<jsp:useBean>` action. This means that the bean instance named in a `<jsp:getProperty>` action must appear in a `<jsp:useBean>` directive in the same translation unit; more precisely, the `<jsp:useBean>` must appear before the `<jsp:getProperty>` action(s) for the bean instance. If the instance does exist, the value of the Bean property specified in the `property="propertyName"` attribute/value pair is converted to a string and placed into the output stream of the current `out` object. If the Bean property value is an object, its `toString()` method is invoked. If it is a primitive, a direct conversion is performed. If the named property does not exist, a request-time exception is raised.

Here is the sample code from file `MiscSystemProperties.java`. It is the Java source for a Bean whose methods return a variety of System properties. Yes, we could simply use the `getProperty()` method of the System class, but that would defeat our purpose of showing Beans at work.

```java
package com.instantjsp.Chapter2;
public class MiscSystemProperties {

  public String getRuntimeEnvironmentVersion() {
    return System.getProperty("java.version");
  }

  public String getRuntimeEnvironmentVendor() {
    return System.getProperty("java.vendor");
  }

  public String getVmSpecVersion() {
    return System.getProperty("java.vm.specification.version");
  }

  public String getVmSpecVendor() {
    return System.getProperty("java.vm.specification.vendor");
  }

  public String getVmSpecName() {
    return System.getProperty("java.vm.specification.name");
  }

  public String getVmVersion() {
    return System.getProperty("java.vm.version");
  }

  public String getVmVendor() {
    return System.getProperty("java.vm.vendor");
  }

  public String getVmName() {
    return System.getProperty("java.vm.name");
```

```
    }

    public String getRteSpecVersion() {
      return System.getProperty("java.specification.version");
    }

    public String getRteSpecVendor() {
      return System.getProperty("java.specification.vendor");
    }

    public String getRteSpecName() {
      return System.getProperty("java.specification.name");
    }

    public String getOperatingSystemName() {
      return System.getProperty("os.name");
    }

    public String getOperatingSystemArchitecture() {
      return System.getProperty("os.arch");
    }

    public String getOperatingSystemVersion() {
      return System.getProperty("os.version");
    }
}
```

The JavaBean resulting from the compilation of this code is referenced in the following JSP page.

```
<jsp:useBean id="props"
    class="com.instantjsp.Chapter2.MiscSystemProperties" />
<html>
<head>
<title>Miscellaneous System Properties</title>
</head>
<body bgcolor="#FFFFFF">
<font face = "Arial, Helvetica"><font size="+1">
<br>
<br>
Operating System Name:
<jsp:getProperty name="props" property="operatingSystemName" />
<br>
<br>
Operating System Architecture:
<jsp:getProperty name="props" property="operatingSystemArchitecture"/>
<br>
<br>
Operating System Version:
<jsp:getProperty name="props" property="operatingSystemVersion" />
<br>
<br>
Runtime Environment Version:
<jsp:getProperty name="props" property="runtimeEnvironmentVersion" />
<br>
<br>
Runtime Environment Vendor:
```

```
<jsp:getProperty name="props" property="runtimeEnvironmentVendor" />
<br>
<br>
VM Spec Version:
<jsp:getProperty name="props" property="vmSpecVersion" />
<br>
<br>
VM Spec Vendor:
<jsp:getProperty name="props" property="vmSpecVendor" />
<br>
<br>
VM Version:
<jsp:getProperty name="props" property="vmVersion" />
<br>
<br>
VM Name:
<jsp:getProperty name="props" property="vmName" />
<br>
<br>
RTE Spec Version:
<jsp:getProperty name="props" property="rteSpecVersion" />
<br>
<br>
RTE Spec Vendor:
<jsp:getProperty name="props" property="rteSpecVendor" />
<br>
<br>
RTE Spec Name:
<jsp:getProperty name="props" property="rteSpecName" />
</font>
</body>
</html>
```

When you store this code in a file named `MiscSystemProperties.jsp` and access it from a browser, you see the page shown in Figure 2-6.

Now, let's discuss what happens when this JSP page executes. The `<jsp:useBean>` action first checks to see if an instance of `com.instantjsp.Chapter2.MiscSystemProperties` with a scripting variable name of `props` exists. It does not, so it creates such an instance and assigns it to the scripting variable `props`. Next, the action `<jsp:getProperty name="props" property="operatingSystemName">` uses the standard introspection methodology (in this case, low-level reflection) to determine the presence of the accessor method `getOperatingSystemName()`. Then, using reflection, it dynamically invokes this method and places the returned result in the output stream of the current `out` object. It repeats this for each of the `<jsp:getProperty>` actions.

Before moving on, let's take a closer look at the `scope` attribute, `ScopeTest.java`, which contains the Java source for a Bean that has a single accessor that returns the value of an instance variable after first incrementing it.

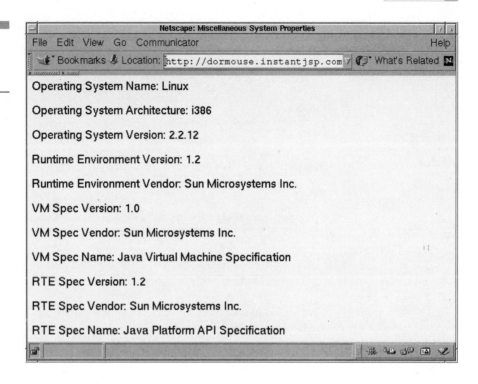

**Figure 2-6**
Output from
MiscSystem-
Properties.jsp

```
package com.instantjsp.Chapter2;

public class ScopeTest {

  private int i;

  public ScopeTest() {
    i = 0;
  }

  public int getNextInt() {
    return ++i;
  }
}
```

The JSP page (ScopeTest.jsp) shown below contains two
<jsp:useBean> actions. Notice that the scope specified for each is differ-
ent. The object contained in the scripting variable appScopeCount has a
scope of application. This means that an instance of ScopeTest is created but once for the life of the application. The object contained in the
scripting variable reqScopeCount has a scope of request. This means
that an instance of ScopeTest will be created each time a request is
processed and will be destroyed when processing for the request is completed.

```
<jsp:useBean id="appScopeCount" scope="application"
  class="com.instantjsp.Chapter2.ScopeTest" />

<jsp:useBean id="reqScopeCount" scope="request"
  class="com.instantjsp.Chapter2.ScopeTest" />

<html>
<head>
<title>Scope Test</title>
</head>
<body bgcolor="#FFFFFF">

<font face = "Arial, Helvetica"><font size="+2">
<br>
<br>
<br>
Counter (scope=application) has a value of 
<jsp:getProperty name="appScopeCount" property="nextInt"/>
<br>
<br>
Counter (scope=request) has a value of 
<jsp:getProperty name="reqScopeCount" property="nextInt"/>
<br>
<br>
</font></font>
<center>
<form method=get action="ScopeTest.jsp">
<input type=submit name="submit" value="INCREMENT">
</form>
</center>
</body>
</html>
```

The first time you access this page, you observe the output shown in Figure 2-7. The instance variable i is initialized to zero and becomes 1 after the first invocation of getNextInt(), which is invoked as the result of the <jsp:getProperty> action for each of the two Beans.

When you access the JSP page a second time, you notice that the value of the appScopeCount variable becomes 2 but the value of the reqScopeCount variable remains as 1. This is because a new instance of ScopeTest is created and the instance variable i is reinitialized to zero. Figure 2-8 shows the page resulting from the second running of the JSP page.

## <jsp:setProperty>

The <jsp:setProperty> action, as its name implies, allows you to set a Bean property to some value. The syntax is:

```
<jsp:setProperty name="beanName" property_expression />
```

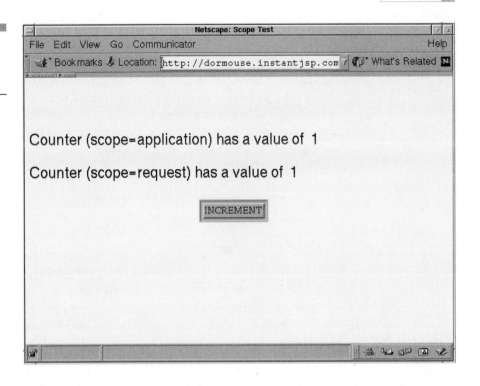

**Figure 2-7**
Output from First
Access of
ScopeTest.jsp

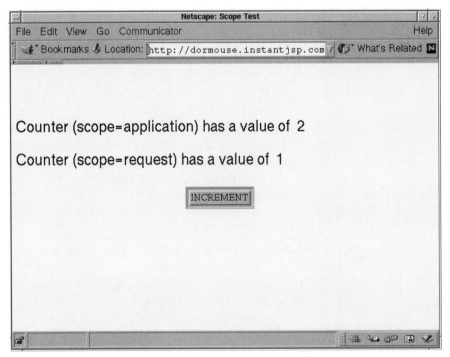

**Figure 2-8**
Output from Second
Access of
ScopeTest.jsp

The beanName in the `name="beanName"` attribute/value pair is the name of an existing instance of a Bean; in other words, it is the value of name in the `id="name"` attribute/value pair. This means that the Bean instance named in a `<jsp:setProperty>` action must appear in a `<jsp:useBean>` directive in the same translation unit; more precisely, the `<jsp:useBean>` directive must appear before the `<jsp:setProperty>` action(s) for the Bean instance.

Possible values of property_expression are:

property = "propertyName" value = "propertyValue"

property = "propertyName" param = "parameterName"

property = "propertyName"

property = "*"

The value of the `property` attribute specified by "propertyName" is the name of the property whose value you wish to set.

The value of the `value` attribute specified by "propertyValue" can be a String or an expression of the form <% = expression %> which, as we have seen earlier, is coerced to a String.

In the case where property_expression is property = "propertyName" param = "parameterName", the value of the specified property becomes the value of the request parameter with the name "parameterName". The parameter name is typically the name of an element in an HTML form.

In the case where property_expression is property = "propertyName", the value assigned to the property is the value of a parameter with the same name if such a parameter exists.

Finally, for the case where property_expression is property = "*", all parameters of the current `ServletRequest` are examined iteratively and wherever the Bean has a setter method corresponding to the parameter name, the value of the parameter is passed as an argument to that setter.

**NOTE:**  *In Chapter 1, when we were dealing with the problem of missing data, we said we would see a better solution. That solution consists of using the* `<jsp:setProperty>` *action to invoke the setter method(s) of a Bean that serves as a holder for the parameters in the HTML form.*

*Each setter method examines the data it receives as an argument and when it detects a value of null, it throws an* Exception *that is handled by a JSP* errorPage.

It's time again for some sample code, so here is the listing of PaintBrush.java, which contains the source for a simple paint brush. At any given time, red, green, or blue can be selected. The initial color is red.

```
package com.instantjsp.Chapter2;

public class PaintBrush {

  private String currentColor = "red";

  public String getCurrentColor() {
    return currentColor;
  }

  public void setCurrentColor(String color) {
    currentColor = color;
  }
}
```

Here's a JSP page (PaintBrush.jsp) that displays color as it first finds it, uses the <jsp:setProperty> action to select a different color and then displays the color again.

```
<jsp:useBean id="brush" class="PaintBrush" />
<html>
<head>
<title>Paint Brush</title>
</head>
<body bgcolor="#FFFFFF">
<font face = "Arial, Helvetica"><font size="+1">
<br>
<br>
Initial brush color:
<jsp:getProperty name="brush" property="currentColor" />
<br>
<br>
<jsp:setProperty name="brush" property="currentColor" value="white"/>
New brush color:
<jsp:getProperty name="brush" property="currentColor" />
<br>
<br>
<jsp:setProperty name="brush" property="currentColor" value="blue"/>
New brush color:
<jsp:getProperty name="brush" property="currentColor" />
</font>
</body>
</html>
```

**Figure 2-9**
Output from
PaintBrush.jsp

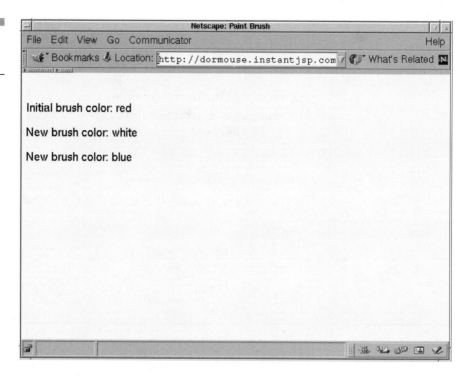

Figure 2-9 shows the page that is displayed in the browser when you access PaintBrush.jsp.

## `<jsp:include>`

The `<jsp:include>` action allows you to specify a static or dynamic resource in the same context as the current page. Now, since we've already seen the `<%@ include>` directive, you may be wondering if this isn't perhaps a case of duplication. The `<@ include>` directive is parsed during the translation phase and can specify only a static resource. The `<jsp:include>` action, which is processed at request time, can specify either a static value or a scriptlet expression that is not parsed but simply included in place. The syntax is:

```
<jsp:include page="urlSpec" />
```

If buffering is in effect, the buffer is flushed before the designated inclusion occurs.

**Figure 2-10**
Menu from Dave's
Diner

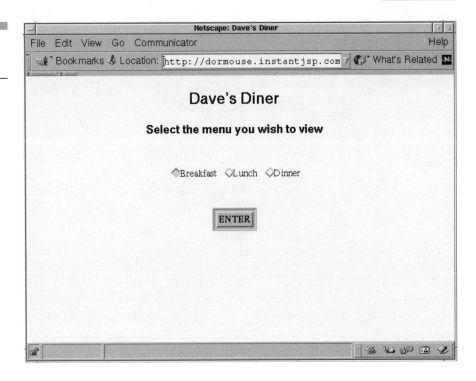

Here's an HTML page that presents the user with a choice a break-fast, lunch, or dinner menu from Dave's Diner. Its output is shown in Figure 2-10.

```html
<html>
<head>
<title>Dave's Diner</title>
</head>
<body bgcolor="#ffffff">
<form method="post" action="Menu.jsp">
<br>
<center>
<b>
<font face = "Arial, Helvetica"><font size="+2">
Dave's Diner
<br>
<br>
</font></font>
<font face = "Arial, Helvetica"><font size="+1">
Select the menu you wish to view
<br>
<br>
<br>
<table>
<tr>
```

```
<td>
<input name="rb" type="radio" value="Breakfast.html" checked>Breakfast
</td>
<td>
<input name="rb" type="radio" value="Lunch.html">Lunch
</td>
<td>
<input name="rb" type="radio" value="Dinner.html">Dinner
</td>
</tr>
</table>
</font></font>
<br>
<br>
<input type="submit" name="submit" value="ENTER">
</b>
</center>
</form>
</center>
</body>
</html>
```

As you can see, the request is sent to Menu.jsp, which contains the following code:

```
<html>
<head>
<title>Menu</title>
</head>
<body bgcolor="#C7C3C7">
<font face = "Arial, Helvetica"><font size="+2">
<center>
<br>
<br>
<b>
Welcome to Dave's Diner
</font></font>
<%! String [] names; %>
<%names = request.getParameterValues("rb"); %>
<jsp:include page="<%= names[0] %>" flush="true" />
</body>
</html>
```

The important lines from the preceding code are:

```
<%! String [] names; %>
<%names = request.getParameterValues("rb"); %>
<jsp:include page="<%= names[0] %>" flush="true" />
```

This code declares a scripting variable names that is an array of Strings and the values returned from the getParameterValues() method of the request object are stored in this array. The <jsp:include> action includes the HTML page whose name is the value of the radio button that the user clicked. This ability to specify a dynamic value is the power behind the `<jsp:include>` action. Without it, you would have to perform a series of tests to determine which of several static pages to include.

Figures 2-11 and 2-12 show the results of clicking ENTER after selecting breakfast and lunch, respectively. Here is the code for `Breakfast.html`:

```
<html>
<br>
<font face = "Arial, Helvetica"><font size="+1">
<br>
Breakfast
<br>
<br>
<table BORDER=6 WIDTH="80%" NOSAVE >
<tr NOSAVE>
<td NOSAVE>Muffin</td>

<td ALIGN=RIGHT NOSAVE>.65</td>
</tr>

<tr NOSAVE>
```

**Figure 2-11**
Dave's Breakfast
Menu

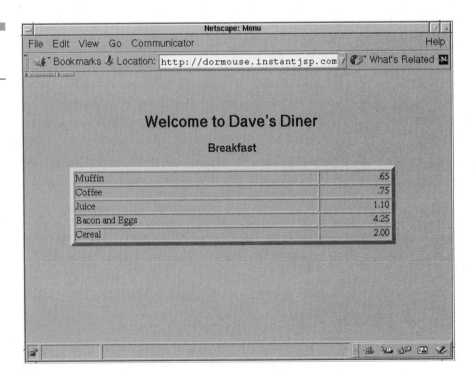

**Figure 2-12**
Dave's Lunch Menu

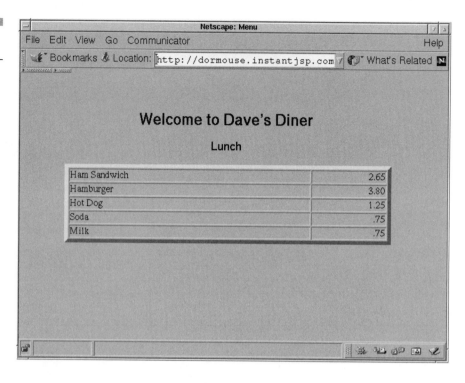

```
<td>Coffee</td>

<td ALIGN=RIGHT NOSAVE>.75</td>
</tr>

<tr NOSAVE>
<td>Juice</td>

<td ALIGN=RIGHT NOSAVE>1.10</td>
</tr>
<tr NOSAVE>
<td>Bacon and Eggs</td>

<td ALIGN=RIGHT NOSAVE>4.25</td>
</tr>

<tr NOSAVE>
<td>Cereal</td>

<td ALIGN=RIGHT NOSAVE>2.00</td>
</tr>
</table>
</html>
```

## `<jsp:forward>`

Sometimes it makes sense at runtime to dispatch a request elsewhere, which is made possible by the `<jsp:forward>` action. The target of the dispatching can be a static resource, a JSP page, or a Servlet. Because execution of this action results in immediate termination of the current page, the buffer is cleared before forwarding takes place. If buffering is not in effect and some output has already been written, an `IllegalStateException` will be raised when the attempt is made to forward the request. The syntax is:

```
<jsp:forward page="relativeURLspec" />
```

The value of `relativeURLspec` does not have to be hard-coded. It can be an expression.

Consider the following code named `Forward.html`, which displays the browser page shown in Figure 2-13:

**Figure 2-13**
Output from
`Forward.html`

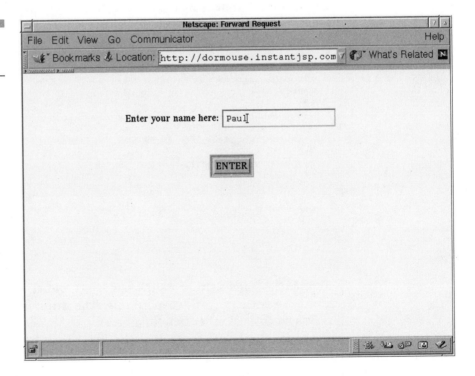

```
<html>
<head>
<title>Forward Request</title>
</head>
<body bgcolor="#FFFFFF">
<form method="post" action="Forward.jsp">
<br>
<br>
<br>
<center>
<b>
Enter your name here:
<input name="userName" type="text">
<br>
<br>
<br>
<input type="submit" name="submit" value="ENTER">
</b>
</center>
</form>
</center>
</body>
</html>
```

The JSP page that processes this page is Forward.jsp. If we examine it, we see that it forwards the request to one of two possible JSP pages depending on the time of day the HTML form shown earlier was received by the server. Here is the code for Forward.jsp:

```
<%@ page import="java.util.*" %>
<html>
<%
GregorianCalendar cal = new GregorianCalendar(new SimpleTimeZone
    (-5*60*60*1000,"EDT"));
   if (cal.get(Calendar.AM_PM) == Calendar.AM) {
%>
<jsp:forward page="AmGreeting.jsp" />

<% } else { %>

<jsp:forward page="PmGreeting.jsp"/>

<% } %>
</html>
```

Figures 2-14 and 2-15 show the pages generated by AmGreeting.jsp and PmGreeting.jsp, respectively. The different color background serves no purpose other than to differentiate between the two pages. The most important data in each of the two pages displayed comprise the name entered in the entry field of the original HTML form.

To understand its importance, examine the code for AmGreeting.jsp:

**Figure 2-14**
Output from
`AmGreeting.jsp`

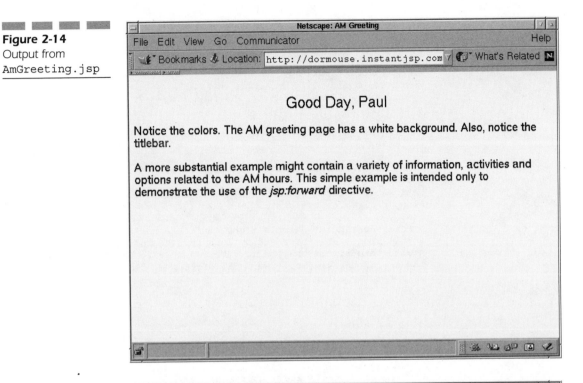

**Figure 2-15**
Output from
`PmGreeting.jsp`

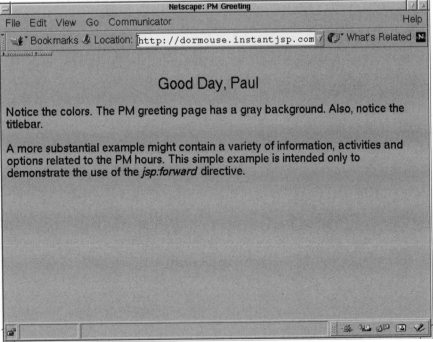

```
<html>
<head>
<title>AM Greeting</title>
</head>
<body bgcolor="white">
<center>
<font face = "Arial, Helvetica"><font size="+2">
<br>
Good Day,
<%= request.getParameter("userName") %>
</font></font>
</center>
<font face = "Arial, Helvetica"><font size="+1">
<br>
Notice the colors. The AM greeting page has a white background.
Also, notice the titlebar.
<p>
A more substantial example might contain a variety of
information, activities and options related to the AM
hours. This simple example is intended only to demonstrate
the use of the <i>jsp:forward</i> directive.
</font></font>
</center>
</body>
</html>
```

This page successfully evaluates the expression:

```
<%= request.getParameter("userName") %>
```

The fact that the `getParameter()` method of the `request` object returns the value that was originally entered shows that the `request` object was forwarded from one JSP page to another. This ability to pass `request` objects is what gives the `<jsp:forward>` action its power.

## Declarations

Like any language, the JSP scripting language uses variables to store data. Such variables are declared by a scripting element called a *declaration*, the syntax of which is:

```
<%! declaration(s) %>
```

All declarations in a JSP page are initialized when the page is initialized. After initialization, the declared variables are available for use by the scripting language. In addition to simple variables, methods can also be declared. Declarations do not produce any output to the current `out` stream.

We have already seen one declaration in `Menu.jsp`. Here's another example that declares the method `addSeven()` and invokes that method in a loop in the body of the page:

```
<html>
<head>
<title>Invoking Declared Method</title>
</head>
<body bgcolor="white">
<font face = "Arial, Helvetica"><font size="+2">
<center>
Count by seven using declared method
<br>
</center>
</font></font>
<b>
<b>
<b>
<%!
   int addSeven(int i) {
     return i + 7;
   }
%>
<%
   int j = 1;
   for (int count = 0; count < 10; ++count) {
%>
        
j= <%= j %>
<br><br>
<%
     j = addSeven(j);
   }
%>
</b>
</body>
</html>
```

Figure 2-16 shows the output produced by this JSP page.

## Scriptlets

We have already seen scriptlets and so we know they take the form:

```
<% code fragment %>
```

Scriptlets are executed at request-processing time and may or may not produce output to the current out stream. Scriptlets can create and modify objects.

**Figure 2-16**
Output from
AddSeven.jsp

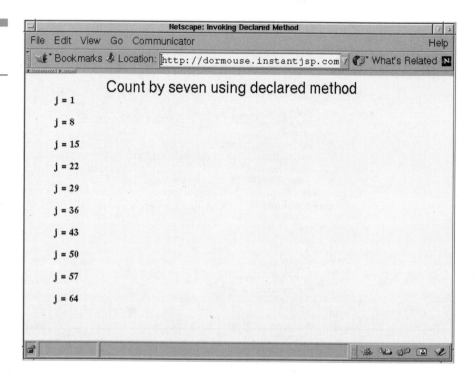

You must keep in mind that the concatenation of all scriptlets in a JSP page in the order in which they appear must yield a Java statement or series of statements considered syntactically valid by a Java compiler. Because the characters %> are used as a scriptlet terminator, if you need to use this character sequence in a scriptlet, you must use the escape sequence %\>.

# Expressions

We have already seen expressions and so we know they look like:

```
<%= expression %>
```

Expressions are evaluated at request-processing time. The result of evaluating an expression is coerced to a string and inserted into the current out stream. If the result cannot be coerced to a string, a ClassCastException is thrown.

We have also already seen that scriptlet expressions can be used to provide request-time attribute values for action elements.

# The `jspInit` and `jspDestroy` Methods

Because the semantic model underlying JSP is that of a servlet, you should expect to be able to use methods from the Servlet class. Let's now look at the extent to which that is the case. The three methods that should come immediately to mind in any discussion of servlets are `init()`, `destroy()`, and `service()`. In any implementation of a JSP page, these manifest themselves as `jspInit()`, `jspDestroy()`, and `_jspService()`. The `_jspService()` method is generated automatically by the JSP container from the JSP page and you may *not* define this method in a JSP page; you may, however, optionally provide code for the `jspInit()` method, which is invoked when a page is initialized, or the `jspDestroy()` method, which is invoked before the JSP page is destroyed, or both.

## `jspInit()`

Before the first time a request is delivered to a JSP page a `jspInit()` method, if present, is invoked. The `jspInit()` method typically creates or initializes resources that will be used during subsequent processing of requests delivered to the page. Such resources might include TCP/IP socket connections to a server or a pool of JDBC connections to a database.

The `jspInit()` method is placed in a declaration. Its signature must be:

```
public void jspInit()
```

Here is some sample code that contains a `jspInit()` method:

```
<html>
<head>
<title>Test JspInit</title>
</head>
<body bgcolor="white">
<%! String s = "initial value"; %>
<%! public void jspInit() {
        s = "value set by <i>jspInit()</i>";
    }
%>
<font face = "Arial, Helvetica"><font size="+2">
```

```
<center>
<br>
<br>
<b>
The value of s is <%= s %>
</center>
</font></font>
</b>
</body>
</html>
```

When this page is saved as `TestJspInit.jsp` and accessed, it produces the output shown in Figure 2-17. The value of s that is displayed demonstrates that the `jspInit()` method was invoked.

## `jspDestroy()`

This method is the counterpart of `jspInit()`, and is invoked before a page is destroyed. The body of the `jspDestroy()` method usually frees resources created by `jspInit()`. For certain resources, it is very important that such housekeeping be performed. On some systems, for example,

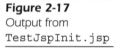

**Figure 2-17**
Output from
`TestJspInit.jsp`

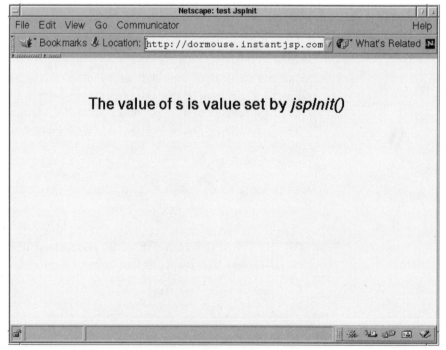

socket connections that are aborted may persist for a long time before being cleaned up. You should be aware of the fact that as resources are required, the JSP container can destroy any page that is not processing a request. If you do not provide a jspDestroy() method and the page is destroyed by the JSP container, you will have no means of releasing resources.

The jspDestroy() method appears in a declaration like jspInit() does.

**NOTE**: *Other than* jspInit *and* jspDestroy, *you must not declare methods that start with* jsp, _jsp, jspx, *or* _jspx. *These are reserved for possible future use.*

# Objects Available to All JSPs

We have already seen two objects that are available to all JSPs: request and response. The request object has the scope of a request; the response object has the scope of the page. Now let's discuss some others.

## pageContext

The pageContext object is an instance of the javax.servlet.jsp.-PageContext class. A pageContext provides an object that encapsulates implementation-dependent features and provides convenience methods. A JSP page implementation class can use a pageContext to run unmodified in any compliant JSP container while taking advantage of implementation-specific improvements like high-performance JspWriters. Generating such an implementation is not a requirement of JSP 1.0–compliant containers, although providing the pageContext implicit object is. JSP 1.1–compliant containers must generate JSP page implementation classes that use this pageContext object to provide insulation from platform implementation details. For the pageContext object, the scope is page.

For additional information on the javax.servlet.jsp.PageContext class, see Appendix C.

## session

The session object of type javax.servlet.http.Httpsession is created for the requesting client. The HttpSession interface is implemented by services to provide an association between an HTTP Client and HTTP Server. This association, or *session*, persists over multiple connections and/or requests during a given time period. Sessions are used to maintain state and user identity across multiple page requests.

In addition to storing standard session properties such as the session identifier, the session object can also store and retrieve application layer data using a dictionary-like interface. The scope of the session object is session.

We have already seen the session object used in SessionInfo.jsp, which generates the output shown in Figures 2-3 and 2-4.

## application

The application object is of type javax.servlet.ServletContext. The ServletContext interface gives servlets access to information about their environment. The scope of the application object is application.

Here is a JSP page that uses the getServerInfo() method of the application object. Its output is shown in Figure 2-18.

```
<html>
<head>
<title>Server Info</title>
</head>
<body bgcolor="#FFFFFF">
<br>
<br>
<font face = "Arial, Helvetica"><font size="+1">
<center>
Info returned by <i>application.getServerInfo()</i> is:
<br>
<br>
<%= application.getServerInfo() %>
</center>
</font></font>
</body>
</html>
```

## out

The out object writes to the output stream and is an instance of javax.servlet.jsp.JspWriter. We have already seen several uses of the out

**Figure 2-18**
Output from
GetServer-
Info.jsp

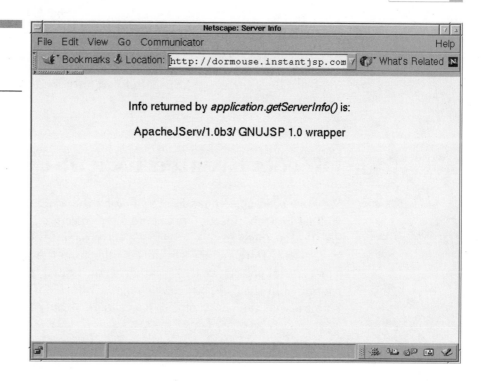

object. The scope of the out object is page. Additional information can be found in Appendix C.

## config

The config object is of type javax.servlet.ServletConfig and is where initialization data are stored and can be retrieved. The scope of the config object is page.

## page

The page object is of type java.lang.Object and is the instance of the JSP page's implementation class processing the current request. The page object can be thought of as a synonym for "this" in the body of the page. The scope of the page object is page.

## exception

The exception object is of type java.lang.Throwable. Unlike the other implicit objects, exception is defined only for a page that specifies errorPage="true".

# Objects Created By a JSP Page

We have seen objects made available by the `<jsp:useBean>` action as well as implicit objects. We should keep in mind, however, that we can create instances of any class. We have seen an example of creating instances of Date and GregorianCalendar from the `java.util` package. The types of objects we can create are not limited to instances of classes contained in the JDK but can be objects we have written ourselves. The result is that the power of JSP pages is practically unlimited.

# Implementing a Typical Web Session

- Login Database
- LoginManager
- Logging In
- Making Login Mandatory
- Limiting Login Attempts
- Enforcing Timeouts
- Measuring Session Time
- Monitoring and Profiling
- Logging Out

Now that we have examined sufficient sample code to see some simple uses of the various elements of JavaServer Pages, it is time to see some practical uses. In this chapter and the remaining chapters, we explore ways in which JavaServer Pages can be used in the real world. In addition to presenting the code for JSP pages, HTML pages, and Java Beans, we also present the layout of any database tables that are used. Detailed information on all database tables can be found in Appendix B.

Before we begin, we should point out that the sample code that we examine is intended only to demonstrate how to use JSP. No emphasis has been placed on design issues and, although portions of the code could certainly be used in an actual system, it should not be treated as industrial strength. Likewise, the database tables have not been normalized or optimized for performance. As is always the case with sample code, you are encouraged to make changes and improvements.

# A Login Scenario

Some Web sites limit access to authorized individuals who can prove their identity by performing a login sequence. Some reasons for this policy are immediately obvious and some are not.

Let's look at an obvious one first. If you have used an intranet, you probably already know and appreciate the reason for enforcing logins. Let's say your intranet allows you to access your salary, your pension fund portfolio, and your last performance review. Don't you feel much more comfortable knowing that a login policy is in effect?

However, what if the only data your site sends to browsers are the results of searches of your product catalog? Since these are not sensitive data, is a login necessary? If you are interested in gathering marketing demographics or selling advertising space, knowing who is visiting your site is important and controlling access using a login procedure becomes helpful. By making the login ID the user's email address, you also provide yourself with a way to contact those who are searching your catalog. Of course, your site would include a privacy statement guaranteeing users that their email addresses would be used only by you and only if they requested mailings.

A simple login involves three data elements—a user ID, a password, and the status of the user's account. For starters, let's create a database table called idpassword that contains these three fields as shown in Table 3-1. Let's then create three accounts so that the contents look like Table 3-2.

**TABLE 3-1**

Definition of
idpassword Table

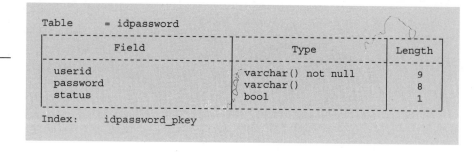

```
Table     = idpassword
```

| Field | Type | Length |
|-------|------|--------|
| userid | varchar() not null | 9 |
| password | varchar() | 8 |
| status | bool | 1 |

```
Index:    idpassword_pkey
```

**TABLE 3-2**

Contents of
idpassword Table

```
Field    | Value

-- RECORD 0 --
userid   | kevin_mc
password | vinthill
status   | t

-- RECORD 1 --
userid   | mike_zab
password | chapin
status   | t

-- RECORD 2 --
userid   | paul_tre
password | x93qvqv
status   | t

(3 rows)
```

Now we're ready to look at a typical login page. Here is the HTML code, which is named `Login.html`:

```html
<html>
<head>
  <title>Login</title>
  <script language="JavaScript">

    function giveFocus() {
      document.login.user.focus()
    }

    function submitForm() {
      document.login.submit()
    }

    function resetForm() {
      document.login.reset()
      document.login.user.focus()
    }
  </script>
```

```
</head>
<body bgcolor="#c0c0c0" link="#999999"
   vlink="#999999" alink="#999999" onLoad="giveFocus()">
<center>
<font size=+2>
<BR>
<BR>
<B>LOGIN</B>
</font>
<br>
<br>
<br>
<br>
<FORM NAME="login" METHOD=POST ACTION=
   "http://dormouse.instantjsp.com/Chapter3/ValidateUser1.jsp">
<TABLE WIDTH="50%">
<TR>
<TD align=right>
<font size=+1>
<B>
User ID:
</B>
</font>
</TD>
<TD>
<font size=+1><INPUT NAME="user" TYPE="TEXT" LENGTH="9"
   MAXLENGTH="9">
</font>
</TD>
</TR>
<TR>
<TD align=right>
<font size=+1>
<B>
Password:
</B>
</font>
</TD>
<TD>
<font size=+1><INPUT NAME="password" TYPE="PASSWORD" LENGTH="8"
   MAXLENGTH="8">
</font>
</TD>
</TR>
</TABLE>
<BR>
<BR>
<BR>
<font size=+1>
<b>
<INPUT TYPE="button" VALUE="LOGIN" onClick="submitForm()">
     
<INPUT TYPE="button" VALUE="RESET" onClick="resetForm()">
</b>
</font>
</FORM>
</CENTER>
</body>
</html>
```

**Figure 3-1**
The Login Page

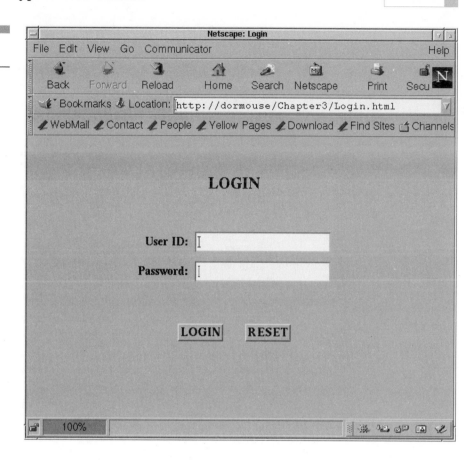

This code produces the output shown in Figure 3-1. As you can see, the request resulting from submission of the HTML form is processed by the JSP page ValidateUser1.jsp.

**NOTE:**  *The URL indicates that* ValidateUser1.jsp *resides on host* dormouse *in the domain* instantjsp.com. *This is a legitimate domain registered by the author but no hosts in this domain are accessible from the Web. When you experiment with the code contained on the CD, you would change the URLs to refer to a host in your own domain.*

Now let's have a look at ValidateUser1.jsp:

```
<jsp:useBean id="loginManager" class="com.instantjsp.LoginManager"
    scope="application" />
```

```
<jsp:useBean id="credentials" class="com.instantjsp.UserCredentials"
  scope="session" />
<jsp:setProperty name="credentials" property="*"/>
<%! String nextPage; %>
<%
  if (loginManager.login(credentials)) {
    nextPage="MainMenu.jsp";
  }
  else if (loginManager.alreadyLoggedIn(credentials)) {
    nextPage="DuplicateLogin1.jsp";
  }
  else {
   nextPage="LoginFailure1.jsp";
  }
%>
<jsp:forward page="<%= nextPage %>"/>
```

The first thing you will notice is that this JSP page contains no HTML. Remember that we defined a JavaServer Page as a text-based document that describes how to process a request to create a response. The document can consist entirely of JSP elements and that is the case here.

So, what does ValidateUser1.jsp do? The first statement it contains is a <jsp:useBean> action. The JSP container searches the namespace that it maintains for the specified scope ("application") and if it does not find an instance of class LoginManager, it creates one using the null constructor. We will see the code for LoginManager shortly but first let's look at the second line in ValidateUser1.jsp. It is a <jsp:useBean> action that defines the scripting variable credentials as being an instance of UserCredentials. Here is UserCredentials.java:

```
package com.instantjsp;

public class UserCredentials {
  private String   user;
  private String   password;
  private String sessionId;

  public UserCredentials( ) {
    user = "";
    password = "";
    sessionId = "";
  }

   public String getUser( ) {
     return user;
  }

   public void setUser( String user ) {
     this.user = user;
  }

   public String getPassword( ) {
```

```
        return password;
    }

    public void setPassword( String password ) {
        this.password = password;
    }

    public String getSessionId() {
        return sessionId;
    }

    public void setSessionId(String sessionId) {
        this.sessionId = sessionId;
    }
}
```

ValidateUser1.jsp sets the user and password instance variables of UserCredentials using the following action:

```
<jsp:setProperty name="credentials" property="*"/>
```

When the property attribute of the <jsp:useBean> action specifies "*", the code generated iterates over the current ServletRequest parameters, matching parameter names and value type(s) to property names and setter method type(s), setting each matched property to the value of the matching parameter. The methods invoked in this case are the setUser() and setPassword() methods of UserCredentials. The values passed to these methods are the values you typed into the fields named "user" and "password," respectively, in the HTML form defined in Login.html.

ValidateUser1.jsp next sets the scripting variable nextPage to one of three values, depending on which of the following is true:

1. the user/password pair is valid and the user is not already logged in from another browser or terminal

2. the user/password pair is valid but the user is already logged in

3. the user/password pair is invalid

It accomplishes this by passing the instance of UserCredentials named by the scripting variable credentials to the login() method of LoginManager. If the method returns true, case (1) is true and the value MainMenu.jsp is assigned to nextPage. If the method returns false, ValidateUser1.jsp invokes the alreadyLoggedIn() method of LoginManager. If this method returns true, case (2) is true and the value DuplicateLogin1.jsp is assigned to nextPage; otherwise, case (3) is true and the value LoginFailure1.jsp is assigned to nextPage.

Finally, `ValidateUser1.jsp` uses the `<jsp:forward>` action to chain to the JavaServer Page specified by the variable `nextPage`.

**NOTE:**   *The code in this book was developed using GNU JSP. Although the JSP Specification does not define the* flush *attribute of* `<jsp:forward>`, *GNU JSP does use it. If you are running the sample code using another JSP container, you should change each occurrence of the* `<jsp:forward>` *action.*

# A Closer Look At LoginManager

Now it's time to take a closer look at LoginManager. If details do not particularly interest you at this time, you can skip ahead to the next section in this chapter entitled "Logging In" (page 83).

Here is the code for LoginManager:

```
package com.instantjsp;

import java.sql.Connection;
import java.sql.ResultSet;
import java.sql.SQLException;
import java.sql.Statement;
import java.util.Date;
import java.util.Hashtable;
import javaservlets.jdbc.ConnectionPool;

public class LoginManager {

    private Hashtable currentLogins;
    private ConnectionPool connectionPool;

    private static final String SELECT_PASSWORD =
        "SELECT password FROM idpassword WHERE userid = ";

    private static final String QUOTE = "'";

    private class LoginProfile extends UserCredentials {
        boolean isLoggedIn = false;

        public LoginProfile(UserCredentials credentials) {
            setUser( credentials.getUser());
            setPassword( credentials.getPassword());
            isLoggedIn = false;
        }
    }

    public LoginManager() throws Exception {
```

```
      connectionPool = new ConnectionPool();
      connectionPool.initialize();
      currentLogins = new Hashtable();
  }

  public boolean alreadyLoggedIn(UserCredentials credentials) {
      boolean loggedIn = false;
      String user = credentials.getUser();
      if (currentLogins.containsKey(user)) {
        LoginProfile aProfile =
          (LoginProfile)currentLogins.get(user);
        loggedIn = aProfile.isLoggedIn;
      }
      return loggedIn;
  }

  public boolean login(UserCredentials credentials)
      throws SQLException {
      if (alreadyLoggedIn(credentials)) {
        return false;
      }

      LoginProfile profile = new LoginProfile(credentials);
      Connection conn = connectionPool.getConnection();
      Statement qs = conn.createStatement();
      ResultSet rs =
        qs.executeQuery(SELECT_PASSWORD + QUOTE +
        credentials.getUser() + QUOTE);
      while (rs.next()) {
        if (rs.getString(1).equals(credentials.getPassword())) {
        profile.isLoggedIn = true;
        currentLogins.put(credentials.getUser(), profile);
        break;
        }
      }
      return profile.isLoggedIn;
  }
}
```

The first action performed by the constructor of LoginManager is
the creation of an instance of ConnectionPool, which is assigned to the
private instance variable `connectionPool`. One of the most expen-
sive database operations is establishing a connection. It's not an operation you'd want to perform each time a user logged in. As its name
implies, the ConnectionPool object preallocates a pool of connections
ready for use. Any code that subsequently requires database connectivity obtains a connection from the pool, uses it, and returns the connection to the pool when it is no longer needed. The ConnectionPool
class we will be using was written by Karl Moss and is discussed in
detail in his book *Java Servlets*, Second Edition, ISBN 0-07-135188-4,
McGraw-Hill.

**NOTE:** *The CD contains a copy of the ConnectionPool class. It can be found in the* javaservlets *directory. Before attempting to run the sample code, you should copy the ENTIRE contents of the* javaservlets *directory to the CLASSPATH as known to your JSP container.*

The next action performed by the constructor is creation of a hashtable called currentLogins. The key to this hashtable is the user ID and the objects it contains are instances of the private inner class LoginProfile. As you can see, LoginProfile extends the UserCredentials class to include an additional instance variable isLoggedIn, which is used to prevent a user from conducting multiple, simultaneous logins from different browsers.

The constructor of LoginProfile takes an instance of UserCredentials as an argument. It invokes the getUser() method to extract the user, which it passes in turn as an argument to the setUser() method of the parent class of LoginProfile.

The two methods we examine in LoginProfile are login() and alreadyLoggedIn(). The login() method, which we have seen was invoked by ValidateUser1.jsp, determines whether a login is active for the user by invoking alreadyLoggedIn().

The actions performed by alreadyLoggedIn() are:

- extracts the user from the instance of UserCredentials received as an argument
- checks if the hashtable currentLogins contains a key whose value matches the value of user
- if currentLogins does not contain the key, it returns false
- if currentLogins contains the key, it retrieves the LoginProfile object stored at that key and returns the value of the isLoggedIn instance variable of that object

If alreadyLoggedIn() returns false, login() returns false; otherwise, it obtains a connection from the pool and performs the following SQL query:

```
SELECT password FROM idpassword WHERE userid = user;
```

If the ResultSet returned by the query contains a password that matches the password contained in the instance of UserCredentials login() received as an argument, login() returns true; otherwise, it returns false.

# Logging In

Now let's go ahead and enter a user ID and password but without starting the database containing the idpassword table. When we do so, we see
none of the pages we just mentioned; rather we see the page shown in
Figure 3-2. As developers, we can interpret the stack trace and conclude
that the database needs to be started, but this is not something we would
ever want a user to see. To improve things, let's add the following directive to ValidateUser1.jsp:

```
<%@ page errorPage="/common/Exception.jsp" %>
```

Now, all exceptions are passed to Exception.jsp, which we have chosen to place in our /common directory, since we will be using it in other
chapters. Exception.jsp looks like this:

```
<%@ page isErrorPage="true" %>
<html>
<head>
<title>FATAL ERROR</title>
</head>
```

**Figure 3-2**
Exception Thrown
with no errorPage
Specified

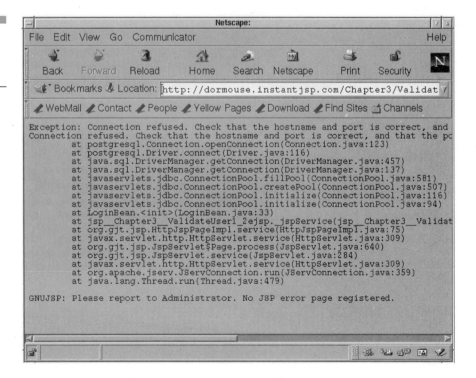

```
<body bgcolor="#ffffff">
<center>
<br>
<br>
<h1>A FATAL ERROR HAS OCCURRED!!!</h1>
</center>
<br>
<b>
<h2>
<%= exception.getMessage() %>
</h2>
<center>
<br>
Report above message to System Administrator
</b>
</center>
</body>
</html>
```

Now let's try to log in again. This time, the output looks like Figure 3-3. The user may not know what the message means but it's a lot less intimidating than the contents of Figure 3-2 and it contains instructions to report the message to the system administrator.

So, let's assume we had reported the message contained in Figure 3-3

**Figure 3-3**
Exception Caught by
an errorPage

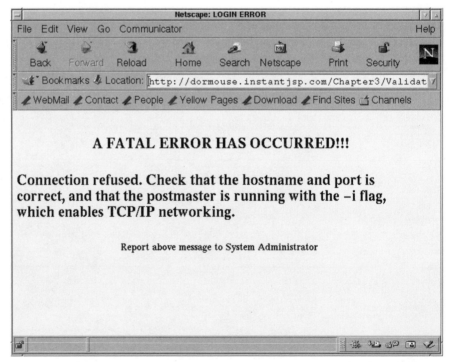

**Figure 3-4**
Successful Login

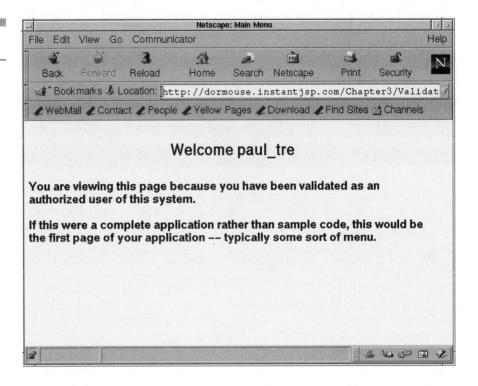

to the system administrator, waited until we are informed that the database was available, and attempted to log in. If the user ID and password we entered are correct, we see the page shown in Figure 3-4. This page is generated by `MainMenu.jsp`, which looks like this:

```
<jsp:useBean id="credentials" class="com.instantjsp.UserCredentials"
  scope="session" />
<html>
<head>
<title>Main Menu</title>
</head>
<body bgcolor="#FFFFFF">
<center>
<b>
<font face = "Arial, Helvetica"><font size="+2">
<br>
Welcome
<%= credentials.getUser() %>
</font></font>
</center>
<br>
<br>
<font face = "Arial, Helvetica"><font size="+1">
You are viewing this page because you have been validated as an
authorized user of this system.
```

```
<p>
If this were a complete application rather 2 than sample code, this would
be the first page of your application — typically some sort of menu.
</font></font>
</b>
</body>
</html>
```

If either the user or password is incorrect (and we are not already logged in from another browser), we see the page shown in Figure 3-5. This page is generated by LoginFailure1.jsp. Here is the code:

```
<jsp:useBean id="credentials" class="com.instantjsp.UserCredentials"
   scope="session" />
<jsp:setProperty name="credentials" property="user" value="" />
<jsp:setProperty name="credentials" property="password" value="" />
<html>
<head>
<title>LOGIN FAILURE</title>
</head>
<body bgcolor="#FFFFFF">
<center>
<br>
<br>
<b>
<font face = "Arial, Helvetica"><font size="+2">
```

**Figure 3-5**
Incorrect User or
Password

```
Login failed for user
<%= request.getParameter ("user") %>
<br>
<br>
<br>
</font></font>
<font face = "Arial, Helvetica"><font size="+1">
Click on the button below to retry your request.
<br>
<br>
</font></font>
</b>
<form method=get action="Login.html">
<input type=submit name="submit" value="OK">
</form>
</center>
</body>
</html>
```

The final case we should consider is when we are already logged in from a browser on a different machine or from a different browser on the same machine. In this case, our user ID is detected as already being present in the `currentLogins` hashtable maintained by LoginManager and we see the page shown in Figure 3-6. This page is generated by `DuplicateLogin1.jsp`. Here is the code:

**Figure 3-6**
Duplicate Login

```
<jsp:useBean id="sessionManager" class="com.instantjsp.SessionManager"
  scope="application" />
<jsp:useBean id="credentials" class="com.instantjsp.UserCredentials"
  scope="session" />
<jsp:setProperty name="credentials" property="user" value="" />
<jsp:setProperty name="credentials" property="password" value="" />
<html>
<head>
<title>LOGIN FAILURE</title>
</head>
<body bgcolor="#FFFFFF">
<center>
<br>
<br>
<h1>
User
<%= credentials.getUser() %>
is already logged in!</h1>
<br>
<b>
Click on the button below to login as another user.
</b>
<form method=get action="Login.html">
<input type=submit name="submit" value="OK">
</form>
</center>
</body>
</html>
```

***NOTE:*** *If you are wondering about the security implications of transmitting passwords in the clear and storing them unencrypted in the database, these are legitimate concerns but are outside the scope of this book.*

# Preventing Users from Bypassing Login

At this point, we think we've secured our site by enforcing a login. Let's think about ways in which an unauthorized person might still gain access. Suppose someone had casually looked over the shoulder of a legitimate user and made a list of all the pages visited as they were displayed in the Location field if Netscape were being used or the Address field if the browser was Internet Explorer. What would happen if this person attempted to access one of the pages in that list? We can easily see for ourselves by entering the URL `http://dormouse.instantjsp.com/Chapter3/MainMenu.jsp`.

**NOTE:**  *As we mentioned before, the actual URL you use should reflect your own host and domain.*

The fact that you end up looking at the screen shown in Figure 3-4, which is the same screen seen by a user who had successfully logged in, is proof that we need to tighten things up. We could resort to an Access Control List (ACL) but that would have two drawbacks. First, the access control mechanism is likely to be server specific. That would make moving our application from one server to another difficult. Second, as we see later, we have a good reason for wanting the user IDs and passwords stored in a database; storing them in an ACL list as well would be a maintenance nightmare. What we really need is a mechanism that will permit each JSP page to determine for itself whether the user who is requesting it has been authenticated as part of the active session.

We now examine such a mechanism, but first let's set up a main Web page that simplifies navigation. We will divide the page into two frames. The left frame, which persists throughout, contains a navigational menu. The right frame is used as our primary display area. Here is the HTML code that is saved as `index.html`:

```html
<html>
<head>
  <title>Chapter 3 Sample Code</title>
</head>
<frameset cols="150,*">
  <frame src="MenuFrame.html"
    frameborder="0" noresize="noresize" name="mainmenuframe">
  <frame src="Intro.html"
    frameborder="0" name="rightframe">
</frameset>
<html>
```

The source for the menu frame is named `MenuFrame.html` and looks like this:

```html
<html>
<body text="#000000" bgcolor="#e0e0e0" link="#555555"
  vlink="#555555" alink="#555555">
<br>
<br>
<table COLS=1 WIDTH="100%" >
  <tr>
    <td><a href="Login2.jsp" target="rightframe">Login</a>
    </td>
  </tr>
```

```
    <tr>
      <td>
      </td>
    </tr>

    <tr>
      <td>
      </td>
    </tr>

    <tr>
      <td><a href="Passage1.jsp" target="rightframe">Passage 1</a>
      </td>
    </tr>

    <tr>
      <td><a href="Passage2.jsp" target="rightframe">Passage 2</a>
      </td>
    </tr>

    <tr>
      <td><a href="Passage3.jsp" target="rightframe">Passage 3</a>
      </td>
    </tr>

    <tr>
      <td>
      </td>
    </tr>

    <tr>
      <td>
      </td>
    </tr>

    <tr>
      <td><a href="LogoutVerification.jsp" target="rightframe">
        Logout</a>
      </td>
    </tr>
  </table>

  </body>
  </html>
```

The contents of the main display frame will change depending on the menu item selected. The initial content is `Intro.html`, which looks like this:

```
<html>
<body bgcolor="#c0c0c0" link="#999999"
  vlink="#999999" alink="#999999">
<center>
<font size=+2>
<br>
<br>
```

```
<b>Welcome!</B>
</font>
</center>
<br>
<br>
<br>
<br>
<font size=+1>
This site contains three passages from one of my favorite authors.
 You can
view any of them by simply clicking on the appropriate link in the
 menu area
on the left.
<p>
Before you can view any of the pages, you must login. Be careful
 typing your
user ID and password because you only get <i><b>three</b></i>
 attempts. After that,
your account will be temporarily deactivated and you will have to
 bother me to
reset your account.
<p>
If you are sharing this browser with someone else, only one of you
 can be
logged on at a time.
<p>
</font>
</body>
</html>
```

Assuming you have your server configured to automatically look for `index.html`, if you enter the URL `http://dormouse.instantjsp.com/Chapter3`, you will see the page displayed in Figure 3-7.

Now, let's try to select "Passage 1" from the menu without logging in and see what happens. The page we see is shown in Figure 3-8. This demonstrates that we have solved the problem of users who bypass login.

It's time now to take a look at `Passage1.jsp` and see how it determines that we have not yet logged in. Here is the code for `Passage1.jsp`:

```
<%@ page info="Paul's #1 Favorite" %>
<%@ page errorPage="/common/Exception.jsp" %>
<jsp:useBean id="sessionManager" class="com.instantjsp.SessionManager"
    scope="application" />
<jsp:useBean id="credentials" class="com.instantjsp.UserCredentials"
    scope="session" />
<%
    if (!sessionManager.keepAlive(credentials,getServletInfo())) {
%>
        <jsp:forward page="RequestLogin.jsp" />
<%
    }
%>
<html>
<body>
```

**Figure 3-7**
Chapter 3 Main Page

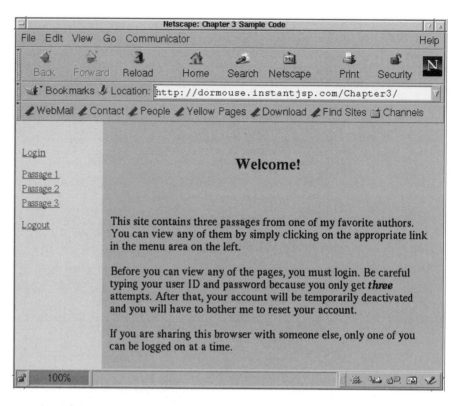

```
<center>
<br>
<br>
This page has been cleared for viewing by user
<%= credentials.getUser() %>
</center>
<br>
<br>
"The time has come," the Walrus said,<p>
"To talk of many things:<p>
Of shoes — and ships — and sealing-wax —<p>
Of cabbages — and kings —<p>
And why the sea is boiling hot —<p>
And whether pigs have wings."<p>
<p>
Through The Looking Glass — Lewis Carroll
</body>
</html>
```

The directive in the first line specifies some information about the page. Later we see how it is used for logging statistics, but we can ignore it for now. The directive in the second line specifies an errorPage that will

**Figure 3-8**
Attempting to Bypass
Login

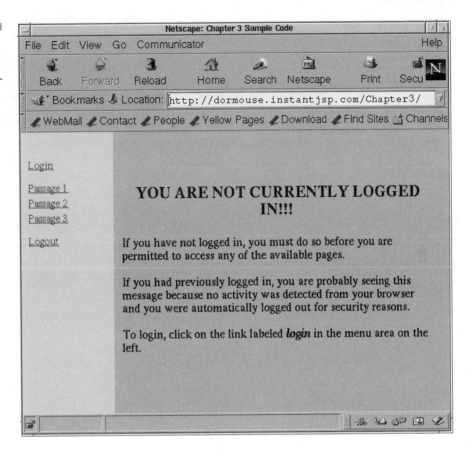

Netscape: Chapter 3 Sample Code

File  Edit  View  Go  Communicator                                    Help

Back    Forward    Reload    Home    Search   Netscape   Print   Secu

Bookmarks  Location: http://dormouse.instantjsp.com/Chapter3/

WebMail  Contact  People  Yellow Pages  Download  Find Sites  Channels

Login

Passage 1
Passage 2
Passage 3

Logout

# YOU ARE NOT CURRENTLY LOGGED IN!!!

If you have not logged in, you must do so before you are permitted to access any of the available pages.

If you had previously logged in, you are probably seeing this message because no activity was detected from your browser and you were automatically logged out for security reasons.

To login, click on the link labeled *login* in the menu area on the left.

handle exceptions. Figure 3-9 shows what we would see if we forgot to start the database. The exception is handled in exactly the same manner as we saw in Figure 3-3, but now we don't have to deal with the browser's BACK button, since the menu frame is persistent.

The next line in Passage1.jsp is a <jsp:useBean> action. The class of the scripting variable sessionManager specified in the action is SessionManager, which is a replacement for the simpler LoginManager we saw before. The complete listing for the SessionManager class is presented at the end of the chapter. This is followed by another <jsp:useBean> whose scripting variable credentials is an instance of UserCredentials, which we have already discussed.

Passage1.jsp passes two arguments to the keepAlive() method of SessionManager. The first is the scripting variable credentials and the second is the string specified in the directive in the first line (i.e.,

**Figure 3-9**
Exception Caught by
errorPage

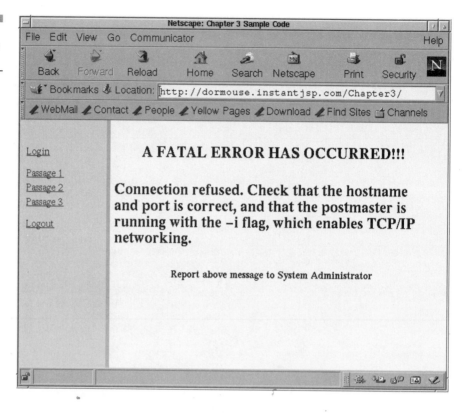

Paul's #1 Favorite). For now, we need to examine only the first few lines of `keepAlive()`. These are as follows:

```
public boolean keepAlive(UserCredentials credentials,
    String pageInfo) throws SQLException {
  if (!alreadyLoggedIn(credentials)) {
    return false;
  }
```

The instance of UserCredentials received as an argument by `keepAlive()` is passed to the method `alreadyLoggedIn()`, which is similar to the identically named method we saw in LoginManager. Here is the code:

```
public boolean alreadyLoggedIn(UserCredentials credentials) {
  boolean loggedIn = false;
  String user = credentials.getUser();
  synchronized (currentLogins) {
    if (currentLogins.containsKey(user)) {
      LoginProfile aProfile =
        (LoginProfile)currentLogins.get(user);
```

```
            loggedIn = aProfile.isLoggedIn;
        }
    }
    return loggedIn;
}
```

In our case, since we have not logged in, the instance variable `user` in credentials has a value of `""`, which is not found in the hashtable `currentLogins` and so `alreadyLoggedIn()` returns false to `keepAlive()`, which returns a value of false to `Passage1.jsp`. This results in execution of the `<jsp:forward>` action, which chains to `RequestLogin.jsp` and generates the page we saw in Figure 3-8. The code involved is:

```
<%
    if (!sessionManager.keepAlive(credentials,getServletInfo())) {
%>
        <jsp:forward page="RequestLogin.jsp" />
<%
    }
```

The code for `RequestLogin.jsp` is as follows:

```
<html>
<body>
<center>
<font size="+2">
<b>
<br>
<br>
<br>
YOU ARE NOT CURRENTLY LOGGED IN!!!
<br>
<br>
</font>
</center>
<font size="+1">
If you have not logged in, you must do so before you are permitted to
access any of the available pages.
<p>
If you had previously logged in, you are probably seeing this message
because no activity was detected from your browser and you were
 automatically
logged out for security reasons.
<p>
To login, click on the link labeled <b><i>login</i></b> in the menu
 area
on the left.
</font>
</body>
</html>
```

If you are wondering why we didn't invoke `alreadyLoggedIn()` directly instead of letting `keepAlive()` invoke it for us, we see why later when we discuss the issue of inactivity.

# An Improved Login Procedure

Now that we've solved the problem of users who bypass login, let's take another look at the login procedure. In the frames version of the page we are now using, Login.html, which we used earlier, has been replaced by Login2.jsp. Here is the code:

```
<jsp:useBean id="sessionManager" class="com.instantjsp.SessionManager"
  scope="application" />
<jsp:useBean id="credentials" class="com.instantjsp.UserCredentials"
  scope="session" />
<%
  if (sessionManager.alreadyLoggedIn(credentials)) {
%>
    <jsp:forward page="LogoutFirst.jsp" />
<%
  }
%>
<html>
<head>
   <title>Login</title>

<script language="JavaScript">

  function giveFocus() {
    document.login.user.focus()
  }

  function submitForm() {
    document.login.submit()
  }

  function resetForm() {
    document.login.reset()
    document.login.user.focus()
  }
</script>
</head>

<body bgcolor="#c0c0c0" link="#999999"
   vlink="#999999" alink="#999999" onLoad="giveFocus()">
<center>
<font size=+2>
<BR>
<BR>
<B>LOGIN</B>
</font>
<br>
<br>
<br>
<br>
<FORM NAME="login" METHOD=POST ACTION=
  "http://dormouse.instantjsp.com/Chapter3/ValidateUser2.jsp">
<TABLE WIDTH="50%">
<TR>
```

```
<TD align=right>
<font size=+1>
<B>
User ID:
</B>
</font>
</TD>
<TD>
<font size=+1><INPUT NAME="user" TYPE="TEXT" LENGTH="9"
  MAXLENGTH="9">
</font>
</TD>
</TR>
<TR>
<TD align=right>
<font size=+1>
<B>
Password:
</B>
</font>
</TD>
<TD>
<font size=+1><INPUT NAME="password" TYPE="PASSWORD" LENGTH="8"
  MAXLENGTH="8">
</font>
</TD>
</TR>
</TABLE>
<BR>
<BR>
<BR>
<font size=+1>
<b>
<INPUT TYPE="button" VALUE="LOGIN" onClick="submitForm()">
     
<INPUT TYPE="button" VALUE="RESET" onClick="resetForm()">
</b>
</font>
</FORM>
</CENTER>
</body>
</html>
```

The first action performed by Login2.jsp is that of determining whether the user is already logged in. It does this by invoking the alreadyLoggedIn() method of SessionManager. If this method returns true, Login2.jsp executes a <jsp:forward> action and chains to LogoutFirst.html, which generates the page shown in Figure 3-10. Here is the code for LogoutFirst.html:

```
<html>
<body>
<center>
<font size="+2">
<b>
```

**Figure 3-10**
Attempting Login
While Already
Logged In

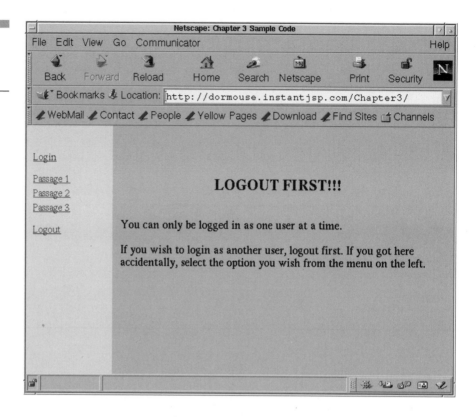

```
<br>
<br>
<br>
LOGOUT FIRST!!!
</font>
</center>
<font size="+1">
<br>
<br>
You can only be logged in as one user at a time.
<p>
If you wish to login as another user, logout first. If you got here
accidentally, select the option you wish from the menu on the left.
</font>
</body>
</html>
```

Now, getting back to Login2.jsp, if no user is logged in, the HTML that generates Figure 3-11 is emitted.

When a user ID and password are entered and the "Login" button is clicked, a request is sent to ValidateUser2.jsp. Here is the code:

**Figure 3-11**
The Login Page

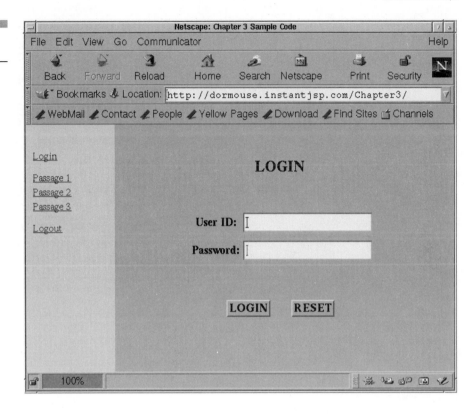

```
<jsp:useBean id="sessionManager" class="com.instantjsp.SessionManager"
  scope="application" />
<jsp:useBean id="credentials" class="com.instantjsp.UserCredentials"
  scope="session" />
<jsp:setProperty name="credentials" property="*"/>
<%! String nextPage; %>
<%
  if (sessionManager.alreadyLoggedIn(credentials)) {
    nextPage = "DuplicateLogin2.jsp";
  }
  else {
    if (sessionManager.login(credentials)) {
      credentials.setSessionId(session.getId());
      sessionManager.initiateSessionLogging(credentials);
      nextPage = "Welcome.jsp";
    }
    else {
      nextPage = "LoginFailure2.jsp";
    }
  }
%>
<jsp:forward page="<%= nextPage %>" flush="true"/>
<%@ page errorPage="/common/Exception.jsp" %>
```

**Figure 3-12**
Successful Login

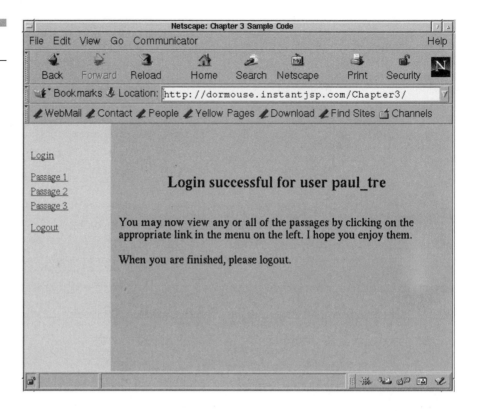

This JSP page is similar to `ValidateUser1.jsp`, which we have already examined. It chains to `Welcome.jsp`, `DuplicateLogin2.jsp`, or `LoginFailure2`, which generate Figures 3-12, 3-13, and 3-14, respectively. The source for the first two of these files is contained on the CD and is not shown here. We examine `LoginFailure2.jsp` in the next section.

If we had logged in successfully, we could then select any of the menu items except "Login". If we selected "Passage 1", which is a hypertext link to `Passage1.jsp`, we would see the page shown in Figure 3-15. We have already seen the code for `Passage1.jsp`.

## Limiting Invalid Login Attempts

One of a hacker's most effective tools is persistence. Hackers also seem to have an abundance of time to devote to their evil pursuits. For these two reasons, it is important that you place a limit on the number of failed login attempts you tolerate for a given user.

**Figure 3-13**
Duplicate Login

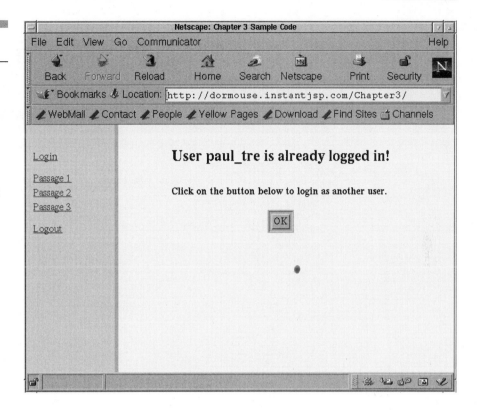

The action you take when a user exceeds the allotted number of failed logins depends largely on the security policy established by your company. In our case, we will temporarily revoke the user's login privileges and notify him or her that such privileges can be reinstated by contacting the system administrator. Now let's see how we implement this. We have already seen in Figure 3-14 what happens when we mistype or forget our user ID or password. The page shown in Figure 3-14 was generated by LoginFailure2.jsp. Here is the code:

```
<jsp:useBean id="sessionManager" class="com.instantjsp.SessionManager"
  scope="application" />
<jsp:useBean id="credentials" class="com.instantjsp.UserCredentials"
  scope="session" />
<html>
<head>
<title>LOGIN FAILURE</title>
</head>
<body bgcolor="#FFFFFF">
<center>
<br>
<h1>Login Unsuccessful for user
```

**Figure 3-14**
Failed Login

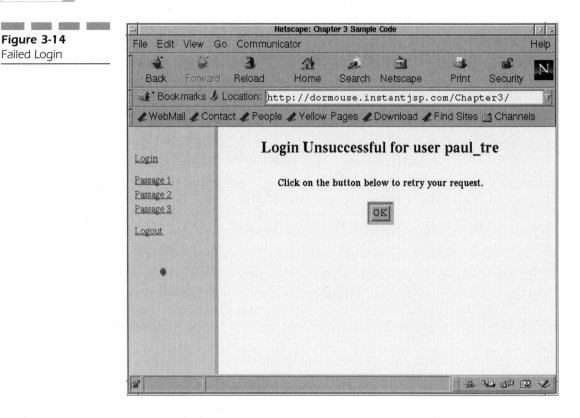

```
<%= credentials.getUser() %>
</h1>
<br>
<b>
<%
  if (sessionManager.isSuspended(credentials)) {
%>
<jsp:forward page="AccountSuspended.jsp" flush="true"/>
<%
  }
  else {
    sessionManager.incrementLoginAttempts(credentials);
    if (sessionManager.getLoginAttempts(credentials) >= 3) {
      sessionManager.suspendAccount(credentials);
%>
<jsp:forward page="AccountSuspended.jsp" flush="true"/>
<%
    }
  }
%>
Click on the button below to retry your request.
</b>
<form method=get action="Login2.jsp">
<input type=submit name="submit" value="OK">
</form>
```

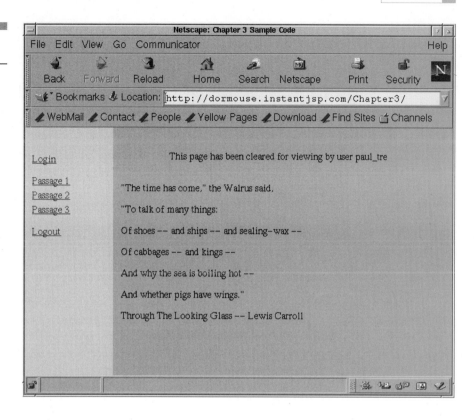

```
</center>
</body>
</html>
```

The first scriptlet passes the `credentials` object as an argument to the `isSuspended()` method of SessionManager. Let's look at the code for that method:

```
public boolean isSuspended(UserCredentials credentials)
    throws SQLException {
  String user = credentials.getUser();
  Connection conn = connectionPool.getConnection();
  Statement qs = conn.createStatement();
  ResultSet rs = qs.executeQuery(SELECT_ACCOUNT_STATUS +
    QUOTE + user + QUOTE);
  boolean tf = (getCount(rs) > 0);
  connectionPool.close(conn);
  return tf;
}
```

You can see that the method issues an SQL query. To understand the nature of this query, we need to examine the variable SELECT_ACCOUNT_STATUS, which is defined as follows:

```
private static final String SELECT_ACCOUNT_STATUS =
  "SELECT COUNT(*) FROM idpassword WHERE status=false AND userid=";
```

The query returns a count of those accounts that match the specified user ID and have a status of false. If the count is greater than zero, this means that the account for the specified user has been suspended. Table 3-3 shows that an account that is suspended, in this case the account for user paul_tre, shows a value of false for the status field.

If the account is suspended, a <jsp forward> action is executed. The target is AccountSuspended.jsp. Here is the code that generates the page shown in Figure 3-16:

```
<%
  session.invalidate();
%>
<html>
<body>
<center>
<font size="+2">
<b>
<br>
<br>
<br>
YOUR USERID HAS BEEN TEMPORARILY REVOKED!
</font>
</center>
<font size="+1">
<br>
<br>
You have exceeded the maximum number of unsuccessful login attempts.
<p>
To have your User ID reinstated, please contact the system
 administrator.
```

**TABLE 3-3**

Suspended Account in idpassword Table

```
Field     | Value

-- RECORD 0 --
userid    | kevin_mc
password  | vinthill
status    | t

-- RECORD 1 --
userid    | mike_zab
password  | chapin
status    | t

-- RECORD 2 --
userid    | paul_tre
password  | x93qvqv
status    | f

(3 rows)
```

**Figure 3-16**
Suspended Account

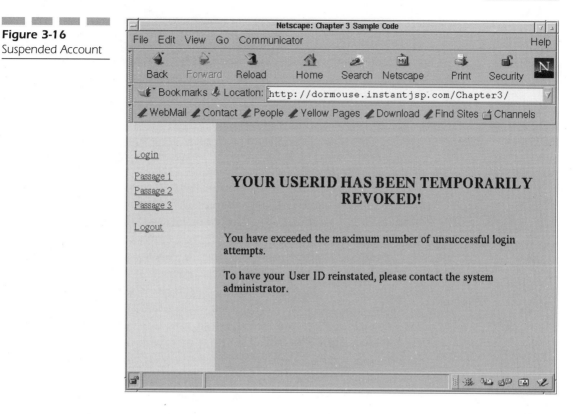

```
    </font>
    </body>
    </html>
```

The scriptlet in the first three lines invalidates the current session. When we discuss measurement of session time later in the chapter, this scriptlet will make sense.

Now, getting back to `LoginFailure2.jsp`, we have one remaining chunk of code to examine:

```
<%
    }
    else {
      sessionManager.incrementLoginAttempts(credentials);
      if (sessionManager.getLoginAttempts(credentials) >= 3) {
        sessionManager.suspendAccount(credentials);
%>
<jsp:forward page="AccountSuspended.jsp" flush="true"/>
<%
      }
    }
%>
```

After invoking the `incrementLoginAttempts()` method, which does exactly as its name implies, a test is performed to determine whether the maximum number of invalid login attempts has been exceeded. If exceeded, a `<jsp:forward>` action is executed and we see the same page we saw earlier in Figure 3-16.

# Catching and Handling Inactivity

As long as we are addressing simple security concerns, let's talk about unattended terminals. Let's say the last thing you were doing before you left work for the evening was using your browser to research a hot technical topic like JavaServer Pages. If you came to work the following morning and discovered that someone had used your browser while you were away, you might be mildly annoyed but probably not be terribly upset. If, on the other hand, the last thing you were doing before you went home was accessing an intranet application that gave you access to your pension fund portfolio, that would be a different case. Finally, let's consider the case where the last thing you were doing was accessing a database containing sensitive corporate data. If the overnight user was someone whose real occupation was corporate espionage and whose night job was a janitor, your boss might very well be waiting for you in the morning to discuss your continued employment. Simply put, unattended terminals present a security concern that must be addressed. One way to address this issue is to terminate a session when no activity has been detected from a user for a prespecified period. Let's see how we do this.

*NOTE:* *All of the major Web servers can be configured to invalidate inactive sessions. Most, however, allow you to specify one value for all sessions. The system administrator may have a valid reason to make this value much greater than you would like or even disable timeout. Handling timeouts yourself guarantees you will get the behavior you desire.*

SessionManager contains an inner class called InactivityMonitor that looks like this:

```
class InactivityMonitor implements Runnable {

  public void run() {
    while (true) {
```

```
        try {
          Thread.sleep(ONE_MINUTE);
          synchronized (currentLogins) {
            Enumeration keyEnumerator = currentLogins.keys();
            Vector expiredKeys = new Vector();
            while (keyEnumerator.hasMoreElements()) {
              String key = (String)keyEnumerator.nextElement();
              processElement(expiredKeys, key);
            }
            Enumeration expiredEnumerator = expiredKeys.elements();
            while (expiredEnumerator.hasMoreElements()) {
              currentLogins.remove(expiredEnumerator.nextElement());
            }
          }
        }
        catch (InterruptedException e) {
        }
    }  // end while
  }

  private void processElement(Vector expiredKeyTable,
      String key){
   LoginProfile profile = (LoginProfile)currentLogins.get(key);
   if (!profile.isLoggingIn) {
    //if (!profile.isAlive) {
     if (profile.minutesToTimeout <= 0) {
       // mark this one for removal
       expiredKeyTable.add(key);
     }
     else {
       // prepare for removal in 5 minutes time...
       //profile.isAlive = false;
       —profile.minutesToTimeout;
       currentLogins.put(key,profile);
     }
    }
   }
  }
}
```

As you can guess from the class name and the fact that it implements the `Runnable` interface, this code is intended to run in a separate thread. If you examine the constructor of the SessionManager class, you will see the following code that creates a Thread containing an instance of InactivityMonitor and starts it running:

```
InactivityMonitor monitor = new InactivityMonitor();
Thread monitorThread = new Thread(monitor);
monitorThread.start();
```

When we examine the `run()` method of InactivityMonitorThread, we see that it basically consists of a loop that sleeps for a minute and then checks every instance of LoginProfile stored in the `currentLogins` hashtable. If the LoginProfile object represents an active login (the isLoggingIn instance variable has a value of false and the isAlive instance variable has a value of true), the instance variable minutesToTimeout is checked. If this variable is not positive, indicating that no activity has been detected for 5 minutes, the LoginProfile object is marked for removal from the currentLogins hashtable; if it is zero or negative, its value is decremented by 1.

You might already guess that timeout can only be prevented if the minutesToTimeout instance variable of LoginProfile is reset at least once every 5 minutes. If we look at Passage1.jsp, we see the following scriptlet:

```
<%
  if (!sessionManager.keepAlive(credentials,getServletInfo())) {
%>
```

The keepAlive() method contains the following code:

```
if (currentLogins.containsKey(user)) {
  LoginProfile aProfile =
    (LoginProfile)currentLogins.get(user);
  aProfile.isAlive = true;
  aProfile.minutesToTimeout = TIMEOUT_MINUTES;
  currentLogins.put(user, aProfile);
}
```

So, each time that the user accesses a page, that page invokes the keepAlive() method, which provides another 5 minutes (or the value of TIMEOUT_MINUTES) and this prevents timeout. We have now addressed another security issue.

# Measuring Total Session Time

Security is important—that is why we discussed it first; however, it is not the only aspect of a login session. Knowing which users are accessing your site, how long they are staying, and what they are doing are also important. Although it is true that every major Web server logs statistics, you discover very quickly that even if you enable every possible option, you can't get the kind of statistics you'd like. The solution can be found in the adage that if you want something done properly, you should do it yourself. With that in mind, let's see how we can capture and record some statistics.

The first thing we will need is a table in our database in which we can

**TABLE 3-4**

Layout of
sessionstats Table

```
Table    = sessionstats
```

| Field | Type | Length |
|-------|------|--------|
| sessionid | varchar() | 64 |
| userid | varchar() | 64 |
| starttime | datetime | 8 |
| endtime | datetime | 8 |
| hits | int2 | 2 |

store statistics. Take a look at Table 3-4 and you will see a table with fields sessionid, userid, starttime, endtime, and hits. The names of the fields are indicative of the data they contain.

When we examined `ValidateUser2.jsp`, we saw the following line of code:

```
sessionManager.initiateSessionLogging(credentials);
```

We said that we would discuss this code later, so now we will. The code simply passes the `credentials` object as an argument to the `initiateSessionLogging()` method, which looks like this:

```
public void initiateSessionLogging(UserCredentials credentials)
    throws SQLException {
  String user = credentials.getUser();
  String sessionId = credentials.getSessionId();
  Connection conn = connectionPool.getConnection();
  Statement qs = conn.createStatement();
  ResultSet rs = qs.executeQuery(SELECT_SESSION_STATS +
    QUOTE + sessionId + QUOTE + " AND userid = " +
    QUOTE + user + QUOTE);
  if (getCount(rs) == 0) {
    java.util.Date dt = new java.util.Date();
    SimpleDateFormat sdf =
      new SimpleDateFormat("yyyy-MM-dd HH:mm:ss");
    String ft = sdf.format(dt);
    Statement us = conn.createStatement();
    us.executeUpdate("insert into sessionstats " +
      "(sessionid, userid, starttime, endtime, hits) VALUES (" +
      QUOTE + sessionId + QUOTE + COMMA +
      QUOTE +user + QUOTE + COMMA +
      QUOTE + ft + QUOTE + COMMA +
      QUOTE + ft + QUOTE + COMMA +
      "0" + RPAREN);
  }
connectionPool.close(conn);
}
```

The code inserts a record into the sessionstats table. The fields sessionid and userid are set to the values extracted from the `credentials` object that was received as an argument. The fields starttime and endtime are both set to the current date/time and the field hits is set to zero.

We have already seen that every page contains a call to `keepAlive()` to prevent timeout. In addition to preventing timeout, `keepAlive()` also passes the `credentials` object to updateSessionStats. Here is the code:

```
public void updateSessionStats(UserCredentials credentials)
    throws SQLException {
  String user = credentials.getUser();
  String sessionId = credentials.getSessionId();
  Connection conn = connectionPool.getConnection();
  Statement qs = conn.createStatement();
  ResultSet rs = qs.executeQuery(SELECT_SESSION_STATS +
    QUOTE + sessionId + QUOTE + " and userid = " +
    QUOTE + user + QUOTE);
  if (getCount(rs) > 0) {
    java.util.Date dt = new java.util.Date();
    SimpleDateFormat sdf =
      new SimpleDateFormat("yyyy-MM-dd HH:mm:ss");
    String ft = sdf.format(dt);
    Statement us = conn.createStatement();
    us.executeUpdate(UPDATE_SESSION_STATS +
      QUOTE + ft + QUOTE + COMMA +
      HITS_PLUS_QUALIFIER + QUOTE + sessionId + QUOTE);
  }
  connectionPool.close(conn);
}
```

The method performs an SQL UPDATE that sets the endtime field to the current time and increments the hit count.

Table 3-5 shows the result of a query issued against the sessionstats table. Although the statistics we have included are quite simple, it would not be a major task to add others.

# Monitoring and Profiling Activities

Monitoring is important. If monitoring a page reveals that it has been visited twice in the last three months, you might want to consider dropping that page. Similarly, you might want to spend time optimizing a page that receives a high volume of hits.

Profiling is even more important. If, over a period of time, you can develop a profile of a user who visits your site, the advertising you display when that user visits your site can be much more targeted.

**TABLE 3-5**

*Some session
Statistics*

```
-- RECORD 1 --
sessionid|  3fbff3d0ed7b50e0.3.946845240449
userid   |  paul_tre
starttime|  Sun Jan 02 15:34:09 2000 EST
endtime  |  Sun Jan 02 15:34:09 2000 EST
hits     |  0

-- RECORD 2 --
sessionid|  3fc3332e11454590.4.946845343516
userid   |  kevin_mc
starttime|  Sun Jan 02 15:35:55 2000 EST
endtime  |  Sun Jan 02 15:36:04 2000 EST
hits     |  3

-- RECORD 3 --
sessionid|  3fd8810a3678d862.5.946845370856
userid   |  mike_zab
starttime|  Sun Jan 02 15:36:19 2000 EST
endtime  |  Sun Jan 02 15:36:29 2000 EST
hits     |  5

(4 rows)
```

**TABLE 3-6**

*Layout of raw-
pagestats Table*

Table    = rawpagestats

| Field | Type | Length |
|-------|------|--------|
| userid | varchar() | 64 |
| sessionid | varchar() | 64 |
| dt | date | 4 |
| tm | time | 8 |
| pagedesc | varchar() | 64 |

Now let's see how to collect some simple data that we might find useful in monitoring and profiling. Table 3-6 shows a database table named raw-pagestats that has fields named userid, sessionid, dt, tm, and pagedesc.

In addition to the actions we have already seen that the keepAlive() method performs, there is yet another, a call to logRawStats(). Here is the code:

```
public void logRawStats(UserCredentials credentials, String pageInfo)
    throws SQLException {
  String user = credentials.getUser();
  String sessionId = credentials.getSessionId();
  java.util.Date dt = new java.util.Date();
  SimpleDateFormat sdfd = new SimpleDateFormat("yyyy-MM-dd");
```

**TABLE 3-7**

Some Raw Statistics

```
instantjsp=> select dt,tm,pagedesc from rawpagestats where
userid='mike_zab' order by pagedesc;

         dt   | tm       | pagedesc
--------------+----------+--------------------------------------------
01-02-2000    | 15:36:22 | Paul's #1 Favorite
01-02-2000    | 15:36:24 | Paul's #2 Favorite
01-02-2000    | 15:36:29 | Paul's #2 Favorite
01-02-2000    | 15:36:29 | Paul's #2 Favorite
01-02-2000    | 15:36:25 | Paul's #3 Favorite

(5 rows)
```

```
    String fd = sdfd.format(dt);
    SimpleDateFormat sdft = new SimpleDateFormat("HH:mm:ss");
    String ft = sdft.format(dt);
    Connection conn = connectionPool.getConnection();
    Statement us = conn.createStatement();
    us.executeUpdate(INSERT_RAW_STATS +
      QUOTE +user + QUOTE + COMMA +
      QUOTE + sessionId + QUOTE + COMMA +
      QUOTE + fd + QUOTE + COMMA +
      QUOTE + ft + QUOTE + COMMA +
      QUOTE + pageInfo.replace('ı'`') + QUOTE + RPAREN);
    connectionPool.close(conn);
  }
```

This code performs an SQL UPDATE to insert the user ID, session ID, date, time, and page description. Table 3-7 shows the results of a simple query against the rawpagestats table. You can see from the results that user mike_zab prefers the page "Paul's # 2 Favorite." Rather than performing ad hoc queries, we would probably extract the raw data each night and use it as input to a batch process that would perform extensive analysis on the data.

**NOTE:** *All our statistics have been logged inline. In a real-world situation, for performance reasons, we would probably just transmit the raw data to a separate logging daemon that would probably be running on a separate computer.*

# Logging Out

The final activity performed by a user at the end of a session is that of logging out. We have provided a "Logout" option in our menu; when selected, it accesses LogoutVerification.jsp. Here is the code:

```
<jsp:useBean id="sessionManager" class="com.instantjsp.SessionManager"
  scope="application"/>
<jsp:useBean id="credentials" class="com.instantjsp.
 UserCredentials"
  scope="session" />
<%
  if (!sessionManager.alreadyLoggedIn(credentials)) {
%>
  <jsp:forward page="NotLoggedIn.jsp" />
<%
  }
%>
<html>
<body bgcolor="#c0c0c0" link="#999999"
    vlink="#999999" alink="#999999" onLoad="giveFocus()">
<center>
<font size=+2>
<BR>
<BR>
<B>LOGOUT VERIFICATION</B>
</font>
</center>
<font size=+1>
<br>
<br>
If you really want to logout, click on the button labeled
<b>CONFIRM LOGOUT</b> below.
<p>
If you do <b>not</b> wish to logout, click on one of the links in the
 menu
area on the left.
<br>
<br>
</font>
<center>
<FORM NAME="logout" METHOD=POST ACTION="http://dormouse.instantjsp.
 com/Chapter3/Logout.jsp">
<BR>
<BR>
<BR>
<font size=+1>
<b>
<INPUT TYPE="submit" VALUE="CONFIRM LOGOUT">
</b>
</font>
</FORM>
</CENTER>
</body>
</html>
```

The first scriptlet invokes the alreadyLoggedIn() method of
SessionManager to see if the user is logged in. If a value of false is
returned by the method, a <jsp:forward> action is executed, specifying
a target of NotLoggedIn.html. This results in the page displayed in
Figure 3-17. Here is the code for NotLoggedIn.html:

**Figure 3-17**
Attempting Logout
but Not Logged In

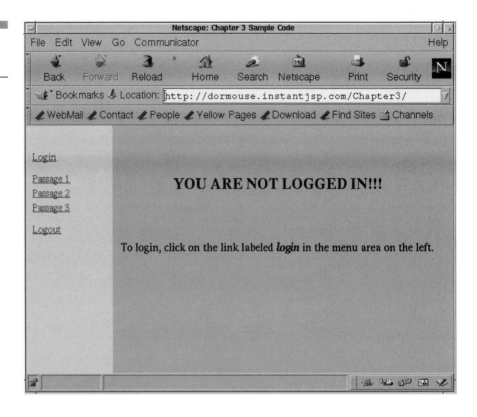

```
<html>
<body>
<center>
<font size="+2">
<b>
<br>
<br>
<br>
YOU ARE NOT LOGGED IN!!!
<br>
<br>
</font>
</center>
<font size="+1">
<br>
<br>
To login, click on the link labeled <b><i>login</i></b> in the menu
  area
on the left.
</font>
</body>
</html>
```

**Figure 3-18**
Logout Verification

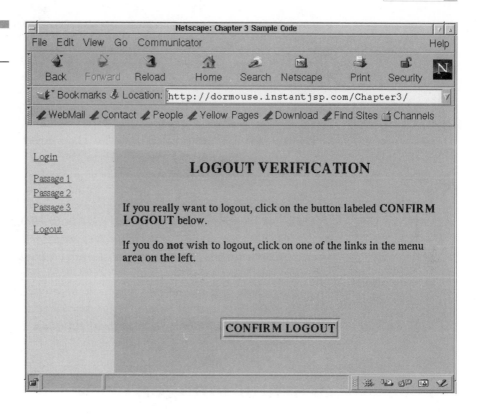

If `alreadyLoggedIn()` returns a value of true, the page shown in Figure 3-18 is displayed. When the CONFIRM LOGOUT button is clicked, a request is sent to `Logout.jsp`. Here is the code:

```
<%@ page errorPage="/common/Exception.jsp" %>
<jsp:useBean id="sessionManager" class="com.instantjsp.SessionManager"
  scope="application" />
<jsp:useBean id="credentials" class="com.instantjsp.UserCredentials"
  scope="session" />
<%
  sessionManager.logout(credentials);
  session.invalidate();
%>
<%@ include file="Intro.html" %>
```

The code in the scriptlet passes the `credentials` object as an argument to the `logout()` method of SessionManager. Here is the code for the `logout()` method:

```
public void logout(UserCredentials credentials) {
  synchronized (currentLogins) {
    currentLogins.remove(credentials.getUser());
  }
}
```

As you can see, the code does nothing more than remove the LoginProfile object for the user from the `currentLogins` hashtable.

The last line in `Logout.jsp` is an `include` directive that specifies file `Intro.html`. This puts us right back to the page we saw displayed in Figure 3-7, and we are ready to handle another login.

*NOTE:* *As you probably noticed, all code in SessionManager that accesses the* `currentLogins` *hashtable is contained in a synchronized block. This maintains the integrity of the hashtable when multiple, simultaneous login/logout activities are attempted from many users. You should also note that use of a hashtable to hold current logins works only if a single instance of SessionManager exists. It would probably be wiser to store current logins in a separate database table.*

# SessionManager Code

We have examined code snippets from the SessionManager class. If you are interested in examining the code in its entirety, here is the complete listing:

```
package com.instantjsp;

import java.sql.Connection;
import java.sql.ResultSet;
import java.sql.SQLException;
import java.sql.Statement;
import java.text.SimpleDateFormat;
import java.util.Date;
import java.util.Enumeration;
import java.util.Hashtable;
import java.util.Vector;

import javax.servlet.ServletContext;

import javaservlets.jdbc.ConnectionPool;

public class SessionManager {

  private Hashtable currentLogins;
  private ConnectionPool connectionPool;
```

```
private static final int TIMEOUT_MINUTES = 5;
private static final long ONE_MINUTE = 60000L;

private static final String POOL_CFG_FILE =
   "javaservlets/jdbc/SessionManagerConnectionPool.cfg";

private static final String SELECT_PASSWORD =
   "SELECT password FROM idpassword WHERE userid = ";

private static final String SELECT_ACCOUNT_STATUS =
   "SELECT COUNT(*) FROM idpassword WHERE status = false AND
    userid = ";

private static final String UPDATE_ACCOUNT_STATUS =
   "UPDATE idpassword SET status = false WHERE userid = ";

private static final String SELECT_SESSION_STATS =
   "SELECT COUNT (*) FROM sessionstats WHERE sessionid = ";

private static final String UPDATE_SESSION_STATS =
   "UPDATE sessionstats SET endtime = ";

private static final String INSERT_RAW_STATS =
   "INSERT INTO rawpagestats" +
   "(userid, sessionid, dt, tm, pagedesc) VALUES (";

private static final String HITS_PLUS_QUALIFIER =
   "hits = hits + 1 WHERE sessionid = ";

private static final String RPAREN = ")";
private static final String COMMA = ",";
private static final String QUOTE = "'";

private class LoginProfile extends UserCredentials{
  boolean isLoggingIn;
  int loginAttempts;
  boolean isLoggedIn;
  Date loginTime;
  Date lastActivity;
  boolean isAlive;
  int minutesToTimeout;

public LoginProfile(UserCredentials credentials) {
  setUser(credentials.getUser());
  setPassword(credentials.getPassword());
  isLoggingIn = true;
  isLoggedIn = false;
  loginAttempts = 0;
  isAlive = false;
  minutesToTimeout = TIMEOUT_MINUTES;
 }
}

class InactivityMonitor implements Runnable {
public void run() {
  while (true) {
    try {
      Thread.sleep(ONE_MINUTE);
      synchronized (currentLogins) {
```

```
        Enumeration keyEnumerator = currentLogins.keys();
        Vector expiredKeys = new Vector();
        while (keyEnumerator.hasMoreElements()) {
          String key = (String)keyEnumerator.nextElement();
          processElement(expiredKeys, key);
        }
        Enumeration expiredEnumerator = expiredKeys.elements();
        while (expiredEnumerator.hasMoreElements()) {
          currentLogins.remove(expiredEnumerator.nextElement());
        }
      }
    }
    catch (InterruptedException e) {
    }
  } // end while
}

private void processElement(Vector expiredKeyTable,
    String key) {
  LoginProfile profile = (LoginProfile)currentLogins.get(key);
  if (!profile.isLoggingIn) {
    //if (!profile.isAlive) {
    if (profile.minutesToTimeout <= 0) {
      // mark this one for removal
      expiredKeyTable.add(key);
    }
    else {
      // prepare for removal in 5 minutes time...
      //profile.isAlive = false;
      —profile.minutesToTimeout;
      currentLogins.put(key,profile);
    }
  }
}


  public SessionManager() throws Exception {
    connectionPool = new ConnectionPool();
    connectionPool.initialize(POOL_CFG_FILE);
    currentLogins = new Hashtable();
    InactivityMonitor monitor = new InactivityMonitor();
    Thread monitorThread = new Thread(monitor);
    monitorThread.start();
  }

  public boolean isLoggingIn(UserCredentials credentials) {
    boolean loggingIn = false;
    String user = credentials.getUser();
    synchronized (currentLogins) {
      if (currentLogins.containsKey(user)) {
        LoginProfile aProfile =
          (LoginProfile)currentLogins.get(user);
        loggingIn = aProfile.isLoggingIn;
      }
    }
    return loggingIn;
  }

  public boolean alreadyLoggedIn(UserCredentials credentials) {
```

```
      boolean loggedIn = false;
      String user = credentials.getUser();
      synchronized (currentLogins) {
        if (currentLogins.containsKey(user)) {
          LoginProfile aProfile =
            (LoginProfile)currentLogins.get(user);
          loggedIn = aProfile.isLoggedIn;
        }
      }
      return loggedIn;
    }

    public int getLoginAttempts(UserCredentials credentials) {
      int loginAttempts = 0;
      String user = credentials.getUser();
      synchronized (currentLogins) {
        if (currentLogins.containsKey(user)) {
          LoginProfile aProfile =
            (LoginProfile)currentLogins.get(user);
          loginAttempts = aProfile.loginAttempts;
        }
      }
      return loginAttempts;
    }

    public void incrementLoginAttempts(UserCredentials credentials) {
      String user = credentials.getUser();
      synchronized (currentLogins) {
        if (currentLogins.containsKey(user)) {
          LoginProfile aProfile =
            (LoginProfile)currentLogins.get(user);
          ++aProfile.loginAttempts;
          currentLogins.put(user, aProfile);
        }
      }
    }

    public boolean keepAlive(UserCredentials credentials,
        String pageInfo) throws SQLException {
      if (!alreadyLoggedIn(credentials)) {
        return false;
      }
      updateSessionStats(credentials);
      String user = credentials.getUser();
        synchronized (currentLogins) {
          if (currentLogins.containsKey(user)) {
            LoginProfile aProfile =
              (LoginProfile)currentLogins.get(user);
            aProfile.isAlive = true;
            aProfile.minutesToTimeout = TIMEOUT_MINUTES;
            currentLogins.put(user, aProfile);
          }
        }
      logRawStats(credentials, pageInfo);
      return true;
    }

    private int getCount(ResultSet rs) throws SQLException {
      rs.next();
```

```
      return rs.getInt(1);
}

public boolean isSuspended(UserCredentials credentials)
    throws SQLException {
  String user = credentials.getUser();
  Connection conn = connectionPool.getConnection();
  Statement qs = conn.createStatement();
  ResultSet rs = qs.executeQuery(SELECT_ACCOUNT_STATUS +
    QUOTE + user + QUOTE);
  boolean tf = (getCount(rs) > 0);
  connectionPool.close(conn);
  return tf;
}

public void suspendAccount(UserCredentials credentials)
    throws SQLException {
  String user = credentials.getUser();
  synchronized (currentLogins) {
    currentLogins.remove(user);
  }
  Connection conn = connectionPool.getConnection();
  Statement us = conn.createStatement();
  us.executeUpdate(UPDATE_ACCOUNT_STATUS +
      QUOTE + user + QUOTE);
  connectionPool.close(conn);
}

public boolean login(UserCredentials credentials)
    throws SQLException {
  if (alreadyLoggedIn(credentials)) {
    return false;
  }
  String user = credentials.getUser();
  LoginProfile profile;
  synchronized (currentLogins) {
    if (currentLogins.containsKey(user)) {
      profile = (LoginProfile)currentLogins.get(user);
    }
    else {
      profile = new LoginProfile(credentials);
    }
  }
  Connection conn = connectionPool.getConnection();
  Statement qs = conn.createStatement();
  ResultSet rs =
    qs.executeQuery(SELECT_PASSWORD +
    QUOTE + user + QUOTE);
  while (rs.next()) {
    if (rs.getString(1).equals(credentials.getPassword())) {
      profile.isLoggingIn = false;
      profile.isLoggedIn = true;
      break;
    }
  }
  synchronized (currentLogins) {
    currentLogins.put(user, profile);
  }
  return profile.isLoggedIn;
```

```
}

public void initiateSessionLogging(UserCredentials credentials)
    throws SQLException {
  String user = credentials.getUser();
  String sessionId = credentials.getSessionId();
  Connection conn = connectionPool.getConnection();
  Statement qs = conn.createStatement();
  ResultSet rs = qs.executeQuery(SELECT_SESSION_STATS +
    QUOTE + sessionId + QUOTE + " AND userid = " +
    QUOTE + user + QUOTE);
  if (getCount(rs) == 0) {
    java.util.Date dt = new java.util.Date();
    SimpleDateFormat sdf = new SimpleDateFormat("yyyy-MM-dd
     HH:mm:ss");
    String ft = sdf.format(dt);
    Statement us = conn.createStatement();
    us.executeUpdate("insert into sessionstats " +
      "(sessionid, userid, starttime, endtime, hits) VALUES (" +
      QUOTE + sessionId + QUOTE + COMMA +
      QUOTE +user + QUOTE + COMMA +
      QUOTE + ft + QUOTE + COMMA +
      QUOTE + ft + QUOTE + COMMA +
      "0" + RPAREN);
  }
  connectionPool.close(conn);
}

public void logRawStats(UserCredentials credentials, String
 pageInfo)
    throws SQLException {
  String user = credentials.getUser();
  String sessionId = credentials.getSessionId();
  java.util.Date dt = new java.util.Date();
  SimpleDateFormat sdfd = new SimpleDateFormat("yyyy-MM-dd");
  String fd = sdfd.format(dt);
  SimpleDateFormat sdft = new SimpleDateFormat("HH:mm:ss");
  String ft = sdft.format(dt);
  Connection conn = connectionPool.getConnection();
  Statement us = conn.createStatement();
  us.executeUpdate(INSERT_RAW_STATS +
    QUOTE +user + QUOTE + COMMA +
    QUOTE + sessionId + QUOTE + COMMA +
    QUOTE + fd + QUOTE + COMMA +
    QUOTE + ft + QUOTE + COMMA +
    QUOTE + pageInfo.replace('ı'`') + QUOTE + RPAREN);
  connectionPool.close(conn);
}

public void updateSessionStats(UserCredentials credentials)
    throws SQLException {
  String user = credentials.getUser();
  String sessionId = credentials.getSessionId();
  Connection conn = connectionPool.getConnection();
  Statement qs = conn.createStatement();
  ResultSet rs = qs.executeQuery(SELECT_SESSION_STATS +
    QUOTE + sessionId + QUOTE + " and userid = " +
    QUOTE + user + QUOTE);
  if (getCount(rs) > 0) {
```

```
            java.util.Date dt = new java.util.Date();
            SimpleDateFormat sdf =
              new SimpleDateFormat("yyyy-MM-dd HH:mm:ss");
            String ft = sdf.format(dt);
            Statement us = conn.createStatement();
            us.executeUpdate(UPDATE_SESSION_STATS +
              QUOTE + ft + QUOTE + COMMA +
              HITS_PLUS_QUALIFIER + QUOTE + sessionId + QUOTE);
          }
        connectionPool.close(conn);
      }

    public void logout(UserCredentials credentials) {
      synchronized (currentLogins) {
        currentLogins.remove(credentials.getUser());
      }
    }
  }
```

# Using JSP on Your Intranet

- Employee Database
- Accessing Employee Data
- Departmental Listings
- Vacation Log
- Check Next Performance Review
- Employee Telephone Directory
- Skills Database
- Sales Literature Repository
- FAQ Database

In the last chapter, we saw how to develop the code required to conduct a Web session. In this chapter, we explore some activities we can perform during such a session. We do so by creating a small intranet application. This application is trivial and is not intended to represent the real world but rather to further demonstrate the use of JSP.

# Creating an Employee Database

Let us begin by creating a table describing the types of employee information required by our intranet application. It is shown in Table 4-1. Next, let's insert records for a few employees. These records are shown in Table 4-2.

Since we are using the employee's ID number as a user ID, we also add a few 9-digit ID numbers to the idpassword table we created in Chapter 3. Table 4-3 reflects these additions.

# Permitting Employees to Access Their Records

Now that we've created the employee database, the next step is to provide employees with a Web interface they can use to access the data it

**TABLE 4-1**

Employee Table Layout

```
Table    = empdata
+------------------------------+--------------------------------------+------+
| Field                        | Type                                 |Length|
+------------------------------+--------------------------------------+------+
|  ssn                         | char() not null                      |   9  |
|  last                        | varchar()                            |  25  |
|  first                       | varchar()                            |  15  |
|  mi                          | char()                               |   1  |
|  hired                       | date                                 |   4  |
|  review                      | date                                 |   4  |
|  dept                        | char()                               |   4  |
|  ext                         | char()                               |   4  |
|  cell                        | char()                               |  10  |
|  pager                       | char()                               |  10  |
|  vacdue                      | int2                                 |   2  |
|  carried                     | int2                                 |   2  |
|  taken                       | int2                                 |   2  |
+------------------------------+--------------------------------------+------+
Index:     empdata_pkey
```

**TABLE 4-2**

Employee Table
Partial Contents

```
-- RECORD 35 --              -- RECORD 36 --
ssn      |  129007275        ssn      |  655121345
last     |  Ridgeway         last     |  Worthington
first    |  Charles          first    |  Michael
mi       |  D                mi       |  K
hired    |  06-20-1992       hired    |  07-11-1997
review   |  04-01-2000       review   |  07-01-2000
dept     |  2001             dept     |  2005
ext      |  3433             ext      |  1052
cell     |  2125559081       cell     |  2125555447
pager    |  2125559082       pager    |  2125555446
vacdue   |  25               vacdue   |  15
carried  |  5                carried  |  0
taken    |  0                taken    |  0
```

**TABLE 4-3**

Partial Contents of
idpassword Table

```
userid      | password |status
------------+----------+------
kevin_mc    | vinthill |t
mike_zab    | chapin   |t
paul_tre    | x93qvqv  |t
661981312   | a65tr30  |t
655121345   | wq03n7a  |t
544218877   | t0q88xc  |t
411032287   | e33t55jj |t
401176655   | r55tsd34 |t
209876612   | gm777d56 |t
```

contains. Since the navigational tool we used in Chapter 3 seems to have satisfied our needs, we will reuse it to the extent that we can. Here is the code for `index.html`. As you can see, it is identical to the `index.html` file we used in Chapter 3.

```
<html>
<head>
  <title>Employee Data</title>
</head>
<frameset cols="165,*">
  <frame src="MenuFrame.html"
    frameborder="0" noresize="noresize" name="mainmenuframe">
  <frame src="Intro.html"
    frameborder="0" name="rightframe">
</frameset>
</html>
```

The contents of the navigational menu are naturally different, so `MenuFrame.html` looks like this:

```
<html>
<body text="#000000" bgcolor="#e0e0e0" link="#555555" vlink="#555555"
 alink="#555555">
<br>
<br>
<table COLS=1 WIDTH="100%" >
  <tr>
    <td>
      <a
href="http://dormouse.instantjsp.com/common/Login.jsp?ok=/Chapter4/
 Welcome.jsp&dup=/common/DuplicateLogin.jsp&fail=/common/LoginFailure.
 jsp" target="rightframe">Login</a>
    </td>
  </tr>

  <tr>
    <td>
    </td>
  </tr>

  <tr>
    <td>
    </td>
  </tr>

  <tr>
    <td><a href="MyDepartment.jsp" target="rightframe">My Department
      </a>
    </td>
  </tr>

  <tr>
    <td><a href="MyVacation.jsp" target="rightframe">My Vacation</a>
    </td>
  </tr>
  <tr>
    <td><a href="NextReview.jsp" target="rightframe">My Next Review
      </a>
    </td>
  </tr>

  <tr>
    <td><a href="PhoneList.jsp" target="rightframe">Phone Directory
      </a>
    </td>
  </tr>

  <tr>
    <td><a href="SkillsSearch.jsp" target="rightframe">Skills
    Database</a>
    </td>
  </tr>

  <tr>
    <td><a href="SalesLiterature.jsp" target="rightframe">Sales
    Literature</a>
    </td>
  </tr>
```

```
<tr>
  <td><a href="KnowledgePool.jsp" target="rightframe">Knowledge
  Pool</a>
  </td>
</tr>

<tr>
  <td>
  </td>
</tr>

<tr>
  <td>
  </td>
</tr>

<tr>
  <td><a href="http://dormouse.instantjsp.com/common/
  LogoutVerification.jsp?nextpage=/Chapter4/Intro.html" target="
  rightframe">Logout</a>
  </td>
</tr>
</table>

</body>
</html>
```

The contents of `Intro.html` are also different. Here is the code:

```
<html>
<body bgcolor="#c0c0c0" link="#999999"
  vlink="#999999" alink="#999999">
<center>
<font size=+2>
<br>
<br>
<b>Welcome!</B>
</font>
</center>
<br>
<br>
<br>
<font size=+1>
Welcome to Employee Info Central. This is only a prototype. It can be
expanded to deliver more data than it does now.
<p>
Before you can view any of the pages, you must login. Be careful
  typing your
user ID and password because you only get <i><b>three</b></i>
  attempts. After that,
your account will be temporarily deactivated and you will have to
  bother me to
reset your account.
<p>
Sharing your browser with someone else is not recommended. If you do,
remember that if you accidently leave yourself logged in, the next
person using the browser can access your personal data.
```

```
<p>
</font>
</body>
</html>
```

If you type the URL `http://dormouse.instantjsp.com/Chapter4`, you will see the page shown in Figure 4-1, which closely resembles Figure 3-7. If we click on "My Department" in the menu, the page shown in Figure 4-2 is displayed; so, the behavior is also similar to the interface we developed in Chapter 3. We now explore the code in detail and see that there is more to reusability than simply copying code. We also see the importance of designing code so that it is reusable and see how JSP technology helps.

The very first problem we encounter when we attempt to reuse code from Chapter 3 is in `Login2.jsp`. It contains a hard-coded reference to `/Chapter3/ValidateUser2.jsp`. It might be tempting to simply copy `ValidateUser2.jsp` into `/Chapter4` and make one simple change, but

**Figure 4-1**
Intranet Initial Page

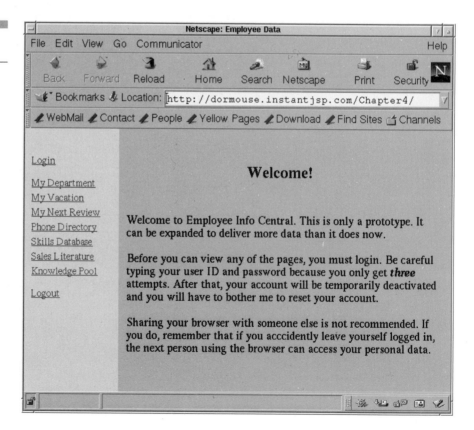

**Figure 4-2**
Attempting Access
Without Proper Login

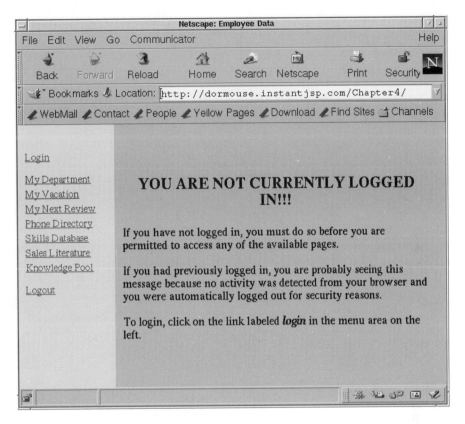

this practice would lead to a maintenance nightmare. If a bug were discovered, we would be faced with the task of locating every mutated version of the original file and changing it. A much better solution would be to eliminate the hard-coded references from `ValidateUser2`. To see how we do this, we need to first look at the version of `MenuFrame.html` we are using here in Chapter 4. We have already listed the code.

Notice that the URL in the hypertext link associated with the "Login" menu option contains a query string that passes the following three key-value pairs to `/common/Login.jsp`:

**1.** `ok=/Chapter4/Welcome.jsp`

**2.** `dup=/common/DuplicateLogin.jsp`

**3.** `fail=/common/LoginFailure.jsp`

So, let's look at `Login.jsp` and see how these are handled. Here is the code:

```
<jsp:useBean id="sessionManager"
class="com.instantjsp.SessionManager"
    scope="application" />
<jsp:useBean id="credentials" class="com.instantjsp.UserCredentials"
    scope="session" />
<%
  if (sessionManager.alreadyLoggedIn(credentials)) {
%>
    <jsp:forward page="LogoutFirst.jsp" />
<%
  }
  String query = request.getQueryString();
  String action =
    "\"http://dormouse.instantjsp.com/common/ValidateUser.jsp?" +
 query + "\"";
%>
<html>
<head>
   <title>Login</title>

<script language="JavaScript">

  function giveFocus() {
    document.login.user.focus()
  }

  function submitForm() {
    document.login.submit()
  }

  function resetForm() {
    document.login.reset()
    document.login.user.focus()
  }
</script>
</head>

<body bgcolor="#c0c0c0" link="#999999"
   vlink="#999999" alink="#999999" onLoad="giveFocus()">
<center>
<font size=+2>
<BR>
<BR>
<B>LOGIN</B>
</font>
<br>
<br>
<br>
<br>
<FORM NAME="login" METHOD=POST ACTION=<%= action%>>
<TABLE WIDTH="50%">
<TR>
<TD align=right>
<font size=+1>
<B>
User ID:
</B>
</font>
```

```
</TD>
<TD>
<font size=+1><INPUT NAME="user" TYPE="TEXT" LENGTH="9" MAXLENGTH="9">
</font>
</TD>
</TR>
<TR>
<TD align=right>
<font size=+1>
<B>
Password:
</B>
</font>
</TD>
<TD>
<font size=+1><INPUT NAME="password" TYPE="PASSWORD" LENGTH="8"
 MAXLENGTH="8">
</font>
</TD>
</TR>
</TABLE>
<BR>
<BR>
<BR>
<font size=+1>
<b>
<INPUT TYPE="button" VALUE="LOGIN" onClick="submitForm()">
     
<INPUT TYPE="button" VALUE="RESET" onClick="resetForm()">
</b>
</font>
</FORM>
</CENTER>
</body>
</html>
```

The second scriptlet in this page contains the following code:

```
String query = request.getQueryString();
  String action =
    "\"http://dormouse.instantjsp.com/common/ValidateUser.jsp?" +
    query + "\"";
```

The code in this scriptlet invokes the `getQueryString()` method, which returns a String containing the key-value pairs we mentioned earlier. The returned String is combined with a URI to form a URL that is saved in the String `action`. We see it used later in the code as:

```
<FORM NAME="login" METHOD=POST ACTION=<%= action%>
```

Since the URI portion of the URL generated by the expression `<%= action %>` specifies `ValidateUser.jsp`, we should now examine that page. It looks like this:

```
<%@ page import="java.util.Hashtable" %>
<jsp:useBean id="sessionManager" class="com.instantjsp.SessionManager"
    scope="application" />
<jsp:useBean id="credentials" class="com.instantjsp.UserCredentials"
    scope="session" />
<jsp:setProperty name="credentials" property="*" />
<%! String nextPage; %>
<%
  String query = request.getQueryString();
  Hashtable qt = HttpUtils.parseQueryString(query);
  if (sessionManager.alreadyLoggedIn(credentials)) {
    nextPage = ((String[])qt.get("dup"))[0];
  }
  else {
    if (sessionManager.login(credentials)) {
      credentials.setSessionId(session.getId());
      sessionManager.initiateSessionLogging(credentials);
      nextPage = ((String[])qt.get("ok"))[0];
    }
    else {
      nextPage = ((String[])qt.get("fail"))[0];
    }
  }
%>
<jsp:forward page="<%= nextPage %>" flush="true"/>
<!%@ page errorPage="/common/Exception.jsp" %>
```

This code uses the same technique as the code we saw in Chapter 3 (i.e., it assigns one of three values to the String nextPage). The difference is that instead of assigning hard values, this code assigns the values passed from Login.jsp, which in turn were passed from MenuFrame. html.

With all of the hard-coded references removed, we store both Login.jsp and ValidateUser.jsp in the /common directory and make them available for use by any login. We now have true reusability. If a bug is discovered in Login.jsp or ValidateUser.jsp, we must fix it in only one place. When a developer wishes to use our common code, he or she simply provides a hyperlink to /common/Login.jsp and specifies the appropriate key-value pairs to handle a successful login, a duplicate login, and a failed login.

If we select the "Login" option from the menu, we see the page displayed in Figure 4-3. If we type an incorrect password, we see the page displayed in Figure 4-4. (Note that we have added an indication of how many unsuccessful attempts have been made.) Finally, if we enter a valid user ID and password, we see the page shown in Figure 4-5.

Notice that in the preceding discussion we took for granted the SessionManager and UserCredential Beans that appear in the <jsp:useBean> actions. We mentioned back in Chapter 1 that reusability is a benefit of Beans and now we have demonstrated it.

**Figure 4-3**
Intranet Login Page

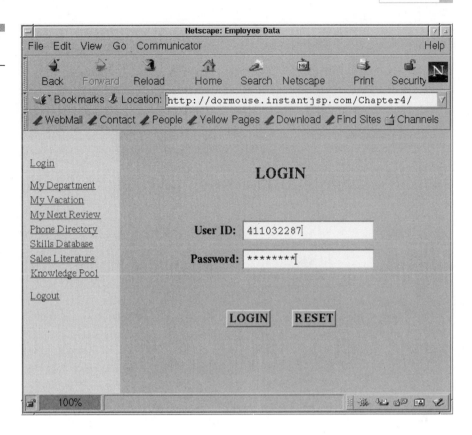

The code for `FailedLogin.jsp` and `Welcome.jsp`, which generates the pages shown in Figures 4-4 and 4-5, respectively, is contained on the CD as is the code for `FailedLogin.jsp`.

Now that we have a working login, we can proceed with developing code that permits an employee to access his or her records in the database we have created.

## Seeing Who Is in My Department

The option labeled "My Department" in the menu links to `MyDepartment.jsp`, which generates the page shown in Figure 4-6. Here is the code for `MyDepartment.jsp`:

```
<%@ include file="/common/EnsureUserLoggedIn.jsp" %>
<jsp:useBean id="eiBean" class="com.instantjsp.EmployeeInfo"
    scope="application" />
<%
```

**Figure 4-4**
Unsuccessful Intranet
Login

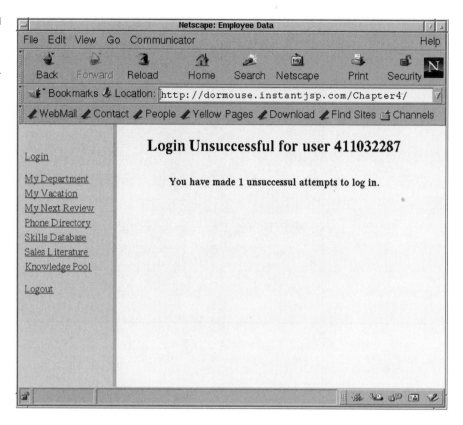

```
    String user = credentials.getUser();
%>
<html>
<body>
<b>
<br>
<br>
You are a member of department
<%= eiBean.getDept(user) %>
.
<br>
<br>
Check the order in which you would like to sort the list of the
members of your department then click on the <i>Generate List</i>
 button.
<br>
<br>
<form method="post" action="http://dormouse.instantjsp.com/Chapter4/
 GetDeptData.jsp">
<input type="radio" name="sortoption" value="last" checked>
  Sort alphabetically by last name
<br>
<br>
```

**Figure 4-5**
Successful Intranet
Login

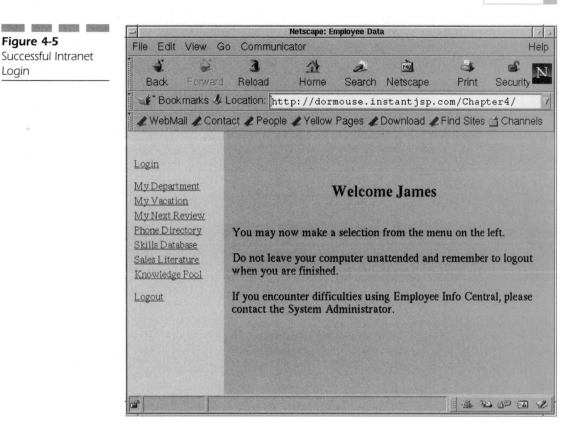

```
<input type="radio" name="sortoption" value="hired">
  Sort by seniority
<br>
<br>
<center>
<input name="submit" type="submit" value="Generate List">
</form>
</center>
</b>
</body>
</html>
```

We enforce login as we did in Chapter 3 by including EnsureUsed-LoggedIn.jsp. Notice that we have moved this file to the /common directory. Here is the code:

```
<jsp:useBean id="sessionManager" class="com.instantjsp.SessionManager"
    scope="application" />
<jsp:useBean id="credentials" class="com.instantjsp.UserCredentials"
    scope="session" />
<%
    if (!sessionManager.alreadyLoggedIn(credentials)) {
```

**Figure 4-6**
Selecting Option for
Presenting
Department Data

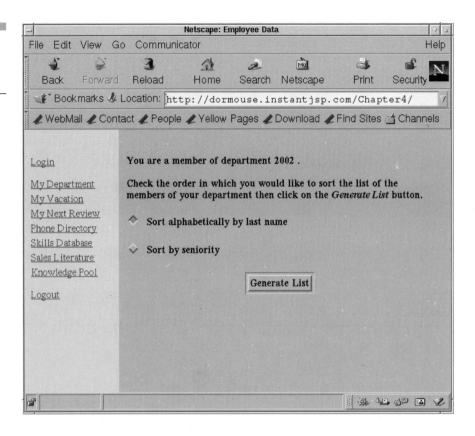

```
%>
    <jsp:forward page="/common/RequestLogin.jsp" />
<%
  }
  else {
    sessionManager.keepAlive(credentials, getServletInfo());
    String l_id = session.getId();
    sessionManager.updateSessionStats(credentials);
    sessionManager.logRawStats(credentials, getServletInfo());
  }
%>
```

*NOTE:* EnsureUserLoggedIn.jsp, *which is included in each of our JSP pages by means of a* page *directive, contains two* <jsp:useBean> *actions. Since the contents of included code are not immediately apparent to the programmer, we face the risk of encountering beans with duplicate names—one in the including code and one in the included code. We must weigh this against the conveniences offered by the* include page *directive (i.e., not having to type redundant code and only having to make changes in only one central piece of code).*

The next thing we notice in `MyDepartment.jsp` is a new Bean. Each Bean should perform a set of related tasks. As its class name implies, the EmployeeInfo Bean accesses employee information. Here is the code:

```java
package com.instantjsp;

import java.sql.Connection;
import java.sql.ResultSet;
import java.sql.SQLException;
import java.sql.Statement;
import java.text.SimpleDateFormat;
import java.util.Date;
import java.util.Enumeration;
import java.util.Hashtable;
import java.util.Vector;

import javaservlets.jdbc.ConnectionPool;

public class EmployeeInfo {
  private ConnectionPool connectionPool;

  private static final String POOL_CFG_FILE =
    "javaservlets/jdbc/EmployeeConnectionPool.cfg";

  private static final String QUERY_DEPT_FOR_USER =
    "SELECT dept FROM empdata WHERE ssn=";

  private static final String QUERY_DEPT_NAMES =
    "SELECT last,first,ext FROM empdata WHERE dept=";

  private static final String ORDER_DEPT_BY =
    " ORDER BY ";

  private static final String QUERY_VACATION =
    "SELECT vacdue,carried,taken FROM empdata WHERE ssn=";

  private static final String QUERY_NEXT_REVIEW =
    "SELECT review FROM empdata WHERE ssn=";

  private static final String QUERY_NAME =
    "SELECT last,first,mi FROM empdata WHERE ssn=";

  private static final String QUERY_PHONE_DATA =
    "SELECT last,first,ext,cell,pager FROM empdata WHERE ";

  private static final String PHONE_QUALIFIER_DEPT =
    "dept=";

  private static final String PHONE_QUALIFIER_NAME =
    "last=";

  private static final String PHONE_QUALIFIER_NAME_WILD =
    "last LIKE ";

  private static final String ORDER_BY_LAST =
    " ORDER BY last ";

  private static final String QUERY_DISTINCT_SKILLS =
```

```
                   "SELECT DISTINCT skill FROM skills";

          private static final String QUERY_SKILLS =
            "SELECT last,first,ext,dept FROM empdata ";

          private static final String RPAREN = ")";
          private static final String COMMA = ",";
          private static final String PERCENT = "%";
          private static final String QUOTE = "'";

          public EmployeeInfo() throws Exception {
            connectionPool = new ConnectionPool();
            connectionPool.initialize(POOL_CFG_FILE);
          }

          public int[] getVacation(String ssn)
              throws SQLException {
            Connection conn = connectionPool.getConnection();
            Statement qs = conn.createStatement();
            ResultSet rs = qs.executeQuery(QUERY_VACATION +
              QUOTE +ssn + QUOTE);
            int[] va = new int[3];
            va[0] = va[1] = va[2] = -32768;
            if (!rs.next()) {
              return va;
            }
            for (int i = 0; i < 3; ++i) {
              va[i] = rs.getInt(i+1);
            }
            connectionPool.close(conn);
            return va;
          }

          public String[] getName(String ssn) throws SQLException{
            Connection conn = connectionPool.getConnection();
            Statement qs = conn.createStatement();
            ResultSet rs = qs.executeQuery(QUERY_NAME +
              QUOTE +ssn + QUOTE);
            String[] na = new String[3];
            na[0] = na[1] = na[2] = "";
            if (!rs.next()) {
              return na;
            }
            for (int i = 0; i < 3; ++i) {
              na[i] = rs.getString(i+1);
            }
            connectionPool.close(conn);
            return na;
          }

          public String getDept(String ssn) throws SQLException{
            Connection conn = connectionPool.getConnection();
            Statement qs = conn.createStatement();
            ResultSet rs = qs.executeQuery(QUERY_DEPT_FOR_USER +
              QUOTE +ssn + QUOTE);
            rs.next();
            String dept = rs.getString(1);
            connectionPool.close(conn);
            return dept;
          }
```

```java
public Vector getSkills() throws SQLException{
  Connection conn = connectionPool.getConnection();
  Statement qs = conn.createStatement();
  ResultSet rs = qs.executeQuery(QUERY_DISTINCT_SKILLS);
  Vector v = new Vector();
  while (rs.next()) {
    v.addElement(rs.getString(1));
  }
  connectionPool.close(conn);
  return v;
}

private String getSkillsQualifier (String[] sl, String t)
    throws SQLException {
  StringBuffer qsb = new StringBuffer();
  Vector v = getSkills();
  switch (Integer.parseInt(t)) {
    case 0: //any
      qsb.append("where ssn in ");
      qsb.append("(select distinct ssn from skills where skill in
(");
      for (int i = 0; i < sl.length; ++i) {
        qsb.append(QUOTE);
        qsb.append(v.elementAt(Integer.parseInt(sl[i].trim())));
        qsb.append(QUOTE);
        if (i < (sl.length - 1)) {
          qsb.append(COMMA);
        }
      }
      qsb.append(RPAREN);
      qsb.append(RPAREN);
      break;
    case 1: //all
      qsb.append(" where ");
      for (int i = 0; i < sl.length; ++i) {
        qsb.append("ssn in ");
        qsb.append("(select distinct ssn from skills where ");
        qsb.append("skill = ");
        qsb.append(QUOTE);
        qsb.append(v.elementAt(Integer.parseInt(sl[i].trim())));
        qsb.append(QUOTE);
        qsb.append(RPAREN);
        if (i < (sl.length -1)){
          qsb.append(" and ");
        }
      }
      break;
  }
  qsb.append(" order by last");
  return qsb.toString();
}

public Vector getSkilledList(String[] choices, String searchType)
    throws SQLException{
  Connection conn = connectionPool.getConnection();
  Statement qs = conn.createStatement();
  ResultSet rs = qs.executeQuery(QUERY_SKILLS +
    getSkillsQualifier(choices, searchType));
  Vector v = new Vector();
  while (rs.next()) {
```

```java
        String[] sa = new String[4];
        for (int i = 0; i < 4; ++i) {
            sa[i] = rs.getString(i+1);
        }
        v.addElement(sa);
    }
    connectionPool.close(conn);
    return v;
}

public String getNextReview(String ssn) throws SQLException {
    Connection conn = connectionPool.getConnection();
    Statement qs = conn.createStatement();
    ResultSet rs = qs.executeQuery(QUERY_NEXT_REVIEW +
        QUOTE + ssn + QUOTE);
    rs.next();
    String rev = rs.getString(1);
    connectionPool.close(conn);
    return rev;
}

public Vector getDeptList(String ssn, String orderopt)
        throws SQLException {
    Connection conn = connectionPool.getConnection();
    Statement qs = conn.createStatement();
    ResultSet rs = qs.executeQuery(QUERY_DEPT_NAMES +
        QUOTE + getDept(ssn) + QUOTE +
        ORDER_DEPT_BY + orderopt);
    Vector v = new Vector();
    while(rs.next()) {
        String[] s = new String[3];
        for (int i = 0; i < 3; ++i) {
            s[i] = rs.getString(i + 1);
        }
        v.addElement(s);
    }
    connectionPool.close(conn);
    return v;
}

public Vector getPhoneList(String ssn, String searchData)
        throws SQLException {
    String qualifier;
    if (searchData.length() == 1) {
        qualifier = PHONE_QUALIFIER_NAME_WILD +
            QUOTE + searchData.toUpperCase() + PERCENT + QUOTE;
    }
    else {
        if (Character.isDigit(searchData.charAt(0))) {
            qualifier = PHONE_QUALIFIER_DEPT +
                QUOTE + getDept(ssn) + QUOTE;
        }
        else {
            qualifier = PHONE_QUALIFIER_NAME +
                QUOTE + searchData + QUOTE;
        }
    }
    Connection conn = connectionPool.getConnection();
    Statement qs = conn.createStatement();
```

```
       ResultSet rs = qs.executeQuery(QUERY_PHONE_DATA +
         qualifier +
         ORDER_BY_LAST);
       Vector v = new Vector();
       while(rs.next()) {
         String[] s = new String[5];
         for (int i = 0; i < 5; ++i) {
           s[i] = rs.getString(i + 1);
         }
         v.addElement(s);
       }
       connectionPool.close(conn);
       return v;
     }
}
```

Getting back to MyDepartment.jsp, we see the expression:

```
<%= eiBean.getDept(user) %>
```

This expression passes the String user as an argument to the method getDept() of eiBean, which is the scripting variable name assigned to the instance of com.instantjsp.EmployeeInfo. The method returns a String containing the department for the specified user.

MyDepartment.jsp also contains an HTML form that contains two radio buttons. When the user clicks on the button labeled GENERATE LIST, the data from the form are sent as a POST request to GetDeptData.jsp. Here is the code:

```
<%@ page import="java.util.Vector" %>
<jsp:useBean id="eiBean" class="com.instantjsp.EmployeeInfo"
    scope="application" />
<jsp:useBean id="credentials" class="com.instantjsp.UserCredentials"
    scope="session" />
<!%@ page errorPage="/common/Exception.jsp" %>
<%
    String[] parms = request.getParameterValues("sortoption");
    String user = credentials.getUser();
    Vector deptList = eiBean.getDeptList(user, parms[0]);
%>
<html>
<body>
<center>
<b>
<font face = "Arial, Helvetica"><font size="+1">
<br>
<br>
Employee List - Department
<%= eiBean.getDept(user) %>
<br>
<br>
<table>
<tr>
```

```
      <td><b>Last Name</b></td>
      <td><b>First Name</b></td>
      <td><b>Ext</b></td>
  </tr>
  <tr>
    <td><b>---------</b></td>
    <td><b>----------</b></td>
    <td><b>---</b></td>
  </tr>
  <%
    for (int i = 0; i < deptList.size(); ++i) {
       String[] sa = (String[])deptList.elementAt(i);
  %>
      <tr>
  <% for (int j = 0; j < sa.length; ++j) { %>
        <td><b>
        <%= sa[j] %>
        </b></td>
  <% }  %>
      </tr>
  <% }  %>
  </table>
  </b>
  </center>
  </body>
  </html>
```

GetDeptData.jsp retrieves the user ID from the credentials object
and passes it along with the value of the clicked radio button, indicating
the user's preferred sort order as arguments to the getDeptList()
method of the EmployeeInfo Bean. This method performs an SQL query
that extracts the desired data and returns the data wrapped in a Vector.
The Vector contains arrays of Strings; these are converted to an HTML
table by the following scriptlet:

```
<%
   for (int i = 0; i < deptList.size(); ++i) {
      String[] sa = (String[])deptList.elementAt(i);
%>
      <tr>
<%
   for (int j = 0; j < sa.length; ++j) {
%>
        <td><b>
        <%= sa[j] %>
        </b></td>
<%
      }
%>
      </tr>
<%
      }
%>
```

The table that is generated is shown in Figure 4-7.

**Figure 4-7**
Department
Members Listed
Alphabetically

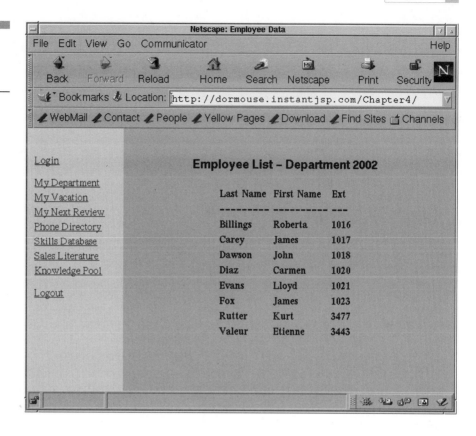

## Checking My Vacation Status

The option labeled "My Vacation" in the menu links to `MyVacation.jsp`, which generates the page shown in Figure 4-8. Here is the code:

```
<%@ include file="/common/EnsureUserLoggedIn.jsp" %>
<jsp:useBean id="eiBean" class="com.instantjsp.EmployeeInfo"
    scope="application" />
<%@ page errorPage="/common/Exception.jsp" %>
<%
  String user = credentials.getUser();
  String[] name = eiBean.getName(user);
%>
<html>
<body>
<font face = "Arial, Helvetica"><font size="+2">
<center>
<br>
<b>
Vacation data for
```

**Figure 4-8**
Output from
`MyVacation.jsp`

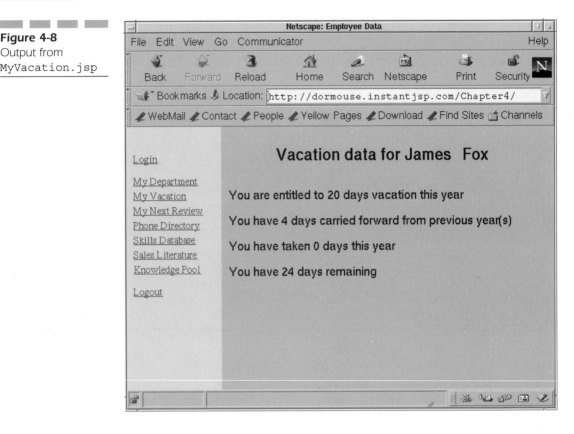

```
<%= name[1] %>
<%= name[0] %>
</b>
</center>
</font></font>
<font face = "Arial, Helvetica"><font size="+1">
<br>
<br>
<%
  int[] va = eiBean.getVacation(user);
%>
You are entitled to
<%= va[0] %>
days vacation this year
<br>
<br>
You have
<%= va[1] %>
days carried forward from previous year(s)
<br>
<br>
You have taken
<%= va[2] %>
days this year
```

```
<br>
<br>
You have
<%= va[0] + va[1] - va[2] %>
days remaining
</font></font>
</body>
</html>
```

The technique here is identical to what we have already seen. The user ID is passed as an argument to the getVacation() method of the instance of EmployeeData. The method performs the appropriate SQL query and returns the result as an array of integers corresponding to the number of days vacation to which the employee is entitled, the number of days carried over from the previous year(s), and the number of days taken to date this year; these three figures are displayed. The amount of vacation remaining is calculated and is displayed as well.

## Checking My Next Review

The option labeled "My Next Review" in the menu links to NextReview.jsp. Here is the code:

```
<%@ include file="/common/EnsureUserLoggedIn.jsp" %>
<jsp:useBean id="eiBean" class="com.instantjsp.EmployeeInfo"
    scope="application" />
<%
  String user = credentials.getUser();
  String[] name = eiBean.getName(user);
%>
<html>
<body>
<center>
<font face = "Arial, Helvetica"><font size="+2">
<br>
<br>
<b>
Information for
<%= name[1] %>
<%= name[0] %>
<br>
<br>
</b>
</font></font>
<font face = "Arial, Helvetica"><font size="+1">
<br>
The date of your next review is:
<%= eiBean.getNextReview(user) %>
</font></font>
</center>
</body>
</html>
```

Figure 4-9
Output from
NextReview.jsp

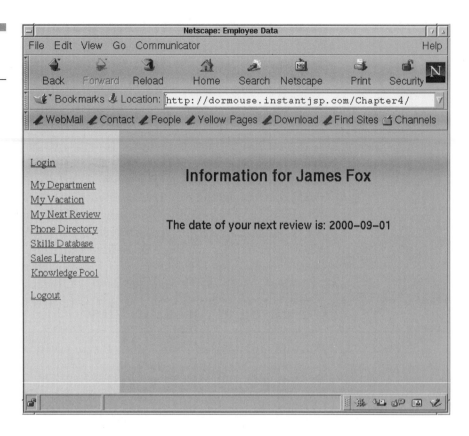

This code first passes the user ID as an argument to the getName()
method of EmployeeInfo. This method performs an SQL query that
returns an array of Strings containing the last name and first name.
These are displayed using JSP expressions.

The user ID is also passed as an argument to the getNextReview()
method, which performs the SQL query that gets the date of the specified
employee's next review. The result is returned as a String and is displayed. The page containing the information returned from the two SQL
queries is shown in Figure 4-9.

## The Employee Telephone Directory

The "Phone Directory" option in the menu links to PhoneList.jsp,
which generates the page shown in Figure 4-10. Here is the code:

**Figure 4-10**
Options Presented by
`PhoneList.jsp`

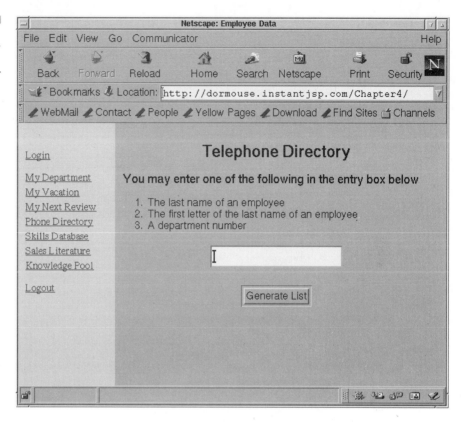

```
<%@ include file="/common/EnsureUserLoggedIn.jsp" %>
<html>
<body>
<center>
<font face = "Arial, Helvetica"><font size="+2">
<b>
<br>
Telephone Directory
</center>
</font></font>
<font face = "Arial, Helvetica"><font size="+1">
<br>
You may enter one of the following in the entry box below
</b>
<ol>
<li>The last name of an employee
</li>
<li>The first letter of the last name of an employee
</li>
<li>A department number
</li>
</ol>
```

```
<form method="post" action="http://dormouse.instantjsp.com/Chapter4/
 GetPhoneList.jsp">
<center>
<input type="text" name="phonedata" length="25">
<br>
<br>
<input name="submit" type="submit" value="Generate List">
</form>
</center>
</font></font>
</b>
</body>
</html>
```

The HTML form generated by PhoneList.jsp is passed to GetPhoneList.jsp, which looks like this:

```
<%@ page import="java.util.Vector" %>
<jsp:useBean id="credentials"
class="com.instantjsp.UserCredentials"
  scope="session" />
<jsp:useBean id="eiBean" class="com.instantjsp.EmployeeInfo"
  scope="application" />
<!%@ page errorPage="/common/Exception.jsp" %>
<%
  String[] parms = request.getParameterValues("phonedata");
  String user = credentials.getUser();
  Vector phoneList = eiBean.getPhoneList(user, parms[0]);
%>
<html>
<body>
<center>
<b>
<font face = "Arial, Helvetica"><font size="+1">
<br>
<br>
Phone List
<br>
<br>
<table>
<tr>
  <td><b>Last Name</b></td>
  <td><b>First Name</b></td>
  <td><b>Extension</b></td>
  <td><b>Cell Phone</b></td>
  <td><b>Pager</b></td>
</tr>
<tr>
  <td><b>--------</b></td>
  <td><b>---------</b></td>
  <td><b>--------</b></td>
  <td><b>----------</b></td>
  <td><b>----------</b></td>
</tr>
<%
  for (int i = 0; i < phoneList.size(); ++i) {
    String[] sa = (String[])phoneList.elementAt(i);
```

```
%>
    <tr>
<% for (int j = 0; j < sa.length; ++j) { %>
        <td><b>
        <%= sa[j] %>
        </b></td>
<%  }  %>
    </tr>
<%  }  %>
</table>
</b>
</center>
</body>
</html>
```

The user ID is retrieved from the `credentials` object and the contents of the text entry field is extracted. These are passed as arguments to the `getPhoneList()` method of EmployeeInfo. This method constructs one of three possible SQL queries as follows:

- If the contents of the text entry field is a single character, the SQL query is:

  ```
  SELECT last,first,ext,cell,pager FROM empdata WHERE last LIKE %c
  ```

- If the text entry field contains more than a single character and the first character is numeric, the SQL query is:

  ```
  SELECT last,first,ext,cell,pager FROM empdata WHERE dept = d
  ```

- For all other cases, the SQL query is:

  ```
  SELECT last,first,ext,cell,pager FROM empdata WHERE last = ln
  ```

The results of the query are stored in a Vector and returned. The contents of the Vector are presented as an HTML table using code similar to what we saw in `GetDeptData.jsp`. Figure 4-11 shows the results of requesting the telephone numbers of all those employees whose name begins with the letter A.

# The Corporate Skills Database

If you are preparing to staff an upcoming project, it is useful to know those employees who have the skills the project will require. Table 4-4 shows the fields in a database table we will use to store the skills of each employee in the company. Table 4-5 shows a few sample rows.

Figure 4-12, which was generated by `SkillsSearch.jsp` when "Skills Database" was selected from the menu, is the page from which we select search criteria. Here is the code for `SkillsSearch.jsp`:

**Figure 4-11**
Output from
`GetPhoneList.jsp`

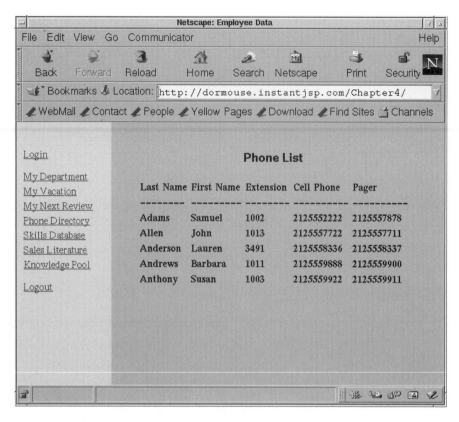

**TABLE 4-4**

Layout of Skills
Table

```
Table     = skills
+-----------------------------+--------------------+-------+
|             Field           |             Type   | Length|
+-----------------------------+--------------------+-------+
|   ssn                       |   char()           |     9 |
|   skill                     |   varchar()        |    16 |
+-----------------------------+--------------------+-------+
```

**TABLE 4-5**

Partial Contents of
Skills Table

```
-- RECORD 174 --              -- RECORD 177 --
ssn   | 207723226             ssn   | 619219665
skill | Fortran               skill | C

-- RECORD 175 --              -- RECORD 178 --
ssn   | 207723226             ssn   |   619219665
skill | C                     skill | Fortran

-- RECORD 176 --              -- RECORD 179 --
ssn   | 207723226             ssn   | 619219665
skill | Java                  skill | Java
```

**Figure 4-12**
Options Presented by
`SkillsSearch.jsp`

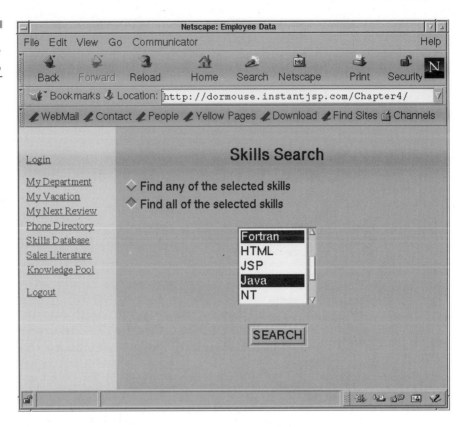

```
<%@ page import="java.util.Vector" %>
<%@ include file="/common/EnsureUserLoggedIn.jsp" %>
<jsp:useBean id="eiBean" class="com.instantjsp.EmployeeInfo"
    scope="application" />
<%
    String user = credentials.getUser();
%>
<html>
<body>
<center>
<b>
<font face = "Arial, Helvetica"><font size="+2">
<br>
Skills Search
</font></font>
</b>
</center>
<font face = "Arial, Helvetica"><font size="+1">
<br>
<form method="post"
action="http://dormouse.instantjsp.com/Chapter4/GetSkills.jsp">
<input type="radio" name="searchType" value="0" checked>
Find any of the selected skills
<br>
```

```
<input type="radio" name="searchType" value="1">
Find all of the selected skills
<br>
<br>
<center>
<select name="skillChoices" size=5 multiple>
<%
  Vector v = eiBean.getSkills();
  for (int i = 0; i < v.size(); ++i) {
%>
  <option value= "<%= i %>">
  <%= v.elementAt(i) %>
<%
  }
%>
</select>
<br>
<br>
<input name="submit" type="submit" value="SEARCH">
</center>
</font></font>
</form>
</body>
</html>
```

The values placed in the listbox are those returned by the `getSkills()` method of EmployeeInfo. The method obtains this data by issuing the SQL query:

```
SELECT DISTINCT skill FROM skills
```

The listbox permits multiple choices and radio buttons are used to specify whether we are interested in employees who have some or all of the specified skills. When the button labeled SEARCH is clicked, the contents of the form are sent to `GetSkills.jsp`. Here is the code:

```
<%@ page import="java.util.Vector" %>
<jsp:useBean id="eiBean" class="com.instantjsp.EmployeeInfo"
    scope="application" />
<%@ page errorPage="/common/Exception.jsp" %>
<%
  String[] types = request.getParameterValues("searchType");
  String[] choices = request.getParameterValues("skillChoices");
  String user = (String)session.getValue("instantjsp.user");
  Vector skilledList = eiBean.getSkilledList(choices, types[0]);
  Vector skills = eiBean.getSkills();
%>
<html>
<body>
<center>
<b>
<font face = "Arial, Helvetica"><font size="+1">
<br>
<br>
Candidate List
<br>
```

```
<br>
<table>
<tr>
  <td><b>Last Name</b></td>
  <td><b>First Name</b></td>
  <td><b>Extension</b></td>
  <td><b>Dept</b></td>
</tr>
<tr>
  <td><b>--------</b></td>
  <td><b>---------</b></td>
  <td><b>--------</b></td>
  <td><b>----</b></td>
</tr>
<%
  for (int i = 0; i < skilledList.size(); ++i) {
    String[] sa = (String[])skilledList.elementAt(i);
%>
    <tr>
<%
    for (int j = 0; j < sa.length; ++j) {
%>
      <td><b>
      <%= sa[j] %>
      </b></td>
<% } %>
    </tr>
<% } %>
</table>
</b>
</center>
</font></font>
<br>
Search was for
<b>
<%
String anyOrAll = (types[0].trim().equals("0")) ? "any" : "all";
%>
<%= anyOrAll %>
</b>
of:
<br>
<%
  for (int i = 0; i < choices.length; ++i) {
%>
<%= (String)skills.elementAt(Integer.parseInt(choices[i].trim()))
%>
<%
    if (i < choices.length - 1) {
%>
      <br>
<%
    }
  }
%>
<br>
<br>
</body>
</html>
```

**Figure 4-13**
Results of Search

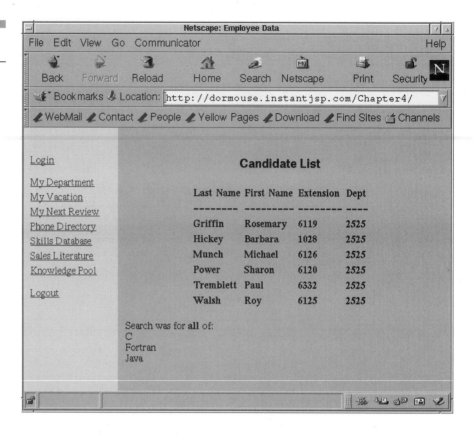

The processing is similar to what was done in pages we have already seen and consists of passing the user ID, search data, and options to a method of EmployeeInfo—in this case, `getSkills()`—and displaying the contents of the Vector that are returned as an HTML table. A summary of the type of search and the specified skills is also displayed. Figure 4-13 shows the results of a typical search.

# Creating a Sales Literature Repository

As long as we are building repositories for company resources, what about our collection of sales literature? Table 4-6 shows the fields in a database table that might be useful for a business that sells kitchen supplies to restaurants and homeowners. As you can see from Table 4-7, the database contains entries for sales literature describing these supplies,

**TABLE 4-6**

Sales Literature
Table Layout

```
:Table     = saleslit
+----------------------------+----------------------+----------+
|          Field             |        Type          | Length   |
+----------------------------+----------------------+----------+
|   id                       | char() not null      |     4    |
|   cat                      | varchar()            |    16    |
|   subcat                   | varchar()            |    16    |
|   title                    | varchar()            |    32    |
|   file                     | varchar()            |    32    |
+----------------------------+----------------------+----------+
Index:     saleslit_pkey
```

**TABLE 4-7**

Partial Contents of
Sales Literature
Table

```
 id|cat        |subcat    |title                   |file
+---+----------+----------+------------------------+-----------
1101|Cookware   |Home      |Glass Stovetop Cookware |hmgstckw.pdf
2107|Appliances |Home      |Blenders                |hblend.pdf
2110|Appliances |Home      |Toasters                |htoast.pdf
2112|Appliances |Home      |Electric Waffle Makers  |hwaff.pdf
1112|Dishware   |Restaurant|Dishware For Restaurants|rdish.pdf
1107|Appliances |Restaurant|Heavy Duty Blenders     |rblend.pdf
2101|Cookware   |Home      |Glass Ovenware          |hglovnw.pdf
2103|Cookware   |Home      |Aluminum Ovenware       |halovnw.pdf
2104|Cookware   |Home      |Cast Iron Ovenware      |hcaovw.pdf
 (9 rows)
```

categorized according to the type of customer and further grouped into subcategories of cookware, dishware, and appliances. Each table entry contains the name of a file that can be viewed or printed.

The data in the table we just created will be accessed by a Bean that will be used by our JSP pages. The Java code for this Bean, which will also be used to access other data that we create later, is found in `CompanyInfo.java`. Here is the source:

```
package com.instantjsp;
import java.sql.Connection;
import java.sql.ResultSet;
import java.sql.SQLException;
import java.sql.Statement;
import java.util.Vector;

import javaservlets.jdbc.ConnectionPool;

import com.instantjsp.FaqHolder;

public class CompanyInfo {
```

```java
    private ConnectionPool connectionPool;

    private static final String POOL_CFG_FILE =
     "javaservlets/jdbc/CompanyConnectionPool.cfg";

    private static final String QUERY_DISTINCT_PRODUCTS =
      "SELECT DISTINCT cat FROM saleslit";

    private static final String QUERY_SALES_LIT_TITLES =
      "SELECT id,title FROM saleslit WHERE ";

    private static final String QUERY_FAQ_TITLES =
      "SELECT id,title FROM faqs ORDER BY id";

    private static final String SELECT_FAQ =
      "SELECT title,text FROM faqs WHERE id=";

    private static final String GET_NEXT_FAQ_ID =
      "SELECT nextval('faq_seq')";

    private static final String INSERT_FAQ =
      "INSERT INTO faqs (id,title,text) VALUES";

    private static final String CAT_QUALIFIER =
      "cat=";

    private static final String SUBCAT_QUALIFIER =
      "subcat=";
    private static final String AND = " and ";
    private static final String LPAREN = "(";
    private static final String RPAREN = ")";
    private static final String COMMA = ",";
    private static final String PERCENT = "%";
    private static final String QUOTE = "'";

    public CompanyInfo() throws Exception {
      connectionPool = new ConnectionPool();
      connectionPool.initialize(POOL_CFG_FILE);
    }

    public Vector getProductCategories() throws SQLException{
      Connection conn = connectionPool.getConnection();
      Statement qs = conn.createStatement();
      ResultSet rs = qs.executeQuery(QUERY_DISTINCT_PRODUCTS);
      Vector v = new Vector();
      while (rs.next()) {
        v.addElement(rs.getString(1));
      }
      connectionPool.close(conn);
      return v;
    }

    public Vector getLiteratureList(String[] cat, String subcat)
        throws SQLException{
      Connection conn = connectionPool.getConnection();
      Statement qs = conn.createStatement();
      Vector pv = getProductCategories();
      String query = QUERY_SALES_LIT_TITLES +
        CAT_QUALIFIER +
        QUOTE + pv.elementAt(Integer.parseInt(cat[0].trim())) + QUOTE +
```

```
          AND + SUBCAT_QUALIFIER +
          QUOTE + subcat + QUOTE;
      ResultSet rs = qs.executeQuery(query);
      Vector v = new Vector();
      while (rs.next()) {
        String[] sa = new String[2];
        for (int i = 0; i < 2; ++i) {
          sa[i] = rs.getString(i+1);
        }
        v.addElement(sa);
      }
      connectionPool.close(conn);
      return v;
    }

    public Vector getFaqTitles( ) throws SQLException{
      Connection conn = connectionPool.getConnection();
      Statement qs = conn.createStatement();
      ResultSet rs = qs.executeQuery(QUERY_FAQ_TITLES);
      Vector v = new Vector();
      while (rs.next()) {
        String[] sa = new String[2];
        for (int i = 0; i < 2; ++i) {
          sa[i] = rs.getString(i+1);
        }
        v.addElement(sa);
      }
      connectionPool.close(conn);
      return v;
    }

    public String[] getFaq(int id) throws SQLException{
      Connection conn = connectionPool.getConnection();
      Statement qs = conn.createStatement();
      ResultSet rs = qs.executeQuery(SELECT_FAQ + id);
      rs.next();
      String[] sa = new String[2];
      sa[0] = rs.getString(1);
      sa[1] = rs.getString(2);
      connectionPool.close(conn);
      return sa;
    }

    public int insertFaq(FaqHolder faqHolder)
        throws SQLException {
      Connection conn = connectionPool.getConnection();
      Statement qs = conn.createStatement();
      ResultSet rs = qs.executeQuery(GET_NEXT_FAQ_ID);
      rs.next();
      int id = rs.getInt(1);
      Statement us = conn.createStatement();
        us.executeUpdate(INSERT_FAQ + LPAREN +
        QUOTE + Integer.toString(++id) + QUOTE + COMMA +
        QUOTE + faqHolder.getQuestion() + QUOTE + COMMA +
        QUOTE + faqHolder.getAnswer() + QUOTE + RPAREN);
      connectionPool.close(conn);
      return id;
    }
  }
```

# Making Life Easier for the Sales Force

Now that we have created a database containing pointers to our sales literature, we can provide tools that can help make a salesperson's job a little easier. This is especially true if the salesperson was recently hired or transferred from another division where different products were sold.

The menu option "Sales Literature" links to `SalesLiterature.jsp`, which generates the page shown in Figure 4-14. Here is the code:

```
<%@ include file="/common/EnsureUserLoggedIn.jsp" %>
<%@ page import="java.util.Vector" %>
<jsp:useBean id="ciBean" class="com.instantjsp.CompanyInfo"
    scope="application" />
<%
    String user = credentials.getUser();
%>
```

**Figure 4-14**
Searching for Sales Literature

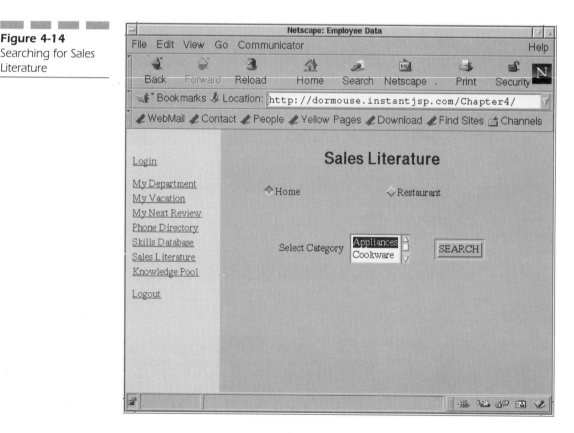

```
<html>
<body>
<center>
<b>
<font face = "Arial, Helvetica"><font size="+2">
<br>
Sales Literature
</font></font>
</b>
<font face = "Arial, Helvetica"><font size="+1">
<br>
<br>
<form method="post"
action="http://dormouse.instantjsp.com/Chapter4/GetSalesLiterature.
 jsp">
<table cols="2" width="80%">
<tr>
<td>
<input type="radio" name="subcategory" value="Home" checked>
Home
</td>
<td>
<input type="radio" name="subcategory" value="Restaurant">
Restaurant
</td>
</tr>
</table>
<br>
<br>
<table rows="2" width="80%">
<tr>
<td valign="center" align="right">
Select Category
</td>
<td align="left" valign="center">
<select name="category" size=2>
<%
  Vector v = ciBean.getProductCategories();
  for (int i = 0; i < v.size(); ++i) {
%>
    <option value="<%= i %>">
    <%= v.elementAt(i) %>
<%
  }
%>
</select>
</td align="left valign="center">
<td>
<input name="submit" type="submit" value="SEARCH">
</td>
</tr>
</table>
<br>
<br>
<br>
<br>
</center>
</font></font>
```

```
</form>
</body>
</html>
```

As you can see, the page in Figure 4-14 is similar to what we saw in the Skills Search example. When the user makes the desired choices using the controls in the HTML form and clicks on the SEARCH button, GetSalesLiterature.jsp performs an SQL query and returns the results as shown in Figure 4-15. Here is the code for GetSales Literature.jsp:

```
<%@ include file="/common/EnsureUserLoggedIn.jsp" %>
<%@ page import="java.util.Vector" %>
<jsp:useBean id="ciBean" class="com.instantjsp.CompanyInfo"
    scope="application" />
<%@ page errorPage="/common/Exception.jsp" %>
<%
   String[] category = request.getParameterValues("category");
```

**Figure 4-15**
Result of Sales
Literature Search

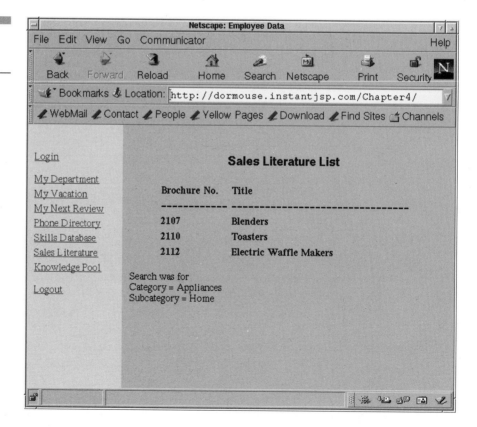

```
      String[] subcategory = request.getParameterValues("subcategory");
      String user = (String)session.getValue("instantjsp.user");
      Vector litList = ciBean.getLiteratureList(category, subcategory[0]);
      Vector catv = ciBean.getProductCategories();
%>
<html>
<body>
<center>
<b>
<font face = "Arial, Helvetica"><font size="+1">
<br>
<br>
Sales Literature List
<br>
<br>
<table>
<tr>
   <td><b>Brochure No.</b></td>
   <td><b>Title</b></td>
</tr>
<tr>
   <td><b>--------------</b></td>
   <td><b>-------------------------------</b></td>
</tr>
<%
   for (int i = 0; i < litList.size(); ++i) {
      String[] sa = (String[])litList.elementAt(i);
%>
   <tr>
<%
      for (int j = 0; j < sa.length; ++j) {
%>
      <td><b>
      <%= sa[j] %>
      </b></td>
<%
      }
%>
   </tr>
<%
   }
%>
</table>
</b>
</center>
</font></font>
<br>
Search was for
<br>
Category =
<%= (String)catv.elementAt(Integer.parseInt(category[0].trim())) %>
<br>
Subcategory =
<%= subcategory[0] %>
<br>
<br>
</body>
</html>
```

**TABLE 4-8**

FAQ Table Layout

```
Table     = faqs
+----------------------------+--------------------------+----------+
|            Field           |           Type           | Length   |
+----------------------------+--------------------------+----------+
|   id                       | int4 not null            |        4 |
|   title                    | varchar()                |       64 |
|   text                     | varchar()                |     1024 |
+----------------------------+--------------------------+----------+
Index:      faqs_pkey
```

# Creating a Knowledge Pool

A common problem workers encounter is knowing that someone in the company knows the answer to a question they need answered to perform a task but not knowing who that person is. Searching for such a person is time consuming. One solution is email but that bothers every recipient except the one who has the answer to the question. It also means that the person with the answer receives duplicate requests for an answer to the same question. A better solution is to ask employees who are experts in a given field to contribute to a "Frequently Asked Questions" (FAQ) database. An employee with a question would then first search the database before resorting to email. The email recipient would enter the question and answer into the database. Over a period of time, the database would grow and the need for email solicitation would diminish.

Table 4-8 shows the fields in a database table that might be used to store FAQs. Identifiers for the FAQs are obtained using the nextval function of a sequence named faq_seq that we create using the SQL statement:

```
CREATE SEQUENCE faq_seq START 1 INCREMENT 1;
```

# Using the Knowledge Pool

When a user selects the "Knowledge Pool" option from the menu, KnowledgePool.jsp generates the page shown in Figure 4-16. Here is the code for KnowledgePool.jsp:

```
<%@ include file="/common/EnsureUserLoggedIn.jsp" %>
<html>
<body>
```

**Figure 4-16**
FAQ Options

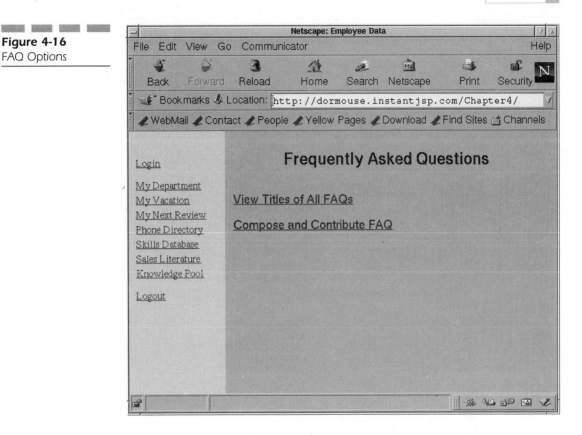

```
<center>
<b>
<font face = "Arial, Helvetica"><font size="+2">
<br>
Frequently Asked Questions
</font></font>
</b>
</center>
<font face = "Arial, Helvetica"><font size="+1">
<br>
<br>
<a href="http://dormouse.instantjsp.com/Chapter4/GetFaqTitles.jsp">
View Titles of All FAQs</a>
<br>
<br>
<a
href="http://dormouse.instantjsp.com/Chapter4/ContributeFaq.jsp">
Compose and Contribute FAQ</a>
</font></font>
</form>
</body>
</html>
```

The user is presented with the choice of viewing the list of FAQs or contributing a FAQ. If the view option is chosen, `GetFaqTitles.jsp` generates the page shown in Figure 4-17. The code for `GetFaqTitles.jsp` follows:

```
<%@ include file="/common/EnsureUserLoggedIn.jsp" %>
<%@ page import="java.util.Vector" %>
<jsp:useBean id="ciBean" class="com.instantjsp.CompanyInfo"
    scope="application" />
<%@ page errorPage="/common/Exception.jsp" %>
<%
  Vector faqTitles = ciBean.getFaqTitles();
%>
<html>
<body>
<center>
<b>
<font face = "Arial, Helvetica"><font size="+1">
<br>
<br>
Available FAQs
```

**Figure 4-17**
Titles of Available
FAQs

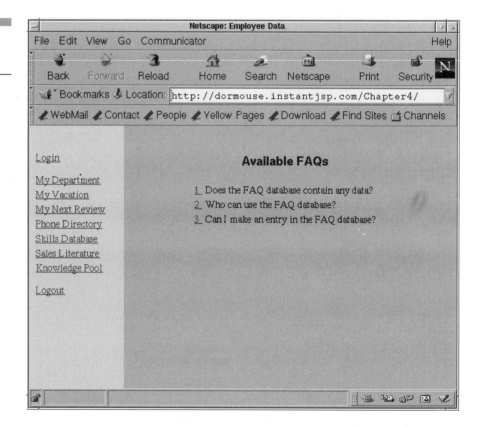

```
<br>
<br>
<table>
<%
  for (int i = 0; i < faqTitles.size(); ++i) {
    String[] sa = (String[])faqTitles.elementAt(i);
%>
    <tr>
      <td>
<%
       StringBuffer sb = new StringBuffer(1);
       sb.setLength(1);
       sb.setCharAt(0,'"');
       String href = "<a href=" +
         "\"http://dormouse.instantjsp.com/Chapter4/GetFaq.jsp?" +
         "id=" + sa[0] + "\">" + sa[0];
%>
         <%= href %>
      </a>
      </td>
      <td>
      <%= sa[1] %>
      </td>
    </tr>
<%
  }
%>
</table>
</b>
</body>
</html>
```

The number of each FAQ is a hyperlink to `GetFaq.jsp` with the FAQ id passed as a query parameter. `GetFaq.jsp` uses this id to perform an SQL query that retrieves the question and answer from the database and displays it as shown in Figure 4-18. Here is the code for `GetFaq.jsp`:

```
<%@ page import="java.util.Hashtable" %>
<jsp:useBean id="ciBean" class="com.instantjsp.CompanyInfo"
    scope="application" />
<%@ page errorPage="/common/Exception.jsp" %>
<%
  String query = request.getQueryString();
  Hashtable qt = HttpUtils.parseQueryString(query);
  String idstr = ((String[])qt.get("id"))[0];
  int id = Integer.parseInt(idstr.trim());
  String[] faqData= ciBean.getFaq(id);
%>
<html>
<body>
<center>
<b>
<font face = "Arial, Helvetica"><font size="+1">
<br>
<br>
<%= faqData[0] %>
```

**Figure 4-18**
Detailed Listing of
Selected FAQ

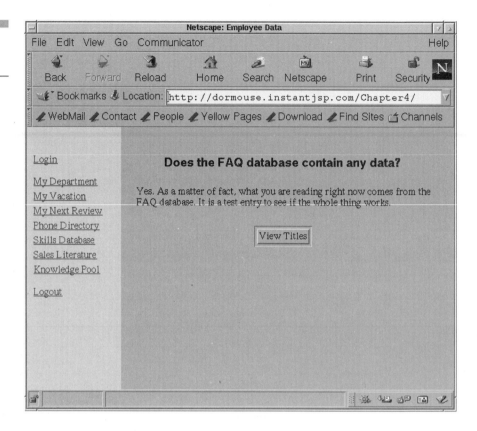

```
<br>
<br>
<table>
<tr>
  <td>
      <%= faqData[1] %>
  </td>
</tr>
</table>
</b>
</font></font>
<form method="get"
action="http://dormouse.instantjsp.com/Chapter4/ GetFaqTitles.jsp">
<input name="submit" type="submit" value="View Titles">
</form>
</center>
</body>
</html>
```

If the user chooses the "Contribute" option in Figure 4-16,
ContributeFaq.jsp generates the page shown in Figure 4-19. Here is
the code for ContributeFaq.jsp:

**Figure 4-19**
Contributing
a Question and
Answer

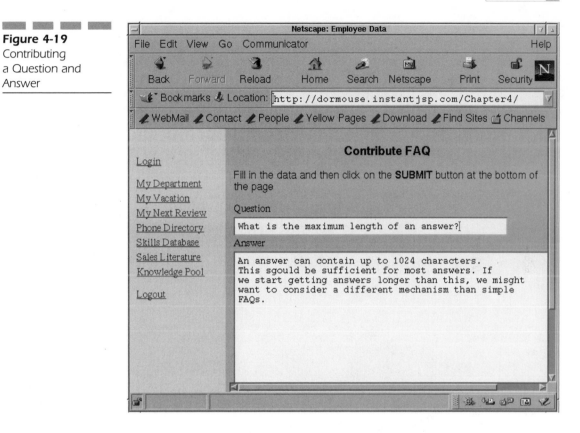

```
<%@ include file="/common/EnsureUserLoggedIn.jsp" %>
<html>
<body>
<center>
<font face = "Arial, Helvetica"><font size="+1">
<b>
<br>
Contribute FAQ
</b>
</font></font>
</center>
<font face = "Arial, Helvetica"><font size="+0">
<br>
Fill in the data and then click on the <b>SUBMIT</b> button at the
  bottom of the page
<br>
</font></font>
<br>
<form method="post"
action="http://dormouse.instantjsp.com/Chapter4/ InsertFaq.jsp">
Question
<input type="text" name="question" size="48" maxlength="64">
<br>
```

```
Answer
<br>
<textarea name="answer" cols=64 rows=16>
</textarea>
<br>
<br>
<center>
<input name="submit" type="submit" value="SUBMIT">
</form>
</center>
</b>
</body>
</html>
```

The contributor enters a question and the corresponding answer and clicks on SUBMIT. Insert.Faq then issues the SQL command that inserts the data into the database and generates a confirmation like the one shown in Figure 4-20. Here is the code for InsertFaq.jsp:

**Figure 4-20**
Confirmation of FAQ Contribution

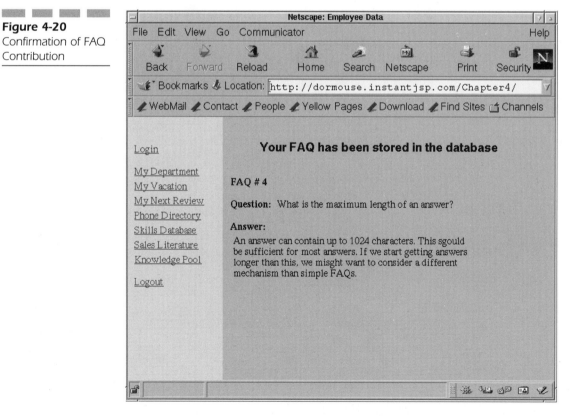

```jsp
<%@ include file="/common/EnsureUserLoggedIn.jsp" %>
<jsp:useBean id="ciBean" class="com.instantjsp.CompanyInfo"
    scope="application" />
<jsp:useBean id="faqHolder" class="com.instantjsp.FaqHolder"
    scope="request" />
<%@ page errorPage="/common/Exception.jsp" %>
<jsp:setProperty name="faqHolder" property="*" />
<%
   int faqid = ciBean.insertFaq(faqHolder);
%>
<br>
<html>
<body>
<center>
<b>
<font face = "Arial, Helvetica"><font size="+1">
<br>
Your FAQ has been stored in the database
<br>
</font></font>
</b>
</center>
<br>
<br>
<b>FAQ #
<%= faqid %>
</b>
<p>
<b>Question: </b>
<jsp:getProperty name="faqHolder" property="question" />
<p>
<b>Answer: </b>
<br>
<table cols=1 width="80%">
<tr>
  <td>
    <jsp:getProperty name="faqHolder" property="answer" />
</td>
</tr>
</table>
</body>
</html>
```

The question and answer are extracted from the HTML form and saved in an instance of FaqHolder by the action:

```jsp
<jsp:setProperty name="faqHolder" property="*" />
```

The insertFaq() method of CompanyInfo receives the instance of FaqHolder as an argument and inserts the data into the database. Here is the code for FaqHolder:

```java
package com.instantjsp;

public class FaqHolder {
```

```
private String answer;
private String question;

public String getAnswer () {
  return answer;
}

public String getQuestion() {
  return question;
}

public void setAnswer(String answer) {
  this.answer = answer;
}

public void setQuestion(String question) {
  this.question = question;
}
}
```

As the size of our FAQ database grows, so too does the list the user sees as the result of selecting the "View Titles" choice. We could improve things by creating a database containing keywords extracted from the question and the answer. We could then provide the user with the option of searching by keyword. We get to see how this might be done in the next chapter.

# The First Step Toward an Online Store— Showing Your Wares

- A Product Database
- The Online Store
- Viewing the Online Catalog
- Searching the Online Catalog
- Tracking Customers

In just a few short years, cybershopping has catapulted from an interesting novelty to a booming business. In this chapter we examine how we can use JavaServer Pages to start constructing an online store.

# Creating a Product Database

We start our online store by creating database tables that hold information about the products that we intend to sell. The first table is named products and the fields it contains are shown in Table 5-1. A few records are shown in Table 5-2.

The first column contains an SKU (unique product identifier) for each product. Each product belongs to a category and each category can be further divided into one or more subcategories. The second and third

**TABLE 5-1**

The Products
Database Table
Layout

```
Table      = products
+---------------------+-------------------------------+--------+
|         Field       |              Type             | Length |
+---------------------+-------------------------------+--------+
|    sku              | int4 not null default nextva  |   4    |
|    cat              | int4                          |   4    |
|    subcat           | int4                          |   4    |
|    prod_desc        | varchar()                     |  48    |
+---------------------+-------------------------------+--------+
Index:     products_pkey
```

**TABLE 5-2**

Some Records in
the Products
Database Table

| sku | cat | subcat | prod_desc |
|--------|------|--------|------------------------------|
| 100014 | 100\| | 1002 | Wipes 90 ct |
| 100015 | 100\| | 1002 | PC Mini Vacuum |
| 100016 | 100\| | 1002 | CD Restorer Polish |
| 100017 | 100\| | 1002 | CD Laser Lens Cleaner |
| 100018 | 100\| | 1002 | CD Scratch Remover |
| 100019 | 100\| | 1003 | 2 pos manual rotary switch |
| 100020 | 100\| | 1003 | 4 pos manual rotary switch |
| 100021 | 100\| | 1003 | Parallel Auto Switch |
| 100022 | 100\| | 1003 | IEEE 1284 Auto Switch |
| 100001 | 100\| | 1001 | IMB Parallel Printer cable 6 ft |

columns contain the numeric identifiers of the category and subcategory, respectively. The fourth column contains a description of the product.

Descriptions for the categories and subcategories are contained in tables product_categories and product_subcats as shown in Tables 5-3 and 5-4. Some representative records are shown is Tables 5-5 and 5-6.

The final table we need is one that is used to store the prices of our products. This table is shown in Table 5-7 and some representative records are shown in Table 5-8.

**TABLE 5-3**

The product_cate-gories Database Table Layout

```
Table   = product_categories
+---------------+-----------------------------------------+--------+
|     Field     |                  Type                   | Length |
+---------------+-----------------------------------------+--------+
| cat           | int4 not null default nextval           |    4   |
| cat_desc      | varchar()                               |   32   |
+---------------+-----------------------------------------+--------+

Index:      product_categories_pkey
```

**TABLE 5-4**

The product_sub-cats Database Table Layout

```
Table   = product_subcats
+---------------+-----------------------------------------+--------+
|     Field     |                  Type                   | Length |
+---------------+-----------------------------------------+--------+
| subcat        | int4 not null default nextval           |    4   |
| subcat_desc   | varchar()                               |   32   |
+---------------+-----------------------------------------+--------+

Index:      product_subcategories_pkey
```

**TABLE 5-5**

Some Records in the product_cate-gories Database Table

```
cat      cat_desc
----+----------------
100 | Accessories
200 | Hardware
300 | Media
400 | Paper Supplies
500 | Print Supplies
```

**TABLE 5-6**

Some Records in the product_sub-cats Database Table

```
subcat   subcat_desc
--------+--------------------
 1001   | Cables
 1002   | Cleaning Supplies
 1003   | Data Switches
 1004   | Diskette Accessories
 1005   | Keyboard Accessories
 1006   | Monitor Accessories
 1007   | Mouse Accessories
 1008   | Printer Accessories
 1009   | Tool Kits
 2001   | Add-In-Boards
 2002   | CPU Fans
 2003   | CD-RW Drives
```

**TABLE 5-7**

The Prices Database Table Layout

```
Table   = prices
+---------------+------------------------------------+--------+
|     Field     |                Type                | Length |
+---------------+------------------------------------+--------+
| sku           | int4 not null                      |    4   |
| price         | float8                             |    8   |
+---------------+------------------------------------+--------+

Index:       prices_pkey
```

**TABLE 5-8**

Some Records in the Prices Database Table

```
sku        price
--------+-------
100014  |     5
100015  | 32.95
100016  |  3.25
100017  |  3.75
100018  |     4
100019  | 49.95
100020  | 59.95
100021  | 29.95
100022  | 24.95
100001  | 14.95
100002  | 16.95
100003  | 18.95
```

# The Online Store

We will be using the same navigational tool as we did in Chapter 4, so Figure 5-1 should look familiar. The only file we will show here is `MenuFrame.html`. All other files can be found on the CD. Here is the code for `MenuFrame.html`:

```html
<<html>
<body text="#000000" bgcolor="#666666" link="#555555" vlink="#555555"
 alink="#555555">
<br>
<br>
<br>
<table COLS=1 WIDTH="100%" >
  <tr bgcolor="#ffffff">
    <td><a href="ViewCatalog.jsp"
```

**Figure 5-1**
Our Online Store

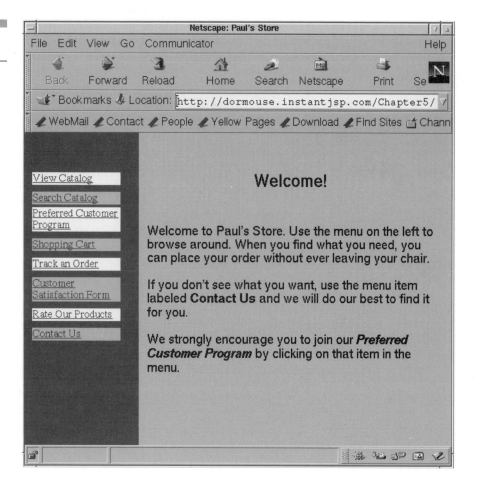

```
          target="rightframe">View Catalog</a>
    </td>
</tr>

<tr><td></td></td>

<tr bgcolor="#c0c0c0">
   <td><a href="GetSearchCriteria.jsp"
        target="rightframe">Search Catalog</a>
   </td>
</tr>
<tr bgcolor="#ffffff">
   <td><a href="PreferredCustomerProgram.jsp"
        target="rightframe">Preferred Customer Program</a>
   </td>
</tr>

<tr><td></td></td>

<tr bgcolor="#c0c0c0">
    <td><a href="ShoppingCart.jsp"
         target="rightframe">Shopping Cart</a>
    </td>
</tr>

<tr><td></td></td>

<tr bgcolor="#ffffff">
   <td><a href="TrackOrder.jsp"
        target="rightframe">Track an Order</a>
   </td>
  </tr>

<tr><td></td></td>

<tr bgcolor="#c0c0c0">
   <td><a href="CustomerSatisfaction.jsp"
         target="rightframe">Customer Satisfaction Form</a>
   </td>
</tr>

<tr><td></td></td>

<tr bgcolor="#ffffff">
   <td><a href="ProductReview.jsp"
        target="rightframe">Rate Our Products</a>
   </td>
</tr>

<tr><td></td></td>

<tr bgcolor="#c0c0c0">
   <td><a href="CustomerFeedback.jsp"
        target="rightframe">Contact Us</a>
   </td>
</tr>

<tr><td></td></td>
```

```
</table>
</body>
</html>
```

# Viewing the Online Catalog

As is the case with traditional brick-and-mortar stores, purchases from an online store are preceded by browsing or window-shopping. In the case of our online store, the customer starts by clicking on "View Catalog" in the menu. As you can see in MenuFrame.html, this menu item is a link to ViewCatalog.jsp. Here is the code:

```
<%@ page import="com.instantjsp.CatalogEntry" %>
<jsp:useBean id="sb" class="com.instantjsp.StoreBean"
  scope="request" />
<%
  String[] categories = sb.getCategories();
  String[] subcategories = sb.getSubcategories();
%>
<html>
<body>
<font face = "Arial, Helvetica" size="+2">
<center>
Catalog
</center>
<br>
</font>
<table>
<%
  for (int i = 0; i < categories.length; ++i) {
%>
    <tr>
      <td>
        <font face = "Arial, Helvetica" size="+1">
        <%= sb.getCategoryName(categories[i]) %>
        </font>
      <td>
    </tr>
<%
    for (int j = 0; j < subcategories.length; ++j) {
      CatalogEntry[] cev =
        sb.getCatalogEntries(categories[i],subcategories[j]);
      if (cev.length == 0) {
        continue;
      }
      String href = "<a href=\"GetProductsInSubcategory.jsp?" +
        "cat=" + categories[i] +
        "&subcat=" + subcategories[j] + "\">";
%>
      <tr>
        <td>
        </td>
```

```
              <td>
                <%= href %>
                <%=sb.getSubcategoryName(subcategories[j]) %></a>
              </td>
          </tr>
    <%
        }
      }
    %>
    </table>
    </body>
    </html>
```

The first scriptlet in this JSP page invokes the `getCategories()` and `getSubcategories()` methods of StoreBean. These methods both return an array of Strings containing the results of the following SQL queries:

```
SELECT DISTINCT cat FROM products

SELECT DISTINCT subcat FROM products
```

The arrays returned by `getCategories()` and `getSubcategories()` are saved in the variables `categories` and `subcategories`, respectively.

Using two nested loops, each major category is shown followed by a list of each of the subcategories in that category. For example, the category Accessories contains subcategories Cables, Cleaning Supplies, and Data Switches. A subcategory list is generated only for a category that contains at least one subcategory. This is determined by checking the size of the array returned by the `getCatalogEntries()` method. This is an array of `CatalogEntry` objects. We will see the `CatalogEntry` class shortly.

Each subcategory is written to the output stream not as simple text but rather as a hypertext link of the form:

<a href="GetProductsInSubcategory.jsp?cat=catstring&subcat=
subcatstring">subcategory</a>

The full output is shown in Figure 5-2.

Clicking on one of the hypertext links mentioned previously results in a "drill-down" to a list of products for a given category/subcategory. As we have already shown, the target of each of the hypertext links is `GetProductsInSubcategory.jsp`. Here is the code:

```
<%@ page import="java.util.Hashtable" %>
%@ page import="com.instantjsp.CatalogEntry" %>
<jsp:useBean id="sb" class="com.instantjsp.StoreBean"
```

**Figure 5-2**
Online Catalog Top-
Level View

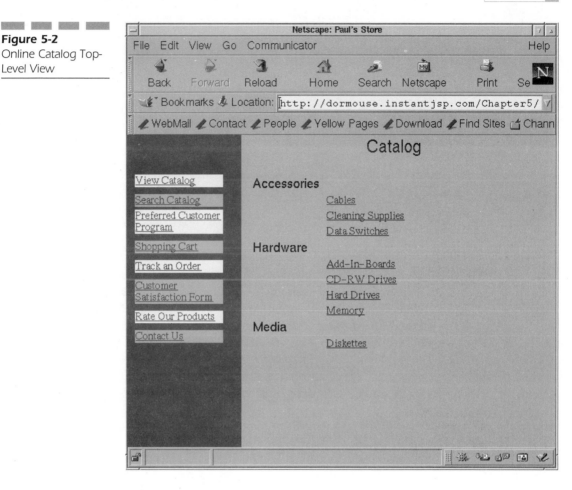

```
    scope="session" />
<%
  String query = request.getQueryString();
  Hashtable qt = HttpUtils.parseQueryString(query);
  String cat = ((String[])qt.get("cat"))[0];
  String subcat = ((String[])qt.get("subcat"))[0];
  CatalogEntry[] cea = sb.getCatalogEntries(cat, subcat);
%>
<html>
<body>
<center>
<font face = "Arial, Helvetica" font size="+1">
Product List
<br>
<br>
```

```
    </font>
    </center>
    <table border width="80%" align="center">
    <%
      for (int i = 0; i < cea.length; ++i) {
    %>
        <tr>
          <td>
            <%= cea[i].getSKU() %>
          </td>
          <td>
            <%= cea[i].getDescription() %>
          </td>
        </tr>
    <%
      }
    %>
    </table>
    </body>
    </html>
```

The first scriptlet extracts the values of cat and subcat from the query string. These are passed as arguments to the getCatalogEntries() method of StoreBean. This method returns an array of CatalogEntry objects. We mentioned the CatalogEntry class before; here is the source:

```
package com.instantjsp;

import java.util.Hashtable;
import java.util.StringTokenizer;

public class CatalogEntry {
  public int category;
  public int subcategory;
  public int sku;
  public String description;
  public float price;

  public CatalogEntry() {
  }

  public int getCategory() {
    return category;
  }

  public int getSubcategory() {
    return subcategory;
  }

  public int getSKU() {
    return sku;
  }
```

```java
    public String getDescription() {
      return description;
    }

    public void setCategory(int category) {
      this.category = category;
    }

    public void setSubcategory(int subcategory) {
      this.subcategory = subcategory;
    }

    public void setSKU(int sku) {
      this.sku = sku;
    }

    public void setDescription(String description) {
      this.description = description;
    }

    public float getPrice() {
      return price;
    }

    public void setPrice(float price) {
      this.price = price;
    }

    public boolean matchesDesc(String keywords,boolean all) {
      String dl = description.toLowerCase();
      StringTokenizer kst = new StringTokenizer(keywords);
      String[] keys = new String[kst.countTokens()];
      while (kst.hasMoreTokens()) {
      String tok = kst.nextToken();
      int ix = dl.indexOf(tok.toLowerCase());
      if (ix  >= 0) {
        if (!all) {
          return true;
        }
      }
      else {
        if (all) {
          return false;
        }
      }
      }
      return (all) ? true: false;
    }
}
```

For each element in the array of `CatalogEntry` objects, the `getSKU()` and `getDescription()` methods are invoked to obtain the product number and description, respectively, and these are displayed in a table as shown in Figure 5-3.

**Figure 5-3**
Drill-down to
Products in Selected
Category/Subcategory

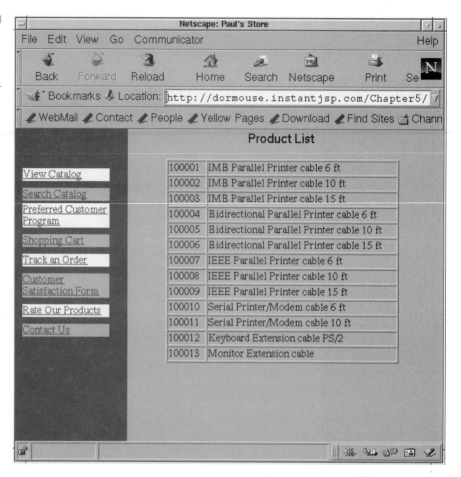

## Searching the Online Catalog

A customer appreciates a tool that provides the ability to browse our catalog online; however, the usefulness of the tool diminishes as the size of the catalog grows. To address this issue, we provide a simple search tool, which the user accesses by selecting SEARCH CATALOG from the menu. As you can see in `MenuFrame.html`, this menu item is a link to `GetSearchCriteria.jsp`. The code is as follows:

```
<jsp:useBean id="sb" class="com.instantjsp.StoreBean"
  scope="session" />
<%
```

```
 String[] cats = sb.getCategories();
%>
<html>
<body>
<form method="post" action="SearchCatalog.jsp">
<font face = "Arial, Helvetica" size="+2">
<center>
Product Locator
<br>
<br>
</center>
</font>
<font face = "Arial, Helvetica" size="+0">
Enter the word(s) you are searching for in the box below.
<p>
Specify whether you want to search for <b>any</b> or <b>all</b>
of the words.
<p>
To limit the search to one section of the catalog, select
that category from the drop-down list.
</font>
<font face = "Arial, Helvetica" size="+0">
<br>
<br>
<hr width="100%">
Search for
<select name="all" size=1>
<option value="false">any
<option value="true">all
</select>
of
<input type="text" name="keywords">
<br>
<br>
Limit search to this category
    <select name="category" size=1>
        <option>All
<%
  for (int i = 0; i < cats.length; ++i) {
%>
      <option value="<%= cats[i] %>"><%= sb.getCategoryName(cats[i]) %>
<%
  }
%>
    </select>
<br>
<br>
<br>
<center>
<input type=submit name="submit" value="SEARCH">
</center>
</form>
</body>
</html>
```

This JSP generates the page shown in Figure 5-4. The page contains a text field into which keywords can be entered, a selection list that we can

**Figure 5-4**
The Search Tool

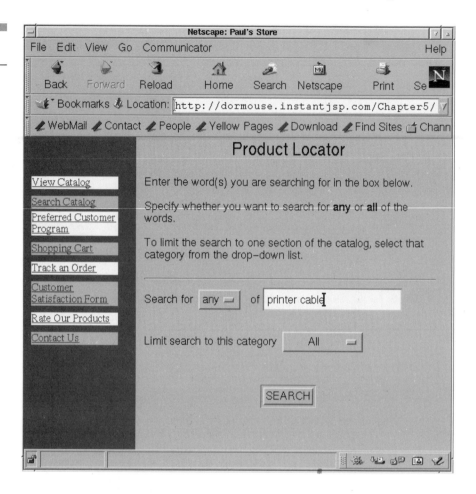

use to indicate that any or all of the keywords must be found, and a second selection list that we can use to limit the search to a specified category. The contents of this second list are obtained using the getCategories() method of the StoreBean.

As you can see from Figure 5-4, we have entered the keywords printer cable and have specified that *any* of these words will satisfy the search. When we click on the SEARCH button, a request containing the contents of the HTML form is sent to SearchCatalog.jsp. Here is the code:

```
<%@ page import="com.instantjsp.CatalogEntry" %>
<jsp:useBean id="sb" class="com.instantjsp.StoreBean"
```

```
       scope="session" />
<%
  boolean all = new
     Boolean(request.getParameter("all")).booleanValue();
  String keywords = request.getParameter("keywords");
  String cat = request.getParameter("category");
  CatalogEntry[] cea = sb.getCatalogEntries(cat,keywords,all);
%>
<html>
<body>
<center>
<font face = "Arial, Helvetica" font size="+1">
<%
  if (cea.length == 0) {
%>
<br>
<br>
<br>
<br>
<br>
No matches found
<%
  }
  else {
%>
Product List
<%
  }
%>
<br>
<br>
</font>
<table border width="80%" align="center">
<%
  for (int i = 0; i < cea.length; ++i) {
%>
    <tr>
      <td>
        <%= cea[i].getSKU() %>
      </td>
      <td>
        <%= cea[i].getDescription() %>
      </td>
    </tr>
<%
  }
%>
</table>
<center>
</body>
</html>
```

The first scriptlet uses the getParameter() method of the implicit request object to get the values of the request parameters. These values are passed to the getCatalogEntries() method of StoreBean. The results of the search are returned as an array of CatalogEntry objects.

**Figure 5-5**
An Unsuccessful
Search

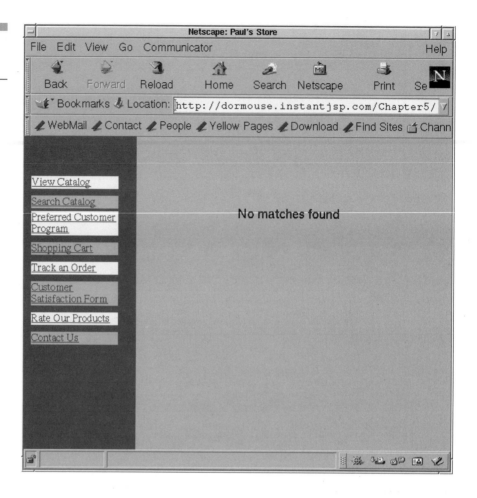

If the array returned by `getCatalogEntries()` contains no entries, the message `No matches found` is sent to the output stream and the customer sees the pages shown in Figure 5-5; otherwise, for each element of the array, the `getSKU()` and `getDescription()` methods are invoked to obtain the product number and product description, respectively. These values are displayed in a table as shown in Figure 5-6.

You will notice that the results shown in Figure 5-6 include cables for monitors and keyboards as well as for printers. To help narrow the search, we could specify the "any" option as shown in Figure 5-7. We would then see Figure 5-8, which is a smaller set of search results.

**Figure 5-6**
Results of a
Successful Search

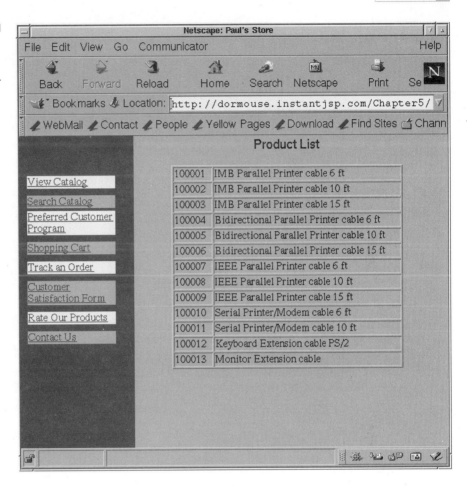

## Keeping Track of What They're Interested In

If you simply provide your customers with Web-based tools to view and search your catalog and—as we'll see in the next chapter—order online, you'll discover rather quickly that there's little truth to "If you build it, they will come." You have to be aggressive but not to the point of driving the customer away. You have to advertise in such a manner that it does not blatantly smack of advertising. You have to get to know your customers' shopping habits without conveying the impression that you are spying on them.

**Figure 5-7**
A More Restrictive
Search

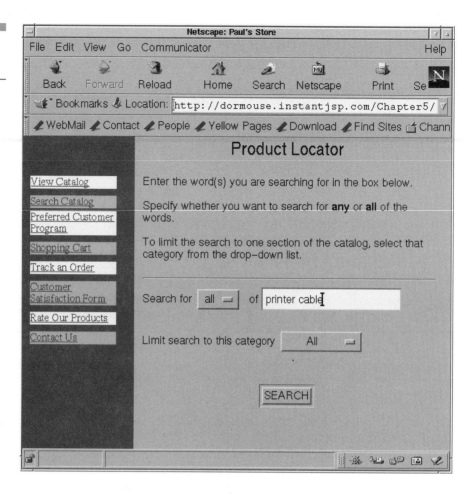

The most effective way to accomplish all this is the widely used, often misunderstood cookie. Let's see how to present the user with a cookie from a JSP page. Later, in Chapter 7 and Chapter 8, we take a look at how we can leverage use of this cookie.

The first issue we must address is the manner in which we present the cookie to customers. We could do what many sites do and simply send a cookie to any visitor who doesn't already have one. We will choose not to go this route because when customers discover that's what you are doing, there's a good chance they'll be annoyed—perhaps to the point of never visiting your site again. Instead, we will institute a "Preferred Customer Program," which the customer chooses to join or not. As part of this program, we let customers know that we are using some means of remem-

**Figure 5-8**
Results of Narrower
Search

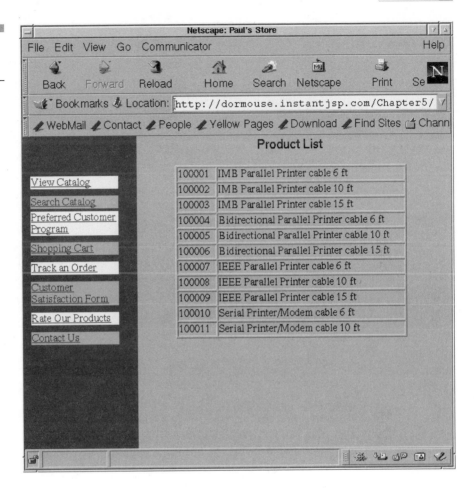

**Figure 5-8**
Results of Narrower
Search

bering who they are between visits and that we are learning their shopping preferences so that we can offer them discounts and other rewards.

The customer either reads our welcome page and takes our suggestion to join the Preferred Customer Program or wonders what the menu item labeled "Preferred Customer Program" is and clicks on it. As you can see by examining MenuFrame.html, the menu item is a link to Preferred-CustomerProgram.jsp. Here is the code:

```
<%@ page import="javax.servlet.http.Cookie" %>
<%@ include file="GetPrefCustId.jsp" %>
<jsp:useBean id="custBean" class="com.instantjsp.Customer"
  scope="session" >
 <jsp:setProperty name="custBean" property="customerInfo"
   value="<%= getPrefCustID(request)%>" />
</jsp:useBean>
```

```
<%
  if (custBean.isPreferredCustomer()) {
%>
    <jsp:forward page="PreferredCustomerStatus.jsp" />
<%
  }
  else {
%>
    <jsp:forward page="PreferredCustomerIntro.html" />
<%
  }
%>
```

The menu item labeled "Preferred Customer Program" serves a dual purpose. It presents an application form to customers who have not yet joined but wish to do so. For customers who are already members of the program, it enables them to update their profile. The decision is made based on the presence or absence of a cookie. As we see in later chapters, this check is performed in numerous JSP pages; therefore, to save typing and to make maintenance easier, we use a directive to include the code that performs the check. This directive is:

```
<%@ include file="GetPrefCustId.jsp" %>
```

The code in the file GetPrefCustId.jsp looks like this:

```
<%! public String getPrefCustID(HttpServletRequest request) {
    String custID = null;
    Cookie[] cookies = request.getCookies();
    for (int i = 0; i < cookies.length; ++i) {
      if (cookies[i].getName().equals("preferred.customer")) {
        custID = cookies[i].getValue();
        break;
      }
    }
    return custID;
  }
%>
```

The included file consists of a declaration that declares the method getPrefCustID(), which simply gets the array of cookies found in the request. If a cookie named "preferred.customer" is found, its value is obtained and returned as the preferred customer ID. If no such cookie is found, null is returned.

If an instance of Customer having a name of custBean does not already exist in the name space for session scope, one is created and the body of the <jsp:useBean> uses a <jsp:setProperty> action to invoke the setter setCustomerInfo() using as an argument the value returned by the getPrefCustID() method contained in the included code. The code for the Customer Bean is shown at the end of this chapter and you can see that when the `setCustomerInfo()` method receives an argument that is not null, it invokes `getCustomerInfo()`, which retrieves a customer profile from the prefcust database and uses the retrieved information to set appropriate instance variables. One of these instance variables is `isPreferredCustomer`.

The first scriptlet in `PreferredCustomerProgram.jsp` tests the boolean value returned by the `isPreferredCustomer()` method. Since we have not yet joined the program, our customer ID will be null and the value returned by `isPreferredCustomer()` will be false, which was assigned when the instance was created. When `isPreferredCustomer()` returns false, a `<jsp:forward>` action is executed with a target of `PreferredCustomerIntro.html`. Here is the code, which produces the page shown in Figure 5-9:

**Figure 5-9**
Introducing the
Preferred Customer
Program

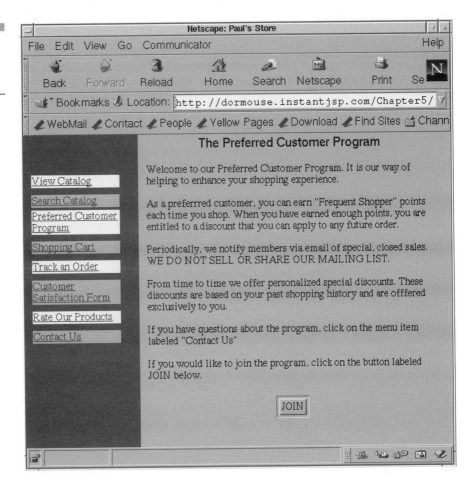

```
<html>
<body>
<center>
<font face = "Arial, Helvetica" size="+1">
The Preferred Customer Program
<br>
<br>
</font>
</center>
Welcome to our Preferred Customer Program. It is our way of helping
to enhance your shopping experience.
<p>
As a preferred customer, you can earn "Frequent Shopper" points
each time you shop. When you have earned enough points, you are
entitled to a discount that you can apply to any future order.
<p>
Periodically, we notify members via email of special, closed sales.
WE DO NOT SELL OR SHARE OUR MAILING LIST.
<p>
From time to time we offer personalized special discounts. These
discounts are based on your past shopping history and are offered
exclusively to you.
<p>
If you have questions about the program, click on the menu item
labeled "Contact Us"
<p>
If you would like to join the program, click on the button labeled
JOIN below.
<center>
<form method="get"

action="http://dormouse.instantjsp.com/Chapter5/PreferredCustomerAp
plication.html">
<input type="submit" name="submit" value="JOIN">
</form>
</center>
</html>
```

Since we have not yet joined the program, we will do so now by clicking
on the JOIN button in Figure 5-9. The submit action of the form containing
this button sends a request to `PreferredCustomerApplication.html`,
which produces the page shown in Figure 5-10. Here is the code:

```
<html>
<body>
<center>
<font face="Arial,Helvetica" size=+1>
Preferred Customer Program
Application
</font>
</center>
<form method="post"

action="http://dormouse.instantjsp.com/Chapter5/CreatePreferredCusto-
mer.jsp">
<table cols=3 width="100%" nosave>
  <tr nosave>
```

**Figure 5-10**
The Preferred
Customer Program
Application Form

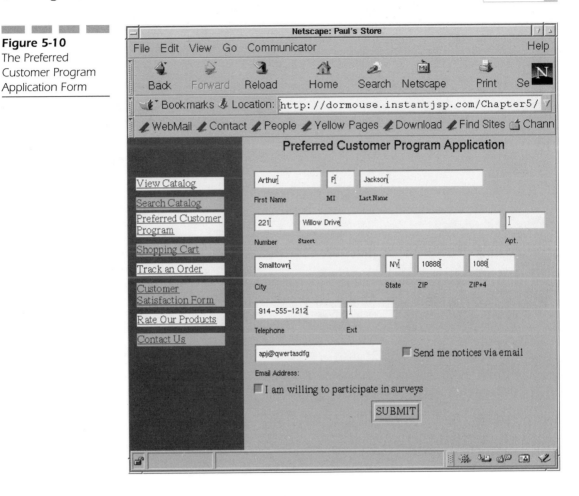

**Figure 5-10**
The Preferred
Customer Program
Application Form

```html
<td width="25%" nosave>
  <font face="Arial,Helvetica" size=0>
  <input type="text" name="firstName" size=15>
  </font>
</td>

<td width="10%" nosave>
  <font face="Arial,Helvetica" size=0>
  <input type="text" name="middleInitial" size=5>
  </font>
</td>

<td width="65%" nosave>
  <font face="Arial,Helvetica" size=0>
  <input type="text" name="lastName" size=30>
  </font>
</td>
</tr>
```

```
        <tr nosave>
          <td width="25%" nosave>
            <font face="Arial,Helvetica" size=-2>
            First Name
            </font>
          </td>

          <td width="10%" nosave>
            <font size=-2>
            MI
            </font>
          </td>

          <td width="65%" nosave>
            <font size=-2>
            Last Name
            </font>
          </td>
        </tr>
</table>

<table width="80%" nosave >
  <tr nosave>
    <td width="10%" nosave>
      <font face="Arial,Helvetica" size=0>
      <input type="text" name="streetNumber" size=8>
      </font>
    </td>

    <td width="80%" nosave>
      <font face="Arial,Helvetica" size=0>
      <input type="text" name="street" size=50>
      </font>
    </td>

    <td width="10%" nosave>
      <font face="Arial,Helvetica" size=0>
      <input type="text" name="apt" size=8>
      </font>
    </td>
  </tr>

  <tr nosave>
    <td width="10%" nosave>
      <font face="Arial,Helvetica" size=-2>
      Number
      </font>
    </td>

    <td width="80%" nosave>
      <font size=-2>
      Street
      </font>
    </td>

    <td width="10%" nosave>
      <font face="Arial,Helvetica"><font size=-2>
      Apt.
      </font></font>
```

```
          </td>
        </tr>
   </table>

<table cols=4 width="80%" nosave >
  <tr nosave>
    <td WIDTH="70%" NOSAVE>
      <font face="Arial,Helvetica" size=0>
      <input type="text" name="city" size=30>
      </font>
    </td>

    <td WIDTH="10%" NOSAVE>
      <font face="Arial,Helvetica" size=0>
      <input type="text" name="state" size=5>
      </font>
    </td>

    <td WIDTH="10%" NOSAVE>
      <font face="Arial,Helvetica" size=0>
      <input type="text" name="zip" size=10>
      </font>
    </td>

    <td WIDTH="10%" NOSAVE>
      <font face="Arial,Helvetica" size=0>
      <input type="text" name="zipPlusFour" size=10>
      </font>
    </td>
  </tr>

  <tr nosave>
    <td width="70%">
      <font face="Arial,Helvetica">
      <font size=-2>City</font></font>
    </td>

   <td width="10%">
     <font face="Arial,Helvetica">
     <font size=-2>
     State
     </font>
     </font>
   </td>

   <td width="10%">
     <font face="Arial,Helvetica">
     <font size=-2>
     ZIP
     </font>
     </font>
   </td>

   <td width="10%">
     <font face="Arial,Helvetica">
     <font size=-2>
     ZIP+4
     </font>
     </font>
```

```
      </td>
    </tr>
  </table>

  <table WIDTH="50%" nosave >
    <tr nosave>
      <td width="75%"nosave>
        <font face="Arial,Helvetica" size=0>
        <input type="text" name="telephoneNumber" size=20>
        </font>
      </td>

      <td width="25%" nosave>
        <font face="Arial,Helvetica" size=0>
        <input type="text" name="telephoneExtension" size=10>
        </font>
      </td>
    </tr>

    <tr nosave>
      <td width="75%" nosave>
        <font face="Arial,Helvetica" size=-2>
        Telephone
        </font>
      </td>

      <td width="25%" nosave>
        <font face="Arial,Helvetica" size=-2>
        Ext
        </font>
      </td>
    </tr>
  </table>

  <table cols=3 width="100%" nosave >
    <tr nosave>
      <td width="45%" nosave>
      <font face="Arial,Helvetica" size=0>
      <input type="text" name="emailAddress" size=30>
      </font>
    </td>

    <td width="5%" nosave>
    </td>

    <td width="50%" nosave>
      <input type="checkbox" name="sendEmail" value="true" checked>
      Send me notices via email
    </td>
  </tr>

  <tr nosave>
    <td width="50%" nosave>
      <font face="Arial,Helvetica" size=0>
      Email Address:
      </font>
    </td>

    <td width="5%" nosave>
```

```
    </td>

    <td width="45%" nosave>
    </td>
</tr>

</table>
<input type="checkbox" name="survey" value="true" checked>
I am willing to participate in surveys
<br>
<center>
<input type="submit" name="submit" value="SUBMIT">
</center>
</form>
</body>
</html>
```

After we fill in the form and click on SUBMIT, a request containing the contents of the form is sent to CreatePreferredCustomer.jsp, which looks like this:

```
<%@ page errorPage="/common/Exception.jsp" %>
<%@ page import="javax.servlet.http.Cookie" %>
<%@include file="GetPrefCustId.jsp" %>
<jsp:useBean id="custBean" class="com.instantjsp.Customer"
  scope="session" >
</jsp:useBean>
<jsp:setProperty name="custBean" property="*" />
<%
  String survey = request.getParameter("survey");
  if (survey == null) {
    survey = "false";
  }
  String sendEmail = request.getParameter("sendEmail");
  if (sendEmail == null) {
    sendEmail = "false";
  }
%>
<jsp:setProperty name="custBean" property= "survey"
  value="<%= survey %>" />
<jsp:setProperty name="custBean" property= "sendEmail"
  value="<%= sendEmail %>" />
<%
  String custno = custBean.createPreferred();
  Cookie c = new Cookie("preferred.customer",custno);
  c.setVersion(1);
  c.setPath("/");
  c.setComment("Preferred Customer");
  c.setDomain(".instantjsp.com");
  c.setMaxAge(365 * 24 * 60 * 60);
  response.addCookie(c);
%>
<html>
<body text="#000000" bgcolor="#e0e0e0">
<font face = "Arial, Helvetica" size="+1">
<center>
Welcome,
```

```
<jsp:getProperty name="custBean" property="firstName" />
<br>
<br>
</center>
</font>
Your new Preferred Customer Number is
<%= custno %>
<br>
<br>
We have recorded the following data in your profile. To change
your profile, click on "Preferred Customer Profile" in the menu.
<br>
<br>
First Name = <jsp:getProperty name="custBean" property="firstName" />
<br>
Middle Initial = <jsp:getProperty name="custBean" property=
"middleInitial" />
<br>
Last Name = <jsp:getProperty name="custBean" property="lastName" />
<br>
Street Number = <jsp:getProperty name="custBean" property=
"streetNumber" />
<br>
Street = <jsp:getProperty name="custBean" property="street" />
<br>
Apt = <jsp:getProperty name="custBean" property="apt" />
<br>
City = <jsp:getProperty name="custBean" property="city" />
<br>
State = <jsp:getProperty name="custBean" property="state" />
<br>
Zip = <jsp:getProperty name="custBean" property="zip" />
<br>
Zip+4 = <jsp:getProperty name="custBean" property="zipPlusFour" />
<br>
Tel = <jsp:getProperty name="custBean" property="telephoneNumber" />
<br>
Ext = <jsp:getProperty name="custBean" property="telephoneExtension" />
<br>
Wants email = <jsp:getProperty name="custBean" property="sendEmail" />
<br>
Email Addr = <jsp:getProperty name="custBean" property="emailAddress"/>
<br>
Will take surveys = <jsp:getProperty name="custBean" property="survey"
/>
<br>
</body>
</html>
```

The first statement we will examine is:

```
<jsp:setProperty name="custBean" property="*" />
```

The value of * for `property` causes the JSP container to iterate over the current `ServletRequest` parameters and invoke all the setter methods of Customer that match a parameter name. The `sendEmail` and `survey` parameters are handled individually, because if one or both are not checked (as indicated by `getParameter()` returning null), we still want to invoke the setter method.

The next code that is executed is the following scriptlet:

```
<%
    String custno = custBean.createPreferred();
    Cookie c = new Cookie("preferred.customer",custno);
    c.setVersion(1);
    c.setPath("/");
    c.setComment("Preferred Customer");
    c.setDomain(".instantjsp.com");
    c.setMaxAge(365 * 24 * 60 * 60);
    response.addCookie(c);
%>
```

The scriptlet first invokes the `createdPreferred()` method of Customer. Using all of the instance variables we populated earlier with the `<jsp:setProperty>` action, this method constructs and executes an SQL statement that inserts a record into the prefcust database table. This table is shown in Table 5-9.

**NOTE:** *The code was developed using PostgreSQL. Some relational database managers may have a different interpretation of a column type of "date." If you find this to be the case with your relational database manager, use "char" instead.*

**TABLE 5-9**

The prefcust Database Table Layout

```
Table   = prefcust
+--------------------------+------------------------+----------+
|      Field               |         Type           |  Length  |
+--------------------------+------------------------+----------+
|  custno                  | int4 not null          |    4     |
|  joined                  | date                   |    4     |
|  lastordered             | date                   |    4     |
|  lastordno               | date                   |    4     |
|  sendemail               | bool                   |    1     |
|  emailaddr               | varchar()              |   128    |
|  oktosurvey              | bool                   |    1     |
|  dp_current_survey       | bool                   |    1     |
|  freq_shop_pts           | int4                   |    4     |
+--------------------------+------------------------+----------+
Index:    prefcust_pkey
```

The one remaining task is that of creating a cookie containing the preferred customer ID and presenting it to the browser. The cookie is created by passing the name of the cookie (in our case "preferred.customer") and the value (the preferred customer ID) to the constructor. The `setVersion()` method does exactly what its name implies. The `setPath()` method with an argument of / guarantees that we will be able to access the cookie from other chapters, since / is the most general case that will match any of our URLs that are of the form http://dormouse.instantjsp.-com/Chapter?. The `setDomain()` method with an argument of ".instantjsp.com" ensures that any host in the instantjsp.com domain can ask for the cookie. The life of the cookie, which is specified in seconds, is set as one year (365 days $\times$ 24 h/day $\times$ 60 min/h $\times$ 60 s/min). The `addCookie()` method of `request()` presents the cookie to the browser. If we have requested to be notified when cookies are received, we see a page like the one shown in Figure 5-11. When the customer accepts the cookie, the page shown in Figure 5-12 is displayed. We will see later how the cookie can be used in a variety of ways.

From this point on, when the user selects "Preferred Customer Program" from the menu, `PreferredCustomerProgram.jsp` will forward the request to `PreferredCustomerStatus.jsp` since our cookie will be found and `isPreferredCustomer()` returns true. Here is the code for `PreferredCustomerStatus.jsp`:

```
<%@ page errorPage="/common/Exception.jsp" %>
<jsp:useBean id="custBean" class="com.instantjsp.Customer"
```

**Figure 5-11**
The Cookie is Presented to the Browser

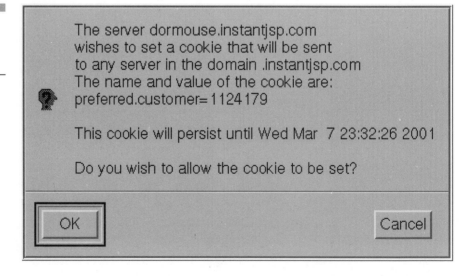

The server dormouse.instantjsp.com
wishes to set a cookie that will be sent
to any server in the domain .instantjsp.com
The name and value of the cookie are:
preferred.customer=1124179

This cookie will persist until Wed Mar  7 23:32:26 2001

Do you wish to allow the cookie to be set?

OK                    Cancel

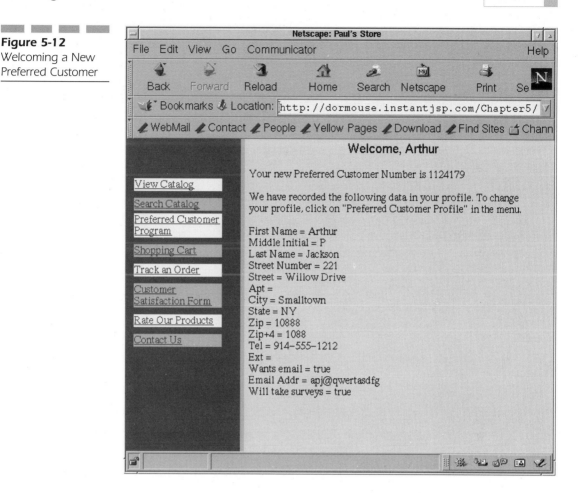

```
    scope="session" />
<html>
<body text="#000000" bgcolor="#e0e0e0">
<font face = "Arial, Helvetica" size="+1">
<center>
Welcome,
<jsp:getProperty name="custBean" property="firstName" />
<br>
<br>
</center>
</font>
We have recorded the following data in your profile. To change
your profile, click on the "UPDATE" button below.
<br>
<br>
Preferred Customer Number
<jsp:getProperty name="custBean" property="customerID" />
<br>
```

```
First Name = <jsp:getProperty name="custBean" property="firstName" />
<br>
Middle Initial = <jsp:getProperty name="custBean" property=
 "middleInitial" />
<br>
Last Name = <jsp:getProperty name="custBean" property="lastName" />
<br>
Street Number = <jsp:getProperty name="custBean" property="street-
 Number" />
<br>
Street = <jsp:getProperty name="custBean" property="street" />
<br>
Apt = <jsp:getProperty name="custBean" property="apt" />
<br>
City = <jsp:getProperty name="custBean" property="city" />
<br>
State = <jsp:getProperty name="custBean" property="state" />
<br>
Zip = <jsp:getProperty name="custBean" property="zip" />
<br>
Zip+4 = <jsp:getProperty name="custBean" property="zipPlusFour" />
<br>
Tel = <jsp:getProperty name="custBean" property="telephoneNumber" />
<br>
Ext = <jsp:getProperty name="custBean" property="telephone-
 Extension" />
<br>
Wants email = <jsp:getProperty name="custBean" property="sendEmail" />
<br>
Email Addr = <jsp:getProperty name="custBean" property="email-
 Address" />
<br>
Will take surveys = <jsp:getProperty name="custBean" property="survey"
 />
<br>
<center>
<form method="post"
action="http://dormouse.instantjsp.com/Chapter5/UpdatePreferredCus-
 tomer.jsp">
<input type="submit" value="UPDATE">
</form>
</center>
</body>
</html>
```

This JSP page simply uses a <jsp:getProperty> for each field in the profile and displays the results as shown in Figure 5-13.

If the customer clicks on the UPDATE button, a request is sent to UpdatePreferredCustomer.jsp, which presents the customer with the prepopulated form shown in Figure 5-14. Here is the code for UpdatePreferredCustomer.jsp:

```
<jsp:useBean id="custBean" class="com.instantjsp.Customer"
  scope="session" />
<html>
```

**Figure 5-13**
Viewing Current
Customer Profile

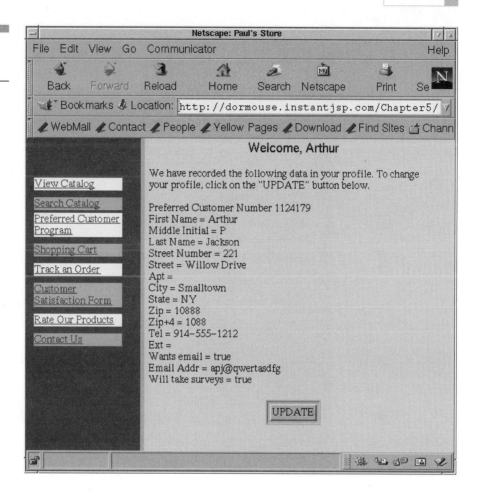

```
<body>
<center>
<font face="Arial,Helvetica" size=+1>
Preferred Customer Program Profile
</font>
</center>
<br>
Make any changes you wish and click on the SUBMIT button
<form

action="http://dormouse.instantjsp.com/Chapter5/NewPreferredCustomer-
  Profile.jsp">
<table cols=3 width="100%" nosave>
  <tr nosave>
    <td width="25%" nosave>
      <font face="Arial,Helvetica" size=0>
      <input type="text" name="firstName" size=15
        value="<jsp:getProperty name="custBean"
```

**Figure 5-14**
Updating the
Customer Profile

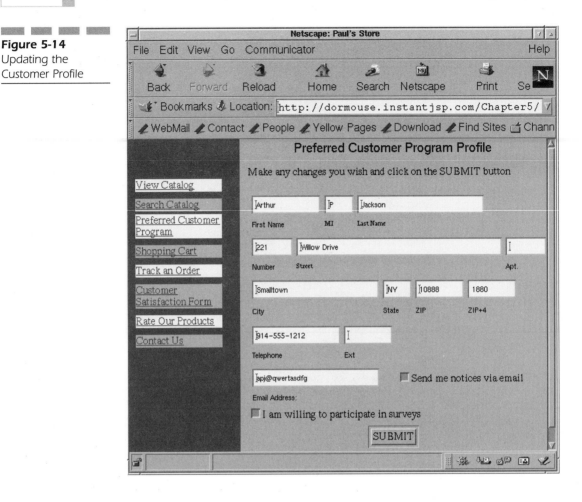

```
                    property="firstName" />">
              </font>
          </td>

          <td width="10%" nosave>
            <font face="Arial,Helvetica" size=0>
            <input type="text" name="middleInitial" size=5
              value="<jsp:getProperty name="custBean"
                property="middleInitial" />">
              </font>
          </td>

          <td width="65%" nosave>
            <font face="Arial,Helvetica" size=0>
            <input type="text" name="lastName" size=30
              value="<jsp:getProperty name="custBean"
                property="lastName" />">
              </font>
```

```
            </td>
          </tr>

        <tr nosave>
          <td width="25%" nosave>
            <font face="Arial,Helvetica" size=-2>
            First Name
            </font>
          </td>

          <td width="10%" nosave>
            <font size=-2>
            MI
            </font>
          </td>

          <td width="65%" nosave>
            <font size=-2>
            Last Name
            </font>
          </td>
        </tr>
    </table>

    <table width="80%" nosave >
      <tr nosave>
        <td width="10%" nosave>
          <font face="Arial,Helvetica" size=0>
          <input type="text" name="streetNumber" size=8
            value="<jsp:getProperty name="custBean"
              property="streetNumber" />">
          </font>
        </td>

        <td width="80%" nosave>
          <font face="Arial,Helvetica" size=0>
          <input type="text" name="street" size=50
            value="<jsp:getProperty name="custBean" property="street" />">
          </font>
        </td>

        <td width="10%" nosave>
          <font face="Arial,Helvetica" size=0>
          <input type="text" name="apt" size=8
            value="<jsp:getProperty name="custBean" property="apt" />">
          </font>
        </td>
      </tr>

      <tr nosave>
        <td width="10%" nosave>
          <font face="Arial,Helvetica" size=-2>
          Number
          </font>
        </td>

        <td width="80%" nosave>
          <font size=-2>
          Street
```

```
        </font>
      </td>

    <td width="10%" nosave>
      <font face="Arial,Helvetica"><font size=-2>
      Apt.
      </font></font>
    </td>
  </tr>
</table>

<table cols=4 width="80%" nosave >
  <tr nosave>
    <td WIDTH="70%" NOSAVE>
      <font face="Arial,Helvetica" size=0>
      <input type="text" name="city" size=30
        value="<jsp:getProperty name="custBean" property="city" />">
      </font>
    </td>

    <td WIDTH="10%" NOSAVE>
      <font face="Arial,Helvetica" size=0>
      <input type="text" name="state" size=5
        value="<jsp:getProperty name="custBean" property="state" />">
      </font>
    </td>

    <td WIDTH="10%" NOSAVE>
      <font face="Arial,Helvetica" size=0>
      <input type="text" name="zip" size=10
        value="<jsp:getProperty name="custBean" property="zip" />">
      </font>
    </td>

    <td WIDTH="10%" NOSAVE>
      <font face="Arial,Helvetica" size=0>
      <input type="text" name="zipPlusFour" size=10
        value="<jsp:getProperty name="custBean"
          property="zipPlusFour" />">
      </font>
    </td>
  </tr>

  <tr nosave>
    <td width="70%">
      <font face="Arial,Helvetica">
      <font size=-2>City</font></font>
    </td>

    <td width="10%">
      <font face="Arial,Helvetica">
      <font size=-2>
      State
      </font>
      </font>
    </td>

    <td width="10%">
      <font face="Arial,Helvetica">
```

```
            <font size=-2>
            ZIP
            </font>
            </font>
         </td>

         <td width="10%">
            <font face="Arial,Helvetica">
            <font size=-2>
            ZIP+4
            </font>
            </font>
         </td>
     </tr>
</table>

<table WIDTH="50%" nosave >
   <tr nosave>
      <td width="75%"nosave>
         <font face="Arial,Helvetica" size=0>
         <input type="text" name="telephoneNumber" size=20
           value="<jsp:getProperty name="custBean"
             property="telephoneNumber" />">
         </font>
      </td>

      <td width="25%" nosave>
         <font face="Arial,Helvetica" size=0>
         <input type="text" name="telephoneExtension" size=10
           value="<jsp:getProperty name="custBean"
             property="telephoneExtension" />">
         </font>
      </td>
   </tr>

   <tr nosave>
      <td width="75%" nosave>
         <font face="Arial,Helvetica" size=-2>
         Telephone
         </font>
      </td>

     <td width="25%" nosave>
         <font face="Arial,Helvetica" size=-2>
         Ext
         </font>
      </td>
   </tr>
</table>

<table cols=3 width="100%" nosave >
   <tr nosave>
      <td width="45%" nosave>
         <font face="Arial,Helvetica" size=0>
         <input type="text" name="emailAddress" size=30
           value="<jsp:getProperty name="custBean"
             property="emailAddress" />">
         </font>
      </td>
```

```
        <td width="5%" nosave>
        </td>

         <td width="50%" nosave>
           <input type="checkbox" name="sendEmail" value="true"
<%
   if (new Boolean(custBean.getSendEmail()).booleanValue()) {
%>
           checked
<%
    }
%>
>
           Send me notices via email
        </td>
     </tr>

     <tr nosave>
        <td width="50%" nosave>
          <font face="Arial,Helvetica" size=0>
          Email Address:
          </font>
        </td>

        <td width="5%" nosave>
        </td>

        <td width="45%" nosave>
        </td>
     </tr>

</table>
<input type="checkbox" name="survey" value="true"
<%
   if (new Boolean(custBean.getSurvey()).booleanValue()) {
%>
        checked
<%
    }
%>
>
I am willing to participate in surveys
<br>
<center>
<input type="submit" name="submit" value="SUBMIT">
</center>
</form>
</body>
</html>
```

After the customer makes changes to one or more of the fields and/or checkboxes and clicks on SUBMIT, a request containing the contents of the form is sent to NewPreferredCustomerProfile.jsp. This JSP page is almost identical to CreatePreferredCustomer.jsp, which we have already seen. It differs in that it does not create and store a cookie. Here is the code:

```
<%@ page errorPage="/common/Exception.jsp" %>
<jsp:useBean id="custBean" class="com.instantjsp.Customer"
  scope="session" />
<jsp:setProperty name="custBean" property="*" />
<%
  String survey = request.getParameter("survey");
  if (survey == null) {
    survey = "false";
  }
  String sendEmail = request.getParameter("sendEmail");
  if (sendEmail == null) {
    sendEmail = "false";
  }
%>
<jsp:setProperty name="custBean" property= "survey"
  value="<%= survey %>" />
<jsp:setProperty name="custBean" property= "sendEmail"
  value="<%= sendEmail %>" />
<%
  custBean.updateProfile();
%>
<html>
<body text="#000000" bgcolor="#e0e0e0">
<font face = "Arial, Helvetica" size="+1">
<center>
New Profile for
<jsp:getProperty name="custBean" property="firstName" />
<jsp:getProperty name="custBean" property="lastName" />
<br>
<br>
</center>
</font>
Preferred Customer Number:
<jsp:getProperty name="custBean" property="customerID" />
<br>
<br>
First Name = <jsp:getProperty name="custBean" property="firstName" />
<br>
Middle Initial = <jsp:getProperty name="custBean" property="middle-
  Initial" />
<br>
Last Name = <jsp:getProperty name="custBean" property="lastName" />
<br>
Street Number = <jsp:getProperty name="custBean" property="street-
  Number" />
<br>
Street = <jsp:getProperty name="custBean" property="street" />
<br>
Apt = <jsp:getProperty name="custBean" property="apt" />
<br>
City = <jsp:getProperty name="custBean" property="city" />
<br>
State = <jsp:getProperty name="custBean" property="state" />
<br>
Zip = <jsp:getProperty name="custBean" property="zip" />
<br>
Zip+4 = <jsp:getProperty name="custBean" property="zipPlusFour" />
<br>
Tel = <jsp:getProperty name="custBean" property="telephoneNumber" />
```

```
<br>
Ext = <jsp:getProperty name="custBean" property="telephone-
Extension" />
<br>
Wants email = <jsp:getProperty name="custBean" property="sendEmail" />
<br>
Email Addr = <jsp:getProperty name="custBean" property="email-
Address" />
<br>
Will take surveys = <jsp:getProperty name="custBean" property="survey"
/>
<br>
</body>
</html>
```

See Figure 5-15 for an updated profile.

**Figure 5-15**
An Updated Profile

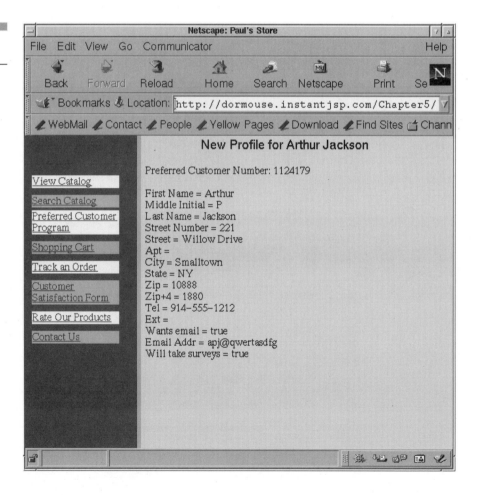

## Code for `StoreBean`

```
package com.instantjsp;

import java.sql.Connection;
import java.sql.ResultSet;
import java.sql.SQLException;
import java.sql.Statement;
import java.util.Date;
import java.util.Random;
import java.text.SimpleDateFormat;
import java.util.Vector;

import javaservlets.jdbc.ConnectionPool;

public class StoreBean {

  private ConnectionPool connectionPool;

  private static final String POOL_CFG_FILE =
    "javaservlets/jdbc/BusinessPool.cfg";

  private static final String SELECT_CATEGORIES =
    "(SELECT DISTINCT cat FROM products)";

  private static final String SELECT_SUBCATEGORIES =
    "(SELECT DISTINCT subcat FROM products)";

  private static final String SELECT_CATEGORY_NAME =
    "SELECT cat_desc FROM product_categories WHERE ";

  private static final String SELECT_SUBCATEGORY_NAME =
    "SELECT subcat_desc FROM product_subcats WHERE ";

  private static final String SELECT_PRODUCTS =
    "SELECT * FROM products";

  private static final String SELECT_PRODUCTS_QUALIFIED =
    "SELECT * FROM products WHERE ";

  private static final String INSERT_ORDER_DETAIL =
    "INSERT INTO orderdetail VALUES (";

  private static final String INSERT_ORDER =
    "INSERT INTO orders (ordno, custno, placed, status) VALUES (";

  private static final String CAT_QUALIFIER =
    " cat = ";

  private static final String SUBCAT_QUALIFIER =
    " subcat = ";

  private static final String SKU_QUALIFIER =
    " sku = ";

  private static final String GET_ORDER_NUMBER =
    "SELECT nextval('seq_ord')";
```

```java
  private static final String AND = " AND ";
  private static final String QUOTE = "'";
  private static final String RPAREN = ")";
  private static final String COMMA = ",";

  public StoreBean() throws Exception {
    connectionPool = new ConnectionPool();
    connectionPool.initialize(POOL_CFG_FILE);
  }

  public CatalogEntry[] getCatalogEntries()
    throws SQLException {
  Connection conn = connectionPool.getConnection();
  Statement us = conn.createStatement();
  ResultSet rs = us.executeQuery(SELECT_PRODUCTS);
  Vector v = new Vector();
  while (rs.next()) {
    CatalogEntry ce = new CatalogEntry();
    ce.setSKU(rs.getInt(1));
    ce.setCategory(rs.getInt(2));
    ce.setSubcategory(rs.getInt(3));
    ce.setDescription(rs.getString(4));
    ce.setPrice(rs.getFloat(5));
    v.add(ce);
  }
  connectionPool.close(conn);
  CatalogEntry[] cev = new CatalogEntry[v.size()];
  for (int i = 0; i < v.size(); ++i) {
    cev[i] = (CatalogEntry)v.elementAt(i);
  }
  return cev;
}

public CatalogEntry[] getCatalogEntries(String cat, String subcat)
    throws SQLException {
  Connection conn = connectionPool.getConnection();
  Statement us = conn.createStatement();
  ResultSet rs = us.executeQuery(SELECT_PRODUCTS_QUALIFIED +
    CAT_QUALIFIER + cat + AND +
    SUBCAT_QUALIFIER + subcat);
  Vector v = new Vector();
  while (rs.next()) {
    CatalogEntry ce = new CatalogEntry();
    ce.setSKU(rs.getInt(1));
    ce.setCategory(rs.getInt(2));
    ce.setSubcategory(rs.getInt(3));
    ce.setDescription(rs.getString(4));
    ce.setPrice(rs.getFloat(5));
    v.add(ce);
  }
  connectionPool.close(conn);
  CatalogEntry[] cev = new CatalogEntry[v.size()];
  for (int i = 0; i < v.size(); ++i) {
    cev[i] = (CatalogEntry)v.elementAt(i);
  }
  return cev;
}

public CatalogEntry getCatalogEntry(int sku)
```

```
    throws SQLException {
  Connection conn = connectionPool.getConnection();
  Statement us = conn.createStatement();
  ResultSet rs = us.executeQuery(SELECT_PRODUCTS_QUALIFIED +
    SKU_QUALIFIER + Integer.toString(sku));
  rs.next();
  CatalogEntry ce = new CatalogEntry();
  ce.setSKU(rs.getInt(1));
  ce.setCategory(rs.getInt(2));
  ce.setSubcategory(rs.getInt(3));
  ce.setDescription(rs.getString(4));
  ce.setPrice(rs.getFloat(5));
  connectionPool.close(conn);
  return ce;
}

public CatalogEntry[] getCatalogEntries(String cat, String keywords,
    boolean all) throws SQLException {
  Connection conn = connectionPool.getConnection();
  Statement us = conn.createStatement();
  StringBuffer  sb = new StringBuffer(SELECT_PRODUCTS);
  if (!cat.equals("All")) {
    sb.append(" WHERE cat=");
    sb.append(QUOTE);
    sb.append(cat);
    sb.append(QUOTE);
  }
  ResultSet rs = us.executeQuery(sb.toString());
  Vector v = new Vector();
  while (rs.next()) {
    CatalogEntry ce = new CatalogEntry();
    ce.setSKU(rs.getInt(1));
    ce.setCategory(rs.getInt(2));
    ce.setSubcategory(rs.getInt(3));
    ce.setDescription(rs.getString(4));
    ce.setPrice(rs.getFloat(5));
    if (!ce.matchesDesc(keywords, all)) {
      continue;
    }
    v.add(ce);
  }
  connectionPool.close(conn);
  CatalogEntry[] cev = new CatalogEntry[v.size()];
  for (int i = 0; i < v.size(); ++i) {
    cev[i] = (CatalogEntry)v.elementAt(i);
  }
  return cev;
}

public String[] getCategories()
    throws SQLException {
  Connection conn = connectionPool.getConnection();
  Statement us = conn.createStatement();
  ResultSet rs = us.executeQuery(SELECT_CATEGORIES);
  Vector v = new Vector();
  while (rs.next()) {
    String s = rs.getString(1);
    v.add(s);
  }
```

```
        connectionPool.close(conn);
        String[] sa = new String[v.size()];
        for (int i = 0; i < v.size(); ++i) {
          sa[i] = (String)v.elementAt(i);
        }
        return sa;
      }

      public String[] getSubcategories()
          throws SQLException {
        Connection conn = connectionPool.getConnection();
        Statement us = conn.createStatement();
        ResultSet rs = us.executeQuery(SELECT_SUBCATEGORIES);
        Vector v = new Vector();
        while (rs.next()) {
          String s = rs.getString(1);
          v.add(s);
        }
        connectionPool.close(conn);
        String[] sa = new String[v.size()];
        for (int i = 0; i < v.size(); ++i) {
          sa[i] = (String)v.elementAt(i);
        }
        return sa;
      }

      public String getCategoryName(String cat)
          throws SQLException {
        Connection conn = connectionPool.getConnection();
        Statement us = conn.createStatement();
        ResultSet rs = us.executeQuery(SELECT_CATEGORY_NAME +
          CAT_QUALIFIER + cat);
        rs.next();
        String catname = rs.getString(1);
        connectionPool.close(conn);
        return catname;
      }

      public String getSubcategoryName(String subcat)
          throws SQLException {
        Connection conn = connectionPool.getConnection();
        Statement us = conn.createStatement();
        ResultSet rs = us.executeQuery(SELECT_SUBCATEGORY_NAME +
          SUBCAT_QUALIFIER + subcat);
        rs.next();
        String subcatname = rs.getString(1);
        connectionPool.close(conn);
        return subcatname;
      }

      public int placeOrder(Customer customer, ShoppingCart cart)
          throws SQLException {
        String custno;
        if (customer.isPreferredCustomer()) {
          custno = customer.getCustomerID();
        }
        else {
          custno = customer.recordCustomer();
        }
```

```
Connection conn = connectionPool.getConnection();
Statement st = conn.createStatement();
ResultSet rs = st.executeQuery(GET_ORDER_NUMBER);
rs.next();
int ordno = rs.getInt(1);
OrderItem[] contents = cart.getContents();
for (int i = 0; i < contents.length; ++i) {
  st.executeUpdate(INSERT_ORDER_DETAIL +
    Integer.toString(ordno) + COMMA +
    custno + COMMA +
    Integer.toString(contents[i].getSKU()) + COMMA +
    Integer.toString(contents[i].getQuantity()) + COMMA +
    Float.toString(contents[i].getPrice()) + RPAREN);
}
String now =
  new SimpleDateFormat("MM-dd-yyyy HH:mm").format(new Date());
st.executeUpdate(INSERT_ORDER +
  Integer.toString(ordno) + COMMA +
  custno + COMMA +
  QUOTE + now + QUOTE + COMMA +
  "0" + RPAREN);
connectionPool.close(conn);
return ordno;
}

public void finalize() {
  connectionPool.destroy();
}
}
```

# Code for Customer Bean

```
package com.instantjsp;

import java.sql.Connection;
import java.sql.ResultSet;
import java.sql.SQLException;
import java.sql.Statement;
import java.text.SimpleDateFormat;
import java.util.Date;

import javaservlets.jdbc.ConnectionPool;

import javax.servlet.http.Cookie;
import javax.servlet.http.HttpServletRequest;

public class Customer {

  private ConnectionPool connectionPool;

  private boolean isPreferredCustomer = false;
  private String customerID = "";
  private String firstName = "";
  private String lastName = "";
  private String middleInitial = "";
```

```
private String streetNumber = "";
private String street = "";
private String apt = "";
private String city = "";
private String state = "";
private String zip = "";
private String zipPlusFour = "";
private String telephoneNumber = "";
private String telephoneExtension = "";
private Date joined;
private Date lastordered;
private String lastordno;
private boolean sendEmail = false;
private String emailAddress = "";
private boolean okToSurvey = false;
private boolean doCurrentSurvey = false;

private static final String POOL_CFG_FILE =
  "javaservlets/jdbc/BusinessPool.cfg";

private static final String GET_CUSTOMER_INFO =
   "SELECT * FROM customer";

private static final String GET_PREFCUST_INFO =
   "SELECT * FROM prefcust";

private static final String CUSTNO_QUALIFIER =
   " WHERE custno=";

private static final String GET_NEXT_CUSTNO =
   "SELECT nextval('seq_cust')";

private static final String INSERT_CUST =
   "INSERT INTO customer VALUES";

private static final String INSERT_PREF =
   "INSERT INTO prefcust VALUES";

private static final String UPDATE_CUST =
   "UPDATE customer SET ";

private static final String UPDATE_PREF =
   "UPDATE prefcust SET ";

private static final String UPDATE_OK_TO_SURVEY =
   "UPDATE prefcust SET oktosurvey=";

private static final String UPDATE_DO_CURRENT_SURVEY =
   "UPDATE prefcust SET do_current_survey=";

private static final String AND = " and ";
private static final String LPAREN = "(";
private static final String RPAREN = ")";
private static final String COMMA = ",";
private static final String PERCENT = "%";
private static final String QUOTE = "'";
private static final String NULL = "null";

public Customer() throws Exception {
```

```
      connectionPool = new ConnectionPool();
      connectionPool.initialize(POOL_CFG_FILE);
  }

  public void setCustomerInfo(String custno)
      throws Exception {
      if (custno != null) {
        customerID = custno;
        getCustomerInfo(custno);
      }
  }

  public void setOkToSurvey(boolean tf)
        throws SQLException {
      Connection conn = connectionPool.getConnection();
      Statement us = conn.createStatement();
      us.executeUpdate(UPDATE_OK_TO_SURVEY +
        new Boolean(tf).toString() +
        CUSTNO_QUALIFIER +
        QUOTE + customerID + QUOTE);
      connectionPool.close(conn);
      okToSurvey = tf;
  }

  public void setDoCurrentSurvey(boolean tf)
        throws SQLException {
      Connection conn = connectionPool.getConnection();
      Statement us = conn.createStatement();
      us.executeUpdate(UPDATE_DO_CURRENT_SURVEY +
        new Boolean(tf).toString() +
        CUSTNO_QUALIFIER +
        QUOTE + customerID + QUOTE);
      connectionPool.close(conn);
      doCurrentSurvey = tf;
  }

  private void getCustomerInfo(String custno)
        throws SQLException {
      Connection conn = connectionPool.getConnection();
      Statement qs = conn.createStatement();
      ResultSet rs = qs.executeQuery(GET_CUSTOMER_INFO +
        CUSTNO_QUALIFIER +
         QUOTE + custno + QUOTE);
      rs.next();
      lastName = rs.getString(2);
      firstName = rs.getString(3);
      middleInitial = rs.getString(4);
      streetNumber = rs.getString(5);
      street = rs.getString(6);
      apt = rs.getString(7);
      city = rs.getString(8);
      state = rs.getString(9);
      zip = rs.getString(10);
      zipPlusFour = rs.getString(11);
      telephoneNumber = rs.getString(12);
      telephoneExtension = rs.getString(13);
      rs = qs.executeQuery(GET_PREFCUST_INFO +
        CUSTNO_QUALIFIER +
        QUOTE + customerID + QUOTE);
```

```
    if (rs.next()) {
      isPreferredCustomer = true;
      joined = rs.getDate(2);
      lastordered = rs.getDate(3);
      lastordno = rs.getString(4);
      sendEmail = rs.getBoolean(5);
      emailAddress = rs.getString(6);
      okToSurvey = rs.getBoolean(7);
      doCurrentSurvey = rs.getBoolean(8);
    }
    connectionPool.close(conn);
  }

  public String recordCustomer() throws SQLException {
    Connection conn = connectionPool.getConnection();
    Statement st = conn.createStatement();
    ResultSet rs = st.executeQuery(GET_NEXT_CUSTNO);
    rs.next();
    customerID = Integer.toString(rs.getInt(1));
    st.executeUpdate(INSERT_CUST + LPAREN +
      QUOTE + customerID + QUOTE + COMMA +
      QUOTE + lastName + QUOTE + COMMA +
      QUOTE + firstName + QUOTE + COMMA +
      QUOTE + middleInitial + QUOTE + COMMA +
      QUOTE + streetNumber + QUOTE + COMMA +
      QUOTE + street + QUOTE + COMMA +
      QUOTE + apt + QUOTE + COMMA +
      QUOTE + city + QUOTE + COMMA +
      QUOTE + state + QUOTE + COMMA +
      QUOTE + zip + QUOTE + COMMA +
      QUOTE + zipPlusFour + QUOTE + COMMA +
      QUOTE + telephoneNumber + QUOTE + COMMA +
      QUOTE + telephoneExtension + QUOTE + RPAREN);
    return customerID;
  }

  public String createPreferred()
      throws SQLException {
    String now = new SimpleDateFormat("MM-dd-yyyy").format-
      (new Date());
    Connection conn = connectionPool.getConnection();
    customerID = recordCustomer();
    Statement st = conn.createStatement();
    st.executeUpdate(INSERT_PREF + LPAREN +
      QUOTE + customerID + QUOTE + COMMA +
      QUOTE + now + QUOTE + COMMA +
      QUOTE + now + QUOTE + COMMA +
      QUOTE + now + QUOTE + COMMA +
      QUOTE + sendEmail + QUOTE + COMMA +
      QUOTE + emailAddress + QUOTE + COMMA +
      QUOTE + okToSurvey + QUOTE + COMMA +
      QUOTE + okToSurvey + QUOTE + COMMA +
      "0" + RPAREN);
    connectionPool.close(conn);
    isPreferredCustomer = true;
    return customerID;
  }

  public void updateProfile()
```

```
    throws SQLException {
  Connection conn = connectionPool.getConnection();
  Statement us = conn.createStatement();
  us.executeUpdate(UPDATE_CUST +
    "n_last=" + QUOTE + lastName + QUOTE + COMMA +
    "n_first=" + QUOTE + firstName + QUOTE + COMMA +
    "n_mi=" + QUOTE + middleInitial + QUOTE + COMMA +
    "a_number=" + QUOTE + streetNumber + QUOTE + COMMA +
    "a_street=" + QUOTE + street + QUOTE + COMMA +
    "a_apt=" + QUOTE + apt + QUOTE + COMMA +
    "a_city=" + QUOTE + city + QUOTE + COMMA +
    "a_state=" + QUOTE + state + QUOTE + COMMA +
    "a_zip=" + QUOTE + zip + QUOTE + COMMA +
    "a_zip_plus4=" + QUOTE + zipPlusFour + QUOTE + COMMA +
    "a_telno=" + QUOTE + telephoneNumber + QUOTE + COMMA +
    "a_tel_ext=" + QUOTE + telephoneExtension + QUOTE +
    CUSTNO_QUALIFIER + QUOTE + customerID + QUOTE);
  us.executeUpdate(UPDATE_PREF +
    "sendemail=" + new Boolean(sendEmail).toString() + COMMA +
    "emailaddr=" + QUOTE + emailAddress + QUOTE + COMMA +
    "oktosurvey=" + new Boolean(okToSurvey).toString() + COMMA +
    "do_current_survey=" +
      new Boolean(okToSurvey).toString() +
    CUSTNO_QUALIFIER + QUOTE + customerID + QUOTE);
  connectionPool.close(conn);
  isPreferredCustomer = true;
}

public boolean isPreferredCustomer() {
  return isPreferredCustomer;
}

public String getCustomerID() {
  return customerID;
}

public boolean isSurveyCandidate() {
  return isPreferredCustomer & okToSurvey & doCurrentSurvey;
}

public String getFirstName() {
  return firstName;
}

public void setFirstName(String firstName) {
  this.firstName  = firstName;
}

public String getLastName() {
  return lastName;
}

public void setLastName(String lastName) {
  this.lastName = lastName;
}

public String getMiddleInitial() {
  return middleInitial;
}
```

```java
public void setMiddleInitial(String middleInitial) {
  this.middleInitial = middleInitial;
}

public void getMiddleInitial(String middleInitial) {
  this.middleInitial = middleInitial;
}

public String getStreetNumber() {
  return streetNumber;
}

public void setStreetNumber(String streetNumber) {
  this.streetNumber = streetNumber;
}

public String getStreet() {
  return street;
}

public void setStreet(String street) {
  this.street = street;
}

public String getApt() {
  return apt;
}

public void setApt(String apt) {
  this.apt = apt;
}

public String getCity() {
  return city;
}

public void setCity(String city) {
  this.city = city;
}

public String getState() {
  return state;
}

public void setState(String state) {
  this.state = state;
}

public String getZip() {
  return zip;
}

public void setZip(String zip) {
  this.zip = zip;
}

public String getZipPlusFour() {
  return zipPlusFour;
}
```

```java
public void setZipPlusFour(String zipPlusFour) {
  this.zipPlusFour = zipPlusFour;
}

public String getTelephoneNumber() {
  return telephoneNumber;
}

public void setTelephoneNumber(String telephoneNumber) {
  this.telephoneNumber = telephoneNumber;
}

public String getTelephoneExtension() {
  return telephoneExtension;
}

public void setTelephoneExtension(String telephoneExtension) {
  this.telephoneExtension = telephoneExtension;
}

public String getEmailAddress() {
  return emailAddress;
}

public void setEmailAddress(String emailAddress) {
  this.emailAddress = emailAddress;
}

public String getSurvey() {
  return new Boolean(okToSurvey).toString();
}

public void setSurvey(String tf) {
  okToSurvey = new Boolean(tf).booleanValue();
}

public String getSendEmail() {
  return new Boolean(sendEmail).toString();
}

public void setSendEmail(String tf) {
  sendEmail = new Boolean(tf).booleanValue();
}

public void finalize() {
  connectionPool.destroy();
  }
}
```

# Moving Up to Online Sales

- Taking Online Orders
- Tracking Online Orders

In the last chapter, we saw how to provide customers with tools they could use to browse and search our online catalog. In this chapter, we devote our attention to the next logical step in building an online store—providing a means of ordering online.

# Taking Online Orders

One of the most important goals when designing an online ordering system should be to make things as easy as possible on the user. The easiest thing a customer can do is to simply click on a product he or she wishes to order. Implementing this requires only a very simple modification to GetProductsInSubcategory.jsp and SearchCatalog.jsp. We will not show the complete source for these JSP pages. Instead, we show the modified code that transforms each entry in the SKU column into a hypertext link that sends a request to PurchaseItem.jsp, passing the SKU as a query string of the form sku=skunumber. Here is the modified code:

```
<%
    for (int i = 0; i < cea.length; ++i) {
      String href = "<a href=\"PurchaseItem.jsp?" +
        "sku=" + cea[i].getSKU() + "\">";
%>
      <tr>
        <td>
            <%= href %>
            <%= cea[i].getSKU() %></a>
        </td>
        <td>
          <%= cea[i].getDescription() %>
        </td>
      </tr>
<%
    }
%>
```

Now, when the customer selects "View Catalog" or "Search Catalog" the output looks like Figure 6-1. Notice the hypertext links.

So now let's look at PurchaseItem.jsp. Here is the code:

```
<%@ page import="java.util.Hashtable" %>
<%@ page import="com.instantjsp.CatalogEntry" %>
<jsp:useBean id="sb" class="com.instantjsp.StoreBean"
  scope="session" />
<%
  String query = request.getQueryString();
```

**Figure 6-1**
New Catalog Entries
with "click-to-order"
Hyperlinks

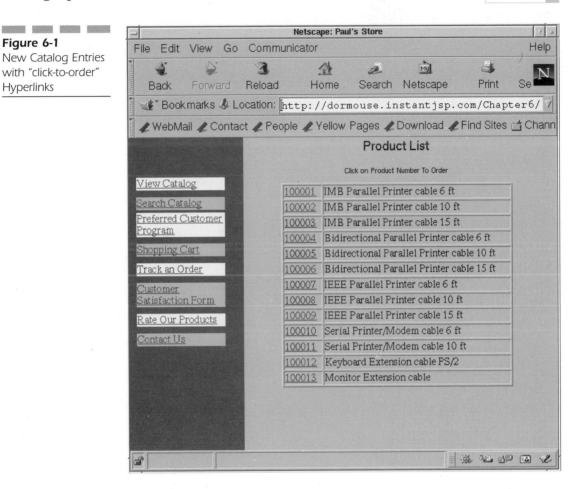

```
    Hashtable qt = HttpUtils.parseQueryString(query);
    String skuString = ((String[])qt.get("sku"))[0];
    int sku = Integer.parseInt(skuString);
    CatalogEntry ce = sb.getCatalogEntry(sku);
    String action = "AddItemToCart.jsp?" +
       "sku=" + skuString + "\"";
%>
<html>
<body>
<center>
<font face = "Arial, Helvetica" size="+1">
Add Item to Shopping Cart
<br>
<br>
</font>
</center>
<form method="post" action="<%= action %>">
<table border width="100%" align="center">
```

```
<tr>
  <td>
    SKU:
  </td>
  <td>
      <%= ce.getSKU() %>
  </td>
</tr>
<tr>
    <td>
      Description:
    </td>
    <td>
        <%= ce.getDescription() %>
    </td>
  </tr>
    <td>
      Price:
    </td>
    <td>
        <%= ce.getPrice() %>
    </td>
  </tr>
</table>
<br>
<br>
Enter how many of the above items you would like to order.
<br>
Then click on "ADD TO SHOPPING CART".
<br>
<br>
Quantity:
<input type="text" name="quantity" size=5>
<input type="submit" name="submit" value="ADD TO SHOPPING CART">
</form>
</body>
</html>
```

This JSP page extracts the product number (SKU) from the query string, passes it as an argument to `getCatalogEntry()` and presents the SKU, description, and price as shown in Figure 6-2.

When the customer enters the desired quantity and clicks on ADD TO SHOPPING CART, a request containing the contents of the HTML form is sent to `AddItemToCart.jsp`. The SKU is passed as a query string. Here is the code for `AddItemToCart.jsp`:

```
<%@ page import="java.util.Hashtable" %>
<%@ page import="com.instantjsp.CatalogEntry" %>
<%@ page import="com.instantjsp.OrderItem" %>
<jsp:useBean id="sb" class="com.instantjsp.StoreBean"
  scope="session" />
<jsp:useBean id="cart" class="com.instantjsp.ShoppingCart"
  scope="session" />
<%
  String query = request.getQueryString();
```

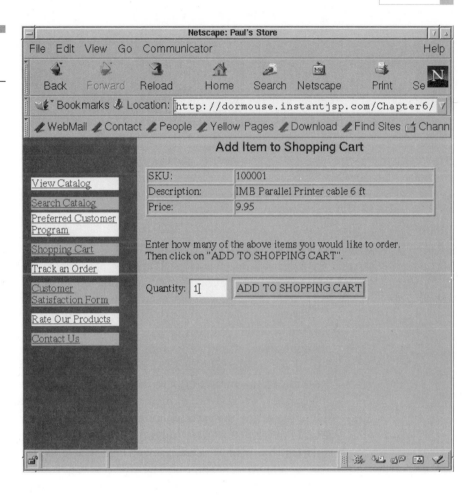

**Figure 6-2**
Adding an Entry to
the Shopping Cart

```
    Hashtable qt = HttpUtils.parseQueryString(query);
    int sku = Integer.parseInt(((String[])qt.get("sku"))[0]);
    CatalogEntry ce = sb.getCatalogEntry(sku);
    int qty = Integer.parseInt(request.getParameter("quantity"));
    cart.addItem(new OrderItem(ce,qty));
    OrderItem[] contents = cart.getContents();
%>
<jsp:forward page="ShoppingCart.jsp" />
```

This JSP page introduces a new Bean, ShoppingCart. The full code is
shown at the end of the chapter.

After AddItemToCart.jsp extracts the SKU from the query string
and uses request.getParameter("quantity") to get the quantity, it
passes these two values to the constructor of OrderItem. Here is the
code for OrderItem:

```
package com.instantjsp;

public class OrderItem extends CatalogEntry {
  int quantity;

  public OrderItem(CatalogEntry ce, int quantity) {
    setCategory(ce.getCategory());
    setSubcategory(ce.getSubcategory());
    setSKU(ce.getSKU());
    setDescription(ce.getDescription());
    setPrice(ce.getPrice());
    this.quantity = quantity;
  }

  public int getQuantity() {
    return quantity;
  }

  public void setQuantity(int quantity) {
    this.quantity = quantity;
  }
}
```

The new instance of `OrderItem` is then passed to the `addItem()` method of `ShoppingCart`. The `addItem()` method checks to see if the shopping cart already contains an item with the same product number (i.e., if the hashtable the `ShoppingCart` object uses to hold its contents contains a key matching the SKU). If it does, it retrieves the existing object from the hashtable, increments its instance variable `quantity` by the value of the instance variable `quantity` in the object received as an argument, and stores the updated object back in the hashtable.

If the hashtable does not contain a key matching the SKU, then `addItem()` inserts the instance of `OrderItem` into the hashtable.

After `addItem()` returns, a `<jsp:forward>` action is executed specifying `ShoppingCart.jsp` as a target. Here is the code:

```
<%@ page import="com.instantjsp.OrderItem" %>
<jsp:useBean id="cart" class="com.instantjsp.ShoppingCart"
  scope="session" />
<%
  OrderItem[] contents = cart.getContents();
  if (contents.length == 0) {
%>
    <jsp:forward page="CartEmpty.html" />
<%
  }
%>
<html>
<body>
<center>
<font face = "Arial, Helvetica" size="+2">
Shopping Cart
```

```
</font>
</center>
<form method="post" action="UpdateCart.jsp">
<table border width="100%">
<%
  for (int i = 0; i < contents.length; ++i) {
%>
    <tr>
      <td align="center">
        <%= contents[i].getSKU() %>
      </td>
      <td>
        <%= contents[i].getDescription() %>
      </td>
      <td>
        <font face = "Arial, Helvetica" size="+0">
        <input type="input" size=3
          name="<%= contents[i].getSKU() %>"
          value="<%= contents[i].getQuantity() %>">
        </font>
      </td>
      <td align="right">
        <%= contents[i].getPrice() %>
      </td>
      <td align="right">
        <%= cart.totalAsString(contents[i].getSKU()) %>
      </td>
    </tr>
<%
  }
%>
    <tr>
      <td></td>
      <td></td>
      <td></td>
      <td></td>
      <td align="right">
        <%= cart.totalAsString() %>
      </td>
    </tr>

</table>
<br>
<table align="center">
  <tr>
    <td>
      <input type="submit" name="clear" value="EMPTY CART">
    </td>
    <td>
      <input type="submit" name="recalc" value="RECALCULATE">
    </td>
    <td>
      <input type="submit" name="checkout" value="CHECK OUT">
    </td>
  </tr>
</table>
</form>
</body>
</html>
```

The first scriptlet in `ShoppingCart.jsp` invokes the `getContents()` method of `ShoppingCart`. This method returns an array of `OrderItem` objects. If the array has a length of zero, the following action is executed:

```
<jsp:forward page="CartEmpty.html" />
```

`CartEmpty.html` produces the page shown in Figure 6-3. If the cart is not empty, `ShoppingCart.jsp` produces the page shown in Figure 6-4. Here is the code for `CartEmpty.html`:

```
<html>
<body bgcolor="#c0c0c0" link="#999999"
   vlink="#999999" alink="#999999">
<center>
```

**Figure 6-3**
Empty Shopping Cart

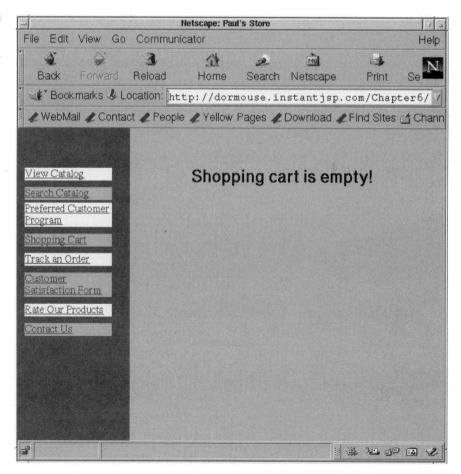

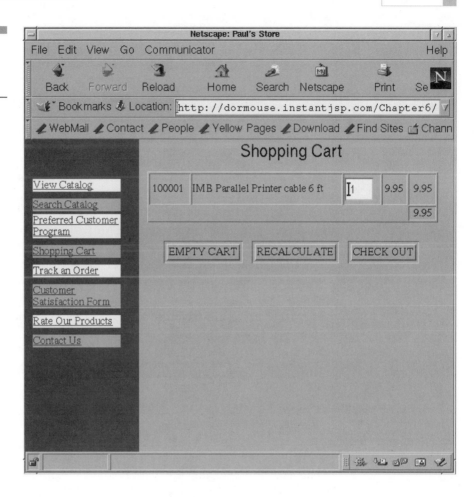

**Figure 6-4**
Shopping Cart
Containing a Single
Item

```
<font face = "Arial, Helvetica" size="+2">
<br>
<br>
<b>Shopping cart is empty!
</font>
</center>
</body>
</html>
```

In addition to the cart contents, ShoppingCart.jsp displays three buttons labeled EMPTY CART, RECALCULATE, and CHECK OUT. Clicking on any of these sends a request to UpdateCart.jsp. Here is the code:

```
<%
  String target = "CheckOut.jsp";
  if (request.getParameter("clear") != null) {
```

```
      target = "EmptyShoppingCart.jsp";
    }
    else {
      if (request.getParameter("recalc") != null) {
        target = "RecalculateShoppingCart.jsp";
      }
    }
  %>
  <jsp:forward page="<%= target %>" />
```

UpdateCart.jsp does nothing more than use the getParameter() method to determine which of the three buttons was clicked and set the variable target to one of EmptyShoppingCart.jsp, Recalculate-ShoppingCart.jsp, or CheckOut.jsp. The variable target is then used in a <jsp:forward> action. We will examine each of the three pages.

In the case where the customer clicks on EMPTY CART, Empty-ShoppingCart.jsp receives the request from UpdateCart.jsp, invokes the empty() method of ShoppingCart and forwards to ShoppingCart.jsp, which produces the page we have already seen in Figure 6-3. Here is the code for EmptyShoppingCart.jsp:

```
<jsp:useBean id="cart" class="com.instantjsp.ShoppingCart"
  scope="session" />
<%
  cart.empty();
%>
<jsp:forward page="ShoppingCart.jsp" />
```

Now let's see what happens when the customer changes the contents of the cart and clicks on RECALCULATE. If we examine Figure 6-5, we see from the position of the cursor at the end of the text field on the third line that the customer has just changed the quantity from 1 to 2. We know it was 1 because the last two columns are 9.95.

When the customer clicks on RECALCULATE, RecalculateShopping-Cart.jsp receives the request from UpdateCart.jsp. Here is the code for RecalculateShoppingCart.jsp:

```
<%@ page import="java.util.Enumeration" %>
<jsp:useBean id="cart" class="com.instantjsp.ShoppingCart"
  scope="session" />
<%
  Enumeration parmNames = request.getParameterNames();
  while (parmNames.hasMoreElements()) {
    String sku = (String)parmNames.nextElement();
    if (sku.equals("recalc")) {
      continue;
    }
```

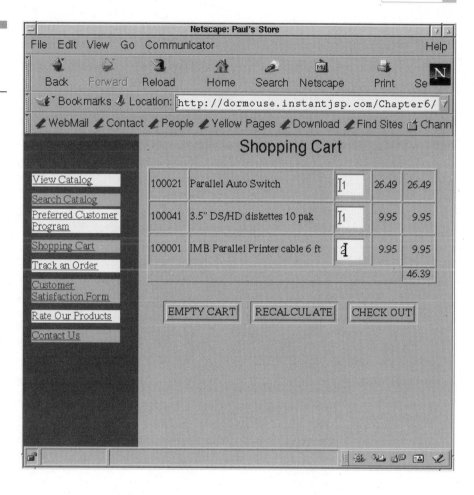

**Figure 6-5**
Changing the
Quantity of an Item
in the Cart

```
        int q = Integer.parseInt(request.getParameter(sku));
        cart.setQuantity(sku,q);
    }
%>
<jsp:forward page="ShoppingCart.jsp" />
```

RecalculateShoppingCart.jsp gets the names of all the parameters in the request (i.e., the names of all the fields in the HTML form). The name of each of the text fields in the form is the value of the product ID (SKU) and the value is the quantity as can be seen from the following code from ShoppingCart.jsp that generates each of these fields:

```
<input type="input" size=3
    name="<%= contents[i].getSKU() %>"
    value="<%= contents[i].getQuantity() %>">
```

`RecalculateShoppingCart.jsp` iterates across all of the parameter names and for each name except `recalc` (the name of the button), it passes the SKU and the quantity to the `setQuantity()` method of `ShoppingCart`. When the iteration is complete, a `<jsp:forward>` action sends a request to `ShoppingCart.jsp`. In this case, we see Figure 6-6 and can see the change we made to the quantity and the resultant change to the totals column.

When the customer finishes shopping and clicks on CHECK OUT, `UpdateCart.jsp` forwards the request to `CheckOut.jsp`. Here is the code:

```
<%@ page import="com.instantjsp.OrderItem" %>
<%@ include file="GetPrefCustId.jsp" %>
<jsp:useBean id="custBean" class="com.instantjsp.Customer"
```

**Figure 6-6**
The Cart after
Changing the
Quantity of an Item

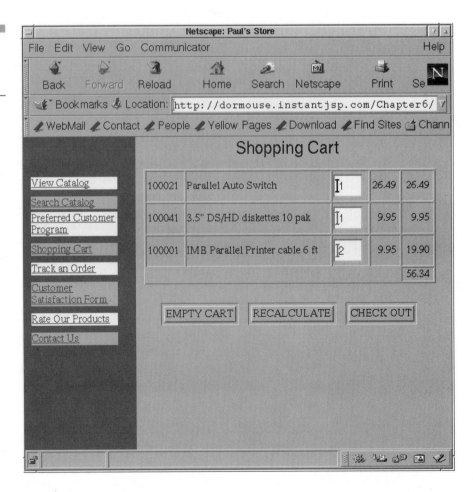

```
      scope="session" >
      <jsp:setProperty name="custBean" property="customerInfo"
        value="<%= getPrefCustID(request)%>" />
  </jsp:useBean>
  <jsp:useBean id="cart" class="com.instantjsp.ShoppingCart"
    scope="session" />
  <%
    OrderItem[] contents = cart.getContents();
  %>
  <html>
  <body>
  <center>
  <font face = "Arial, Helvetica" size="+1">
  Place Order
  <br>
  </font>
  </center>
  <font face = "Arial, Helvetica">
  <ul>
  <li>Verify the contents of the order
  <li>Supply the required information
  <li>Click on PLACE ORDER
  </ul>
  </font>
  <form method="post" action="PlaceOrder.jsp">
  <table border width="100%">
  <%
    for (int i = 0; i < contents.length; ++i) {
  %>
    <tr>
      <td>
        <%= contents[i].getSKU() %>
      </td>
      <td>
        <%= contents[i].getDescription() %>
      </td>
      <td>
        <font face = "Arial, Helvetica" size="+0">
        <input type="input" size=3
          name="<%= contents[i].getSKU() %>"
          value="<%= contents[i].getQuantity() %>">
        </font>
      </td>
      <td align="right">
        <%= contents[i].getPrice() %>
      </td>
      <td align="right">
        <%= cart.totalAsString(contents[i].getSKU()) %>
      </td>
    </tr>
  <%
    }
  %>
    <tr>
      <td></td>
      <td></td>
      <td></td>
      <td></td>
      <td align="right">
```

```
          <%= cart.totalAsString() %>
        </td>

</table>
<hr width="100%">
<%
  if (!custBean.isPreferredCustomer()) {
%>
<font face = "Arial, Helvetica" size="0">
If you want us to remember your address for future orders,
now would be a good time to use the menu on the left to
join the Preferred Customer Program.
</font>
<%
  }
%>
<table cols=3 width="100%" nosave>
  <tr nosave>
    <td width="25%" nosave>
      <font face="Arial,Helvetica" size=0>
      <input type="text" name="firstName" size=15
        value="<jsp:getProperty name="custBean"
          property="firstName" />">
      </font>
    </td>

     <td width="10%" nosave>
       <font face="Arial,Helvetica" size=0>
       <input type="text" name="middleInitial" size=5
         value="<jsp:getProperty name="custBean"
           property="middleInitial" />">
       </font>
     </td>

     <td width="65%" nosave>
       <font face="Arial,Helvetica" size=0>
       <input type="text" name="lastName" size=30
         value="<jsp:getProperty name="custBean"
           property="lastName" />">
       </font>
     </td>
   </tr>

  <tr nosave>
    <td width="25%" nosave>
      <font face="Arial,Helvetica" size=-2>
      First Name
      </font>
    </td>

    <td width="10%" nosave>
      <font size=-2>
      MI
      </font>
    </td>

     <td width="65%" nosave>
       <font size=-2>
       Last Name
```

```
          </font>
        </td>
      </tr>
    </table>

    <table width="80%" nosave >
      <tr nosave>
        <td width="10%" nosave>
          <font face="Arial,Helvetica" size=0>
          <input type="text" name="streetNumber" size=8
            value="<jsp:getProperty name="custBean"
              property="streetNumber" />">
          </font>
        </td>

        <td width="80%" nosave>
          <font face="Arial,Helvetica" size=0>
          <input type="text" name="street" size=50
            value="<jsp:getProperty name="custBean"
              property="street" />">
          </font>
        </td>

        <td width="10%" nosave>
          <font face="Arial,Helvetica" size=0>
          <input type="text" name="apt" size=8
            value="<jsp:getProperty name="custBean"
              property="apt" />">
          </font>
        </td>
      </tr>

      <tr nosave>
        <td width="10%" nosave>
          <font face="Arial,Helvetica" size=-2>
          Number
          </font>
        </td>

        <td width="80%" nosave>
          <font size=-2>
          Street
          </font>
        </td>

        <td width="10%" nosave>
          <font face="Arial,Helvetica"><font size=-2>
          Apt.
          </font></font>
        </td>
      </tr>
    </table>

    <table cols=4 width="80%" nosave >
      <tr nosave>
        <td WIDTH="70%" NOSAVE>
          <font face="Arial,Helvetica" size=0>
          <input type="text" name="city" size=30
            value="<jsp:getProperty name="custBean"
```

```
                property="city" />">
            </font>
         </td>

         <td WIDTH="10%" NOSAVE>
            <font face="Arial,Helvetica" size=0>
            <input type="text" name="state" size=5
              value="<jsp:getProperty name="custBean"
                property="state" />">
            </font>
         </td>

         <td WIDTH="10%" NOSAVE>
            <font face="Arial,Helvetica" size=0>
            <input type="text" name="zip" size=10
              value="<jsp:getProperty name="custBean"
                property="zip" />">
            </font>
         </td>

         <td WIDTH="10%" NOSAVE>
            <font face="Arial,Helvetica" size=0>
            <input type="text" name="zipPlusFour" size=10
              value="<jsp:getProperty name="custBean"
                property="zipPlusFour" />">
            </font>
         </td>
      </tr>

      <tr nosave>
        <td width="70%">
          <font face="Arial,Helvetica">
          <font size=-2>City</font></font>
        </td>

        <td width="10%">
          <font face="Arial,Helvetica">
          <font size=-2>
          State
          </font>
          </font>
        </td>

        <td width="10%">
          <font face="Arial,Helvetica">
          <font size=-2>
          ZIP
          </font>
          </font>
        </td>

        <td width="10%">
          <font face="Arial,Helvetica">
          <font size=-2>
          ZIP+4
          </font>
          </font>
        </td>
      </tr>
```

```
    </table>

    <table WIDTH="50%" nosave >
      <tr nosave>
        <td width="75%"nosave>
          <font face="Arial,Helvetica" size=0>
          <input type="text" name="telephoneNumber" size=20
            value="<jsp:getProperty name="custBean"
              property="telephoneNumber" />">
          </font>
        </td>

        <td width="25%" nosave>
          <font face="Arial,Helvetica" size=0>
          <input type="text" name="telephoneExtension" size=10
            value="<jsp:getProperty name="custBean"
              property="telephoneExtension" />">
          </font>
        </td>
      </tr>

      <tr nosave>
        <td width="75%" nosave>
          <font face="Arial,Helvetica" size=-2>
          Telephone
          </font>
        </td>

        <td width="25%" nosave>
          <font face="Arial,Helvetica" size=-2>
          Ext
          </font>
        </td>
      </tr>
    </table>

    <table cols=3 width="100%" nosave >
      <tr nosave>
        <td width="45%" nosave>
          <font face="Arial,Helvetica" size=0>
          <input type="text" name="emailAddress" size=30
            value="<jsp:getProperty name="custBean"
              property="emailAddress" />">
          </font>
        </td>
      </tr>

      <tr nosave>
        <td width="50%" nosave>
          <font face="Arial,Helvetica" size=0>
          Email Address:
          </font>
        </td>

      </tr>

    </table>
    <hr width="100%">
    <br>
```

```
<center>
<input type="submit" name="submit" value="PLACE ORDER">
</center>
</form>
</body>
</html>
```

CheckOut.jsp generates a page containing a form into which the user enters the name and address information we need to ship the order. Since this page is scrollable, it is shown in Figures 6-7 and 6-8. Figure 6-9 shows a completed order form.

The following code from CheckOut.jsp bears further examination:

```
<%
    if (!custBean.isPreferredCustomer()) {
```

**Figure 6-7**
Checkout 1 of 2

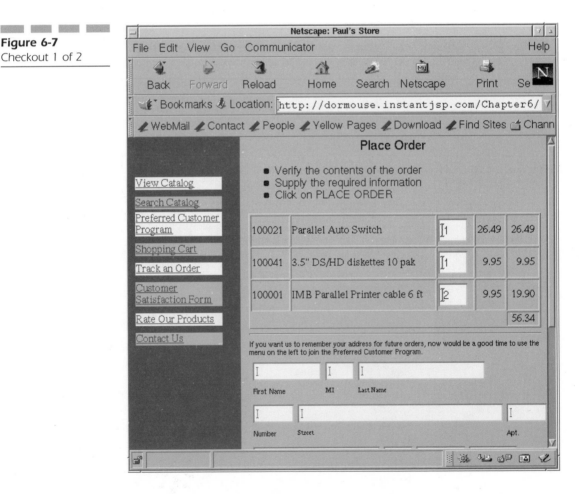

**Figure 6-8**

Checkout 2 of 2

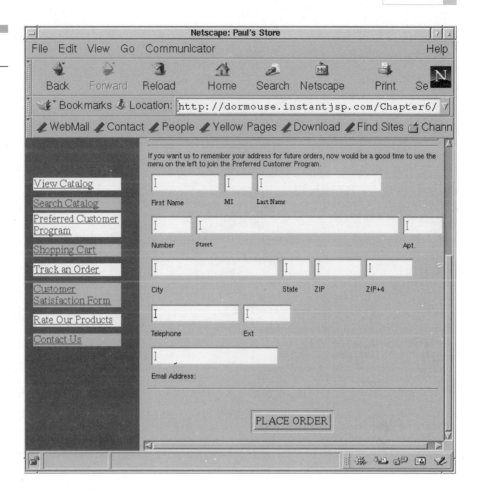

```
%>
<font face = "Arial, Helvetica" size="0">
If you want us to remember your address for future orders,
now would be a good time to use the menu on the left to
join the Preferred Customer Program.
</font>
<%
   }
%>
```

We have now reached the point where we see another use for the cookie we discussed in the last chapter. We only display this message when isPreferredCustomer() returns false. That's because, as each field in the form is generated, it is assigned a value by a <jsp:getProperty> action of the form:

**Figure 6-9**
A Completed Order
Form

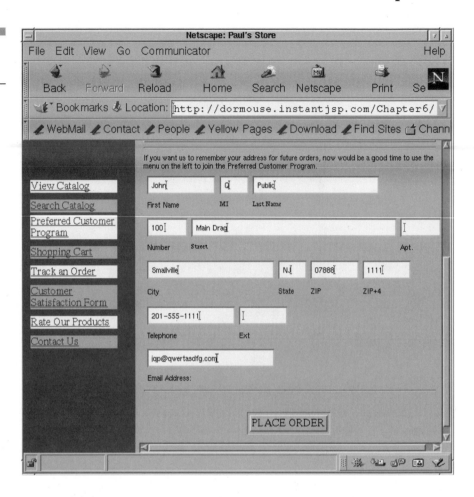

```
<jsp:getProperty name="custBean" property="filedName" />
```

In the case of a customer who has not joined the Preferred Customer Program, the value of the property would be the default value of `""`, which was assigned when the instance of the Bean was created. For a preferred customer, it would be the value retrieved from the database when the body of the `<jsp:useBean>` that created the Bean instance was executed.

After the order form has been filled in and the customer clicks on PLACE ORDER, a request containing the contents of the form is sent to `PlaceOrder.jsp`. Here is the code:

```
<%@ page import="com.instantjsp.Order" %>
<%@ include file="GetPrefCustId.jsp" %>
<jsp:useBean id="custBean" class="com.instantjsp.Customer"
```

```
    scope="session" >
    <jsp:setProperty name="custBean" property="customerInfo"
       value="<%= getPrefCustID(request)%>" />
</jsp:useBean>
<jsp:useBean id="cart" class="com.instantjsp.ShoppingCart"
    scope="session" />
<jsp:useBean id="sb" class="com.instantjsp.StoreBean"
    scope="session" />
<%
    if (!custBean.isPreferredCustomer()) {
%>
       <jsp:setProperty name="custBean" property="*" />
<%
    }
    int ordnum = sb.placeOrder(custBean,cart);
%>
<html>
<body>
<center>
<font face = "Arial, Helvetica" size="+2">
<br>
<br>
<b>Thank you for your order</b>
<br>
<br>
</font>
<font face = "Arial, Helvetica" size="+1">
Your order number is
<%= Integer.toString(ordnum) %>
<br>
<br>
</font>
</center>
Your order will be shipped immediately. You can use the menu
item labeled "Track an Order" on the left to track your order.
</body>
</html>
```

If `isPreferredCustomer()` returns false, the following action is executed:

```
<jsp:setProperty name="custBean" property="*" />
```

This is not necessary when `isPreferredCustomer()` returns true because the data is already stored in the `Customer` Bean.

The instances of the `Customer` Bean and the `ShoppingCart` Bean are passed as arguments to the `placeOrder()` method of `StoreBean`. This method creates records like those shown in Tables 6-1 and 6-2. Some representative records are shown in Tables 6-3 and 6-4.

After the records have been created and inserted into the appropriate databases, `PlaceOrder.jsp` displays the order number in a confirmation message as shown in Figure 6-10.

**TABLE 6-1**

The Orders
Database Table
Layout

```
Table   = orders
+----------------+-------------------------------+--------+
|     Field      |             Type              | Length |
+----------------+-------------------------------+--------+
| ordno          | int4 not null default next    |    4   |
| custno         | int4                          |    4   |
| placed         | datetime                      |    8   |
| shipped        | datetime                      |    8   |
| status         | int4                          |    4   |
+----------------+-------------------------------+--------+
Index:    orders_pkey
```

**TABLE 6-2**

The Orderdetail
Database Table
Layout

```
Table   = orderdetail
+----------------+-------------------------------+--------+
|     Field      |             Type              | Length |
+----------------+-------------------------------+--------+
| ordno          | int4                          |    4   |
| custno         | int4                          |    4   |
| sku            | int4                          |    4   |
| qty            | int4                          |    4   |
| price          | float8                        |    8   |
+----------------+-------------------------------+--------+
```

**TABLE 6-3**

Some Records from
the Orders
Database Table

```
-- RECORD 6 --
ordno  | 1212100212
custno | 1124178
placed | Tue Feb 29 15:33:00 2000 EST
status | 0
-- RECORD 7 --
ordno  | 1212100210
custno | 1124172
placed | Sun Feb 27 16:27:00 2000 EST
status | 1
-- RECORD 8 --
ordno  | 1212100213
custno | 1124175
placed | Tues Feb 29 15:50:00 20000 EST
status | 1
```

**TABLE 6-4**

Some Records from
the Orderdetail
Database Table

```
Field    Value
-- RECORD 0 --
ordno   | 1212100212
custno  | 1124178
sku     | 100021
qty     | 1
price   | 26.49
-- RECORD 1 --
ordno   | 1212100212
custno  | 1124178
sku     | 100041
qty     | 1
price   | 9.95
-- RECORD 2 --
ordno   | 1212100212
custno  | 1124178
sku     | 100001
qty     | 2
price   | 9.95
```

# Order Tracking—Keeping the Customer in the Loop

Customers are reassured when they can determine the status of their order at any point in time, and so our final chore consists of providing them with a tool they can use to track their orders. This tool is accessed by selecting "Track an Order" from the menu. This menu item is a link to `TrackOrder.jsp`, which looks like this:

```
<%@ page import="javax.servlet.http.Cookie" %>
<%@ include file="GetPrefCustId.jsp" %>
<jsp:useBean id="custBean" class="com.instantjsp.Customer"
  scope="session" >
  <jsp:setProperty name="custBean" property="customerInfo"
    value="<%= getPrefCustID(request)%>" />
</jsp:useBean>
<jsp:useBean id="orderBean" class="com.instantjsp.Order"
  scope="session" />
<html>
<body text="#000000" bgcolor="#c0c0c0">
<center>
```

Figure 6-10
Order Confirmation

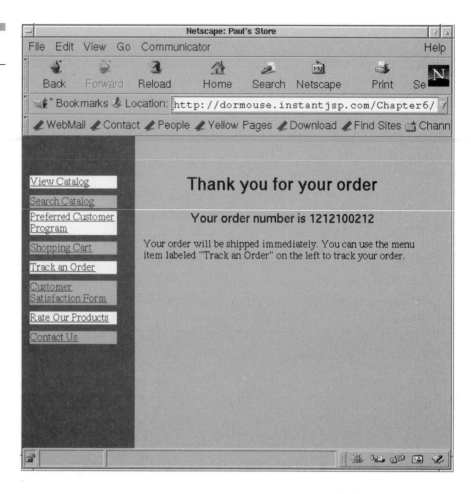

Figure 6-10
Order Confirmation

```
<font face = "Arial, Helvetica"><font size="+1">
Track Order
</font></font>
</center>
<form method="post" name="track" action="GetOrder.jsp">
<table cols="3" width="100%" nosave>
<tr nosave>
<%
  if (custBean.isPreferredCustomer()) {
    String custID = custBean.getCustomerID();
    int[] recentOrders = orderBean.getOrdersForCustomer(custID);
    if (recentOrders.length == 0) {
%>
<td>
<font face="Arial,Helvetica">
Your order number:
</font>
</td>
```

```
<td>
<font face="Arial,Helvetica">
<input type="text" name="orderNumber">
</font>
</td>
<%
    }
    else {
%>
<td>
<font face="Arial,Helvetica">
Select order number to track:
</font>
</td>
<td>
<font face="Arial,Helvetica">
<select name="orderNumber" size="1">
<%
      for (int i = 0; i < recentOrders.length; ++i) {
          String ordnum = Integer.toString(recentOrders[i]);
%>
<option value="<%= ordnum %>"><%= ordnum %>
<%
      }
%>
</select>
</font>
</td>
<%
    }
  }
    else {
%>
<td>
<font face="Arial,Helvetica">
Your order number:
</td>
<td>
<font face="Arial,Helvetica">
<input type="text" name="orderNumber">
</font>
</td>
<%
    }
%>
</tr>
</table>
<br>
<center>
<br>
<font face="Arial,Helvetica"><font size="-1">
<b>
<input type="submit" name="submit" value="TRACK">
</b>
</font></font>
</center>
</form>
</body>
</html>
```

TrackOrder.jsp produces a page like the one shown in Figure 6-11 or 6-12, depending on whether isPreferredCustomer() returns true or false. When the user types or selects the order number and clicks on TRACK, a request containing the order number is sent to GetOrder.jsp. Here is the code:

```
<%@ page import="com.instantjsp.OrderStatus" %>
<jsp:useBean id="orderBean" class="com.instantjsp.Order"
  scope="session" />
<%
  int ordnum= Integer.parseInt(request.getParameter("orderNumber"));
  OrderStatus orderStatus = orderBean.getOrderStatus(ordnum);
%>
<html>
<body>
<center>
```

**Figure 6-11**
Track Order
(Anonymous
Customer)

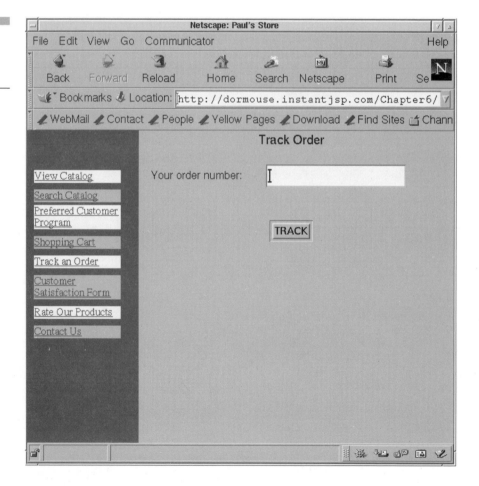

**Figure 6-12**
Track Order
(Preferred Customer)

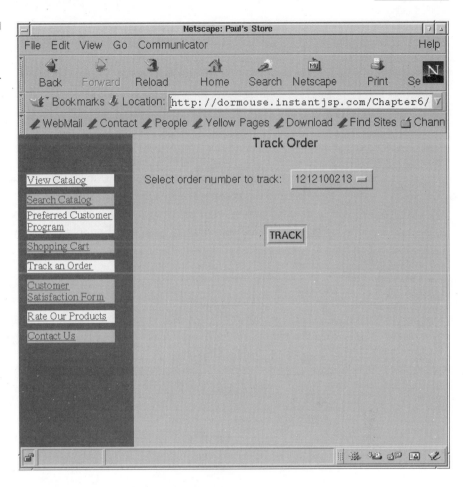

```
<font face = "Arial, Helvetica" size="+2">
Order Status
<br>
<br>
</font>
</center>
Order Number:
<%= ordnum %>
<br>
<br>
Date placed:
<%= orderStatus.placed %>
<br>
<br>
Status:
<%= orderStatus.status %>
<%
  if (orderStatus.shipped != null) {
```

```
%>
<br>
<br>
Shipped:
<%= orderStatus.shipped %>
<%
   }
%>
<br>
</body>
</html>
```

GetOrder.jsp gets the order number using the getParameter()
method and passes it to the getOrderStatus() method of Order. The
OrderStatus object that is returned contains the date placed, the status,
and the date shipped and these are displayed as shown in Figure 6-13.

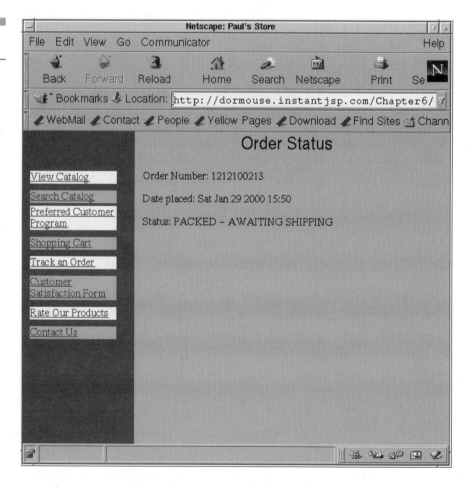

# Code for ShoppingCart

```java
package com.instantjsp;

import java.text.NumberFormat;
import java.util.Enumeration;
import java.util.Hashtable;

public class ShoppingCart {

  Hashtable contents;
  public ShoppingCart() {
    contents = new Hashtable();
  }

  public void empty() {
    contents.clear();
  }

  public boolean isEmpty() {
    return (contents.size() > 0);
  }

  public OrderItem[] getContents() {
    OrderItem[] sca = new OrderItem[contents.size()];
    int i = 0;
    for (Enumeration e = contents.elements(); e.hasMoreElements();) {
      sca[i++] = (OrderItem)e.nextElement();
    }
    return sca;
  }

  public void setQuantity(String sku, int quantity) {
    if (!contents.containsKey(sku)) {
      return;
    }
    if (quantity == 0) {
      contents.remove(sku);
      return;
    }
    OrderItem item = (OrderItem)contents.get(sku);
    item.setQuantity(quantity);
    contents.put(sku,item);
  }

  public void addItem(OrderItem item) {
    String sku = Integer.toString(item.getSKU());
    if (contents.containsKey(sku)) {
      OrderItem itemInCart =
        (OrderItem)contents.get(sku);
      item.setQuantity(item.getQuantity() +
        itemInCart.getQuantity());
    }
    contents.put(sku,item);
  }

  public String totalAsString(int sku) {
    OrderItem item =
```

```
        (OrderItem)contents.get(Integer.toString(sku));
      NumberFormat nf = NumberFormat.getCurrencyInstance();
      return nf.format((double)item.getQuantity() *
        (double)item.getPrice());
   }

   public String totalAsString() {
      double total = 0;
      for (Enumeration e = contents.elements(); e.hasMoreElements();) {
        OrderItem item = (OrderItem)e.nextElement();
          total = total + (double)item.getQuantity() *
            (double)item.getPrice();
      }
      NumberFormat nf = NumberFormat.getCurrencyInstance();
      return nf.format(total);
   }
}
```

# How're We Doing?— Hearing from the Customer

- Customer Feedback Form
- Customer Satisfaction Form
- Product Evaluation Form
- Random Surveys

The e-business landscape is already strewn with the shuttered stores of companies who failed to understand and meet the needs of their customers. If our customers have found better prices or higher-quality products than we are offering, we need to know. If they are considering switching to another company that offers goods or services that are not in our catalog, we need to know that, too. If our shipper failed to deliver on time, our customer needs a way to let us know. If we are about to make changes in the way we conduct business, it is far better to put out feelers before doing so than to find ourselves wishing we had done so after our customers leave us.

In this chapter, we examine some tools we can use to keep the lines of communication open between our customers and us.

# Customer Feedback Form

The most effective communication tool we can offer our customer is the feedback form. It also happens to be the simplest. Unlike questionnaires, whose content is decided by the person composing the questions, the feedback form is nothing more than a blank piece of paper on which the customer can write anything.

The customer accesses the feedback form by selecting the menu item labeled CONTACT US, which is a link to `CustomerFeedback.jsp`. Here is the code:

```
<jsp:useBean id="custBean" class="com.instantjsp.Customer"
  scope="session" >
</jsp:useBean>
<html>
<body>
<form method="post" name="feedback"

action="http://dormouse.instantjsp.com/Chapter7/ProcessCustomerFeed-
  back.jsp">
<center>
<font face = "Arial, Helvetica" size="+1">
<br>
Customer Feedback
</font>
</center>
<br>
<table nosave>
<tr nosave>
<td>
<font face = "Arial, Helvetica">
Your email address:
</font>
```

```
</td>
<td>
<font face = "Arial, Helvetica">
<%
  if (custBean.isPreferredCustomer()) {
%>
<input type="text" name="emailAddress"
  value="<jsp:getProperty name="custBean" property="emailAddress" />">
<%
  }
  else {
%>
<input type="text" name="emailAddress">
<%
  }
%>
</font>
</td>
</tr>
<%
  if (custBean.isPreferredCustomer()) {
%>
<tr nosave>
<td>
<font size="-1">
</font>
</td>
<td>
<font size="-1">
(please correct your address if it is not current)
</font>
</td>
</tr>
<%
  }
%>
</table>
<br>
<br>
<br>
<center>
<table>
<tr>
<td>
Enter your comments in the box below:
</td>
<tr>
<td>
<textarea name="feedback" rows=6 cols=40>
</textarea>
</td>
</tr>
</table>
<input type="submit" name="submit" value="SUBMIT">
</center>
</font>
</form>
</body>
</html>
```

The first `<jsp:useBean>` action creates an instance of class `Customer` if a similarly named instance is not found in the session scope namespace. It is assigned to the scripting variable `custBean`. We have already seen the `Customer` Bean in Chapters 5 and 6. The page the customer sees looks like either Figure 7-1 or 7-2. The difference is that in Figure 7-1 the email address field is populated. `CustomerFeedback.-jsp` determines whether it should populate this field by testing the value returned by the `isPreferredCustomer()` method of `custBean`, which we have already seen. The value assigned to the email address field is obtained by the action:

```
<jsp:getProperty name="custBean" property="emailAddress" />
```

**Figure 7-1**
Customer Feedback
Form for Known
Customer

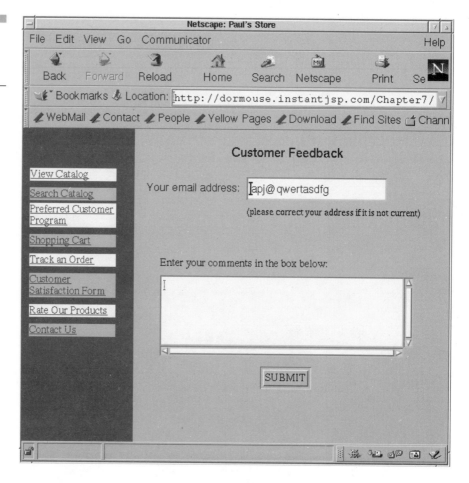

**Figure 7-2**
Customer Feedback
Form for Anonymous
Customer

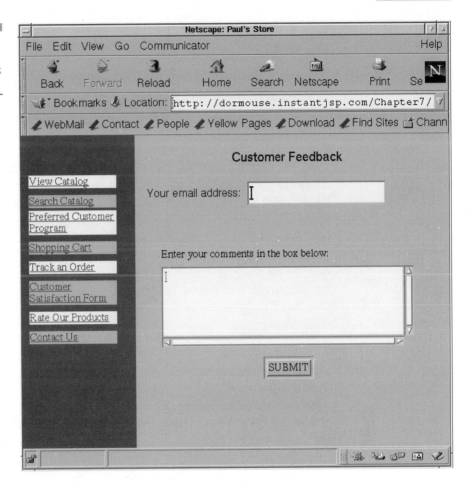

When the user enters comments into the text area labeled "Enter your comments in the box below" and clicks on the SUBMIT button, a request containing the contents of the HTML form is sent to Process-CustomerFeedback.jsp. Here is the code:

```
<%@ page errorPage="/common/Exception.jsp" %>
<jsp:useBean id="custInputBean"
class="com.instantjsp.CustomerInput"
  scope="session" />
<jsp:useBean id="feedbackData" class="com.instantjsp.FeedbackData"
  scope="session" />
<jsp:setProperty name="feedbackData" property="*" />
<%
  custInputBean.recordFeedback(feedbackData);
%>
```

```
<html>
<body text="#000000" bgcolor="#FFFFFF">
<center>
<font face = "Arial, Helvetica"><font size="+1">
<br>
Thank you for contacting us. You can expect a reply at the email
address you provided.
</font>
</body>
</html>
```

ProcessCustomerFeedback.jsp saves the request data in an instance of FeedbackData using a <jsp:setProperty> action. FeedbackData is a simple data holder that contains only getters and setters for its instance variables. The code can be found on the CD. The instance of FeedbackData is then passed as an argument to the recordFeedback() method of an instance of CustomerInput. The complete listing for CustomerInput is shown at the end of the chapter. An examination of this code shows that the recordFeedback() method executes the following SQL statement:

```
INSERT INTO feedback VALUES ('emailaddress', 'feedbacktext');
```

This statement creates a new database record containing the fields shown in Table 7-1.

After it saves the data in the database, ProcessCustomerFeedback.-jsp emits HTML code that produces an acknowledgment of receipt like the one shown in Figure 7-3.

Table 7-2 shows a representative sample of a customer feedback record. Such records are extracted from the database at regular intervals by a batch job and sent to a customer service representative who prepares appropriate responses, which are sent to the email address supplied by the customer.

Implementing the customer feedback in this manner has an advantage over simply providing a page containing a MAILTO link. Besides rely-

**TABLE 7-1**

Customer
Feedback
Database Table
Description

```
Table   = feedback
+-------------------+-------------------------------+-----------+
|      Field        |            Type               |  Length   |
+-------------------+-------------------------------+-----------+
| email_address     | varchar()                     |    128    |
| feedback_text     | varchar()                     |   1024    |
+-------------------+-------------------------------+-----------+
```

**Figure 7-3**
Acknowledging
Receipt of Customer
Feedback Form

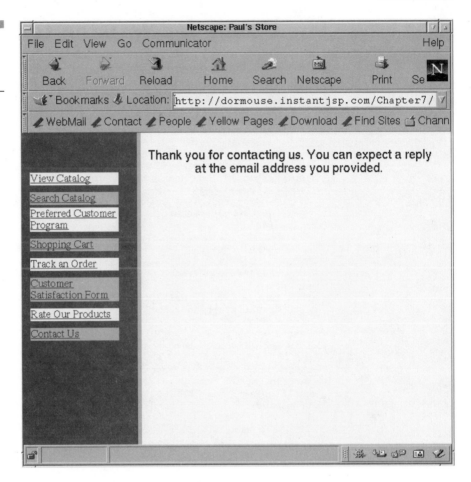

**TABLE 7-2**

Customer
Feedback
Database Contents

```
RECORD 6 --
email_address | jjones@qwertasdf.com
feedback_text | What is your return policy?
              | Do you require an RA number?
```

ing on observations from the customer service representatives who read the contents of the feedback forms, you can use the output of programs that use the feedback database as input. Such programs might detect trends and patterns that might otherwise not be detectable—especially if the job of reviewing feedback is spread out among many persons.

# The Customer Satisfaction Form

Whenever we fulfill an order, we should provide a means whereby the customer can rate us on how well we did. We do this by providing the menu item labeled "Customer Satisfaction Form," which is a link to CustomerSatisfaction.jsp. Here is the code:

```
<%@ page import="javax.servlet.http.Cookie" %>
<%@ include file="GetPrefCustId.jsp" %>
<jsp:useBean id="custBean" class="com.instantjsp.Customer"
  scope="session" >
 <jsp:setProperty name="custBean" property="customerInfo"
   value="<%= getPrefCustID(request)%>" />
</jsp:useBean>
<jsp:useBean id="orderBean" class="com.instantjsp.Order"
  scope="session" />
<html>
<body text="#000000" bgcolor="#c0c0c0">
<center>
<font face = "Arial, Helvetica"><font size="+1">
Customer Satisfaction Form
</font></font>
</center>
<form method="post" name="custsat"

action="http://dormouse.instantjsp.com/Chapter7/RegisterCustomerSatis-
  faction.jsp">
<table cols="3" width="100%" nosave>
<tr nosave>
<%
  if (custBean.isPreferredCustomer()) {
    String custID = custBean.getCustomerID();
    int[] recentOrders = orderBean.getOrdersForCustomer(custID);
    if (recentOrders.length == 0) {
%>
    <%@ include file="RequestOrderNumber.jsp" %>
<%
    }
    else {
%>
    <%@ include file="SelectOrderNumber.jsp" %>
<%
    }
  }
  else {
%>
    <%@ include file="RequestOrderNumber.jsp" %>
<%
  }
%>
</tr>
</table>
<br>
<font face="Arial,Helvetica"><font size="-1">
Please rate each of the categories below by clicking on the
```

```
appropriate button. The meaning of the numbers is as follows:
</font></font>
<br>
<table nosave>
<tr nosave>
<td>
<font face="Arial,Helvetica"><font size="-1">1-poor</font></font>
</td>
<td>
<font face="Arial,Helvetica"><font size="-1">2-fair</font></font>
</td>
<td>
<font face="Arial,Helvetica"><font size="-1">3-good</font></font>
</td>
<td>
<font face="Arial,Helvetica"><font size="-1">4-very good</font></font>
</td>
<td>
<font face="Arial,Helvetica"><font size="-1">5-excellent</font></font>
</td>
</tr>
<br>
</table>
<center><table BORDER WIDTH="100%" BGCOLOR="#e0e0e0" NOSAVE >
<tr NOSAVE>
<td NOSAVE></td>
<font face="Arial,Helvetica"><font size="-1"<

</font></font>
<td>
<font face="Arial,Helvetica"><font size="-1">1</font></font>
</td>

<td>
<font face="Arial,Helvetica"><font size="-1">2</font></font>
</td>

<td>
<font face="Arial,Helvetica"><font size="-1">3</font></font>
</td>

<td>
<font face="Arial,Helvetica"><font size="-1">4</font></font>
</td>

<td>
<font face="Arial,Helvetica"><font size="-1">5</font></font>
</td>

</tr>

<tr NOSAVE>
<td NOSAVE>
<font face="Arial,Helvetica">
Online order process - ease of use
</font>
</td>

<td><input type="radio" name="easeOfOrdering" value="1"</td>
```

```
<td><input type="radio" name="easeOfOrdering" value="2"</td>
<td><input type="radio" name="easeOfOrdering" value="3"</td>
<td><input type="radio" name="easeOfOrdering" value="4"</td>
<td><input type="radio" name="easeOfOrdering" value="5"</td>

</tr>

<tr>
<td>
<font face="Arial,Helvetica">
Ability to track status of your order
</font>
</td>

<td><input type="radio" name="easeOfTracking" value="1"</td>
<td><input type="radio" name="easeOfTracking" value="2"</td>
<td><input type="radio" name="easeOfTracking" value="3"</td>
<td><input type="radio" name="easeOfTracking" value="4"</td>
<td><input type="radio" name="easeOfTracking" value="5"</td>

</tr>

<tr>
<td>
<font face="Arial,Helvetica">
Timliness of delivery
</font>
</td>

<td><input type="radio" name="speedOfDelivery" value="1"</td>
<td><input type="radio" name="speedOfDelivery" value="2"</td>
<td><input type="radio" name="speedOfDelivery" value="3"</td>
<td><input type="radio" name="speedOfDelivery" value="4"</td>
<td><input type="radio" name="speedOfDelivery" value="5"</td>

</tr>

<tr>
<td>
<font face="Arial,Helvetica">
Condition in which shipment arrived
</font>
</td>

<td><input type="radio" name="conditionOfShipment" value="1"</td>
<td><input type="radio" name="conditionOfShipment" value="2"</td>
<td><input type="radio" name="conditionOfShipment" value="3"</td>
<td><input type="radio" name="conditionOfShipment" value="4"</td>
<td><input type="radio" name="conditionOfShipment" value="5"</td>

</tr>

<tr NOSAVE>
<td>
<font face="Arial,Helvetica">
Satisfaction with quality of product
</font>
</td>

<td><input type="radio" name="qualityOfProducts" value="1"</td>
```

```
<td><input type="radio" name="qualityOfProducts" value="2"></td>
<td><input type="radio" name="qualityOfProducts" value="3"></td>
<td><input type="radio" name="qualityOfProducts" value="4"></td>
<td><input type="radio" name="qualityOfProducts" value="5"></td>

</tr>
</table></center>

<center>
<br>
<font face="Arial,Helvetica"><font size="-1">
<b>
<input type="submit" name="submit" value="SUBMIT">
</b>
</font></font>
</center>
</form>
</body>
</html>
```

As was the case with the customer feedback form, the page the user sees after clicking on "Customer Satisfaction Form" depends on whether the customer is known to us or is anonymous. The two pages the user can see are shown in Figures 7-4 and 7-5.

A customer who is known to us but who has not ordered recently will see the same page as a customer who is not known to us (Figure 7-5). We factor out the code required to generate the text entry field and place it in RequestOrderNumber.jsp. That code is as follows:

```
<td>
<font face="Arial,Helvetica">
Your order number:
</font>
</td>
<td>
<font face="Arial,Helvetica">
<input type="text" name="orderNumber">
</font>
</td>
```

Specifying RequestOrderNumber.jsp in an include directive simplifies the page. To simplify the page even further, we store the code required to generate the select list in Figure 7-4 in SelectOrderNumber.jsp, which we also specify in an include directive. This results in the if/else pairs being in closer proximity making the page easier to read. Here is SelectOrderNumber.jsp:

```
<td>
<font face="Arial,Helvetica">
Select the order number on which you wish to comment:
</font>
</td>
```

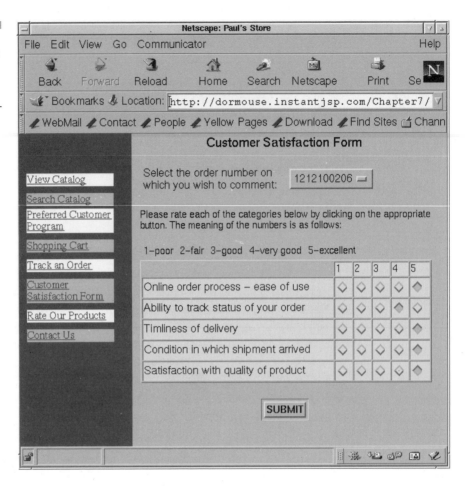

```
<td>
<font face="Arial,Helvetica">
<select name="orderNumber" size="1">
<%
     for (int i = 0; i < recentOrders.length; ++i) {
        String ordnum = Integer.toString(recentOrders[i]);
%>
<option value="<%= ordnum %>"><%= ordnum %>
<%
     }
%>
</select>
</font>
</td>
```

We determine which page is presented to the user by first testing the value returned by the isPreferredCustomer() method. If the method

**Figure 7-5**
Customer Satisfaction
Form for Anonymous
Customer or Known
Customer Who Has
Not Ordered
Recently

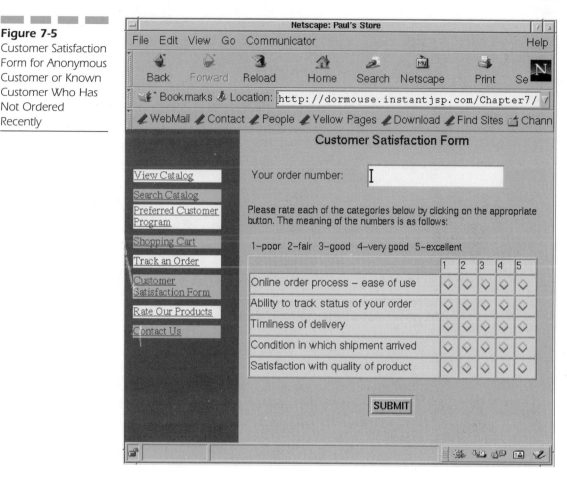

returns true, we pass the customer ID as an argument to the
getOrdersForCustomer() of the Order Bean (we have seen the Order
Bean in Chapter 6). This method gets the order numbers of recent orders
for the specified customer by executing the SQL statement:

```
SELECT ordno FROM orders WHERE custno= custID;
```

The scriptlet that does all this is:

```
<%
  if (custBean.isPreferredCustomer()) {
    String custID = custBean.getCustomerID();
    int[] recentOrders = orderBean.getOrdersForCustomer(custID);
    if (recentOrders.length == 0) {
%>
```

If a nonempty list is returned, we use the order numbers in the list to generate an HTML select list using the following code:

```
<select name="orderNumber" size="1">
<%
    for (int i = 0; i < recentOrders.length; ++i) {
        String ordnum = Integer.toString(recentOrders[i]);
%>
<option value="<%= ordnum %>"><%= ordnum %>
<%
    }
%>
</select>
```

The presence of this prepopulated list of recent order numbers serves as a convenience for the customer. Additionally, it provides a higher level of comfort than simply typing a number and hoping that the order is "somewhere in the system."

A customer can be anonymous or unknown to us for two reasons. The first is that he or she has not joined our Preferred Customer Program. The second is that orders placed by this customer are not sufficiently recent to be in the database. An anonymous customer must type the order number into a text field that is provided, as shown in Figure 7-5.

After selecting or typing an order number, the user rates our processing of that order by checking the appropriate radio buttons and then clicks on the SUBMIT button. This sends a request containing the data in the HTML form to RegisterCustomerSatisfaction.jsp. Here is the code:

```
<%@ page errorPage="/common/UserError.jsp" %>
<jsp:useBean id="custInputBean"
class="com.instantjsp.CustomerInput"
    scope="session" />
<jsp:useBean id="satData" class="com.instantjsp.SatisfactionData"
    scope="session" />
<jsp:setProperty name="satData" property="*" />
<%
    custInputBean.recordSatisfaction(satData);
%>
<html>
<body text="#000000" bgcolor="#FFFFFF">

<center>
<font face = "Arial, Helvetica"><font size="+1">
<br>
Thank you for helping us serve you
</font></font>
</center>
<font face = "Arial, Helvetica">
<br>
We value you as a customer and your satisfaction is important to us.
<p>
```

```
The input you provided has been recorded and will be reviewed. We
will use this input to help us to continue to serve you.
</font>
</body>
</html>
```

`RegisterCustomerSatisfaction.jsp` saves the request data in an instance of `SatisfactionData` using a `<jsp:setProperty>` action. The `SatisfactionData` Bean is a simple data holder that contains only getters and setters for each of its instance variables. The code can be found on the CD. The instance of `SatisfactionData` is then passed as an argument to the `recordSatisfaction()` method of the instance of `CustomerInput`. Since `recordSatisfaction()` has no knowledge of whether the order number was selected from a list or manually entered, it executes an SQL query to find the order number in the database. If a NumberFormatException is thrown because the user typed a nonnumeric order number or if an SQLException is thrown because the order number that was typed is not in the database, the exception is caught by `UserError.jsp`, which is located in the `/common` directory. In this case, the user sees the page shown in Figure 7-6.

If the order number is valid and on file, `recordSatisfaction()` creates a database record containing the fields shown in Table 7-3. After it saves the data in the database, `RegisterCustomerSatisfaction.jsp` emits HTML code that produces an acknowledgment of receipt like the one shown in Figure 7-7.

Table 7-4 shows a few customer satisfaction records. As was the case with customer feedback records, customer satisfaction records are extracted from the database at regular intervals by a batch job that generates reports for our customer relations department. If we are proud of our ratings, we might even publish them on our Web site to attract potential customers. If not, we should take whatever corrective measures are necessary to bring the ratings up.

# Product Evaluation Form

Our customers might find our site easy to use and be perfectly satisfied with the manner in which their order was processed but might have further comments on the products we sell. The product evaluation form, which is designed to handle such comments, is accessed by clicking on the menu item labeled "Rate Our Products," which is a link to `ProductReview.jsp`. Here is the code:

**Figure 7-6**
Order Number Not
on File

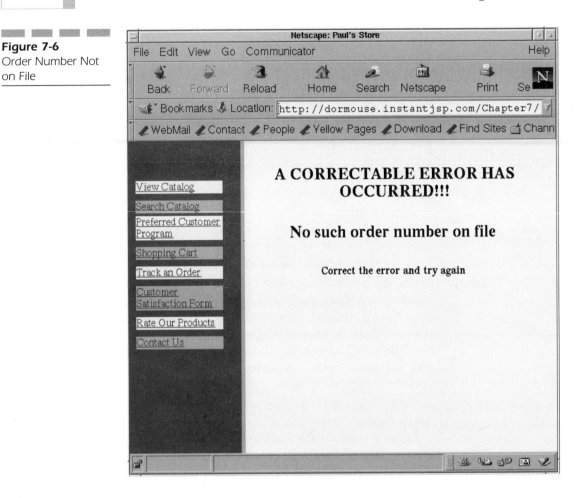

**TABLE 7-3**

Customer
Satisfaction
Database Table
Description

```
Table    = satisfaction
+----------------------------+---------------------------+----------+
|          Field             |           Type            |  Length  |
+----------------------------+---------------------------+----------+
|   survey_date              |   date                    |     4    |
|   ordno                    |   int4                    |     4    |
|   ease_of_ordering         |   int4                    |     4    |
|   ease_of_tracking         |   int4                    |     4    |
|   speed_of_delivery        |   int4                    |     4    |
|   condition_of_shipment    |   int4                    |     4    |
|   quality_of_products      |   int4                    |     4    |
+----------------------------+---------------------------+----------+
```

**Figure 7-7**
Acknowledging
Receipt of Customer
Satisfaction Form

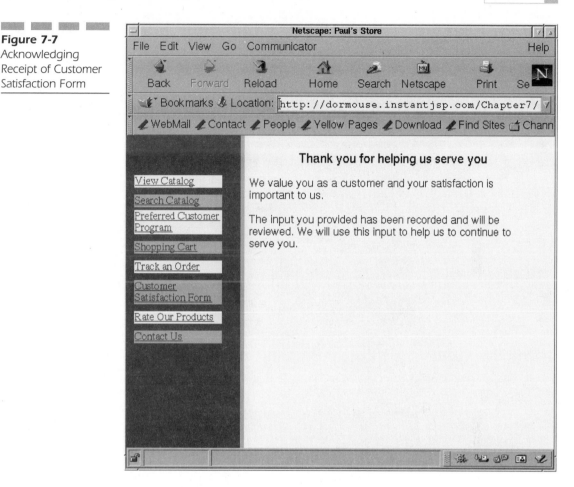

```
<%@ page import="javax.servlet.http.Cookie" %>
<%@ page import="com.instantjsp.Product" %>
<%@ include file="GetPrefCustId.jsp" %>
<jsp:useBean id="custBean" class="com.instantjsp.Customer"
  scope="session" >
  <jsp:setProperty name="custBean" property="customerInfo"
    value="<%= getPrefCustID(request)%>" />
</jsp:useBean>
<jsp:useBean id="orderBean" class="com.instantjsp.Order"
  scope="session" />
<html>
<body text="#000000" bgcolor="#c0c0c0">
<center>
<font face = "Arial, Helvetica"><font size="+1">
Product Review Form
</font></font>
```

**TABLE 7-4**

Customer
Satisfaction
Database Contents

```
-- RECORD 13 --
survey_date            02-06-2000
ordno                  1212100200
ease_of_ordering       5
ease_of_tracking       4
speed_of_delivery      5
condition_of_shipment  4
quality_of_products    5

-- RECORD 14 --
survey_date            02-06-2000
ordno[te[1212100200
ease_of_ordering       5
ease_of_tracking       4
speed_of_delivery      5
condition_of_shipment  4
quality_of_products    5

-- RECORD 15 --
survey_date            02-15-2000
ordno                  1212100200
ease_of_ordering       4
ease_of_tracking       5
speed_of_delivery      5
condition_of_shipment  5
quality_of_products    5
```

```html
</center>
<form method="post" name="custsat"

action="http://dormouse.instantjsp.com/Chapter7/RegisterProductRating.-
 jsp">
<table cols="3" width="100%" nosave>
<tr nosave>
<%
  if (custBean.isPreferredCustomer()) {
    String custID = custBean.getCustomerID();
    Product[] recentProducts =
      orderBean.getProductsForCustomer(custID);
    if (recentProducts.length == 0) {
%>
<td>
<font face="Arial,Helvetica">
SKU Number from invoice:
</font>
</td>
<td>
<font face="Arial,Helvetica">
<input type="text" name="ordno">
</font>
</td>
<%
  }
  else {
%>
```

```
<td>
<font face="Arial,Helvetica">
Select product:
</font>
</td>
<td>
<font face="Arial,Helvetica">
<select name="sku" size="1">
<%
        for (int i = 0; i < recentProducts.length; ++i) {
%>
<option value="<%= recentProducts[i].getSku() %>">
<%= recentProducts[i].getDescription() %>
<%
        }
%>
</select>
</font>
</td>
<%
      }
    }
    else {
%>
<td>
<font face="Arial,Helvetica">
SKU Number from invoice:
</font>
</td>
<td>
<font face="Arial,Helvetica">
<input type="text" name="ordno">
</font>
</td>
<%
      }
%>
</tr>
</table>
<br>
<font face="Arial,Helvetica"><font size="-1">
Please rate the product by clicking on the appropriate button.
The meaning of the numbers is as follows:
</font></font>
<br>
<table nosave>
<tr nosave>
<td>
<font face="Arial,Helvetica"><font size="-1">1-poor</font></font>
</td>
<td>
<font face="Arial,Helvetica"><font size="-1">2-fair</font></font>
</td>
<td>
<font face="Arial,Helvetica"><font size="-1">3-good</font></font>
</td>
<td>
<font face="Arial,Helvetica"><font size="-1">4-very good</font></font>
</td>
```

```
<td>
<font face="Arial,Helvetica"><font size="-1">5-excellent</font></font>
</td>
</tr>
<br>
</table>
<center><table BORDER WIDTH="100%" BGCOLOR="#e0e0e0" NOSAVE >
<tr NOSAVE>
<td NOSAVE></td>
<font face="Arial,Helvetica"><font size="-1"<

</font></font>
<td>
<font face="Arial,Helvetica"><font size="-1">1</font></font>
</td>

<td>
<font face="Arial,Helvetica"><font size="-1">2</font></font>
</td>

<td>
<font face="Arial,Helvetica"><font size="-1">3</font></font>
</td>

<td>
<font face="Arial,Helvetica"><font size="-1">4</font></font>
</td>

<td>
<font face="Arial,Helvetica"><font size="-1">5</font></font>
</td>

</tr>

<tr NOSAVE>
<td NOSAVE>
<font face="Arial,Helvetica">
Quality compared to our competitors
</font>
</td>

<td><input type="radio" name="qualityRating" value="1"</td>
<td><input type="radio" name="qualityRating" value="2"</td>
<td><input type="radio" name="qualityRating" value="3"</td>
<td><input type="radio" name="qualityRating" value="4"</td>
<td><input type="radio" name="qualityRating" value="5"</td>

</tr>

<tr>
<td>
<font face="Arial,Helvetica">
Price compared to our competitors
</font>
</td>

<td><input type="radio" name="priceRating" value="1"</td>
<td><input type="radio" name="priceRating" value="2"</td>
<td><input type="radio" name="priceRating" value="3"</td>
```

```
<td><input type="radio" name="priceRating" value="4"</td>
<td><input type="radio" name="priceRating" value="5"</td>

</tr>

<tr>
<td>
<font face="Arial,Helvetica">
Your overall satisfaction with the product
</font>
</td>

<td><input type="radio" name="satisfactionRating" value="1"</td>
<td><input type="radio" name="satisfactionRating" value="2"</td>
<td><input type="radio" name="satisfactionRating" value="3"</td>
<td><input type="radio" name="satisfactionRating" value="4"</td>
<td><input type="radio" name="satisfactionRating" value="5"</td>

</tr>
</table></center>

<center>
<br>
<font face="Arial,Helvetica"><font size="-1">
<b>
<input type="submit" name="submit" value="SUBMIT">
</b>
</font></font>
</center>
</form>
</body>
</html>
```

As was the case for customer feedback and customer satisfaction, the page generated by `ProductReview.jsp` depends on whether the customer is known to us or is anonymous. Figures 7-8 and 7-9 show the two possibilities.

If `isPreferredCustomer()` returns a value of true, we pass the customer ID to the `getRecentProducts()` method of the `Order` Bean. We have already seen this Bean in Chapter 6. The method returns an array of `Product` objects. The SKU (product number) for each product is obtained by invoking the `getSku()` method and is inserted into a select list by the following code:

```
<select name="sku" size="1">
<%
    for (int i = 0; i < recentProducts.length; ++i) {
%>
<option value="<%= recentProducts[i].getSku() %>">
<%= recentProducts[i].getDescription() %>
<%
    }
%>
</select>
```

**Figure 7-8**
Product Evaluation
Form for Known,
Active Customer

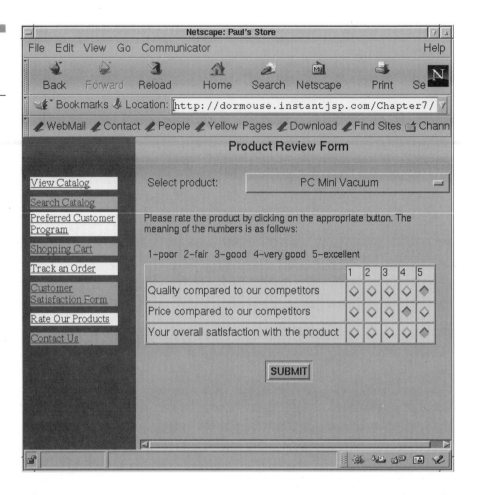

If the customer is anonymous, we simply present a field into which the customer types the product number. The following HTML creates this text field.

```
<input type="text" name="ordno">
```

After selecting or typing a product number, the user rates that product by checking the appropriate radio buttons and then clicks on the SUBMIT button. This sends a request containing the data in the HTML form to RegisterProductRating.jsp. Here is the code:

```
<%@ page errorPage="/common/UserError.jsp" %>
<jsp:useBean id="custInputBean" class="com.instantjsp.CustomerInput"
  scope="session" />
```

**Figure 7-9**
Product Evaluation
Form for Anonymous
or Inactive Customer

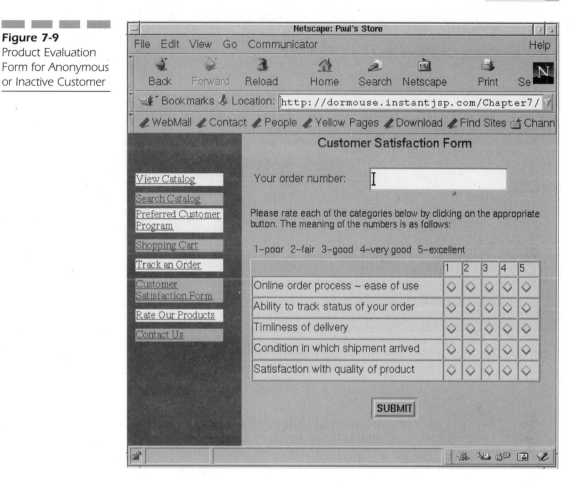

```
<jsp:useBean id="product" class="com.instantjsp.Product"
  scope="session" />
<jsp:setProperty name="product" property="*" />
<%
  custInputBean.recordProductRating(product);
%>
<html>
<body text="#000000" bgcolor="#FFFFFF">
<center>
<font face = "Arial, Helvetica"><font size="+1">
<br>
Your product evaluation has been recorded.
</font></font>
</center>
<font face = "Arial, Helvetica">
<br>
<p>
```

```
The input you provided has been recorded and will be reviewed. We
will use this input to help us to continue to serve you.
<p>
If we can be of assistance to you in any way, please contact
us by clicking on the appropriate menu item on the left.
</font>
</body>
</html>
```

RegisterProductRating.jsp saves the request data in an instance of Product using a <jsp:setProperty> action. This instance is then passed as an argument to the recordProductRating() method of the instance of CustomerInput. Since recordProductRating() has no knowledge of whether the product number was selected from a list or manually entered, it executes an SQL query to find the product number in the database. If a NumberFormatException is thrown because the user typed a nonnumeric product number or if an SQLException is thrown because the product number that was typed is not in the database, the exception is caught by UserError.jsp, which is located in the /common directory. In this case, the user sees the page shown in Figure 7-10.

If the product number is valid and on file, recordProductRating() creates a database record containing the fields shown in Table 7-5. After it saves the data in the database, RegisterProductRating.jsp emits HTML code that produces an acknowledgment of receipt like the one shown in Figure 7-11.

Table 7-6 shows a few product rating records. As was the case with other customer input we have seen, the product evaluation records are extracted from the database at regular intervals by a batch job that generates reports. Such reports might be used to tell us whether we should change our price structure or look for a new supplier for some of our products.

# Conducting Random Customer Surveys

We saw in Chapter 5 that when a customer joins our Preferred Customer Program, he or she is asked to indicate a willingness to participate in random surveys. Let's see how such a survey is conducted.

The survey database table, which is shown in Table 7-7, is used to determine when a survey should be sent to customers who have indicated a desire to participate. This table contains a single row as shown in

**Figure 7-10**
Product Not in
Catalog

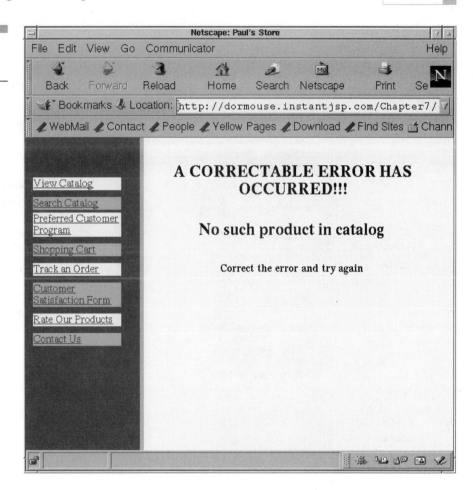

**TABLE 7-5**

Product Evaluation
Database Table
Description

```
Table   = product_rating
+-------------------+-------------------------------------+----------+
|      Field        |                 Type                | Length   |
+-------------------+-------------------------------------+----------+
|   prodno          |   int4                              |      4   |
|   quality         |   int4                              |      4   |
|   price           |   int4                              |      4   |
|   satisfaction    |   int4                              |      4   |
+-------------------+-------------------------------------+----------+
```

Table 7-8. The survey_page field is the name of the page containing the survey form (minus the .html extension).

The steps required to conduct a survey are:

**Figure 7-11**
Acknowledging
Receipt of Product
Evaluation Form

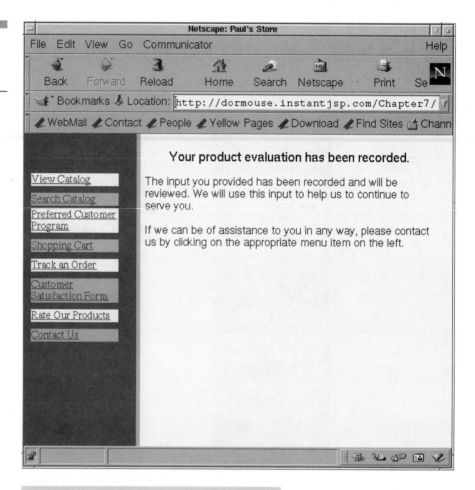

**TABLE 7-6**

Product Evaluation
Database Contents

```
prodno  | quality | price | satisfaction
--------+---------+-------+-------------
100015  |       5 |     4 |            5
100015  |       0 |     0 |            0
100015  |       5 |     4 |            4
100015  |       4 |     5 |            4
100015  |       5 |     5 |            5
```

**TABLE 7-7**

Survey Control
Table Description

```
Table   = survey
+-------------------+---------------------------------+---------+
|      Field        |             Type                | Length  |
+-------------------+---------------------------------+---------+
| start_survey      | date                            |       4 |
| end_survey        | date                            |       4 |
| survey_page       | varchar()                       |     256 |
+-------------------+---------------------------------+---------+
```

**TABLE 7-8**

Survey Control
Table Contents

```
start_survey | end_survey | survey_page
-------------+------------+------------
01-29-2000   | 02-15-2000 | Survey01
```

**TABLE 7-9**

Description of pref-
cust Database
Table

```
Table    = prefcust
+------------------+---------------------------+--------+
|      Field       |           Type            | Length |
+------------------+---------------------------+--------+
| custno           | int4 not null             |    4   |
| joined           | date                      |    4   |
| lastordered      | date                      |    4   |
| lastordno        | date                      |    4   |
| sendemail        | bool                      |    1   |
| emailaddr        | varchar()                 |  128   |
| oktosurvey       | bool                      |    1   |
| do_current_survey| bool                      |    1   |
+------------------+---------------------------+--------+
Index:    prefcust_pkey
```

- Create an HTML file containing the survey
- Use an administrative utility to set the survey_page field to the name of this HTML file
- Use the administrative utility to set the start and end dates in the survey table
- Use the administrative utility to select all customers in the prefcust database table (Table 7-9) and set the do_current_survey field to true for all those records in which the oktosurvey field is true

Now let's look at what happens when a customer accesses our main page and a survey is in progress. An examination of index.html reveals that the source for the main display frame is Intro.jsp. Here is the code:

```
<%@ page import="javax.servlet.http.Cookie" %>
<%@include file="GetPrefCustId.jsp" %>
<jsp:useBean id="custBean" class="com.instantjsp.Customer"
  scope="session">
  <jsp:setProperty name="custBean" property="customerInfo"
    value="<%= getPrefCustID(request) %>" />
</jsp:useBean>
<jsp:useBean id="sb" class="com.instantjsp.SurveyBean"
  scope="request" />
<%
```

```
        if ((custBean.isSurveyCandidate()) &&
            (sb.getSurveyPage() != null)) {
%>
<jsp:forward
  page="SurveyOptions.jsp" />
<%
    }
  else {
%>
<jsp:forward page="Welcome.jsp" />
<%
  }
%>
```

The first scriptlet invokes the isSurveyCandidate() of custBean (an instance of Customer). This method returns true if *all* of the instance variables isPreferredCustomer, okToSurvey, and doCurrent-Survey are true. The latter two reflect the values of the fields oktosurvey and do_current_survey in the preferred customer database table shown in Table 7-9. Table 7-10 shows the contents of the record for a customer who has agreed to participate in surveys.

If isSurveyCandidate returns a value of true, we chain to SurveyOptions.jsp, which results in the page shown in Figure 7-12. Here is the code:

```
<%@ page import="javax.servlet.http.Cookie" %>
<%@ include file="GetPrefCustId.jsp" %>
<jsp:useBean id="custBean" class="com.instantjsp.Customer"
  scope="session" >
  <jsp:setProperty name="custBean" property="customerInfo"
    value="<%= getPrefCustID(request)%>" />
</jsp:useBean>
<html>
<body>
<font face = "Arial, Helvetica">
Hello,
<%= custBean.getFirstName() %>
.
<p>
```

**TABLE 7-10**

Database Record for Customer Who Has Agreed to Participate in Surveys

| Field | Value |
| --- | --- |
| -- RECORD 0 -- | |
| custno | 1124101 |
| joined | 12-15-1999 |
| sendemail | t |
| emailaddr | jjones@qwertasdf.com |
| oktosurvey | t |
| do_current_survey | t |
| (1 row) | |

**Figure 7-12**

Participation in Current Survey Is Optional

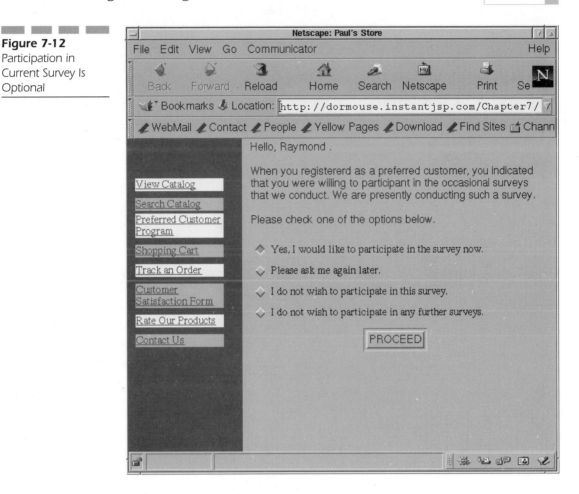

When you registererd as a preferred customer, you indicated that
you were willing to participant in the occasional surveys that we
conduct. We are presently conducting such a survey.
```
<p>
Please check one of the options below.
<br>
<form method="post" name="surveyoptions"

action="http://dormouse.instantjsp.com/Chapter7/ProcessSurveyOptions.-
  jsp">
<table>
<tr>
<td>
<input type="radio" name="opt" value="0" checked>
</td>
<td>
Yes, I would like to participate in the survey now.
```

```
</td>
</tr>
<tr>
<td>
<input type="radio" name="opt" value="1">
</td>
<td>
Please ask me again later.
</td>
</tr>
<tr>
<td>
<input type="radio" name="opt" value="2">
</td>
<td>
I do not wish to participate in this survey.
</td>
</tr>
<tr>
<td>
<input type="radio" name="opt" value="3">
</td>
<td>
I do not wish to participate in any further surveys.
</td>
</tr>
</table>
<center>
<input type="submit" name="submit" value="PROCEED">
</center>
</form>
</font>
</body>
</html>
```

Even though the customer has agreed to participate in surveys, each survey provides the customer with a way of opting out either for the current survey or for all future surveys. The customer indicates his or her preference by checking the appropriate radio button and clicks on the button labeled PROCEED. A request containing the value of the checked radio button is then sent to ProcessSurveyOptions.jsp. Here is the code:

```
<%@ page import="javax.servlet.http.Cookie" %>
<%@ include file="GetPrefCustId.jsp" %>
<jsp:useBean id="custBean" class="com.instantjsp.Customer"
  scope="session" >
  <jsp:setProperty name="custBean" property="customerInfo"
    value="<%= getPrefCustID(request)%>" />
</jsp:useBean>
<jsp:useBean id="sb" class="com.instantjsp.SurveyBean"
  scope="session" />
<%
  switch (Integer.parseInt(request.getParameter("opt"))) {
    case 0: // yes, participate
```

```
                    String surveyPage = sb.getSurveyPage() + ".html";
%>
<jsp:forward page="<%= surveyPage %>" />
<%
       break;
    case 1: // ask later
%>
<jsp:forward page="Welcome.jsp" />
<%
       break;
    case 2: // not this time
%>
<jsp:setProperty name="custBean" property="doCurrentSurvey"
   value="false" />
<jsp:forward page="Welcome.jsp" />
<%
       break;
    case 3: // not ever
%>
<jsp:forward page="NoSurveyEverAgain.jsp" />
<%
       break;
   }
%>
```

ProcessSurveyOptions.jsp uses the class method parseInt() of class Integer to convert the value of the checked radio button to an integer, which it then uses in a switch statement to determine the target of a <jsp:forward> action.

Let's look at the case where the checked radio button has a value of 0, indicating that the customer checked the radio button labeled "Yes, I would like to participate in the survey now." The following code is executed:

```
case 0: // yes, participate
      String surveyPage = sb.getSurveyPage() + ".jsp";
%>
<jsp:forward page="<%= surveyPage %>" />
<%
      break;
```

The getSurveyPage() method returns the value of the survey_page field, which we saw in Table 7-8 is Survey01. The .html extension is added and the result is stored in the String surveyPage, which is used in a scriptlet expression in the <jsp:forward> action. Survey01.html produces the page shown in Figure 7-13. Here is the code:

```
<html>
<body>
<font face = "Arial, Helvetica" size="+1">
<br>
<center>
```

**Figure 7-13**
A Typical Survey

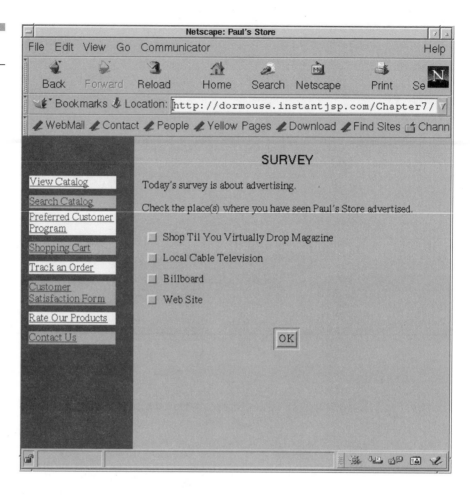

**Figure 7-13**
A Typical Survey

```
SURVEY
<br>
<br>
</center>
</font>
Today's survey is about advertising.
<br>
<br>
Check the place(s) where you have seen Paul's Store advertised.
<br>
<form method="post"

action="http://dormouse.instantjsp.com/Chapter7/RecordSurveyData.jsp">
<input type="hidden" name="surveyPage" value="Survey01">
<table>
<tr>
<td>
```

```
<input name="whereAdvertised" type="checkbox"
  value="Shop Til You Virtually Drop Magazine">
</td>
<td>
Shop Til You Virtually Drop Magazine
</td>
</tr>
<tr>
<td>
<input name="whereAdvertised" type="checkbox"
  value="Local Cable Television">
</td>
<td>
Local Cable Television
</td>
</tr>
<tr>
<td>
<input name="whereAdvertised" type="checkbox"
  value="Billboard">
</td>
<td>
Billboard
</td>
</tr>
<td>
<input name="whereAdvertised" type="checkbox"
  value="Web Site">
</td>
<td>
Web Site
</td>
</tr>
</table>
<br>
<center>
<input type="submit" name="submit" value="OK">
</center>
</form>
</font>
</body>
</html>
```

This survey uses only radio buttons but we could also have included checkboxes, selection lists, or text entry fields. After completing the survey, the customer clicks on the button labeled OK and the data from the HTML form are sent in a request to `RecordSurveyData.jsp`. Here is the code:

```
<%@ page import="javax.servlet.http.Cookie" %>
<%@include file="GetPrefCustId.jsp" %>
<jsp:useBean id="custBean" class="com.instantjsp.Customer"
  scope="session">
  <jsp:setProperty name="custBean" property="customerInfo"
    value="<%= getPrefCustID(request) %>" />
```

```
</jsp:useBean>
<jsp:useBean id="surveyBean" class="com.instantjsp.SurveyBean"
  scope="session" />
<%
  surveyBean.recordSurveyData(request);
%>
<jsp:setProperty name="custBean" property="doCurrentSurvey"
  value="false" />
<html>
<body text="#000000" bgcolor="#FFFFFF">
<center>
<font face = "Arial, Helvetica"><font size="+1">
<br>
Thank you for participating in our survey.
</font></font>
</center>
<font face = "Arial, Helvetica">
<br>
<p>
The input you provided has been recorded and will be reviewed. We
will use this input to help us to continue to serve you.
<p>
If we can be of assistance to you in any way, please contact
us by clicking on the appropriate menu item on the left.
</font>
</body>
</html>
```

RecordSurveydata.jsp invokes the recordSurveydata() method
of an instance of SurveyBean. Here is the code for that method:

```
public void recordSurveyData(HttpServletRequest request)
     throws Exception, SQLException {
  String surveyPage = request.getParameter("surveyPage");
  if (surveyPage == null) {
    throw new Exception("INTERNAL SURVEY ERROR");
  }
  Connection conn = connectionPool.getConnection();
  Statement us = conn.createStatement();
  for (Enumeration e =
      request.getParameterNames();e.hasMoreElements();) {
    String parmName= (String)e.nextElement();
    if ((parmName.equals("surveyPage")) ||
       (parmName.toLowerCase().equals("submit"))) {
      continue;
    }
    String[] pvals = request.getParameterValues(parmName);
    for (int i = 0; i < pvals.length; ++i) {
      us.executeUpdate(INSERT_SURVEY_DATA + LPAREN +
        QUOTE + surveyPage + QUOTE + COMMA +
        QUOTE + parmName + QUOTE + COMMA +
        QUOTE + pvals[i] + QUOTE + RPAREN);
    }
  }
  connectionPool.close(conn);
}
```

The method iterations across an Enumeration of all the parameter names in the request. For each parameter except the two named surveyPage (the name of the HTML form) and submit (the name of the OK button) a record is inserted into the survey_data table shown in Table 7-11. Some survey data are shown in Table 7-12. This survey data can be processed by batch jobs or by ad hoc queries like the two simple examples shown in Table 7-13. The first of these two queries is:

**TABLE 7-11**

Description of survey_data Database Table

```
Table   = survey_data
+----------------------+-------------------------------------------------+--------+
|       Field          |                    Type                         | Length |
+----------------------+-------------------------------------------------+--------+
| survey_page          | varchar()                                       |    256 |
| keyword              | varchar()                                       |     32 |
| value                | varchar()                                       |     64 |
+----------------------+-------------------------------------------------+--------+
```

**TABLE 7-12**

Some Records in the survey_data Database Table

```
Survey01    | whereAdvertised | Web Site
Survey01    | whereAdvertised | Shop Til You Virtually Drop Magazine
Survey01    | whereAdvertised | Local Cable Television
Survey01    | whereAdvertised | Web Site
Survey01    | whereAdvertised | Shop Til You Virtually Drop Magazine
Survey01    | whereAdvertised | Local Cable Television
Survey01    | whereAdvertised | Web Site
Survey01    | whereAdvertised | Shop Til You Virtually Drop Magazine
Survey01    | whereAdvertised | WebSite
Survey01    | whereAdvertised | Shop Til You Virtually Drop Magazine
Survey01    | whereAdvertised | Web site
Survey01    | whereAdvertised | Web site
Survey01    | whereAdvertised | Web site
Survey01    | whereAdvertised | Web site
Survey01    | whereAdvertised | Web site
```

**TABLE 7-13**

Ad Hoc Queries to Analyze Survey Results

```
==> select count (*) from survey_data where value='Billboard';

count
-----
    0
(1 row)

==> select count (*) from survey_data where value='Web Site';

count
-----
   14
(1 row)
```

```
SELECT COUNT(*) FROM survey_data WHERE value='Billboard';
```

The fact that this query returns a count of zero might indicate to us that our use of billboard advertising is totally ineffective.

The second query is:

```
SELECT COUNT(*) FROM survey_data WHERE value='Web Site';
```

This query returns a much higher count and this tells us that advertising on a Web site is very effective.

We do not want to continuously bother a customer who has already taken the survey; therefore, we set the field do_current_survey in the prefcust database table to false. We do so using the following code:

```
<jsp:setProperty name="custBean" property="doCurrentSurvey"
  value="false" />
```

The method `setDoCurrentSurvey()` that is invoked by this JSP action executes the SQL statement that updates the database, which now looks like Table 7-14. It also sets the `doCurrentSurvey` instance variable of `custBean` to false.

Finally, `RecordSurveyData.jsp` generates a thank you like the one shown in Figure 7-14.

If the customer selects "Please ask me again later," the switch variable has a value of 1 and the next page is `Welcome.jsp` as shown in Figure 7-15.

If the customer selects "I do not wish to participate in this survey," the switch variable has a value of 2. Once again, we see `Welcome.jsp` as the next page but the following code is also executed:

```
<jsp:setProperty name="custBean" property="doCurrentSurvey"
  value="false" />
```

**TABLE 7-14**

*Profile Updated to Prevent Multiple Requests for Survey Participation*

```
Field              | Value
-- RECORD 0 --
custno             | 1124101
joined             | 12-15-1999
sendemail          | t
emailaddr          | jjones@qwertasdf.com
oktosurvey         | t
do_current_survey  | f
```

**Figure 7-14**
Thanking Survey
Participant

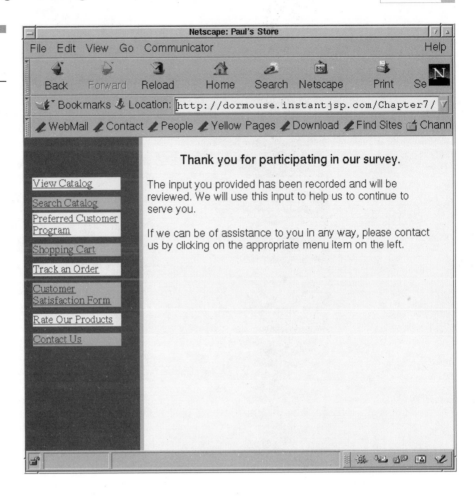

This code updates the prefcust database table so that it looks like Table 7-14.

The last option the user is given is that of opting out of all future surveys. In this case, the switch variable has a value of 3 and the following <jsp:action is executed:

```
<jsp:forward page="NoSurveyEverAgain.jsp" />
```

NoSurveyEverAgain.jsp sets the oktosurvey field in the prefcust database table to false as shown in Table 7-15 and generates the page shown in Figure 7-16.

**Figure 7-15**
Customer Opts to
Bypass Survey

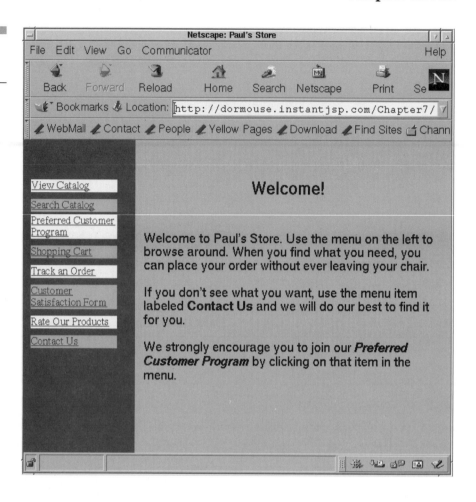

**TABLE 7-15**

Record in prefcust
Table Updated to
Bypass Future
Surveys

```
Field                |  Value
-- RECORD 0 --
custno               |  1124101
joined               |  12-15-1999
sendemail            |  t
emailaddr            |  jjones@qwertasdf.com
oktosurvey           |  f
do_current_survey    |  f
```

**Figure 7-16**
Customer Requests
No Further Surveys

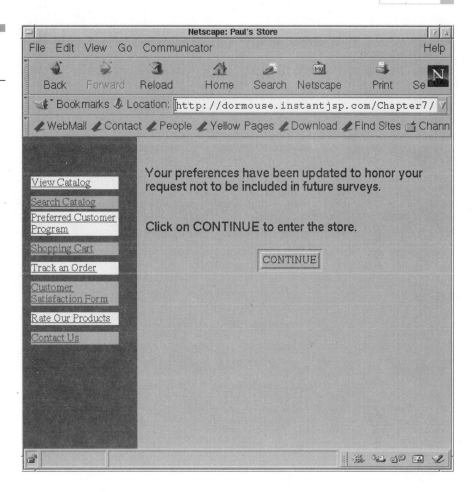

## Source Code for `CustomerInput`

As we saw earlier in the chapter, input from the customer feedback form, the customer satisfaction form, and the product rating form are all handled by the `CustomerInput` Bean. Here is the source code:

```
package com.instantjsp;

import java.sql.Connection;
import java.sql.ResultSet;
import java.sql.SQLException;
import java.sql.Statement;
```

```
import java.text.SimpleDateFormat;
import java.util.Date;

import javax.servlet.http.Cookie;
import javax.servlet.http.HttpServletRequest;

import javaservlets.jdbc.ConnectionPool;

public class CustomerInput {

  private ConnectionPool connectionPool;

  private static final String POOL_CFG_FILE =
    "javaservlets/jdbc/BusinessPool.cfg";

  private static final String VERIFY_ORDER_NUMBER =
    "SELECT COUNT(ordno) FROM orders WHERE ordno =";

  private static final String VERIFY_SKU_NUMBER =
    "SELECT COUNT(sku) FROM products WHERE sku =";

  private static final String INSERT_SATISFACTION_DATA =
    "INSERT INTO satisfaction VALUES";

  private static final String INSERT_PRODUCT_RATING_DATA =
    "INSERT INTO product_rating VALUES";

  private static final String INSERT_FEEDBACK_DATA =
    "INSERT INTO feedback VALUES";

  private static final String COMMA = ",";
  private static final String LPAREN = "(";
  private static final String QUOTE = "`";
  private static final String RPAREN = ")";

  public CustomerInput() throws Exception {
    connectionPool = new ConnectionPool();
    connectionPool.initialize(POOL_CFG_FILE);
  }

  public void recordSatisfaction(SatisfactionData sat)
      throws Exception, SQLException {
    Connection conn = connectionPool.getConnection();
    Statement us = conn.createStatement();
    ResultSet rs = us.executeQuery(VERIFY_ORDER_NUMBER +
      Integer.toString(sat.getOrderNumber())));
    if (DbUtils.getCount(rs) == 0) {
      connectionPool.close(conn);
      throw new Exception("No such order number on file");
    }
    String now = new SimpleDateFormat("MM-dd-yyyy").format(new Date());
    us.executeUpdate(INSERT_SATISFACTION_DATA +
      LPAREN + QUOTE + now + QUOTE + COMMA +
      Integer.toString(sat.getOrderNumber()) + COMMA +
      Integer.toString(sat.getEaseOfOrdering()) + COMMA +
      Integer.toString(sat.getEaseOfTracking()) + COMMA +
      Integer.toString(sat.getSpeedOfDelivery()) + COMMA +
      Integer.toString(sat.getConditionOfShipment()) + COMMA +
      Integer.toString(sat.getQualityOfProducts()) + RPAREN);
```

```
      connectionPool.close(conn);
    }

    public void recordProductRating(Product prod)
      throws Exception, SQLException {
    Connection conn = connectionPool.getConnection();
    Statement us = conn.createStatement();
    ResultSet rs = us.executeQuery(VERIFY_SKU_NUMBER +
      Integer.toString(prod.getSku()));
    if (DbUtils.getCount(rs) == 0) {
      connectionPool.close(conn);
      throw new Exception("No such product in catalog");
    }
    us.executeUpdate(INSERT_PRODUCT_RATING_DATA +
      LPAREN + Integer.toString(prod.getSku()) + COMMA +
      Integer.toString(prod.getQualityRating()) + COMMA +
      Integer.toString(prod.getPriceRating()) + COMMA +
      Integer.toString(prod.getSatisfactionRating()) + RPAREN);
    connectionPool.close(conn);
    }

    public void recordFeedback(FeedbackData fb)
        throws SQLException {
    Connection conn = connectionPool.getConnection();
    Statement us = conn.createStatement();
    us.executeUpdate(INSERT_FEEDBACK_DATA +
      LPAREN + QUOTE + fb.getEmailAddress() + QUOTE + COMMA +
      QUOTE + fb.getFeedback() + QUOTE + RPAREN);
    connectionPool.close(conn);
    }
}
```

# Source Code for the Survey Bean

Here is the code for the Survey Bean:

```
package com.instantjsp;

import java.sql.Connection;
import java.sql.ResultSet;
import java.sql.SQLException;
import java.sql.Statement;
import java.text.SimpleDateFormat;
import java.util.Date;
import java.util.Enumeration;

import javax.servlet.http.HttpServletRequest;

import javaservlets.jdbc.ConnectionPool;

public class SurveyBean {

  Date start;
  Date end;
  String surveyPage;
```

```
private ConnectionPool connectionPool;

private static final String POOL_CFG_FILE =
 "javaservlets/jdbc/BusinessPool.cfg";

private static final String SELECT_SURVEY_PAGE =
  "SELECT survey_page FROM survey WHERE ";

private static final String START_SURVEY =
  "start_survey";

private static final String END_SURVEY =
  "end_survey";

private static final String INSERT_SURVEY_DATA =
  "INSERT INTO  survey_data VALUES";

private static final String AND = " and ";
private static final String GTE = " >= ";
private static final String LTE = " <= ";
private static final String LPAREN = "(";
private static final String RPAREN = ")";
private static final String COMMA = ",";
private static final String PERCENT = "%";
private static final String QUOTE = "'";

public SurveyBean() throws Exception {
  connectionPool = new ConnectionPool();
  connectionPool.initialize(POOL_CFG_FILE);
}

public String getSurveyPage() throws SQLException {
  String now =
    new SimpleDateFormat("MM-dd-yyyy").format(new Date());
  Connection conn = connectionPool.getConnection();
  Statement qs = conn.createStatement();
  ResultSet rs = qs.executeQuery(SELECT_SURVEY_PAGE +
    QUOTE + now + QUOTE + GTE + START_SURVEY + AND +
    QUOTE + now + QUOTE +  LTE + END_SURVEY);
  String surveyPage = null;
  if (rs.next()) {
    surveyPage = rs.getString(1);
  }
  connectionPool.close(conn);
  return surveyPage;
}

public void recordSurveyData(HttpServletRequest request)
    throws Exception, SQLException {
  String surveyPage;
  if ((surveyPage = request.getParameter("surveyPage")) == null) {
    throw new Exception("INTERNAL SURVEY ERROR");
  }
  Connection conn = connectionPool.getConnection();
  Statement us = conn.createStatement();
  for (Enumeration e = request.getParameterNames();e.hasMoreElements-
    ();){
    String parmName= (String)e.nextElement();
    if ((parmName.equals("surveyPage")) ||
```

```
                    (parmName.toLowerCase().equals("submit"))) {
                continue;
            }
            String[] pvals = request.getParameterValues(parmName);
            for (int i = 0; i < pvals.length; ++i) {
                us.executeUpdate(INSERT_SURVEY_DATA + LPAREN +
                    QUOTE + surveyPage + QUOTE + COMMA +
                    QUOTE + parmName + QUOTE + COMMA +
                    QUOTE + pvals[i] + QUOTE + RPAREN);
            }
        }
        connectionPool.close(conn);
    }

    public void finalize() {
        connectionPool.destroy();
    }
}
```

# Rewards and Special Offers

- Preferred Customer Newsletter
- Frequent Shopper Program
- Targeted Special Offers

In the last chapter we saw how we can examine the profile each time a customer accesses our main page and send surveys to those who have agreed to participate. Such surveys benefit us directly and benefit the customer indirectly if we use the results of these surveys wisely. Although customers certainly appreciate indirect, long-term benefits, immediate benefits have a greater impact.

In this chapter, we see how to develop a newsletter we will use to notify the customer that they are eligible for rewards or special offers and to report newsworthy items. The newsletter is divided into two sections: the first contains personalized data that is different for each customer; the second contains general news.

# The Frequent Shopper Program

One incentive we might offer those customers who join our Preferred Customer Program is a "Frequent Shopper Program," in which they earn points proportional to the dollar amount of each order. We have already seen the online ordering process and we know that each order progresses through a series of steps toward complete fulfillment. We could quite easily include programs or scripts in our nightly batch processing that identify all completed orders and assign points if the customer is enrolled in the Preferred Customer Program. The points would be saved in the prefcust database that contains records like the one described in Table 8-1. A sample record is shown in Table 8-2.

**TABLE 8-1**

The prefcust Database Table Layout

```
Table   = prefcust
+----------------------+------------------------+--------+
|        Field         |          Type          | Length |
+----------------------+------------------------+--------+
|  custno              |  int4 not null         |   4    |
|  joined              |  date                  |   4    |
|  lastordered         |  date                  |   4    |
|  lastordno           |  bool                  |   4    |
|  sendemail           |  date                  |   1    |
|  emailaddr           |  varchar()             |  128   |
|  oktosurvey          |  bool                  |   1    |
|  do_current_survey   |  bool                  |   1    |
|  freq_shop_pts       |  int4                  |   4    |
+----------------------+------------------------+--------+
Index:    prefcust_pkey
```

**TABLE 8-2**

Contents of pref-
cust Showing
Frequent Shopper
Points

```
Field                    | Value
-- RECORD 6 --
custno                   | 1124101
joined                   | 12-15-1999
sendemail                | t
emailaddr                | jjones@qwertasdf.com
oktosurvey               | f
do_current_survey        | f
freq_shop_pts            | 296
```

Each time a customer who has accumulated points accesses our main page, we remind them of the number of points they have accumulated. Let's see how this is done.

In Chapter 7, we saw that index.html specified Intro.jsp as the source for the main display frame. To accomplish our goals for this chapter, we will modify index.html and replace Intro.jsp with CheckIf-PreferredCustomer.jsp, which looks like this:

```
<%@ page import="javax.servlet.http.Cookie" %>
<%@include file="GetPrefCustId.jsp" %>
<jsp:useBean id="custBean" class="com.instantjsp.Customer"
  scope="session">
  <jsp:setProperty name="custBean" property="customerInfo"
    value="<%= getPrefCustID(request) %>" />
</jsp:useBean>
<jsp:useBean id="sb" class="com.instantjsp.SurveyBean"
  scope="request" />
<%
    if (custBean.isPreferredCustomer()) {
      if ((custBean.isSurveyCandidate()) &&
        (sb.getSurveyPage() != null)) {
%>
        <jsp:forward page="SurveyOptions.jsp" />
<%
      }
      else {
%>
        <jsp:forward page="CheckNews.jsp" />
<%
      }
    }
%>
<jsp:forward page="Welcome.jsp" />
```

As you can see by examining the first scriptlet, we first check to see if the customer who accessed this page is a member of the Preferred Customer Program. If he or she is not, we chain immediately to

Welcome.jsp. A preferred customer is presented with a survey if the appropriate criteria are met. For all preferred customers, whether they participate in a survey or not, the next page that is executed is CheckNews.jsp. Here is the code:

```
<%@ page import="javax.servlet.http.Cookie" %>
<%@ include file="GetPrefCustId.jsp" %>
<jsp:useBean id="custBean" class="com.instantjsp.Customer"
  scope="session" >
  <jsp:setProperty name="custBean" property="customerInfo"
    value="<%= getPrefCustID(request)%>" />
</jsp:useBean>
<jsp:useBean id="specials" class="com.instantjsp.SpecialOffers"
  scope="session" />
<%
  String custId = custBean.getCustomerID();
  String target = "Welcome.jsp";
  if ((specials.getFrequentShopperPoints(custId) > 0) ||
      (specials.getPromoFile(custId) != null)) {
    target = "PreferredCustomerNotices.jsp";
  }
%>
<jsp:forward page="<%= target %>" />
```

CheckNews.jsp contains an instance the SpecialOffers Bean. The full source for SpecialOffers is shown at the end of the chapter. For now, we are interested in the getFrequentShopperPoints() method. Here is the code:

```
public int getFrequentShopperPoints(String custId)
    throws SQLException {
  Connection conn = connectionPool.getConnection();
  Statement qs = conn.createStatement();
  ResultSet rs = qs.executeQuery(SELECT_FREQUENT_SHOPPER_PTS +
    custId);
  int points = 0;
  if (rs.next()) {
    points = rs.getInt(1);
  }
  connectionPool.close(conn);
  return points;
}
```

This method returns the number of points the customer has accumulated, which it determines by executing the following SQL query:

```
SELECT freq_shop_pts FROM prefcust WHERE custno=custId;
```

If the value returned by the method is greater than zero, a <jsp:forward> action is executed to chain to PreferredCustomerNotices.jsp, which contains the following code:

```
<%
   int points  = specials.getFrequentShopperPoints(custId);
   if (points > 0) {
%>
<br>
<br>
You have accumulated
<%= points %>
frequent shopper points.
<%
   }
%>
```

This code reports the customer's accumulated frequent shopper points as the first item in the Preferred Customer Newsletter as shown in Figure 8-1.

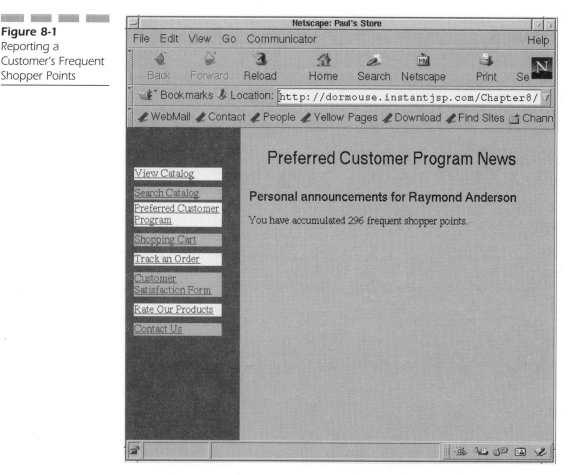

**Figure 8-1**
Reporting a
Customer's Frequent
Shopper Points

# Special Offers

One of the reasons we store the cookie associated with the Preferred Customer Program is to build a profile of the customer over time. Each time we are holding a sale, we can schedule a batch program that analyzes the profiles and selects customers who are most likely to be interested in the items that are on sale. The customer ID and the name of the page describing the sale or special offer are stored in a database that contains records like the one described in Table 8-3. A sample record is shown in Table 8-4.

We have already seen `CheckNews.jsp` and how it chains to `PreferredCustomerNotices.jsp` to report accumulated frequent shopper points. Let's reexamine the code we saw earlier:

```
if ((specials.getFrequentShopperPoints(custId) > 0) ||
    (specials.getPromoFile(custId) != null)) {
  target = "PreferredCustomerNotices.jsp";
}
```

The code invokes the `getPromoFile()` method of `SpecialOffers`. Here is the code:

```
public String getPromoFile(String custId)
    throws SQLException {
```

**TABLE 8-3**

The special_offers Database Table

```
Table    = special offers
+----------------+-----------------------------------+--------+
|     Field      |              Type                 | Length |
+----------------+-----------------------------------+--------+
| custno         | int4 not null                     |      4 |
| promo_file     | varchar()                         |    256 |
+----------------+-----------------------------------+--------+
Index:    special_offers_pkey
```

**TABLE 8-4**

Contents of special_offers Database

```
Field       | Value
-- Record  0 --
custno      | 1124101
promo_file  | Diskettes
```

```
Connection conn = connectionPool.getConnection();
Statement qs = conn.createStatement();
ResultSet rs = qs.executeQuery(SELECT_PROMO_FILE +
  custId);
String promo_file = null;
if (rs.next()) {
  promo_file = rs.getString(1);
}
connectionPool.close(conn);
return promo_file;
}
```

The method returns the name of an HTML page containing details of the special offer (minus the `.html` extension). It retrieves the name using the following SQL query:

```
SELECT promo_file FROM special_offers WHERE custno = custId;
```

If the name returned is not null, `CheckNews.jsp` executes a `<jsp:forward>` action specifying `PreferredCustomerNotices.jsp` as the target page. `PreferredCustomerNotices.jsp` contains the following code:

```
<%
  String pf = specials.getPromoFile(custId);
  if (pf != null) {
  String link = "<a href=\"http://dormouse.instantjsp.com" +
    "/Chapter8/" + pf + ".html\">";
%>
```

This code emits HTML that results in the hyperlink we see in Figure 8-2. When the customer clicks on the link, the page shown in Figure 8-3 is displayed.

# News of General Interest

The second section of our newsletter contains news of general interest. This news is stored in a file called `TodaysNews.html`, which you can see in the following directive in `PreferredCustomerNotices.jsp`. This file is included last since it can potentially be large enough to require scrolling, and we want the customer's personalized information to be immediately visible. Figure 8-4 shows a complete newsletter.

```
<%@ include file="TodaysNews.html" %>
```

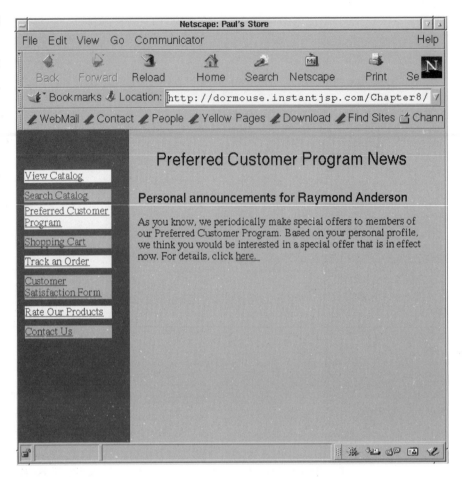

> **NOTE:** JSP containers detect changes in .jsp files and recompile
> when changes are detected; however, no guarantee is made that changes
> made to included files will be detected. To make certain that the latest
> copy of TodaysNews.html is shown to the customer, whenever you
> change it, you should make sure that the date/time stamp of the includ-
> ing file (PreferredCustomerNotices.jsp) is updated.

# The `SpecialOffers` Bean

```
package com.instantjsp;

import java.sql.Connection;
```

**Figure 8-3**
Details of the Special
Offer

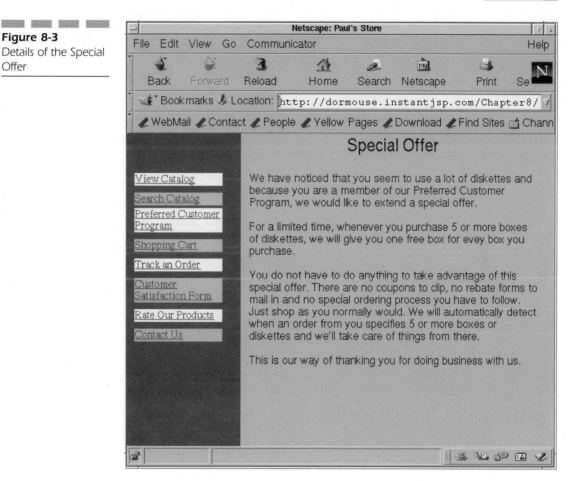

```
import java.sql.ResultSet;
import java.sql.SQLException;
import java.sql.Statement;

import javaservlets.jdbc.ConnectionPool;

public class SpecialOffers {

  private ConnectionPool connectionPool;

  private static final String POOL_CFG_FILE =
    "javaservlets/jdbc/BusinessPool.cfg";

  private static final String SELECT_PROMO_FILE =
    "SELECT promo_file FROM special_offers WHERE custno=";

  private static final String SELECT_FREQUENT_SHOPPER_PTS =
    "SELECT freq_shop_pts FROM prefcust WHERE custno=";
```

**Figure 8-4**
A Complete
Newsletter Showing
Today's News

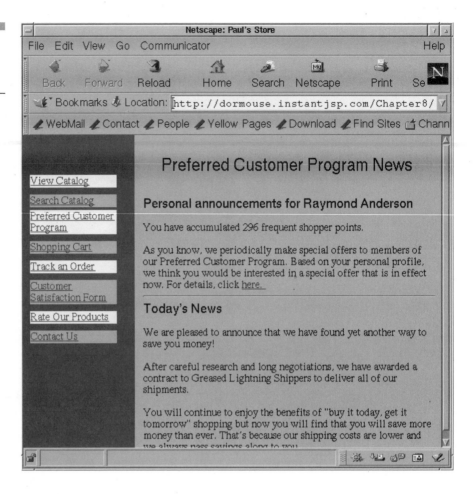

```
private static final String AND = " and ";
private static final String GTE = " >= ";
private static final String LTE = " <= ";
private static final String LPAREN = "(";
private static final String RPAREN = ")";
private static final String COMMA = ",";
private static final String PERCENT = "%";
private static final String QUOTE = "'";

public SpecialOffers() throws Exception {
  connectionPool = new ConnectionPool();
  connectionPool.initialize(POOL_CFG_FILE);
}

public String getPromoFile(String custId)
    throws SQLException {
  Connection conn = connectionPool.getConnection();
  Statement qs = conn.createStatement();
```

```
        ResultSet rs = qs.executeQuery(SELECT_PROMO_FILE +
          custId);
        String promo_file = null;
        if (rs.next()) {
          promo_file = rs.getString(1);
        }
        connectionPool.close(conn);
        return promo_file;
    }

    public int getFrequentShopperPoints(String custId)
        throws SQLException {
      Connection conn = connectionPool.getConnection();
      Statement qs = conn.createStatement();
      ResultSet rs = qs.executeQuery(SELECT_FREQUENT_SHOPPER_PTS +
        custId);
      int points = 0;
      if (rs.next()) {
        points = rs.getInt(1);
      }
      connectionPool.close(conn);
      return points;
    }
}
```

# PreferredCustomerNotices.jsp

```
<jsp:useBean id="custBean" class="com.instantjsp.Customer"
  scope="session" />
<jsp:useBean id="specials" class="com.instantjsp.SpecialOffers"
  scope="session" />
<html>
<body>
<% String custId = custBean.getCustomerID(); %>
<center>
<font face = "Arial, Helvetica" size="+2">
<br>
Preferred Customer Program News
</font>
</center>
<br>
<br>
<font face = "Arial, Helvetica" size="+1">
Personal announcements for
<jsp:getProperty name="custBean" property="firstName" />
<jsp:getProperty name="custBean" property="lastName" />
</font>
<%
  int points  = specials.getFrequentShopperPoints(custId);
  if (points > 0) {
%>
<br>
<br>
You have accumulated
<%= points %>
frequent shopper points.
```

```
<%
  }
%>
<br>
<br>
<%
  String pf = specials.getPromoFile(custId);
  if (pf != null) {
  String link = "<a href=\"http://dormouse.instantjsp.com" +
    "/Chapter8/" + pf + ".html\">";
%>
<p>
As you know, we periodically make special offers to members of
our Preferred Customer Program. Based on your personal profile,
we think you would be interested in a special offer that is in
effect now. For details, click
<%= link %>
here.
</a>
<%
  }
%>
<%@ include file="TodaysNews.html" %>
</body>
</html>
```

# Some Fun JSPs

- Fortune Cookie
- A Voting Mechanism
- Electronic Postcards
- Chat Room

The examples we have seen in the preceding chapters were from the world of business. JavaServer Pages can also be used to construct applications that are meant for fun. In this chapter, we examine several such applications. You could include these in your personal Web site or use them to encourage return visits to your business site knowing that even visitors who come to play games are exposed to advertisements for your products and services.

# An Old Favorite—the Fortune Cookie

Implementation of a fortune cookie server is so simple it is almost trivial. All you need is an image to represent an unopened fortune cookie, another image to represent a cookie that has been opened, and a database from which you can retrieve random fortunes.

Table 9-1 shows what the database looks like, and Table 9-2 shows several of the fortunes stored in the database.

The initial page is shown in Figure 9-1. It is generated from `Fortune.html`, which looks like this:

**TABLE 9-1**

Tabye Layout for Fortunes

```
Table     = fortunes
+----------------------+----------------------------+----------+
|        Field         |            Type            |  Length  |
+----------------------+----------------------------+----------+
|   message            |    varchar()               |    160   |
+----------------------+----------------------------+----------+
```

**TABLE 9-2**

Partial Contents of Fortunes Table

```
message
-----------------------------------------------------------------------
A friend is a present you give yourself.
A happy event will take place shortly in your home.
A heavy burden is lifted with a phone message or letter.
A person is never too old to learn.
A secret admirer will soon send you a sign of affection.
```

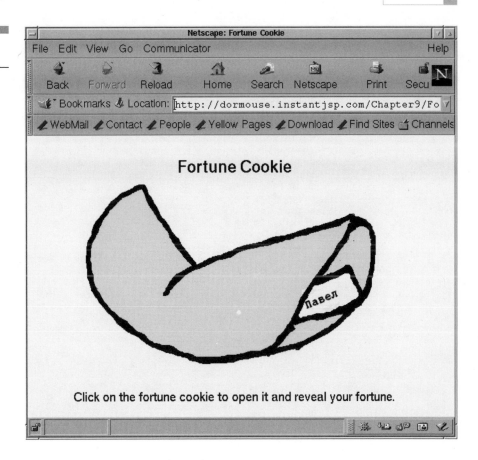

**Figure 9-1**
Fortune Cookie

```
<html>
<head>
<title>Fortune Cookie</title>
</head>
<body bgcolor="#ffffff" vlink="#ffffff" alink="#ffffff">
<center>
<font face = "Arial, Helvetica"><font size="+2">
<br>
<b>Fortune Cookie</b>
</font></font>
<br>
<a href="http://dormouse.instantjsp.com/Chapter9/Fortune.jsp">
<image src="http://dormouse.instantjsp.com/images/Fortune.gif">
</a>
<font face = "Arial, Helvetica"><font size="+1">
<br>
<br>
Click on the fortune cookie to open it and reveal your fortune.
</font></font>
</center>
</body>
</html>
```

As you can see, the image contained in `Fortune.gif` is a hyperlink to `Fortune.jsp`. Here is the code:

```
<%@ page errorPage="/common/Exception.jsp" %>
<jsp:useBean id="fcBean" class="com.instantjsp.FortuneCookie"
    scope="session" />
<html>
<head>
<title>Your Fortune</title>
</head>
<body bgcolor="#ffffff">
<center>
<font face = "Arial, Helvetica"><font size="+2">
<br>
<b>Your Fortune</b>
</font></font>
<br>
<image
src="http://dormouse.instantjsp.com/images/FortuneSplit.gif">
<font face = "Arial, Helvetica"><font size="+1">
<br>
<table border=2 cols=1 bgcolor="#ffffcc" width="80%" >
<tr>
<td align="center">
<jsp:getProperty name="fcBean" property="fortune" />
</td>
</tr>
</table>
<br>
<br>
</font></font>
Click to get
<a href="http://dormouse.instantjsp.com/Chapter9/Fortune.html">
another fortune</a>.
</center>
</form>
</body>
</html>
```

The actual task of generating the fortune is performed by the FortuneCookie Bean named in the `<jsp:useBean>` action. Since `scope=session` is specified, a new instance of this Bean is created each time the user accesses the page from a new session. The Bean contains a single getter, which is invoked by the `<jsp:getProperty>` action. The String returned by the `getFortune()` method is displayed beneath the image representing the opened cookie, as shown in Figure 9-2. Here is the code for the FortuneCookie Bean:

```
package com.instantjsp;
import java.sql.Connection;
import java.sql.ResultSet;
import java.sql.SQLException;
import java.sql.Statement;
```

Figure 9-2
An Open Fortune
Cookie

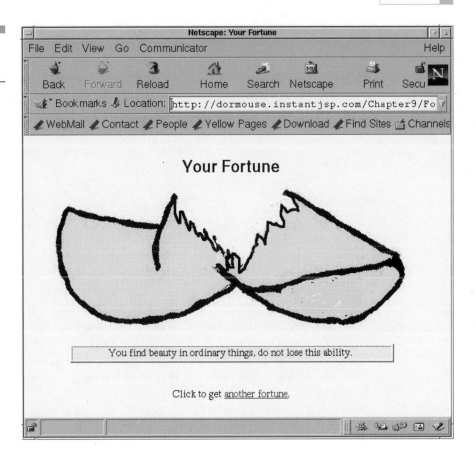

```java
import java.util.Random;
import java.util.Vector;

import javaservlets.jdbc.ConnectionPool;

public class FortuneCookie {

    private ConnectionPool connectionPool;

    private Random rand;

    private Vector fortunes;

    private int fortuneCount;

    private static final String POOL_CFG_FILE =
        "javaservlets/jdbc/FortunePool.cfg";

    private static final String SELECT_FORTUNES =
        "SELECT message FROM fortunes";
```

```
public FortuneCookie() throws Exception {
  connectionPool = new ConnectionPool();
  connectionPool.initialize(POOL_CFG_FILE);
  rand = new Random();
  Connection conn = connectionPool.getConnection();
  Statement us = conn.createStatement();
  ResultSet rs = us.executeQuery(SELECT_FORTUNES);
  fortunes = new Vector();
  while (rs.next()) {
    String f = rs.getString(1);
    fortunes.addElement(f);
  }
  fortuneCount = fortunes.size();
  connectionPool.close(conn);
}
public String getFortune() {
  int fn = Math.abs(rand.nextInt()) % fortuneCount;
  return (String)fortunes.elementAt(fn);
}
}
```

The only connection to the database is made in the constructor. The SQL query SELECT message FROM fortunes is used to retrieve all of the records from the database. They are then stored in the Vector fortunes. The reason for doing this is that the fortune cookie application is of such a nature that we really don't care whether records are added to or deleted from the database during a user session. The amount of data in the database is also small.

The getFortune() method generates a random number using the instance of Random that was created in the constructor. It converts negative results to positive using the abs() class method of Math and then uses the modulo operator to produce a number between 0 and $n$ where $n$ is 1 less than the number of messages contained in the Vector fortunes. Finally, the method retrieves the String from the $n$th element of the Vector and returns it.

# Voting for Your Favorite Song

We now examine some JSP pages that allow you to rate a list of songs. In our case, we are doing it simply for fun; however, a similar technique might be used by a radio or TV station to determine the type of music the listeners or viewers prefer. It could also be used to provide public input to an award ceremony.

As in the fortune cookie application, the data we are dealing with are simple in nature and the volume is small. Table 9-3 shows the database

**TABLE 9-3**

Layout of Songlist
Table

```
Table      = songlist
+------------------------+----------------------------+---------+
|         Field          |           Type             | Length  |
+------------------------+----------------------------+---------+
|  id                    |  int4 not null             |    4    |
|  title                 |  varchar()                 |   32    |
+------------------------+----------------------------+---------+
Index:     songlist_pkey
```

**TABLE 9-4**

Contents of
Songlist

```
id|title
--+------------------------------
 1|Rainy Day Women # 12 & 35
 2|Blowin' in the Wind
 3|The Times They Are A-Changin'
 4|It Ain't Me Babe
 5|Subterranean Homesick Blues
 6|Mr. Tambourine Man
 7|Like A Rolling Stone
 8|I Want You
 9|Positively 4th Street
10|Just Like a Woman
(10 rows)
```

**TABLE 9-5**

Table Used to Hold
Votes

```
Table      = currentvotes
+------------------------+----------------------------+---------+
|         Field          |           Type             | Length  |
+------------------------+----------------------------+---------+
|  id                    |  int4                      |    4    |
|  rating                |  int4                      |    4    |
+------------------------+----------------------------+---------+
```

layout and Table 9-4 shows the contents of the database. Table 9-5 shows the fields of the table used to hold the votes.

The first page you see is the one shown in Figure 9-3. This page is generated by VotingBooth.html, which looks like this:

```html
<html>
<head>
<title>Voting Booth</title>
</head>
<body>
<center>
```

**Figure 9-3**
Voting Options

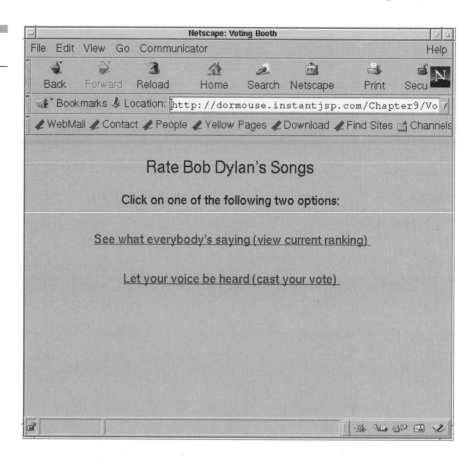

```
<font face = "Arial, Helvetica"><font size="+2">
<br>
Rate Bob Dylan's Songs
<br>
<br>
</font></font>
<font face = "Arial, Helvetica"><font size="+1">
Click on one of the following two options:
<br>
<br>
<br>
<a href="http://dormouse.instantjsp.com/Chapter9/ViewRanking.jsp">
See what everybody's saying (view current ranking)
</a>
<br>
<br>
<br>
<a href="http://dormouse.instantjsp.com/Chapter9/VotingBooth.jsp">
Let your voice be heard (cast your vote)
```

```
</a>
</font></font>
</center>
</body>
</html>
```

You are presented with two choices: to view the current order in which other voters have ranked 10 of Bob Dylan's songs or to cast a vote. Let's first look at what happens when you choose to see the current standings.

The "view current ranking" choice is a hyperlink to `ViewRanking.jsp`, which looks like this:

```
<%@ page errorPage="/common/Exception.jsp" %>
<jsp:useBean id="voteBean" class="com.instantjsp.VoteBean"
    scope="session" />
<%
  String[] titles = voteBean.getTitleList();
  int[][] rankings = voteBean.getRankings();
%>
<html>
<head>
<title>Current Ranking</title>
</head>
<body>
<br>
<center>
<font face = "Arial, Helvetica"><font size="+1">
How You Rated Dylan's Songs
<br>
<br>
</font></font>
<table border width="80%">
<%
  for (int i = 0; i < 10; ++i) {
%>
<tr >
<td >
<%= titles[rankings[i][0]] %>
</td>
<td>
<%= rankings[i][1] %>
</td>
</tr>
<%
  }
%>
</table>
<br>
<br>
<a href="http://dormouse.instantjsp.com/Chapter9/VotingBooth.html">
Back to main page
</a>
</center>
</body>
</html>
```

The JSP page contains a scriptlet that invokes the getTitleList() method of VoteBean; this method does exactly what its name implies. The scriptlet then invokes the getRankings() method; this method returns a two-dimensional array of integers containing the song number and the number of votes received by that song. The title and ranking of each song are displayed in a table as shown in Figure 9-4. Here is the code for VoteBean.java:

```
package com.instantjsp;

import java.sql.Connection;
import java.sql.ResultSet;
import java.sql.SQLException;
import java.sql.Statement;
import javaservlets.jdbc.ConnectionPool;

public class VoteBean {
```

**Figure 9-4**
Votes Received by
Each Song

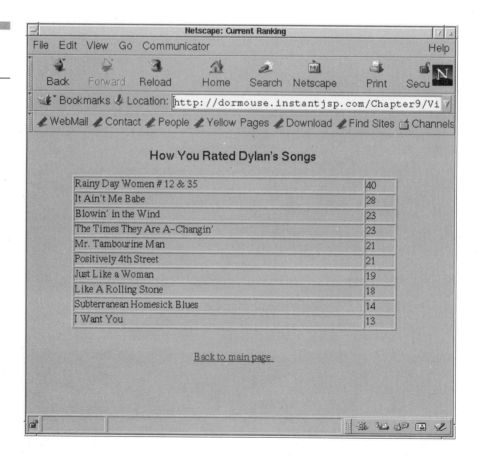

```
    String[] titles;

    private ConnectionPool connectionPool;

    private static final String POOL_CFG_FILE =
     "javaservlets/jdbc/VotePool.cfg";

    private static final String SELECT_TITLES =
       "SELECT title FROM songlist ORDER BY id";

    private static final String INSERT_VOTE =
       "INSERT INTO currentvotes " +
       "(id,rating) VALUES ";

    private static final String GET_RATINGS =
       "SELECT id,SUM(rating) AS x FROM currentvotes " +
       "GROUP BY id ORDER BY x DESC";

    private static final String AND = " and ";
    private static final String LPAREN = "(";
    private static final String RPAREN = ")";
    private static final String COMMA = ",";
    private static final String PERCENT = "%";
    private static final String QUOTE = "'";

public VoteBean() throws Exception {
   connectionPool = new ConnectionPool();
   connectionPool.initialize(POOL_CFG_FILE);
   Connection conn = connectionPool.getConnection();
   Statement qs = conn.createStatement();
   ResultSet rs = qs.executeQuery(SELECT_TITLES);
   titles = new String[10];
   int i = 0;
   while (rs.next()) {
      titles[i++] = rs.getString(1);
   }
   connectionPool.close(conn);
}
public String[] getTitleList() throws SQLException {
   return titles;
}

public void castVotes(int[] votes) throws SQLException {
   Connection conn = connectionPool.getConnection();
   for (int i = 0; i < 10; ++i) {
      Statement us = conn.createStatement();
      us.executeUpdate(INSERT_VOTE + LPAREN +
         Integer.toString(i) + COMMA +
         Integer.toString(11 - votes[i]) + RPAREN);
   }
   connectionPool.close(conn);
}

public int[][] getRankings() throws SQLException {
   int [][] r = new int[10][2];
   Connection conn = connectionPool.getConnection();
   Statement qs = conn.createStatement();
   ResultSet rs = qs.executeQuery(GET_RATINGS);
   for (int i = 0; i < 10; ++i) {
```

```
            rs.next();
            r[i][0] = rs.getInt(1);
            r[i][1] = rs.getInt(2);
        }
        connectionPool.close(conn);
        return r;
    }
}
```

The constructor retrieves the song titles from the database. We can do this because our simple design dictates that the contents of the songlist table will not change.

Now let's look at what happens when you choose to cast a vote. Looking back at VotingBooth.html, we see that the "cast your vote" choice is a hyperlink to VotingBooth.jsp, which looks like this:

```
<%@ page errorPage="/common/Exception.jsp" %>
<jsp:useBean id="voteBean" class="com.instantjsp.VoteBean"
    scope="session" />
<%
    String[] titles = voteBean.getTitleList();
%>
<html>
<head>
<title>Voting Booth</title>
</head>
<body>
<center>
<font size="+1">
<br>
Rate the songs from 1 to 10 (1=highest, 10=lowest) then click on
 <b>VOTE</b>
<form method="post" name="ballot"
  action="http://dormouse.instantjsp.com/Chapter9/CastBallot.jsp">
<table noborder width="80%" nosave >
<%
  int j = 0;
  for (int i = 0; i < 5; ++i) {
%>
<tr nosave>
<td width="5%">
<input type=text name="rank" size="2">
</td>
<td>
<%= titles[j++] %>
</td>
<td width="5%">
<input type=text name="rank" size="2">
</td>
<td>
<%= titles[j++] %>
</td>
</tr>
<%
  }
```

```
%>
</table>
<br>
</font>
<input type="submit" name="submit" value="VOTE">
</center>
</form>
</body>
</html>
```

The page contains a scriptlet that invokes the `getTitleList()` method, which we have already seen. The song titles are displayed with a text field next to each, as shown in Figure 9-5.

After you type a number from 1 to 10 next to each song title and click on VOTE, the contents of the HTML form are sent as a POST request to `CastBallot.jsp`. Here is the code:

**Figure 9-5**
Preparing to Cast
Your Ballot

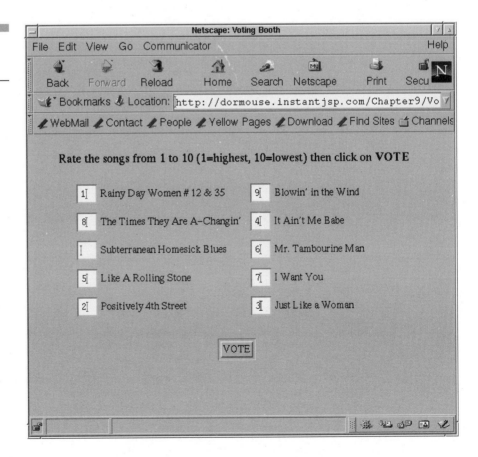

```
<%@ page errorPage="/common/UserError.jsp" %>
<jsp:useBean id="voteBean" class="com.instantjsp.VoteBean"
    scope="session" />
<jsp:useBean id="rankings" class="com.instantjsp.Rankings"
    scope="session" />
<jsp:setProperty name="rankings" property="rank" />
<html>
<head>
<title>Cast Ballot Booth</title>
</head>
<body>
<br>
<%
  if (rankings.processRanking()) {
%>
<jsp:forward page="GoodBallot.jsp" />
<%
  }
  else {
%>
<jsp:forward page="InvalidBallot.html" />
<%
  }
%>
</body>
</html>
```

This JSP page first uses the `<jsp:setProperty>` action to save the ratings you typed into `VotingBooth.jsp` in an instance of Rankings. Here is the code for the Rankings Bean:

```
package com.instantjsp;

public class Rankings {

  private static final int MAX_ITEMS = 10;

  private String[] rank = null;
  private int[] rankings = new int[MAX_ITEMS];

  public Rankings() {
  }

  public String[] getRank() {
    return rank;
  }

  public void setRank(String[] aRanking) {
    rank = aRanking;
  }

  public boolean processRanking() throws Exception {
    boolean ok = true;
    boolean rankNumber[] = new boolean[MAX_ITEMS];
    int i;

    for (i = 0; i < MAX_ITEMS; ++i) {
```

```
          rankNumber[i] = false;
        }

        for (i = 0; i < MAX_ITEMS; ++i) {
          try {
            rankings[i] = Integer.parseInt(rank[i]);
          }
          catch (NumberFormatException e) {
            throw new Exception("One or more fields is blank or
             non-numeric");
          }
          if ((rankings[i] < 1) || (rankings[i] > 10)) {
            ok = false;
            break;
          }
          else {
            rankNumber[rankings[i] - 1] = true;
          }
        }

        for (i = 0; i < MAX_ITEMS; ++i) {
          if (!rankNumber[i]) {
            ok = false;
          }
        }

        return ok;
      }

      public int[] getRankings() {
        return rankings;
      }
    }
  }
```

After the ratings have been saved, VotingBooth.jsp invokes the processRanking() method of the instance of Rankings. This method checks that all of the numbers entered are numeric and have values between 1 and 10. Any NumberFormatException resulting from nonnumeric data is caught. The catch block creates an instance of Exception containing a message appropriate to our application and throws it. This Exception is caught by the errorPage specified in the page directive (i.e., /common/UserError.jsp). Here is the code for UserError.jsp:

```
<%@ page isErrorPage="true" %>
<html>
<head>
<title>USER ERROR</title>
</head>
<body bgcolor="#ffffff">
<center>
<br>
<br>
<h1>A CORRECTABLE ERROR HAS OCCURRED!!!</h1>
<br>
<b>
```

```
<h2>
<%= exception.getMessage() %>
</h2>
<br>
Correct the error and try again
</b>
</center>
</body>
</html>
```

Figure 9-6 shows the page generated by `UserError.jsp`. The reason is that we left a field blank. On seeing this error, you would use the browser's BACK button to return to the ballot page (Figure 9-5) and correct the bad data.

If no Exception is thrown, `CastBallot.jsp` executes one of two `<jsp:forward>` actions, depending on whether `processRanking()` returns true or false. If the method returns false, the `<jsp:forward>` action specifies `InvalidBallot.html`, which looks like this:

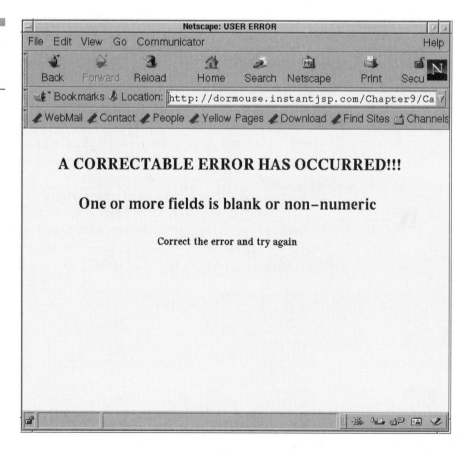

**Figure 9-6**
Error Resulting from Ballot with Missing Data

```
<html>
<head>
<title>good</title>
</head>
<body>
<center>
<font face = "Arial, Helvetica"><font size="+2">
Improper Ballot!
</center>
<br>
<br>
</font></font>
<font face = "Arial, Helvetica"><font size="+1">
You must assign each song a rating of 1 to 10 with 1 being the
 highest and 10 the lowest.
<p>
You are not allowed to assign two songs the same rating.
</font></font>
<br>
<br>
<center>
<a href="http://dormouse.instantjsp.com/Chapter9/VotingBooth.html">
Go back to voting booth
</a>
</center>
</body>
</html>
```

InvalidBallot.html generates a page like that shown in Figure 9-7. In this case, you see the page because you assigned two songs a rating of 9. The page does nothing more than explain the rules and provide a hyperlink to get back to Figure 9-5. Unfortunately, this clears everything you had typed. You might want to consider changing this as an exercise.

If the processRanking() method returns true, the <jsp:forward> action specifies GoodBallot.jsp, which looks like this:

```
<%@ page errorPage="/common/Exception.jsp" %>
<jsp:useBean id="voteBean" class="com.instantjsp.VoteBean"
    scope="session" />
<jsp:useBean id="rankings" class="com.instantjsp.Rankings"
  scope="session" />
<%
  voteBean.castVotes(rankings.getRankings());
%>
<html>
<head>
<title>Ballot Processed</title>
</head>
<body>
<center>
<font face = "Arial, Helvetica"><font size="+2">
Your vote has been recorded
<br>
<br>
<br>
</font></font>
```

**Figure 9-7**

Attempting to Assign
Same Rating to Two
Songs

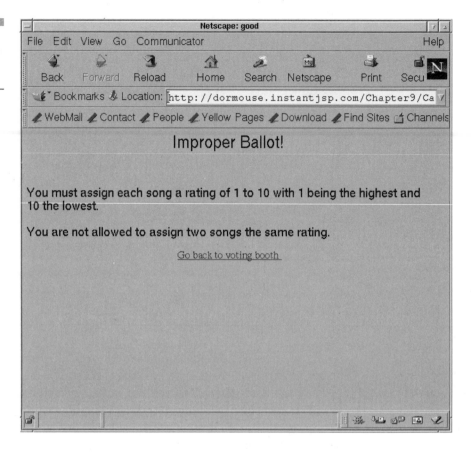

**Figure 9-7**

Attempting to Assign
Same Rating to Two
Songs

```
<font face = "Arial, Helvetica"><font size="+1">
Click on one of the links below
<br>
<br>
</font></font>
<a href="http://dormouse.instantjsp.com/Chapter9/ViewRanking.jsp">
View current rankings.
</a>
           
<a href="http://dormouse.instantjsp.com/Chapter9/VotingBooth.html">
Return to main page.
</a>
</center>
<br>
<br>
</body>
</html>
```

GoodBallot.jsp first retrieves the rankings stored in the
Ranking Bean. The array containing these rankings is passed as an

argument to the castVotes() method of VoteBean. Since 1 is used as the highest rating and 10 as the lowest, the castVotes() method transforms this by recomputing each value as $v = 11 - v$. It then uses the SQL statement

```
"INSERT INTO currentvotes (id,rating) VALUES (i, r)"
```

where $i$ is the song number and $r$ is the computed rating to enter a vote for each song into the currentvotes table.

GoodBallot.jsp then generates the page shown in Figure 9-8. This page provides positive feedback and provides links to view the ratings or return to the main page. Figure 9-9 shows the page you would see if "View Current Rankings" were chosen. You can see that the ratings of each song as first displayed in Figure 9-4 have changed to reflect your vote.

**Figure 9-8**
A Successful Ballot

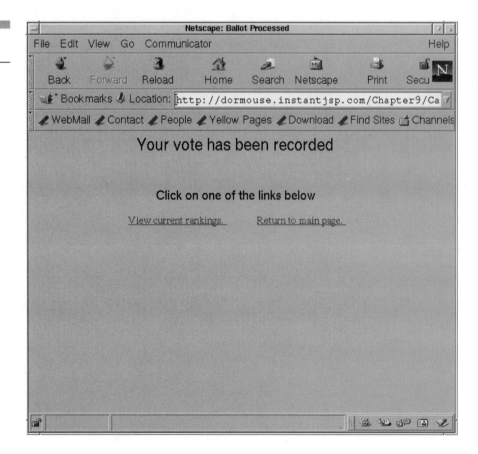

**Figure 9-9**
Ratings Reflecting
Your Vote

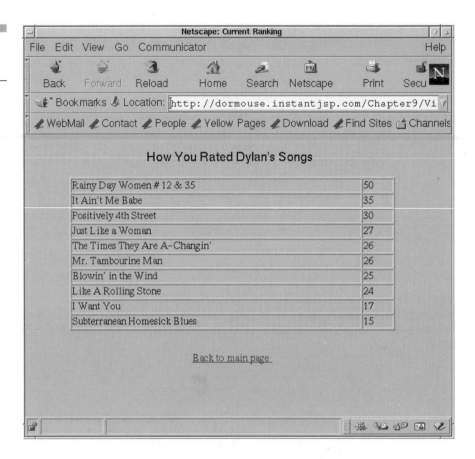

In our example, we are only using `currentvotes`, which could potentially become quite large. As an exercise, you might consider writing a daemon that periodically sums all of the votes in `currentvotes` and stores the summary in `archivedvotes`. Of course, you would also have to modify the `getRankings()` method of VoteBean as well.

## Sending Electronic Postcards

You have undoubtedly visited or used sites that allow you to send a greeting card or postcard to a friend. We now show how you can use JavaServer Pages to create such a site. We start with the database we will need. The layout is shown in Table 9-6.

The first page the user sees is the one shown in Figure 9-10. This page is generated by `Postcards.html`, which looks like this:

**TABLE 9-6**

Layout of Postcards
Table

```
Table     = postcards
+------------------+-----------------------------------+--------+
| Field            | Type                              | Length |
+------------------+-----------------------------------+--------+
| id               | int4 not null default nextva      |    4   |
| sender           | varchar()                         |   64   |
| sender_email     | varchar()                         |  128   |
| recipient        | varchar()                         |   64   |
| recipient_email  | varchar()                         |  128   |
| message          | varchar()                         |  256   |
| file_identifier  | varchar()                         |  128   |
| date_sent        | datetime                          |    8   |
+------------------+-----------------------------------+--------+
Index:    postcards_pkey
```

**Figure 9-10**

Selecting a Postcard

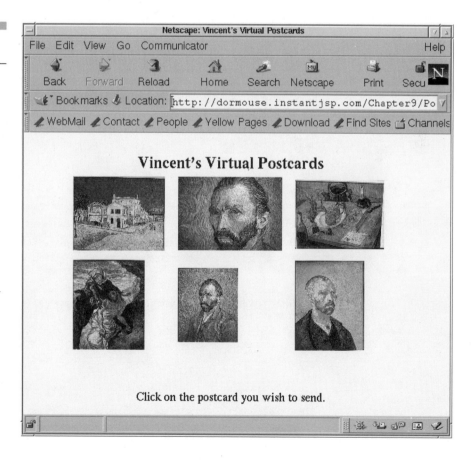

```
<head>
<title>Vincent's Virtual Postcards</title>
</head>
<html>
<body bgcolor="#ffffff" vlink="#ffffff" alink="#ffffff">
<center>
<font size=+2>
<br>
<b>Vincent's Virtual Postcards</b>
</font>
<table>
<tr>
<td>
<a
href="http://dormouse.instantjsp.com/Chapter9/GetPostcardParameters
 .jsp?f=v_yhouse.jpg">
<image
src="http://dormouse.instantjsp.com/images/v_yhouse_thumb.gif">
</a>
<td>
<td>
<a
href="http://dormouse.instantjsp.com/Chapter9/GetPostcardParameters
 .jsp?f=v_self4.jpg">
<image
src="http://dormouse.instantjsp.com/images/v_self4_thumb.jpg">
</a>
<td>
<td>
<a
href="http://dormouse.instantjsp.com/Chapter9/GetPostcardParameters
 .jsp?f=v_still.jpg">
<image src="http://dormouse.instantjsp.com/images/v_still_thumb.gif">
</a>
<td>
</tr>
<tr>
<td>
<a
href="http://dormouse.instantjsp.com/Chapter9/GetPostcardParameters
 .jsp?f=v_tomb.jpg">
<image
src="http://dormouse.instantjsp.com/images/v_tomb_thumb.gif">
</a>
<td>
<td>
<a
href="http://dormouse.instantjsp.com/Chapter9/GetPostcardParameters
 .jsp?f=v_self3.jpg">
<image src="http://dormouse.instantjsp.com/images/v_self3_thumb.gif">
</a>
<td>
<td>
<a
href="http://dormouse.instantjsp.com/Chapter9/GetPostcardParameters
 .jsp?f=v_bonze.jpg">
<image src="http://dormouse.instantjsp.com/images/v_bonze_thumb.gif">
</a>
<td>
```

```
</tr>
</table>
<br>
<br>
<font size=+1
<br>
Click on the postcard you wish to send.
</font>
</center>
</body>
</html>
```

Each of the thumbnail versions of the postcards is a hyperlink to
`GetPostcardParameters.jsp`. The URL for each specifies a different
key/value pair as a query string. In each case the key is `f` (which stands
for file). The value associated with this key is the name of the file containing
the full-sized version of the postcard.

Now let's examine `GetPostcardParameters.jsp`, which produces
the page shown in Figure 9-11. Here is the code:

**Figure 9-11**
Filling Out Your
Postcard

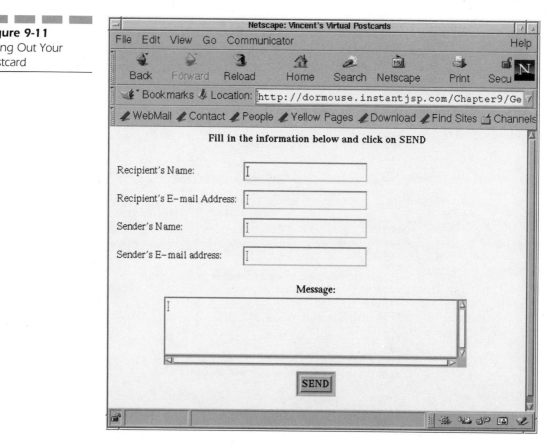

```
<%@ page errorPage="/common/Exception.jsp" %>
<%@page import="java.util.Hashtable" %>
<%@page import="javax.servlet.http.HttpUtils" %>
<jsp:useBean id="pcBean" class="com.instantjsp.PostcardBean"
    scope="session" />
<%
  String query = request.getQueryString();
  Hashtable qt = HttpUtils.parseQueryString(query);
  String file_identifier = ((String[])qt.get("f"))[0];
%>
<html>
<head>
<title>Vincent's Virtual Postcards</title>
</head>
<body bgcolor="#ffffff">
<b>
<center>
Fill in the information below and click on <b>SEND</b>
</center>
<br>
<form method="post" name="postcard"
  action="http://dormouse.instantjsp.com/Chapter9/SendPostcard.jsp">
<input type="hidden" name="fileIdentifier" value="<%= file_identifier
 %>">
<table>
<tr>
<td>
Recipient's Name:
</td>
<td>
<input type="text" name="recipient">
</td>
</tr>
<tr>
<td>
Recipient's E-mail Address:
</td>
<td>
<input type="text" name="recipientEmail">
</td>
</tr>
<tr>
<td>
Sender's Name:
</td>
<td>
<input type="text" name="sender">
</td>
</tr>
<tr>
<td>
Sender's E-mail address:
</td>
<td>
<input type="text" name="senderEmail">
</td>
</tr>
</table>
<br>
<center>
```

```
Message:
<br>
<textarea name="message" rows=5 cols=50>
</textarea>
<br>
<input type="submit" name="submit" value="SEND">
</form>
</body>
</html>
```

When the user enters the required data and clicks on SEND, the contents of the HTML forms are sent to SendPostcard.jsp. Here is the code:

```
<%@ page errorPage="/common/Exception.jsp" %>
<jsp:useBean id="pcBean" class="com.instantjsp.PostcardBean"
    scope="session" />
<jsp:setProperty name="pcBean" property="*" />
<%
   String id = pcBean.send();
%>
<html>
<head>
<title>Confirmation</title>
</head>
<body bgcolor="#ffffff">
<b>
<center>
<font face = "Arial, Helvetica"><font size="+2">
<br>
Confirmation
</center>
<br>
</font></font>
<font face = "Arial, Helvetica"><font size="+0">
Your postcard has been sent to
<jsp:getProperty name="pcBean" property="recipient" />
<br>
<br>
Recipient was notified via email sent to
<jsp:getProperty name="pcBean" property="recipientEmail" />
<br>
<br>
Email will say that sender is
<jsp:getProperty name="pcBean" property="sender" />
<br>
<br>
The ticket number is
<%= id %>
</body>
</html>
```

SendPostcard.jsp first uses a <jsp:setProperty> action to set all of the properties of PostcardBean as indicated by property="*". It then invokes the Bean's send() method. This method uses an SQL

INSERT to create a database record containing all of the data the user entered and then generates a confirmation page like the one shown in Figure 9-12. Here is the code for PostcardBean:

```
package com.instantjsp;

import java.sql.Connection;
import java.sql.ResultSet;
import java.sql.SQLException;
import java.sql.Statement;
import java.text.SimpleDateFormat;
import java.util.Calendar;
import java.util.Date;
import java.util.GregorianCalendar;
import java.util.Random;
import java.util.Vector;

import javaservlets.jdbc.ConnectionPool;

public class PostcardBean {
```

**Figure 9-12**
Confirmation of
Transmission of
Postcard

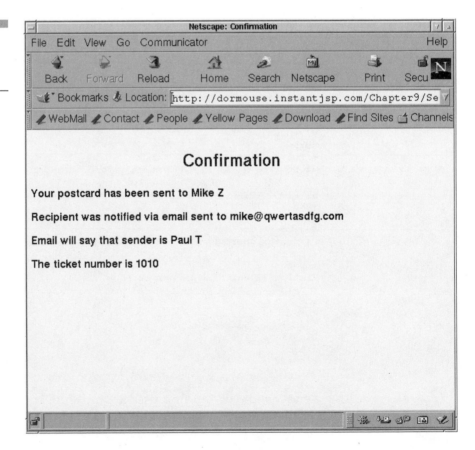

```
private String recipient;
private String recipientEmail;
private String sender;
private String senderEmail;
private String message;
private String fileIdentifier;

private ConnectionPool connectionPool;

private Random rand;

private static final String POOL_CFG_FILE =
  "javaservlets/jdbc/PostcardPool.cfg";

private static final String SELECT_POSTCARD =
  "SELECT * FROM postcards WHERE ID = ";

private static final String INSERT_POSTCARD =
  "INSERT INTO postcards " +
  "(sender,sender_email,recipient,recipient_email," +
  "message,file_identifier,date_sent) " +
  "VALUES ";

private static final String SELECT_ID =
  "SELECT id FROM postcards WHERE ";

private SimpleDateFormat sdtf =
  new SimpleDateFormat("yyyy-MM-dd HH:mm:ss.SSS");

private static final String AND = " and ";
private static final String LPAREN = "(";
private static final String RPAREN = ")";
private static final String COMMA = ",";
private static final String PERCENT = "%";
private static final String QUOTE = "'";

public PostcardBean() throws Exception {
  connectionPool = new ConnectionPool();
  connectionPool.initialize(POOL_CFG_FILE);
  rand = new Random();
}

public String getRecipient() {
  return recipient;
}

public String getRecipientEmail() {
  return recipientEmail;
}

public String getSender() {
  return sender;
}

public String getSenderEmail() {
  return senderEmail;
}

public String getMessage() {
  return message;
```

```
  }

  public String getFileIdentifier() {
    return fileIdentifier;
  }

  public void setRecipient(String recipient) {
    this.recipient = recipient;
  }

  public void setRecipientEmail(String addr) {
    recipientEmail = addr;
  }

  public void setSender(String sender) {
    this.sender = sender;
  }

  public void setSenderEmail(String addr) {
    senderEmail = addr;
  }

  public void setMessage(String message) {
    this.message = message;
  }

  public void setFileIdentifier(String fileIdentifier) {
    this.fileIdentifier = fileIdentifier;
  }

  public String send() throws SQLException {
    String date = sdtf.format(new Date());
    Connection conn = connectionPool.getConnection();
    Statement us = conn.createStatement();
    us.executeUpdate(INSERT_POSTCARD + LPAREN +
      QUOTE + sender + QUOTE + COMMA +
      QUOTE + senderEmail + QUOTE + COMMA +
      QUOTE + recipient + QUOTE + COMMA +
      QUOTE + recipientEmail + QUOTE + COMMA +
      QUOTE + message.replace('\''`') + QUOTE + COMMA +
      QUOTE + fileIdentifier + QUOTE + COMMA +
      QUOTE + date + QUOTE + RPAREN);
    ResultSet rs = us.executeQuery(SELECT_ID +
      "sender=" + QUOTE + sender + QUOTE + AND +
      "sender_email=" + QUOTE + senderEmail + QUOTE + AND +
      "recipient=" + QUOTE + recipient + QUOTE + AND +
      "recipient_email=" + QUOTE + recipientEmail + QUOTE + AND +
      "file_identifier=" + QUOTE + fileIdentifier + QUOTE + AND +
      "date_sent=" + QUOTE + date + QUOTE);
    rs.next();
    String id = Integer.toString(rs.getInt(1));
    connectionPool.close(conn);
    return id;
  }

  public void pickupPostcard(String id) throws SQLException {
    Connection conn = connectionPool.getConnection();
    Statement qs = conn.createStatement();
    ResultSet rs = qs.executeQuery(SELECT_POSTCARD + id);
```

```
        rs.next();
        sender = rs.getString(2);
        senderEmail = rs.getString(3);
        recipient = rs.getString(4);
        recipientEmail = rs.getString(5);
        message = rs.getString(6);
        fileIdentifier = rs.getString(7);
        connectionPool.close(conn);
    }
}
```

Normally, at this point a method would be invoked that would send email to the recipient announcing that he or she has a postcard waiting at your Web site. In our example here, we did not include the code that sends email. If we had, the recipient of the postcard would receive email that looks like:

```
From: paul@instantjsp.com
To: mike@qwerasdfg.com

You have been sent an electronic postcard. To view it, go to:

http://dormouse.instantjsp.com/PickUpPostcard.jsp?id=1010
```

The user then either clicks on the URL or types it into a browser depending on his or her email program. The URL specifies PickUpPostcard.jsp. Here is the code:

```
<%@ page errorPage="/common/Exception.jsp" %>
<jsp:useBean id="pcBean" class="com.instantjsp.PostcardBean"
    scope="session" />
<%@ page import="java.util.Hashtable" %>
<%@ page import="java.util.StringTokenizer" %>
<%!
  public String getImageSrc(String fileIdentifier) {
    return "http://dormouse.instantjsp.com/images/" +
    fileIdentifier;
  }

  public String insertBreaks(String s) {
    StringBuffer sb = new StringBuffer();
    StringTokenizer st = new StringTokenizer(s,",",true);
    while (st.hasMoreTokens()) {
      String t = st.nextToken();
      if (t.equals(",")) {
        sb.append("<br>");
      }
      else {
        sb.append(t);
      }
    }
    return sb.toString();
  }
%>
<%
```

```
      String query = request.getQueryString();
      Hashtable qt = HttpUtils.parseQueryString(query);
      String idstr = ((String[])qt.get("id"))[0];
      long id = Long.parseLong(idstr.trim());
      pcBean.pickupPostcard(idstr);
%>
<html>
<head>
<title>Vincent's Virtual Postcards</title>
</head>
<body bgcolor="#ffffff">
<b>
<font face = "Arial, Helvetica"><font size="+1">
<center>
A postcard for
<jsp:getProperty name="pcBean" property="recipient" />
From
<jsp:getProperty name="pcBean" property="sender" />
<br>
</font></font>
</b>
<center>
<image src="<%= getImageSrc(pcBean.getFileIdentifier()) %>">
</center>
<center>
<br>
<table>
<tr>
<td>
<pre>
<jsp:getProperty name="pcBean" property="message" />
</pre>
</td>
</tr>
</table>
</center>
<br>
<%
   String senderEmail = pcBean.getSenderEmail();
   if (senderEmail != null) {
%>
To send email to
<jsp:getProperty name="pcBean" property="sender" />
click on
<a href="mailto:">
<%= senderEmail %>
</a>
<%
   }
%>
<br>
<br>
<center>
<a href="http://dormouse.instantjsp.com/Chapter9/Postcards.html">
Click on this line to send a postcard.
</a>
</center>
</body>
</html>
```

The page first uses the getQueryString() method to retrieve the query string (in this case, id=1010). It then uses parseQuery, which returns a Hashtable containing the key id and String 1010. The String is retrieved from the Hashtable and is passed as an argument to the pickupPostcard() method of PostcardBean. This method issues the SQL query:

```
SELECT  * FROM postcards WHERE id = '1010'
```

The values returned are used to update the Bean's instance variables that contain the postcard data.

PickupPostcard.jsp then uses appropriate <jsp:getProperty> actions to retrieve the postcard information, which is used to generate the page shown in Figure 9-13.

**Figure 9-13**
Postcard as Viewed by Recipient

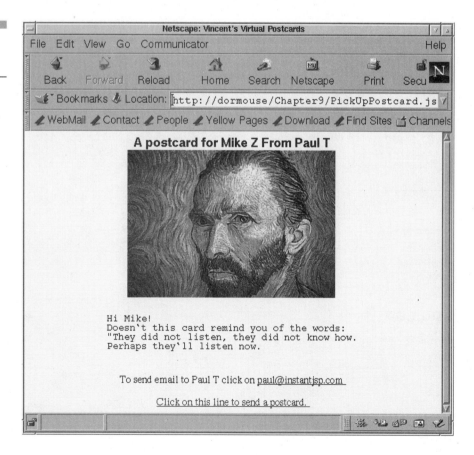

# A Simple Chat Room

One of the more popular attractions of the Internet is the chat room. Let's now see how we can implement a simple chat room using JavaServer Pages.

To keep track of the names by which chat room participants are known and to allow them to make return visits using the same name, we will need a database table in which we can store such names. The description of this database is shown in Table 9-7. The messages that are exchanged by the participants are stored in a table described in Table 9-8.

All users enter the chat room by accessing `ChatRoom.jsp`. Here is the code:

```
<%@ page import="javax.servlet.http.Cookie" %>
<jsp:useBean id="chatBean" class="com.instantjsp.ChatBean"
    scope="session" />
<%@ page errorPage="/common/Exception.jsp" %>
<%
  String user = null;
  Cookie[] cookies = request.getCookies();
  for (int i = 0; i < cookies.length; ++i) {
    if (cookies[i].getName().equals("instantjsp.chatuser")) {
      user = cookies[i].getValue();
```

**TABLE 9-7**

Participants Table Layout

```
Table     = participants
+-----------------------+-----------------------+----------+
|         Field         |         Type          |  Length  |
+-----------------------+-----------------------+----------+
| user_id               | varchar() not null    |    16    |
| last_visit            | date                  |     4    |
+-----------------------+-----------------------+----------+
Index:     participants_pkey
```

**TABLE 9-8**

Partial Contents of Participants Table

```
Table     = messages
+-----------------------+-----------------------+----------+
|         Field         |         Type          |  Length  |
+-----------------------+-----------------------+----------+
| dt                    | datetime              |     8    |
| from_user             | varchar()             |    16    |
| message               | varchar()             |    80    |
+-----------------------+-----------------------+----------+
```

```
      }
    }
    if (user == null) {
%>
    <jsp:forward page="/Chapter9/NewParticipant.jsp" />
<%
    }
%>
    <jsp:setProperty name="chatBean" property="user"
        value="<%= user %>" />
<%
    chatBean.enterRoom();
%>
<%@ include file="/Chapter9/ChatFrameSet.html" %>
```

As you can guess from the very first line, we will be using cookies to store the user's preferred name in the browser. The first scriptlet uses the `getCookies()` method to obtain a list of those cookies the browser is willing to send back. If one of the returned cookies has a name of "instantjsp.chatuser", the value of that cookie is stored in the variable `user`. Let's start with the case of a user who has not visited the chat room before. This user's browser would not send back the required cookie and so the variable `user` would contain the value of null that was initially assigned to it. This would result in the request's being forwarded to `NewParticipant.html`, which generates a page like the one shown in Figure 9-14. Here is the code:

```
<html>
<head>
    <title>The Ramblin' Room</title>
</head>
<body bgcolor="#ffffff">
<center>
<font size=+1>
<b>The Ramblin' Room</b>
<br>
<br>
</font>
</center>
<font size=+0>
Welcome to our chat room. To the uninitiated, it might seem that
our conversations consist of non-sequiturs. In reality (to the extent
that the participants know reality), it all makes perfect sense.
You'll see once you get to know us.
<p>
Anyone may join. The rules are as follows:
<ol>
<li>All participants must choose a <b>one-word</b> name by which they
will be known in the room. You can use your real name or one you make
 up.</li>
<li>You <b>MUST</b> enable cookies in your browser.</li>
<li>Conversations may be monitored for content. If you are the type
of person who can't limit what you type to that which is not offensive,
please just go away now and look for a room where you will be accepted.
```

**Figure 9-14**
New Participant in
Chat Room

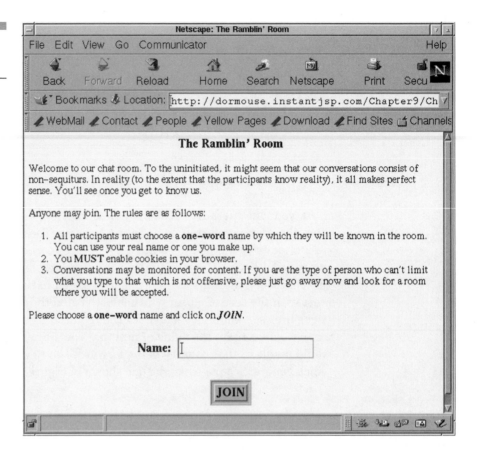

```
</ol>
<p>
Please choose a <b>one-word</b> name and click on <b><i>JOIN</i></b>.
</font>
<br>
<center>
<FORM NAME="newuser" METHOD=POST
 ACTION="http://dormouse.instantjsp.com/Chapter9/AddParticipant.jsp">
<TABLE WIDTH="50%">
<TR>
<TD align=right>
<font size=+1>
<B>
Name:
</B>
</font>
</TD>
<TD>
<font size=+1><INPUT NAME="user" TYPE="TEXT" LENGTH="9" MAXLENGTH="9">
</font>
</TD>
```

```
</TR>
<TR>
</TABLE>
<BR>
<font size=+1>
<b>
<INPUT TYPE="submit" VALUE="JOIN">
</b>
</font>
</FORM>
</CENTER>
</body>
</html>
```

The page contains a statement of what the chat room is about and what the rules are. A user who wishes to participate enters a name in the entry field that is provided and clicks on JOIN, thus sending the contents of the HTML form to AddParticipant.jsp. Here is the code:

```
<%@ page import="javax.servlet.http.Cookie" %>
<jsp:useBean id="chatBean" class="com.instantjsp.ChatBean"
    scope="session" />
<%@ page errorPage="/common/Exception.jsp" %>
<%
  String user = request.getParameter("user");
  if (!chatBean.addParticipant(user)) {
%>
    <jsp:forward page="/Chapter9/AddUserFailed.jsp" />
<%
  }
  Cookie c = new Cookie("instantjsp.chatuser",user);
  c.setComment("Your pass to the Ramblin' Room");
  c.setDomain(".instantjsp.com");
  c.setMaxAge(365 * 24 * 60 * 60);
  response.addCookie(c);
%>
<html>
<body bgcolor="#ffffff">
<center>
<b>
<font face = "Arial, Helvetica"><font size="+2">
<br>
<br>
Welcome,
<%= user %>
<br>
<br>
</font></font>
</b>
</center>
<font face = "Arial, Helvetica"><font size="+1">
<p>
We will remember the name you have chosen so whenever you come back to
visit, you will be taken immediately to the chat room.
<p>
To enter the chat room now, simply click on the button labeled
```

```
<b>ENTER</b> below.
</font></font>
</b>
<form name="welcome" method="get"
  action="http://dormouse.instantjsp.com/Chapter9/ChatRoom.jsp">
<center>
<input type="submit" name="submit" value="ENTER">
</center>
</form>
</body>
</html>
```

The first scriptlet in the page retrieves the user's proposed name by invoking:

```
request.getParameter("user");
```

It then passes the value read from the entry field named "user" to the addParticipant() method of ChatBean. This method returns true if the SQL INSERT it issues to add the user to the participants table succeeds and false if it fails, because the database already contains a record with that key. Here is the code for ChatBean.java:

```
package com.instantjsp;

import java.sql.Connection;
import java.sql.ResultSet;
import java.sql.SQLException;
import java.sql.Statement;
import java.text.ParseException;
import java.text.SimpleDateFormat;
import java.util.Date;
import java.util.Random;
import java.util.Vector;

import javax.servlet.http.Cookie;

import javaservlets.jdbc.ConnectionPool;

public class ChatBean {

  private ConnectionPool connectionPool;

  private String user;

  private String lastViewed;

  private String[][] lastUnreadMessages = {
  {"***","no new messages"} } ;

  private SimpleDateFormat dateFormatter =
    new SimpleDateFormat("yyyy-MM-dd");

  private SimpleDateFormat dateTimeFormatter =
```

```
        new SimpleDateFormat("yyyy-MM-dd HH:mm:ss.SSS");

private SimpleDateFormat dateTimeParser =
    new SimpleDateFormat("EEE MMM dd HH:mm:ss.SS YYYY");

private static final String POOL_CFG_FILE =
    "javaservlets/jdbc/ChatPool.cfg";

private static final String INSERT_PARTICIPANT =
    "INSERT INTO participants (user_id,last_visit)";

private static final String VALUES = "VALUES";

private static final String UPDATE_PARTICIPANTS =
    "UPDATE PARTICIPANTS SET last_visit=";

private static final String WHERE_USERID =
    "WHERE user_id = ";

private static final String SELECT_MESSAGES =
    "SELECT from_user,message FROM  messages WHERE dt >= ";

private static final String ORDER_BY_DATETIME =
    " ORDER BY dt";

private static final String INSERT_MESSAGE =
    "insert into messages (dt,from_user,message) values (";

private static final String SELECT_MIN_DATE =
    "select min(dt) from messages";

private static final String AND = " and ";
private static final String LPAREN = "(";
private static final String RPAREN = ")";
private static final String COMMA = ",";
private static final String PERCENT = "%";
private static final String QUOTE = "'";

public ChatBean() throws Exception {
  connectionPool = new ConnectionPool();
  connectionPool.initialize(POOL_CFG_FILE);
}

public void setUser(String user) {
  this.user = user;
}

public String getUser() {
  return user;
}

public boolean addParticipant(String user) {
  boolean ok = true;
  Connection conn = null;
  try {
    conn = connectionPool.getConnection();
    Statement us = conn.createStatement();
      us.executeUpdate(INSERT_PARTICIPANT +
      VALUES + LPAREN +
```

```
            QUOTE + user + QUOTE + COMMA +
            QUOTE + dateFormatter.format(new Date()) + QUOTE +
            RPAREN);
      }
      catch (SQLException e) {
        ok = false;
      }
      connectionPool.close(conn);
      return ok;
  }

  public void enterRoom()
      throws SQLException,ParseException {
      Connection conn = connectionPool.getConnection();
      Statement stmnt = conn.createStatement();
      stmnt.executeUpdate(UPDATE_PARTICIPANTS +
        QUOTE + dateFormatter.format(new Date()) + QUOTE +
        WHERE_USERID +
        QUOTE + user + QUOTE);
      ResultSet rs = stmnt.executeQuery(SELECT_MIN_DATE);
      rs.next();
      lastViewed = rs.getString(1);
      if (lastViewed == null) {
        lastViewed = dateTimeFormatter.format(new Date());
      }
      connectionPool.close(conn);
      addMessage(">> NOW IN ROOM <<<");
  }

  public void addMessage(String message) throws SQLException {
      String mtime = dateTimeFormatter.format(new Date());
      Connection conn = connectionPool.getConnection();
      Statement us = conn.createStatement();
      us.executeUpdate(INSERT_MESSAGE +
        QUOTE + mtime + QUOTE + COMMA +
        QUOTE + user + QUOTE + COMMA +
        QUOTE + message.replace('\'', '`') + QUOTE +
        RPAREN);
      connectionPool.close(conn);
  }

  public String[][] getUnread() throws SQLException {
      Date now = new Date();
      Vector v = new Vector();
      Connection conn = connectionPool.getConnection();
      Statement us = conn.createStatement();
      ResultSet rs = us.executeQuery(SELECT_MESSAGES +
        QUOTE + lastViewed + QUOTE +
        ORDER_BY_DATETIME);
      while (rs.next()) {
        String[] row = new String[2];
        row[0] = rs.getString(1);
        row[1] = rs.getString(2);
        v.addElement(row);
      }
      connectionPool.close(conn);
      if (v.size() == 0) {
        return lastUnreadMessages;
      }
```

```
String[][] msgs = new String[v.size()][2];
lastUnreadMessages = new String[v.size() + 1][2];
String[] s;
for (int i = 0; i < v.size(); ++i) {
  s = (String[])v.get(i);
  lastUnreadMessages[i][0] = msgs[i][0] = s[0];
  lastUnreadMessages[i][1] = msgs[i][1] = s[1];
}
lastUnreadMessages[v.size()][0] = "***";
lastUnreadMessages[v.size()][1] = "NO NEW MESSAGES";
lastViewed = dateTimeFormatter.format(now);
return msgs;
}
}
```

Let's first look at what happens when a name is chosen that is already being used by another participant. You can see from `AddParticipant.jsp` that when the Bean's `addParticipant()` method returns false, the request is forwarded to `AddUserFailed.jsp`, which produces the page shown in Figure 9-15. Here is the code for `AddUserFailed.jsp`:

**Figure 9-15**
Choosing a Name That Is Already Being Used

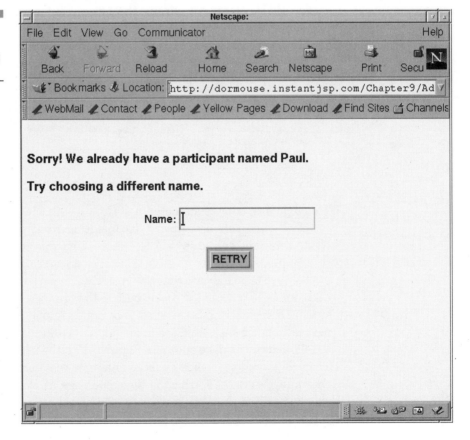

```
<html>
<body bgcolor="#ffffff">
<b>
<font face = "Arial, Helvetica"><font size="+1">
<br>
<br>
Sorry! We already have a participant named
<%= request.getParameter("user") %>.
<p>
Try choosing a different name.
<br>
</b>
<center>
<form name="retry" method="get"
 action="http://dormouse.instantjsp.com/Chapter9/AddParticipant.jsp">
Name:
<input type="text" name="user">
<br>
<br>
<input type="submit" name="submit" value="RETRY">
</form>
</body>
</html>
```

The HTML form containing the entry field named "user" is sent to AddParticipant.jsp after the user enters a new name and clicks on RETRY. When AddParticipant.jsp eventually receives a name that is not already being used, it executes the following scriptlet:

```
<%
  }
  Cookie c = new Cookie("instantjsp.chatuser",user);
  c.setComment("Your pass to the Ramblin' Room");
  c.setDomain(".instantjsp.com");
  c.setMaxAge(365 * 24 * 60 * 60);
  response.addCookie(c);
%>
```

This code first creates an instance of Cookie with the name "instantjsp.cha-tuser". It then sets a comment documenting what the cookie is used for. Next, it invokes setDomain() to indicate that this cookie can be sent back to any host in the instantjsp.com domain. After then invoking setMaxAge() to indicate that this cookie will have a life of 1 year, it invokes addCookie() to send the cookie back to the browser as part of the response stream. If the user had requested to be notified upon receipt of a cookie, the next page he or she would see is the one shown in Figure 9-16. This would be followed by the page shown in Figure 9-17 if the user accepted the cookie. The user would then click on OK to enter the room and would see the page shown in Figure 9-18, which is the same page as would be seen by a user who had visited the room previously and had chosen a name.

**Figure 9-16**
Request to Accept
Chat Room Cookie

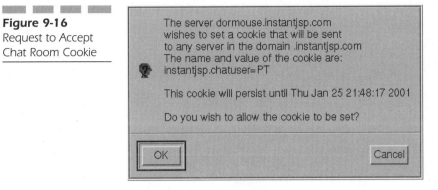

The server dormouse.instantjsp.com
wishes to set a cookie that will be sent
to any server in the domain .instantjsp.com
The name and value of the cookie are:
instantjsp.chatuser=PT

This cookie will persist until Thu Jan 25 21:48:17 2001

Do you wish to allow the cookie to be set?

OK    Cancel

**Figure 9-17**
Welcoming a New
Participant

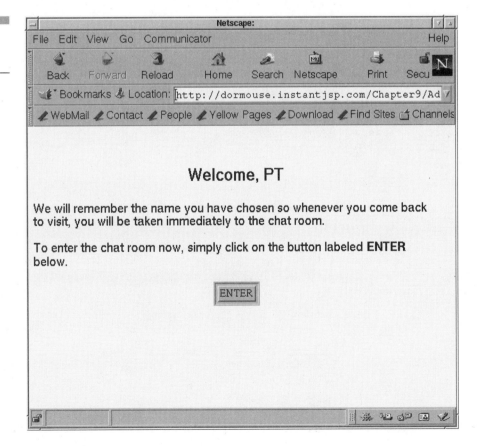

# Welcome, PT

We will remember the name you have chosen so whenever you come back
to visit, you will be taken immediately to the chat room.

To enter the chat room now, simply click on the button labeled **ENTER**
below.

ENTER

**Figure 9-18**
Chat Room Main
Page

Figure 9-18 is produced by `ChatFrameSet.html`, which looks like this:

```
<html>
<head>
   <title>The Ramblin' Room</title>
</head>
<frameset rows="250,*">
  <frame src="ChatWelcome.html"
    frameborder="1" noresize="noresize" name="messageframe">
  <frame src="ChatMessage.html"
    frameborder="1" name="bottomframe">
</frameset>
</html>
```

The frame that occupies the top of the screen initially contains the welcome generated by `ChatWelcome.html`. Here is the code:

```
<html>
<body bgcolor="#ffffff" link="#999999"
  vlink="#999999" alink="#999999">
<center>
<font size=+2>
<br>
<br>
<b>Welcome to The Ramblin' Room!</B>
</font>
<br>
<br>
<br>
<font size=+1>
Use the frame below this one to participate.
</font>
</center>
</body>
</html>
```

The frame that occupies the bottom of the screen is used to participate in the chat room. This frame is generated by ChatMessage.html, which looks like this:

```
<html>
<head>
<script language="JavaScript">

  function giveFocus() {
    document.msgform.chatmessage.focus()
  }

  function submitForm(n) {
    document.msgform.chatmessage.value=
      document.msgform.inputmessage.value
    document.msgform.submittype.value = n
    document.msgform.inputmessage.value = ""
    document.msgform.submit()
  }

</script>
</head>
<body bgcolor="#ffffff" link="#999999"
  vlink="#999999" alink="#999999" onLoad=giveFocus()>
<center>
Enter message in box and click on <i>SUBMIT</i>
<b>OR</b>
click on <i>REFRESH</i>
<form name="msgform" method="post" target="messageframe"
 action="http://dormouse.instantjsp.com/Chapter9/PostMessage.jsp">
<input type=hidden name="chatmessage">
<input type=hidden name="submittype">
<input name="inputmessage" type="text" size=60>
<br>
<input type="button" name="button" value="SUBMIT" onClick=submitForm("S")>
    
<input type="button" name="button" value="REFRESH" onClick=submitForm("R")>
</form>
```

```
</center>
</body>
</html>
```

If you are a "lurker," you can simply use the REFRESH button, which will result in all the messages added since you last checked being displayed in the top frame. If you wish to add a message, you type the message into the text filed and click on SUBMIT. Your message and any other new messages are displayed in the top frame.

Both the REFRESH and the SUBMIT buttons call the JavaScript function submitForm(), which copies the user's message to a hidden field before clearing out the entry field into which it was typed (we do this in preparation for reuse of the bottom frame). The submitForm() function also copies the argument passed to it to the hidden field named "submittype". This argument is "S" when the SUBMIT button is clicked and "R" when the REFRESH button is clicked. The contents of the HTML form are then sent to PostMessage.jsp. Here is the code:

```jsp
<%@ page errorPage="/common/Exception.jsp" %>
<jsp:useBean id="chatBean" class="com.instantjsp.ChatBean"
    scope="session" />
<%
  String msg = request.getParameter("chatmessage");
  if ((request.getParameter("submittype").equals("S")) &&
    (msg.length() > 0)) {
    chatBean.addMessage(msg);
  }
  String[][] newMessages = chatBean.getUnread();
%>
<html>
<body bgcolor="#ffffff" link="#999999"
    vlink="#999999" alink="#999999">
<br>
<table>
<%
  for (int i = 0; i < newMessages.length; ++i) {
%>
<tr>
<td><b>
<%= newMessages[i][0] + ":"%>
</b></td>
<td>
<%= newMessages[i][1] %>
</td>
</tr>
<%
  }
%>
</table>
</font>
</body>
</html>
```

The page contains a scriptlet that retrieves the user's message using the getParameter() method. Likewise, it uses getParameter() to get the value of submittype. If the value of submittype is "S" and the text hidden field contains a message, the addMessage() method of ChatBean is invoked to insert the message into the database. Whether SUBMIT or REFRESH was clicked, the scriptlet next invokes the getUnread() method of ChatBean, which returns a two-dimensional array of Strings. The first column contains a user name and the second contains a message entered by that user. These values are displayed in the top frame in the form of a table. Figure 9-19 shows some typical messages in the top frame and a message about to be sent in the bottom frame.

**Figure 9-19**
Some Typical Chat Messages

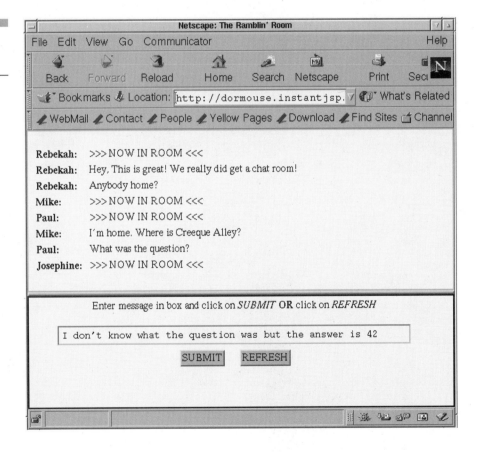

# Beyond HTML

- Working with XML
- Retrieving a PostScript File

Back in Chapter 1 we said that although JavaServer Pages are most often used to generate HTML, they can be used to generate any textual output. In this chapter, we demonstrate this. We develop Java code that sends a request to a JavaServer Page and saves the content sent back by the JSP in a file on the computer on which the Java code executes. Noticeably absent from the JSP pages we use are HTML tags.

# Working with XML

The Extensible Markup Language (XML) is enjoying widespread usage in business-to-business applications. We next see how we can use JSP to respond to requests for an XML document that contains entries from a product database. The products are grouped by category and subcategory and for each product an SKU and description are presented.

The Java application we use to request the XML file is GetFileFromJSP. This program, which executes on our local computer, looks like this:

```java
import java.io.BufferedReader;
import java.io.BufferedWriter;
import java.io.FileWriter;
import java.io.InputStreamReader;
import java.io.IOException;
import java.io.PrintWriter;
import java.net.MalformedURLException;
import java.net.URL;
import java.net.URLConnection;

public class GetFileFromJSP {

  public static void main(String[] args) {
    URL url = null;
    URLConnection connection = null;
    BufferedReader br = null;
    PrintWriter out = null;
    boolean dumpingBeforeXMLTag = true;
    if (args.length != 2) {
      System.out.println("Usage: java GetFileFromJSP URL targetFile");
      System.exit(0);
    }
    try {
      url = new URL(args[0]);
      connection = url.openConnection();

      br = new BufferedReader(
        new InputStreamReader(url.openStream()));

      out = new PrintWriter(new BufferedWriter(
        new FileWriter(args[1])));
```

```
        String line;

        dumpingBeforeXMLTag =
          connection.getContentType().equals("text/xml");

        while ((line = br.readLine()) != null) {
          if (dumpingBeforeXMLTag) {
            if (line.length() == 0) {
              continue;
            }
            else {
              dumpingBeforeXMLTag = false;
            }
          }
          out.println(line);
        }
        br.close();
        out.close();
      }
      catch (MalformedURLException e) {
        System.out.println("malformed URL");
        System.exit(0);
      }
      catch (IOException e) {
        System.out.println("IOE1 " + e.getMessage());
        System.exit(0);
      }
    }
  }
}
```

The program does the following:

- Creates an instance of URL from the first argument
- Opens a URL connection to the URL
- Opens a BufferedReader to read data from the connection
- Reads data one line at a time and writes them to the file specified by the second argument

**NOTE**:  *A minor quirk in the version of the JSP container used to run the sample program required that code be inserted to discard superfluous lines emitted before the* `<?xml?>` *tag.*

The program takes two arguments. The first is a URL. We will use:

"http://dormouse.instantjsp.com/Chapter10/GetCatalogInfo.jsp"

The second argument is the name of a file on `out` local hard drive in which the retrieved document will be stored. We will use `CatalogInfo.-xml`.

The URL in the first argument points to `GetCatalogInfo.jsp`. Here is the code:

```jsp
<%@ page contentType="text/xml" %>
<?xml version="1.0"?>
<%@ page import="com.instantjsp.CatalogEntry" %>
<jsp:useBean id="sb" class="com.instantjsp.StoreBean"
  scope="request" />
<%
  String[] categories = sb.getCategories();
  String[] subcategories = sb.getSubcategories();
%>
<CATALOG>
<%
  for (int i = 0; i < categories.length; ++i) {
%>
  <CATEGORY>
    <CATEGORY_NUMBER><%= categories[i] %></CATEGORY_NUMBER>
    <CATEGORY_NAME>
      <%= sb.getCategoryName(categories[i]) %>
    </CATEGORY_NAME>
<%
  for (int j = 0; j < subcategories.length; ++j) {
    CatalogEntry[] cev =
      sb.getCatalogEntries(categories[i],subcategories[j]);
    if (cev.length == 0) {
      continue;
    }
%>
  <SUBCATEGORY>
    <SUBCATEGORY_NUMBER><%= subcategories[j] %></SUBCATEGORY_NUMBER>
    <SUBCATEGORY_NAME>
      <%= sb.getSubcategoryName(subcategories[j]) %>
    </SUBCATEGORY_NAME>
<%
    for (int k = 0; k < cev.length; ++k) {
%>
    <PRODUCT>
      <SKU>
      <%= cev[k].sku %>
      </SKU>
      <PRODUCT_DESCRIPTION>
      <%= cev[k].description %>
      </PRODUCT_DESCRIPTION>
    </PRODUCT>
<%
    }
%>
    </SUBCATEGORY>
<%
    }
%>
    </CATEGORY>
<%
    }
%>
</CATALOG>
```

The JSP page contains a `<jsp:useBean>` action that names an instance of StoreBean. Here is the code for `StoreBean.java`:

```java
package com.instantjsp;

import java.sql.Connection;
import java.sql.ResultSet;
import java.sql.SQLException;
import java.sql.Statement;
import java.util.Random;
import java.util.Vector;

import javaservlets.jdbc.ConnectionPool;

public class StoreBean {

  private ConnectionPool connectionPool;

  private static final String POOL_CFG_FILE =
    "javaservlets/jdbc/BusinessPool.cfg";

  private static final String SELECT_CATEGORIES =
    "(SELECT DISTINCT cat FROM products)";

  private static final String SELECT_SUBCATEGORIES =
    "(SELECT DISTINCT subcat FROM products)";

  private static final String SELECT_CATEGORY_NAME =
    "SELECT cat_desc FROM product_categories WHERE ";

  private static final String SELECT_SUBCATEGORY_NAME =
    "SELECT subcat_desc FROM product_subcats WHERE ";

  private static final String SELECT_PRODUCTS =
    "SELECT * FROM products";

  private static final String SELECT_PRODUCTS_QUALIFIED =
    "SELECT * FROM products WHERE ";

  private static final String CAT_QUALIFIER =
    " cat = ";

  private static final String SUBCAT_QUALIFIER =
    " subcat = ";

  private static final String AND =
    " AND ";

  public StoreBean() throws Exception {
    connectionPool = new ConnectionPool();
    connectionPool.initialize(POOL_CFG_FILE);
  }

  public CatalogEntry[] getCatalogEntries()
      throws SQLException {
    Connection conn = connectionPool.getConnection();
    Statement us = conn.createStatement();
    ResultSet rs = us.executeQuery(SELECT_PRODUCTS);
```

```
  Vector v = new Vector();
  while (rs.next()) {
    CatalogEntry ce = new CatalogEntry();
    ce.setSKU(rs.getInt(1));
    ce.setCategory(rs.getInt(2));
    ce.setSubcategory(rs.getInt(3));
    ce.setDescription(rs.getString(4));
    v.add(ce);
  }
  connectionPool.close(conn);
  CatalogEntry[] cev = new CatalogEntry[v.size()];
  for (int i = 0; i < v.size(); ++i) {
    cev[i] = (CatalogEntry)v.elementAt(i);
  }
  return cev;
}

public CatalogEntry[] getCatalogEntries(String cat, String subcat)
    throws SQLException {
  Connection conn = connectionPool.getConnection();
  Statement us = conn.createStatement();
  ResultSet rs = us.executeQuery(SELECT_PRODUCTS_QUALIFIED +
    CAT_QUALIFIER + cat + AND +
    SUBCAT_QUALIFIER + subcat);
  Vector v = new Vector();
  while (rs.next()) {
    CatalogEntry ce = new CatalogEntry();
    ce.setSKU(rs.getInt(1));
    ce.setCategory(rs.getInt(2));
    ce.setSubcategory(rs.getInt(3));
    ce.setDescription(rs.getString(4));
    v.add(ce);
  }
  connectionPool.close(conn);
  CatalogEntry[] cev = new CatalogEntry[v.size()];
  for (int i = 0; i < v.size(); ++i) {
    cev[i] = (CatalogEntry)v.elementAt(i);
  }
  return cev;
}

public String[] getCategories()
    throws SQLException {
  Connection conn = connectionPool.getConnection();
  Statement us = conn.createStatement();
  ResultSet rs = us.executeQuery(SELECT_CATEGORIES);
  Vector v = new Vector();
  while (rs.next()) {
    String s = rs.getString(1);
    v.add(s);
  }
  connectionPool.close(conn);
  String[] sa = new String[v.size()];
  for (int i = 0; i < v.size(); ++i) {
    sa[i] = (String)v.elementAt(i);
  }
  return sa;
}
```

```
public String[] getSubcategories()
    throws SQLException {
  Connection conn = connectionPool.getConnection();
  Statement us = conn.createStatement();
  ResultSet rs = us.executeQuery(SELECT_SUBCATEGORIES);
  Vector v = new Vector();
  while (rs.next()) {
    String s = rs.getString(1);
    v.add(s);
  }
  connectionPool.close(conn);
  String[] sa = new String[v.size()];
  for (int i = 0; i < v.size(); ++i) {
    sa[i] = (String)v.elementAt(i);
  }
  return sa;
}

public String getCategoryName(String cat)
    throws SQLException {
  Connection conn = connectionPool.getConnection();
  Statement us = conn.createStatement();
  ResultSet rs = us.executeQuery(SELECT_CATEGORY_NAME +
    CAT_QUALIFIER + cat);
  rs.next();
  String catname = rs.getString(1);
  connectionPool.close(conn);
  return catname;
}

public String getSubcategoryName(String subcat)
    throws SQLException {
  Connection conn = connectionPool.getConnection();
  Statement us = conn.createStatement();
  ResultSet rs = us.executeQuery(SELECT_SUBCATEGORY_NAME +
    SUBCAT_QUALIFIER + subcat);
  rs.next();
  String subcatname = rs.getString(1);
  connectionPool.close(conn);
  return subcatname;
}
}
```

Both the JSP page and the Bean refer to the CatalogEntry class. Here is the code:

```
package com.instantjsp;

public class CatalogEntry {
  public int category;
  public int subcategory;
  public int sku;
  public String description;

  public int getCategory() {
    return category;
```

```
      }

      public int getSubcategory() {
        return subcategory;
      }

      public int getSKU() {
        return sku;
      }

      public String getDescription() {
        return description;
      }

      public void setCategory(int category) {
        this.category = category;
      }

      public void setSubcategory(int subcategory) {
        this.subcategory = subcategory;
      }

      public void setSKU(int sku) {
        this.sku = sku;
      }

      public void setDescription(String description) {
        this.description = description;
      }
    }
```

The JSP page invokes three methods of StoreBean to retrieve product categories, product subcategories, and product information from the same database that we saw in earlier chapters. These arrays are traversed using simple `for` loops. The data elements in the arrays are inserted between `start` and `end` XML tags, which appear in the JSP page as fixed template data. Again, note the absence of HTML.

The XML file is quite large and so we show only the following portion of it:

```
<?xml version="1.0"?>

<CATALOG>

  <CATEGORY>
    <CATEGORY_NUMBER>100</CATEGORY_NUMBER>
    <CATEGORY_NAME>
      Accessories
    </CATEGORY_NAME>

    <SUBCATEGORY>
      <SUBCATEGORY_NUMBER>1001</SUBCATEGORY_NUMBER>
      <SUBCATEGORY_NAME>
        Cables
```

```
</SUBCATEGORY_NAME>

<PRODUCT>
  <SKU>
  100001
  </SKU>
  <PRODUCT_DESCRIPTION>
  IMB Parallel Printer 6 ft
  </PRODUCT_DESCRIPTION>
</PRODUCT>

<PRODUCT>
  <SKU>
  100002
  </SKU>
  <PRODUCT_DESCRIPTION>
  IMB Parallel Printer 10 ft
  </PRODUCT_DESCRIPTION>
</PRODUCT>
```

Using the appropriate APIs (which are outside the scope of this book), we could process the XML file in a variety of ways. We choose to use the Extensible Style Language (XSL) to format the data in the XML file as a catalog that can be viewed locally using a Web browser. Here is the XSL file:

```
<xsl:stylesheet xmlns:xsl="http://www.w3.org/1999/XSL/Transform">
  <xsl:template match="/">
    <HTML>
      <HEAD>
        <STYLE>
          BODY {margin:0}
          .bg1 {font:8pt Verdana; background-color:#CCCCCC;
                color:black}
          .bg2 {font:8pt Verdana; background-color:navy; color:white}
          .bg3 {font:8pt Verdana; background-color:teal; color:white}
          .bg4 {font:8pt Verdana; background-color:white; color:white}
          H1 {font:bold 14pt Verdana; background-color:white;
                color:olive}
        </STYLE>
        <TITLE>CATALOG</TITLE>
      </HEAD>

      <BODY BGCOLOR="#FFFFFF" LEFTMARGIN="0" TOPMARGIN="0">
        <CENTER>
          <H1>Catalog</H1>
        </CENTER>
        <TABLE cols="5" width="100%" cellspacing="0">
          <TR><TD></TD><TD></TD><TD></TD><TD></TD></TR>
          <xsl:for-each select="CATALOG/CATEGORY">
            <xsl:apply-templates select="CATEGORY_NAME"/>
            <xsl:for-each select="SUBCATEGORY">
              <xsl:apply-templates select="SUBCATEGORY_NAME"/>
              <xsl:for-each select="PRODUCT">
          <TR>
            <TD></TD><TD></TD>
```

```
                    <xsl:apply-templates select="SKU"/>
                    <xsl:apply-templates select="PRODUCT_DESCRIPTION"/>
            </TR>
                  </xsl:for-each>
               </xsl:for-each>
            </xsl:for-each>
         </TABLE>
       </BODY>
     </HTML>
   </xsl:template>

   <xsl:template match="CATEGORY_NAME">
     <TR>
       <TD class="bg4">xx</TD>
     </TR>
     <TR>
       <TD colspan="4" class="bg2">
         CATEGORY: <xsl:value-of select="." />
       </TD>
     </TR>
   </xsl:template>

   <xsl:template match="SUBCATEGORY_NAME">
     <TR>
       <TD></TD>
       <TD colspan="3" class="bg3">
         SUBCATEGORY: <xsl:value-of select="." />
       </TD>
     </TR>
   </xsl:template>

   <xsl:template match="SKU">
     <TD class="bg1">
       SKU: <xsl:value-of select="." />
     </TD>
   </xsl:template>

   <xsl:template match="PRODUCT_DESCRIPTION">
     <TD colspan="2" class="bg1">
       <xsl:value-of select="." />
     </TD>
   </xsl:template>

 </xsl:stylesheet>
```

If the preceding XSL file is saved as `Products.xsl` and the output of the GetFileFromJSP program is saved as `Products.html`, then using the Xalan processor produces the translated file `Products.html`. This file produces Figure 10-1 when viewed using a browser.

The Xalan processor is freely available from IBM Alphaworks (http://www.alphaworks.ibm.com) as the Lotus XSL package. You would invoke it in this case by typing:

```
java org.apache.xalan.xslt.Process -in Products.xml -xsl Products.xsl
  -out Products.html
```

**Figure 10-1**
Visual Representation
of Retrieved XML
Document

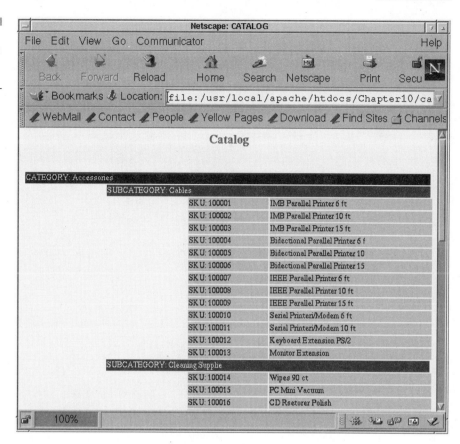

## Retrieving a PostScript File

Imagine you work for a company that stores engineering diagrams in PostScript format on a central computer. You are given an assignment to provide the engineers with a way to retrieve copies of the diagrams and store them on their workstations so that they can be viewed using a PostScript viewer or sent to a PostScript printer. You are told that the engineers already use a large number of Java applications and so the Java Runtime Environment is installed on each workstation. This means we can use the same GetFileFromJSP program we just used to retrieve an XML document.

If we wanted to retrieve a diagram of a traffic light that is stored on the central computer as `trafficlight.ps` and store it on our local workstation as `MyTrafficLight.ps`, we would run our Java program using the following as the first argument:

"http://dormouse.instantjsp.com/GetPostScriptFile.jsp?fn=/engineering/psfiles/trafficlight.ps"

The second argument would be "MyTrafficLight.ps".

As you can see, the URL in the first argument refers to the JSP page `GetPostscriptFile.jsp`. Here is the code:

```
<%@ page contentType="application/postscript" %>
<%@ page import="java.util.Hashtable" %>
<%@ page import="javax.servlet.http.HttpUtils" %>
<jsp:useBean id="ff" class="com.instantjsp.FileFetcher"
    scope="request" />
<%
  String qs = request.getQueryString();
  Hashtable qt = HttpUtils.parseQueryString(qs);
  String fn = ((String[])qt.get("fn"))[0];
  ff.fetchFile(response, fn);
%>
```

This page does nothing more than extract the file name specified in the URL and pass it as an argument to the `fetchFile()` method of the instance of FileFetcher named in the `<jsp:useBean>` action. Note the absence of HTML tags.

This leaves us one more component to examine—the FileFetcher class. Here is `FileFetcher.java`:

```
package com.instantjsp;

import java.io.BufferedReader;
import java.io.FileReader;
import java.io.IOException;
import java.io.PrintWriter;

import javax.servlet.http.HttpServletResponse;

public class FileFetcher {

  public boolean fetchFile(HttpServletResponse resp, String fname)
      throws IOException {
    boolean ok = true;
    PrintWriter pr = resp.getWriter();

    BufferedReader br = new BufferedReader(new FileReader(fname));
    String line;
    while ((line = br.readLine()) != null) {
      pr.println(line);
      pr.flush();
    }
    br.close();
    pr.flush();
```

```
        return ok;
    }

}
```

The `fetchFile()` method takes two arguments. The first is an `HttpServletResponse` object and the second is a String. The method uses `getWriter()` to get the PrintWriter it can use to send data back to the originator of the request. It then creates a BufferedReader that it uses to read the contents of the file specified by the second argument. A simple loop reads the specified file one line at a time using `readLine()` and writes each line to the PrintWriter.

When you run GetFileFromJSP using the URL we just saw as the first argument and `MyTrafficLight.ps` as the second argument, the file `MyTrafficLight.ps` is created on your hard drive. The first few lines look like this:

```
%!PS-Adobe-2.0 EPSF-2.0
%%Title: /home/paul_jsp/trafficlight.ps
%%Creator: XV Version 3.10a Rev: 12/29/94 (PNG patch 1.2) - by John
 Bradley
%%BoundingBox: 173 214 440 578
%%Pages: 1
%%DocumentFonts:
%%EndComments
%%EndProlog

%%Page: 1 1

% remember original state
/origstate save def

% build a temporary dictionary
20 dict begin

% define string to hold a scanline's worth of data
/pix 267 string def

% define space for color conversions
/grays 267 string def  % space for gray scale line
/npixls 0 def
/rgbindx 0 def

% lower left corner
173 214 translate

% size of image (on paper, in 1/72inch coords)
266.97600 364.03200 scale

267 364 8                % dimensions of data
[267 0 0 -364 0 364]           % mapping matrix
{currentfile pix readhexstring pop}
image
```

You can either print the PostScript file you retrieved or view it using a PostScript viewer. When viewed using Ghostview, `MyTrafficLight.ps` looks like Figure 10-2.

**Figure 10-2**
Using GhostView to
View PostScript
Delivered from a JSP

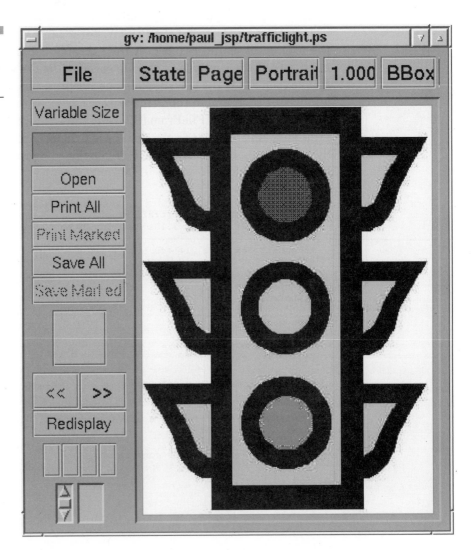

# APPENDIX A

## Creating a JSP Environment

This Appendix describes the environment that was used to develop and test the sample code discussed in the book.

## The Operating System

The operating system used was TurboLinux Workstation 4.0. Any of the major Linux distributions will work equally well.

All of the software components we discuss in this Appendix are also available for Windows NT.

## The JSP Environment

The first package you should install is the Java Development Kit (JDK) for Linux. JDK 1.2 was used for the book. The JDK is available from any of the mirror sites listed at `www.blackdown.org`. It is also available from `java.sun.com`. You should also install the Java Servlet Development Kit (JSDK).

**NOTE:** *From this point forward, it is very important that you install the packages in the proper order. If you fail to do so, your environment will be unusable. Before proceeding, you might want to take a few minutes to read the installation and configuration notes for Apache, JServ, and PostgreSQL that can be found at the end of this Appendix.*

The next package you should install is Apache. This package is included with most Linux distributions. Some vendors install Apache in a directory other than `/usr/local/apache`, which is the directory in which it was installed on the host computer used for the book. This directory is also the one referenced in most documents that discuss Apache. If your Linux distribution does not have Apache installed in

/usr/local/apache, you might find it useful to remove the server and reinstall it in this directory. The CD contains Apache 1.3.9.

After you install and configure Apache according to the directions contained in the package, you should start the server by typing:

```
/usr/local/apache/bin/apachectl start
```

With Apache running, you can use your browser to test the installation by entering the URL http://myhost, where myhost is the name of your host. If everything is working properly, you should see a page like the one shown in Figure A-1.

You should not proceed past this point until you are satisfied that

**Figure A-1**
Testing Apache

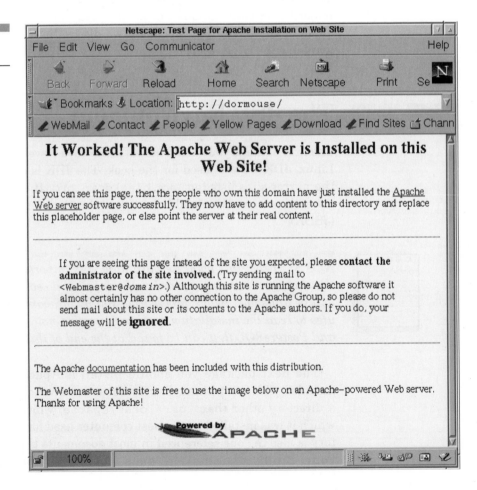

Apache is working properly. Since most problems are caused by incorrect configuration, you might find it useful to compare the contents of your httpd.conf file (the main Apache configuration file) to the listing shown below. This is httpd.conf from dormouse.instantjsp.com (the host on which the code in the book was tested):

```
##
## httpd.conf - Apache HTTP server configuration file
##


#
# Based upon the NCSA server configuration files
# originally by Rob McCool.
#
# This is the main Apache server configuration file.
# It contains the configuration directives that give the
# server its instructions.
# See <URL:http://www.apache.org/docs/> for detailed
# information about the directives.
#
# Do NOT simply read the instructions in here without
# understanding what they do. They're here only as hints
# or reminders. If you are unsure consult the online docs.
# You have been warned.
#


### Section 1: Global Environment
#
# The directives in this section affect the overall operation
# of Apache, such as the number of concurrent requests it can
# handle or where it can find its configuration files.
#


#
# ServerType is either inetd, or standalone. Inetd mode is
# only supported on Unix platforms.
#
ServerType standalone


#
# ServerRoot: The top of the directory tree under which the
# server's configuration, error, and log files are kept.
#
# Do NOT add a slash at the end of the directory path.
#
ServerRoot "/usr/local/apache"


#
# PidFile: The file in which the server should record its
# process identification number when it starts.
#
PidFile /usr/local/apache/logs/httpd.pid


#
# Timeout: The number of seconds before receives and sends
```

```
# time out.
#
Timeout 300


#
# KeepAlive: Whether or not to allow persistent connections
# (more than one request per connection). Set to "Off" to
# deactivate.
#
KeepAlive On


#
# MaxKeepAliveRequests: The maximum number of requests to
# allow during a persistent connection. Set to 0 to allow
# an unlimited amount.
# We recommend you leave this number high, for maximum
# performance.
#
MaxKeepAliveRequests 100


#
# KeepAliveTimeout: Number of seconds to wait for the next
# request from the same client on the same connection.
#
KeepAliveTimeout 15


#
# Server-pool size regulation. Rather than making you guess
# how many server processes you need, Apache dynamically
# adapts to the load it sees -- that is, it tries to maintain
# enough server processes to handle the current load, plus a
# few spare servers to handle transient load spikes (e.g.,
# multiple simultaneous requests from a single Netscape browser).
#
# It does this by periodically checking how many servers are
# waiting for a request. If there are fewer than MinSpareServers,
# it creates a new spare. If there are more than MaxSpareServers,
some of the spares die off. The default values are probably OK
# for most sites.
#
MinSpareServers 5
MaxSpareServers 10


#
# Number of servers to start initially -- should be a reasonable
# ballpark figure.
#
StartServers 5


#
# Limit on total number of servers running, i.e., limit on the
# number of clients who can simultaneously connect -- if this
# limit is ever reached, clients will be LOCKED OUT, so it should
# NOT BE SET TOO LOW.
# It is intended mainly as a brake to keep a runaway server from
# taking the system with it as it spirals down...
#
MaxClients 150
```

```
#
# MaxRequestsPerChild: the number of requests each child process
# is allowed to process before the child dies.
#
MaxRequestsPerChild 0


#
# Dynamic Shared Object (DSO) Support
#

LoadModule vhost_alias_module libexec/mod_vhost_alias.so
LoadModule env_module          libexec/mod_env.so
LoadModule config_log_module   libexec/mod_log_config.so
LoadModule mime_magic_module   libexec/mod_mime_magic.so
LoadModule mime_module         libexec/mod_mime.so
LoadModule negotiation_module  libexec/mod_negotiation.so
LoadModule status_module       libexec/mod_status.so
LoadModule info_module         libexec/mod_info.so
LoadModule includes_module     libexec/mod_include.so
LoadModule autoindex_module    libexec/mod_autoindex.so
LoadModule dir_module          libexec/mod_dir.so
LoadModule cgi_module          libexec/mod_cgi.so
LoadModule asis_module         libexec/mod_asis.so
LoadModule imap_module         libexec/mod_imap.so
LoadModule action_module       libexec/mod_actions.so
LoadModule speling_module      libexec/mod_speling.so
LoadModule userdir_module      libexec/mod_userdir.so
LoadModule alias_module        libexec/mod_alias.so
LoadModule rewrite_module      libexec/mod_rewrite.so
LoadModule access_module       libexec/mod_access.so
LoadModule auth_module         libexec/mod_auth.so
LoadModule anon_auth_module    libexec/mod_auth_anon.so
LoadModule dbm_auth_module     libexec/mod_auth_dbm.so
LoadModule digest_module       libexec/mod_digest.so
LoadModule proxy_module        libexec/libproxy.so
LoadModule cern_meta_module    libexec/mod_cern_meta.so
LoadModule expires_module      libexec/mod_expires.so
LoadModule headers_module      libexec/mod_headers.so
LoadModule usertrack_module    libexec/mod_usertrack.so
LoadModule unique_id_module    libexec/mod_unique_id.so
LoadModule setenvif_module     libexec/mod_setenvif.so

# Reconstruction of the complete module list from
# all available modules(static and shared ones) to
# achieve correct module execution order.
# [WHENEVER YOU CHANGE THE LOADMODULE SECTION ABOVE UPDATE
# THIS, TOO]
ClearModuleList
AddModule mod_vhost_alias.c
AddModule mod_env.c
AddModule mod_log_config.c
AddModule mod_mime_magic.c
AddModule mod_mime.c
AddModule mod_negotiation.c
AddModule mod_status.c
AddModule mod_info.c
AddModule mod_include.c
AddModule mod_autoindex.c
```

```
AddModule mod_dir.c
AddModule mod_cgi.c
AddModule mod_asis.c
AddModule mod_imap.c
AddModule mod_actions.c
AddModule mod_speling.c
AddModule mod_userdir.c
AddModule mod_alias.c
AddModule mod_rewrite.c
AddModule mod_access.c
AddModule mod_auth.c
AddModule mod_auth_anon.c
AddModule mod_auth_dbm.c
AddModule mod_digest.c
AddModule mod_proxy.c
AddModule mod_cern_meta.c
AddModule mod_expires.c
AddModule mod_headers.c
AddModule mod_usertrack.c
AddModule mod_unique_id.c
AddModule mod_so.c
AddModule mod_setenvif.c

### Section 2: 'Main' server configuration
#
# Port: The port to which the standalone server listens. For
# ports < 1023, you will need httpd to be run as root initially.
#
Port 80

#
# If you wish httpd to run as a different user or group, you
# must run httpd as root initially and it will switch.
#
# User/Group: The name (or #number) of the user/group to run
# httpd as.
# . On SCO (ODT 3) use "User nouser" and "Group nogroup".
# . On HPUX you may not be able to use shared memory as nobody,
# and the suggested workaround is to create a user www and
# use that user.
# NOTE that some kernels refuse to setgid(Group) or semctl
# (IPC_SET) when the value of (unsigned)Group is above 60000;
# don't use Group nobody on these systems!
#
User nobody
Group nobody

#
# ServerAdmin: Your address, where problems with the server
# should be e-mailed. This address appears on some
# server-generated pages, such as error documents.
#
ServerAdmin root@dormouse.instantjsp.com

#
# ServerName allows you to set a host name which is sent back
# to clients for your server if it's different than the one the #
# program would get (i.e., use "www" instead of the host's real name).
```

```
#
ServerName dormouse.instantjsp.com

#
# DocumentRoot: The directory out of which you will serve your
# documents. By default, all requests are taken from this
# directory, but symbolic links and aliases may be used to point
# to other locations.
#
DocumentRoot "/usr/local/apache/htdocs"

#
# Each directory to which Apache has access, can be configured
# with respect to which services and features are allowed
# and/or disabled in that directory (and its subdirectories).
#
# First, we configure the "default" to be a very restrictive
# set of permissions.
#
<Directory />
    Options FollowSymLinks
    AllowOverride None
</Directory>

#
# Note that from this point forward you must specifically allow
# particular features to be enabled - so if something's not
# working as you might expect, make sure that you have
# specifically enabled it below.
#

#
# This should be changed to whatever you set DocumentRoot to.
#
<Directory "/usr/local/apache/htdocs">

#
# Controls who can get stuff from this server.
#
    Order allow,deny
    Allow from all
</Directory>
```

**NOTE:** *Most of the actual content of the* httpd.conf *file from* dormouse.instantjsp.com *has been removed from the listing for clarity. You should use this abbreviated file to help you concentrate on those areas that have been identified as where you should first look for configuration errors.*

When you are satisfied that Apache is working properly, you should install Apache JServ. The instructions are contained in the package, which is on the CD or is available from java.apache.org/jserv.

When JServ is installed properly, you should see the following lines appended to the end of your `httpd.conf` file:

```
#############################################
#        Apache JServ Configuration File  #
#############################################

# Note: this file should be appended to httpd.conf
# Tell Apache on win32 to load the Apache JServ
# communication module
LoadModule jserv_module libexec/mod_jserv.so

# Whether Apache must start JVM or not
# (On=Manual Off=Autostart)
# Syntax: ApJServManual [on/off]
# Default: "Off"
ApJServManual off

# Properties filename for Apache JServ in Automatic Mode.
# In manual mode this directive is ignored
# Syntax: ApJServProperties [filename]
# Default: "./conf/jserv.properties"
ApJServProperties /usr/local/apache/etc/jserv.properties

# Log file for this module operation relative to Apache
# root directory.
# Syntax: ApJServLogFile [filename]
# Default: "./logs/mod_jserv.log"
# Note: when set to "DISABLED", the log will be redirected to
# Apache error log
ApJServLogFile /usr/local/apache/var/log/jserv.log

# Protocol used by this host to connect to Apache JServ
# (see documentation for more details on available protocols)
# Syntax: ApJServDefaultProtocol [name]
# Default: "ajpv11"
ApJServDefaultProtocol ajpv11

# Default host on which Apache JServ is running
# Syntax: ApJServDefaultHost [hostname]
# Default: "localhost"
# ApJServDefaultHost

# Default port that Apache JServ is listening to
# Syntax: ApJServDefaultPort [number]
# Default: protocol-dependent (for ajpv11 protocol this is "8007")
ApJServDefaultPort 8007

# Passes parameter and value to specified protocol.
# Syntax: ApJServProtocolParameter [name] [parameter] [value]
# Default: NONE
# Note: Currently no protocols handle this. Introduced for
# future protocols.

# Apache JServ secret key file relative to Apache root
# directory.
# Syntax: ApJServSecretKey [filename]
# Default: "./conf/jserv.secret.key"
```

```
# Warning: if authentication is DISABLED, everyone on this
# machine (not just this module) may connect to your servlet
# engine and execute servlet bypassing web server restrictions.
# See the documentation for more information
ApJServSecretKey DISABLED

# Mount point for Servlet zones
# (see documentation for more information on servlet zones)
# Syntax: ApJServMount [name] [jserv-url]
# Default: NONE
# Note: [name] is the name of the Apache URI path to mount
# jserv-url on
# [jserv-url] is something like "protocol://host:port/zone"
# If protocol, host or port are not specified, the values
# from "ApJServDefaultProtocol", "ApJServDefaultHost" or
# "ApJServDefaultPort" will be used.
# If zone is not specified, the zone name will be the first
# subdirectory of the called servlet.
# Example: "ApJServMount /servlets /myServlets"
# if user requests "http://host/servlets/TestServlet"
# the servlet "TestServlet" in zone "myServlets" on default host
# thru default protocol on default port will be requested
# Example: "ApJServMount /servlets ajpv11://localhost:8007"
# if user requests "http://host/servlets/myServlets/TestServlet"
# the servlet "TestServlet" in zone "myServlets" will be requested
# Example: "ApJServMount /servlets
# ajpv11://jserv.mydomain.com:15643/myServlets"
# if user requests "http://host/servlets/TestServlet" the servlet
# "TestServlet" in zone "myServlets" on host "jserv.mydomain.com"
# using
# "ajpv11" protocol on port "15643" will be executed
ApJServMount /servlet /servlet
ApJServMount /jsp /jsp

# Whether <VirtualHost> inherits base host mount points or not
# Syntax: ApJServMountCopy [on/off]
# Default: "On"
# Note: This directive is meaningful only when virtual hosts are
# being used
ApJServMountCopy on

# Executes a servlet passing filename with proper extension in
# PATH_TRANSLATED
# property of servlet request.
# Syntax: ApJServAction [extension] [servlet-uri]
# Defaults: NONE
# Notes: This is used for external tools such as JSP (Java Servlet
# Pages),
# GSP (GNU Server Pages) or Java server side include.
ApJServAction .jsp /jsp/gnujsp
# ApJServAction .gsp /servlets/com.bitmechanics.gsp.GspServlet
# ApJServAction .jhtml /servlets/org.apache.ssi.SSIServlet

# Enable the Apache JServ status handler with the URL of
# "http://servername/jserv/" (note the trailing slash!)
# Change the ".your_domain.com" to match your domain to enable.
<Location /jserv/>
  SetHandler jserv-status
```

```
   order deny,allow
   deny from all
   allow from localhost 127.0.0.1
</Location>
########## W A R N I N G ###########################
# Remember to disable or otherwise protect the      #
# execution of the Apache JServ on a production      #
# environment since this may give untrusted users    #
# to gather restricted information on your servlets  #
# and their initialization arguments                 #
####################################################
```

You should now test JServ using the URL http://myhost/servlet/ Hello. You should see a page like the one shown in Figure A-2.

The JServ package includes a dynamic status self-test, which you can access using the URL http://myhost/jserv. Figure A-3 shows the

**Figure A-2**
Testing JServ

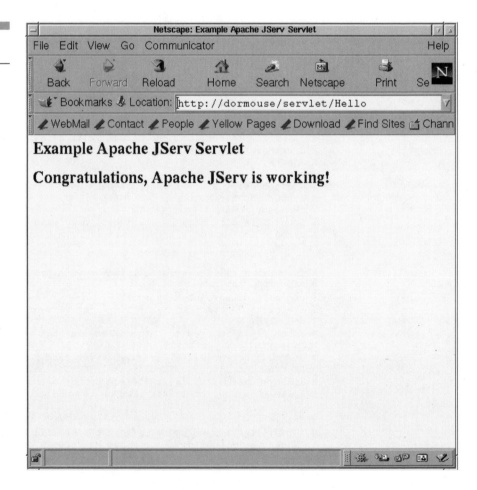

**Figure A-3**
Apache JServ
Dynamic Status Page

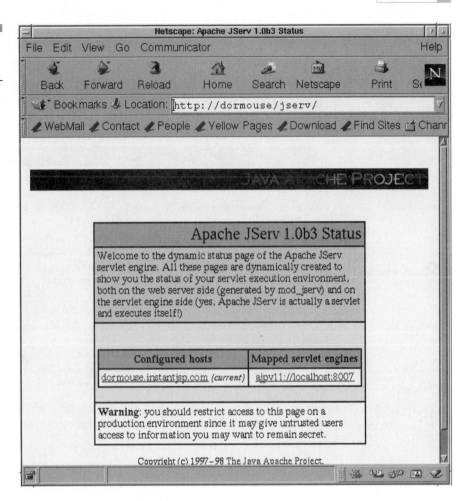

page displayed by the self-test program. Select your host and you should see the page shown in Figure A-4.

As was the case with the Apache server, you should not proceed past this point until you are satisfied that JServ is working properly.

The final package to install is GNU JSP, which is contained on the CD and is also available from www.klomp.org. GNU JSP is distributed under the terms of the GNU General Public License.

After you have installed GNU JSP, you can test it using the examples from Chapter 1. If the JSP pages do not behave as expected, you might want to compare the contents of the following two files to the corresponding files on your system.

**Figure A-4**
Apache JServ
Dynamic Status for
Host dormouse.-
instantjsp.com

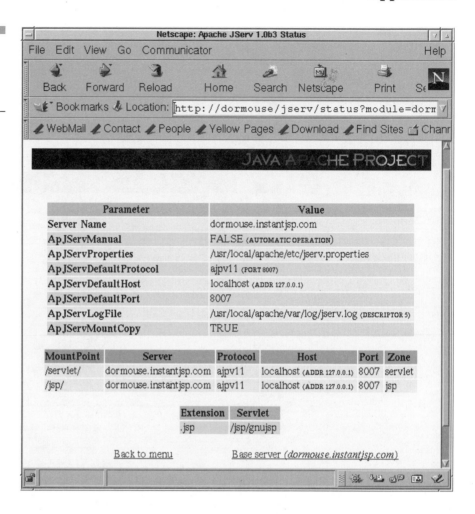

## jserv.properties

```
####################################
# Apache JServ Configuration File #
####################################

######### WARNING ####################################
# Unlike normal Java properties, JServ configurations #
# have some important extensions:                      #
#                                                      #
# 1) commas are used as token separators               #
# 2) multiple definitions of the same key              #
#    are concatenated in a comma-separated list         #
#                                                      #
#                                                      #
# Execution parameters                                  #
#######################################################
```

```
# The Java Virtual Machine interpreter
# Syntax: wrapper.bin=[filename]
# Default: "/usr/bin/java" for Unix systems
#          "c:\jdk\bin\java.exe" for Win32 systems
wrapper.bin=/usr/local/jdk1.2/bin/java

# Arguments passed to java interpreter (optional)
# Syntax: wrapper.bin.parameters=[string]
# Default: NONE

# Apache JServ entry point class
# Syntax: wrapper.class=[classname]
# Default: "org.apache.jserv.JServ"
wrapper.class=org.apache.jserv.JServ

# Arguments passed to main class after the properties filename
# Syntax: wrapper.class.parameters=[string]
# Default: NONE
# Note: currently not used

# PATH environment value passed to the JVM
# Syntax: wrapper.path=[path]
# Default: "/bin:/usr/bin:/usr/local/bin" for Unix systems
#          "c:\(windows-dir);c:\(windows-system-dir)" for Win32
# systems
# Notes: if more than one line is supplied these will be concatenated
# using
#        ":" or ";" (depending whether Unix or Win32) characters
#    Under Win32 (windows-dir) and (windows-system-dir) will be
#    automatically evaluated to match your system requirements

# CLASSPATH environment value passed to the JVM
# Syntax: wrapper.classpath=[path]
# Default: NONE (Sun's JDK/JRE already have a default classpath)
# Notes: if more than one line is supplied these will be concatenated
# using
#        ":" or ";" (depending whether Unix or Win32) characters.
#        JVM must be able to find JSDK and JServ classes and any
#        utility classes used by your servlets.
wrapper.classpath=/usr/local/src/Apache-JServ-1.0b3/src/java/Apache-
 JServ.jar
#wrapper.classpath=/dosd/jswdk-1.0.1/lib/servlet.jar
wrapper.classpath=/usr/local/gnujsp-1.0.0/lib/servlet-2.0-plus.jar
#wrapper.classpath=/usr/local/JSDK2.0/lib/jsdk.jar
wrapper.classpath=/usr/local/jdk1.2/lib/tools.jar
#wrapper.classpath=/usr/local/apache/beans
#wrapper.classpath=/usr/local/apache/classes

# An environment name with value passed to the JVM
# Syntax: wrapper.env=[name]=[value]
# Default: NONE on Unix Systems
#          SystemDrive and SystemRoot with appropriate values on Win32
#systems

# An environment name with value copied from caller to Java Virtual
# Machine
# Syntax: wrapper.env.copy=[name]
# Default: NONE
```

```
# Copies all environment from caller to Java Virtual Machine
# Syntax: wrapper.env.copyall=[true,false]
# Default: false

# Protocol used for signal handling
# Syntax: wrapper.protocol=[name]
# Default: ajpv11

# General parameters
######################

# Set the port JServ will listen to.
# Syntax: port=[1024,65535] (int)
# Default: 8007
port=8007

# Servlet Zones parameters
############################

# List of servlet zones JServ manages
# Syntax: zones=<servlet zone>,<servlet zone>... (Comma-separated list
# of String)
# Default: <empty>
zones=servlet,jsp

# Configuration file for each servlet zone
# Syntax: <servlet zone name as on the zones list>.properties=<full
# path to configFile> (String)
# Default: <empty>
servlet.properties=/usr/local/apache/etc/servlet.properties
jsp.properties=/usr/local/apache/etc/jsp.properties

# Security parameters
#####################

# Enable/disable the execution of org.apache.jserv.JServ as a servlet.
# This is disabled by default because it may give information that
# should
# be restricted.
# Note that the execution of JServ as a servlet is filtered by
# mod_jserv
# by default so that both sides should be enabled to let this service
# work.
# This service is useful for installation and configuration since it
# gives
# feedback about the exact configurations JServ is set with, but it
# should
# be disabled when both installation and configuration processes are
# done.
# Syntax: security.selfservlet=[true,false] (boolean)
# Default: false
# security.selfservlet=true

# Set the maximum number of socket connections JServ may handle
# simultaneously.
# (this number does not identify the maximum number of concurrent
# servlet
# requests: see the JServ protocol specification for more info on
```

```
# this)
# Syntax: security.maxConnections=(int)>1
# Default: 50
security.maxConnections=50

# List of IP addresses allowed to connect to JServ. This is a first
# security
# filtering to reject possibly unsecure connections and avoid the
# overhead
# of connection authentication.
# Syntax: security.allowedAddresses=<IP address>,<IP Address>...
# (Comma-separated list of IP adresses)
# Default: <empty list>
security.allowedAddresses=127.0.0.1

# Enable/disable connection authentication.
# NOTE: unauthenticated connections are a little faster since
# authentication
# handshake is not performed at connection creation.
# WARNING: disable authentication only if you can protect the
# intrusion on
# the port JServ listens on with other systems or do it at your own
# risk.
# Syntax: security.authentication=[true,false] (boolean)
# Default: true
security.authentication=false

# Authentication secret key.
# The secret key is passed as a file that must be kept secure and must
# be exactly the same as those used by clients to authenticate
# themselves.
# Syntax: security.secretKey=<secret key file> (String)
# Default: <empty>
# security.secretKey=

# Length of the randomly generated challenge string (in bytes) used to
# authenticate connections. 5 is the lowest possible choice to force a
# safe
# level of security and reduce connection creation overhead.
# Syntax: security.challengeSize=(int)>5
# Default: 5
security.challengeSize=5

# Logging parameters
###################

# Enable/disable JServ tracing, used for debugging and development.
# WARNING: tracing is a very costly operation in terms of performance
# and
# it's disabled by default. Note that trace logs may become really big
# since each servlet connection may generate many Kb of log.
# Syntax: log=[true,false] (boolean)
# Default: false
log=true

# Set the name of the trace/log file. To avoid possible confusion
# about
# the location of this file, an absolute pathname is recommended.
```

```
# Syntax: log.file=<log file name> (String)
# Default: NONE
# log.file=jserv.log
log.file=/usr/local/apache/var/log/trace.log

# Enable the timestamp before the log message
# Syntax: log.timestamp=[true,false] (boolean)
# Default: true
log.timestamp=true

# Use the given string as a data format
# (see java.text.SimpleDateFormat for the list of options)
# Syntax: log.dateFormat=(String)
# Default: [dd/MM/yyyy HH:mm:ss:SSS zz]
log.dateFormat=[dd/MM/yyyy HH:mm:ss:SSS zz]

# Enable/disable channels, each logging a different part of the code
# self-explained by their names.
# Syntax: log.channel.<channel name>=[true,false] (boolean)
# Default: false
log.channel.init=false
log.channel.terminate=true
log.channel.serviceRequest=true
log.channel.authentication=false
log.channel.requestData=false
log.channel.responseHeaders=false
log.channel.signal=true
log.channel.exceptionTracing=true
log.channel.servletManager=true
log.channel.singleThreadModel=true
```

## servlet.properties

```
##############################################
#       Servlet Zone Configuration File      #
##############################################

#### W A R N I N G ##########################
#                                           #
# Unlike normal Java properties, JServ       #
# configurations have some  important        #
# extensions:                                #
#                                           #
#    1) commas are used as token separators #
#    2) multiple definitions of the same key#
# are concatenated in a comma-separated list#
#                                           #
##############################################

# List of Repositories
#######################

# The list of servlet repositories controlled by this servlet zone
# Syntax: repositories=[repository],[repository]...
# Default: NONE
```

```
repositories=/usr/local/src/Apache-JServ-1.0b3/example

# Classloader parameters
#########################

# Enable servlet class autoreloading.
# Syntax: autoreload.classes=[true,false] (boolean)
# Default: true
autoreload.classes=true

# Enable servlet resourced autoreloading (properties and other loaded
# resources)
# Syntax: autoreload.file=[true,false] (boolean)
# Default: true
autoreload.file=true

# Set the number of milliseconds to wait before giving up on
# initializing a servlet.
# (a timeout of zero means no timeout)
# Syntax: init.timeout=(long)>0
# Default: 10000 (10 secs)
init.timeout=10000

# Set the number of milliseconds to wait before giving up on destroying
# a servlet.
# (a timeout of zero means no timeout)
# Syntax: destroy.timeout=(long)>0
# Default: 10000 (10 secs)
destroy.timeout=10000

# Set the number of milliseconds to wait before invalidating an unused
# session.
# Syntax: session.timeout=(long)>0
# Default: 1800000 (30 mins)
session.timeout=1800000

# Set how frequently (milliseconds) to check for timed-out sessions.
# Syntax: session.checkFrequency=(long)>0
# Default: 30000 (30 secs)
session.checkFrequency=30000

# SingleThreadModel Servlets parameters
#######################################

# Set the initial capacity of the STM servlets pool.
# Syntax: singleThreadModelServlet.initialCapacity=(int)>1
# Default: 5
singleThreadModelServlet.initialCapacity=5

# Set the number of servlet instances should be added to the pool if
# found empty.
# Syntax: singleThreadModelServlet.incrementCapacity=(int)>1
# Default: 5
singleThreadModelServlet.incrementCapacity=5

# Set the maximum capacity of the STM pool
# Syntax: singleThreadModelServlet.maximumCapacity=(int)>1
# Default: 10
```

```
singleThreadModelServlet.maximumCapacity=10

################## S E R V L E T     P A R A M E T E R S
######################

################################### N O T E
####################################
# When "classname" is specified, it means a Java dot-formatter full
# class name
# without the ".class". For example, a class with source file named
# "Dummy.java" with a package name "org.fool" is defined as
# "org.fool.Dummy".
#
# Since each servlet may have lots of private initialization data,
# Apache JServ
# allows you to store those servlet initArgs in a separate file. To do
# this,
# simply do not set any initArgs in this file: Apache JServ will then
# look for
# a file named "[servlet classname].initargs" in the same directory of
# that
# class. Note that this may work with even class archives.
###################################################################
#########

# Startup Servlets
##################

# Comma- or space-delimited list of servlets to launch on startup.
# This can be either a class name or alias.
# Syntax: servlets.startup=[classname or alias],[classname or
# alias],...
# Default: NONE
# servlets.startup=hello,snoop,org.fool.Dummy


# Servlet Aliases
#################

# This defines aliases from which servlets can be invoked.
# Each alias gives a new instance of the servlet. This means that if a
# servlet
# is invoked both by class name and by alias name, it will result in
#_TWO_
# instances of the servlet being created.
# Syntax: servlet.[alias].code=[classname]  (String)
# Default: NONE
# servlet.snoop.code=SnoopServlet
# servlet.hello.code=org.fool.Dummy


# Global Init Parameters
#########################

# Parameters passed here are given to each of the servlets. You should put
# configuration information that is common to all servlets.
#
# The value of the property is a comma-delimited list of "name=value"
```

```
# pairs
# that are accessible to the servlet via the method getInitParameter()
# in ServletConfig.
# Syntax: servlets.default.initArgs=[name]=[value],[name]=[value],...
# Default: NONE
# servlets.default.initArgs=common.to.everybody=Hi everybody!


# Servlet Init Parameters
###########################

# These properties define init parameters for each servlet that is
# invoked
# by its classname.
# Syntax:
# servlet.[classname].initArgs=[name]=[value],[name]=[value],...
# Default: NONE
# servlet.org.fool.Dummy.initArgs=message=I'm a dummy servlet


# Aliased Servlet Init Parameters
##################################

# These properties define init parameters for each servlet that is
# invoked
# by its alias.
# Syntax: servlet.[alias].initArgs=[name]=[value],[name]=[value],...
# Default: NONE
# servlet.snoop.initArgs=message=I'm a snoop servlet
# servlet.hello.initArgs=message=I say hello world to everyone
```

# The Database

Any relational database manager that can be accessed using JDBC should be suitable. PostgreSQL was chosen. This RDBM is included with most of the major Linux Distributions. It can also be downloaded from www.postgresql.org.

A type 4 JDBC driver is also required. A discussion of JDBC with PostgreSQL can be found at www.postgresql.org/docs/postgres/jdbc.htm.

If you choose to use Windows NT, you should use a relational database manager that works with that operating system. Depending on the RDBM you use, you might have to make some changes to some database tables described in the book. Some RDBMs do not support the boolean type, so you would use integer values of 1 and 0 instead and change the Java code in the appropriate Beans. Some RDBMs do not support the nextval function, which is used throughout the book to supply unique values for key fields. Some RDBMs use an autoincrement facility.

A discussion of the database tables used can be found in Appendix B.

# Apache Installation

The following applies only to UNIX users.

## Introduction

Like all good things, there are two ways to configure, compile, and install Apache. You can go for the three-minute installation process using the APACI process described below; or, you can opt for the same mechanism used in previous versions of Apache, as described in the file src/INSTALL. Each mechanism has its benefits and drawbacks. APACI is newer and a little more raw, but it gets you up and running in the least amount of time, whereas the Configuration.tmpl mechanism may be more familiar and give you some more flexibility to the power user. We'd be very interested in your comments and feedback regarding each approach.

## Installing the Apache 1.3 HTTP Server with APACI

### Overview for the Impatient

```
$ ./configure —prefix=PREFIX
$ make
$ make install
$ PREFIX/bin/apachectl start
```

**NOTE:** PREFIX *is not the string* PREFIX. *Instead use the UNIX filesystem path under which Apache should be installed. For instance use* /usr/local/apache *for* PREFIX *above.*

### Requirements

The following requirements exist for building Apache:

- Disk Space:
  Make sure you have approximately 12 MB of temporary free disk space available. After installation, Apache occupies approximately

3 MB of disk space (the actual required disk space depends on the amount of compiled in third-party modules, etc.).

- ANSI-C Compiler:

  Make sure you have an ANSI-C compiler installed. The GNU C compiler (GCC) from the Free Software Foundation (FSF) is recommended (version 2.7.2 is fine). If you don't have GCC then at least make sure your vendor's compiler is ANSI compliant. You can find the homepage of GNU at `http://www.gnu.org/` and the GCC distribution under `http://www.gnu.org/order/ftp.html`.

- Perl 5 Interpreter (Optional):

  For some of the support scripts like `apxs` or `dbmmanage` (which are written in Perl) the Perl 5 interpreter is required (versions 5.003 and 5.004 are fine). If no such interpreter is found by APACI's `configure` script, this is fine. Of course, you still can build and install Apache 1.3. Only those support scripts cannot be used. If you have multiple Perl interpreters installed (perhaps a Perl 4 from the vendor and a Perl 5 from your own), then it is recommended to use the `—with-perl` option (see below) to make sure the correct one is selected by APACI.

- Dynamic Shared Object (DSO) support (Optional):

  To provide maximum flexibility Apache now is able to load modules under runtime via the DSO mechanism by using the pragmatic `dlopen()`/`dlsym()` system calls. These system calls are not available under all operating systems, and therefore you cannot use the DSO mechanism on all platforms. And Apache currently has only limited built-in knowledge on how to compile shared objects because it is heavily platform-dependent. The current state is:

- Out-of-the-box supported platforms are:

| | |
|---|---|
| Linux | SCO |
| SunOS | OpenStep/Mach |
| UnixWare | NetBSD |
| Mac OS X Server | HPUX |
| FreeBSD | ReliantUNIX |
| Solaris | DYNIX/ptx |
| AIX | BSDI |
| Max OS | DigitalUnix |
| OpenBSD | DGUX |
| IRIX | |

- Entirely unsupported platforms are:
  Ultrix

If your system is not on these lists but has the dlopen-style interface, you either have to provide the appropriate compiler and linker flags (see CFLAGS_SHLIB, LDFLAGS_SHLIB, and DFLAGS_SHLIB_EXPORT below) manually or at least make sure a Perl 5 interpreter is installed from which Apache can guess the options.

For more in-depth information about DSO support in Apache 1.3 please read the document htdocs/manual/dso.html carefully, particularly the section entitled "Advantages & Disadvantages" because using the DSO mechanism can have strange side-effects if you are not careful.

### Configuring the Source Tree

**NOTE:** *Although we'll often advise you to read the* src/Configuration.- tmpl *file parts to better understand the various options in this section, there is at no time any need to edit this file. The complete configuration takes place via command-line arguments and local shell variables for the* ./configure *script. The* src/Configuration.tmpl *file is just a read-only resource here.*

**INTRODUCTION**  The next step is to configure the Apache source tree for your particular platform and personal requirements. The most important setup here is the location prefix where Apache is to be installed later, because Apache has to be configured for this location to work correctly. But there are a lot of other options available to you.

As an idea of what possibilities you have, here is a typical example which compiles Apache for the installation tree /sw/pkg/apache with a particular compiler and flags plus the two additional modules mod_rewrite and mod_proxy for later loading through the DSO mechanism:

```
$ CC="pgcc" OPTIM="-O2" \
  ./configure --prefix=/sw/pkg/apache \
              --enable-module=rewrite --enable-shared=rewrite \
              --enable-module=proxy   --enable-shared=proxy
```

The complete reference of all configuration possibilities follows. For more real-world configuration examples, please check out the file README.configure.

Reference:

```
$ [CC=...]          [CFLAGS_SHLIB=...]              [TARGET=...]
  [OPTIM=...]       [LD_SHLIB=...]
  [CFLAGS=...]      [LDFLAGS_SHLIB=...]
  [INCLUDES=...]    [LDFLAGS_SHLIB_EXPORT=...]
  [LDFLAGS=...]     [RANLIB=...]
  [LIBS=...]        [DEPS=...]
  ./configure
    [--quiet]          [--prefix=DIR]              [--enable-rule=NAME]
    [--verbose]        [--exec-prefix=PREFIX]      [--disable-rule=NAME]
    [--shadow[=DIR]]   [--bindir=EPREFIX]          [--add-module=FILE]
    [--show-layout]    [--sbindir=DIR]             [--activate-module=FILE]
    [--help]           [--libexecdir=DIR]          [--enable-module=NAME]
                       [--mandir=DIR]              [--disable-module=NAME]
                       [--sysconfdir=DIR]          [--enable-shared=NAME]
                       [--datadir=DIR]             [--disable-shared=NAME]
                       [--includedir=DIR]          [--permute-module=N1:N2]
                       [--localstatedir=DIR]
                       [--runtimedir=DIR]          [--enable-suexec]
                       [--logfiledir=DIR]          [--suexec-caller=UID]
                       [--proxycachedir=DIR]       [--suexec-docroot=DIR]
                       [--with-layout=[FILE:]ID]   [--suexec-logfile=FILE]
                                                   [--suexec-userdir=DIR]
                       [--with-perl=FILE]          [--suexec-uidmin=UID]
                       [--without-support]         [--suexec-gidmin=GID]
                       [--without-confadjust]      [--suexec-safepath=PATH]
                       [--without-execstrip]
```

Use the CC, OPTIM, CFLAGS, INCLUDES, LDFLAGS, LIBS, CFLAGS_SHLIB, LD_SHLIB, LDFLAGS_SHLIB, LDFLAGS_SHLIB_ EXPORT, RANLIB, DEPS and TARGET environment variables to override the corresponding default entries in the src/Configuration.tmpl file (see the file for more information about their usage).

**NOTE:** *The syntax* KEY=VALUE./configure... *(one single line!) is the GNU Autoconf compatible way of specifying defines and can be used with Bourne shell-compatible shells only (sh, bash, ksh). If you use a different type of shell either use* env KEY=VALUE ./configure ... *when the* env *command is available on your system or use* setenv KEY VALUE; ./configure ... *if you use one of the C-shell variants (csh, tcsh).*

**NOTE:** *The above parameter names are the canonical ones used in Autoconf-style interfaces. But because* src/Configuration.tmpl *uses the prefix* EXTRA ... *for some variables (e.g.,* EXTRA_CFLAGS*) these variants are accepted for backward-compatibility reasons, too. But please use the canonical Autoconf-style names and don't rely on this.*

Use the `--prefix=PREFIX` and `--exec-prefix=EPREFIX` options to configure Apache to use a particular installation prefix. The default is `PREFIX=/usr/local/apache` and `EPREFIX=PREFIX`.

Use the `--bindir=DIR`, `--sbindir=DIR`, `--libexecdir=DIR`, `--mandir=DIR`, `--sysconfdir=DIR`, `--datadir=DIR`, `--includedir=DIR`, `--localstatedir=DIR`, `--runtimedir=DIR`, `--logfiledir=DIR` and `proxycachedir=DIR` option to change the paths for particular subdirectories of the installation tree.

Defaults are `bindir=EPREFIX/bin`, `sbindir=EPREFIX/sbin`, `libexecdir=EPREFIX/libexec`, `mandir=PREFIX/man`, `sysconfdir=PREFIX/etc.`, `datadir=PREFIX/share`, `includedir=PREFIX/include`, `localstatedir=PREFIX/var`, `runtimedir=PREFIX/var/run`, `logfiledir=PREFIX/var/log` and `proxycachedir=PREFIX/var/proxy`.

To reduce the pollution of shared installation locations (like `/usr/local/` or `/etc.`) with Apache files to a minimum the string `/apache` is automatically appended to `libexecdir`, `sysconfdir`, `datadir`, `localstatedir`, and `includedir` if (and only if) the following points apply for each path individually:

**1.** the path doesn't already contain the word `apache`

**2.** the path was not directly customized by the user

Keep in mind that per default, these paths are derived from `prefix` and `exec-prefix`, so usually it's only a matter of whether these paths contain `apache` or not. Although the defaults were defined with experience in mind, you always should make sure the paths fit your situation by checking the final paths via the `--layout option`.

Use the `--with-layout=[F:]ID` option to select a particular installation path base-layout. You always have to select a base-layout. There are currently two layouts pre-defined in the file `config.layout`: `Apache` for the classical Apache path layout and GNU for a path layout conforming to the GNU standards document. When you want to use your own custom layout FOO, either add a corresponding `<Layout FOO>...</Layout>` section to `config.layout` and use `--with-layout=FOO` or place it into your own file, say `config.mypaths`, and use `--with-layout=config.mypaths:FOO`.

Use the `--show-layout` option to check the final installation path layout while fiddling with the options above.

Use the `--enable-rule=NAME` and `--disable-rule=NAME` options to enable or disable a particular Rule from the Apache `src/Configuration.tmpl` file. The defaults (yes=enabled, no=disabled) can either be seen when running `./configure --help` or manually referenced in the `src/Configuration.tmpl` file.

Use the `--add-module=FILE` option to copy a module source file to the Apache `src/modules/extra/` directory and add an entry on-the-fly for it in the configuration file. `FILE` has to be a valid path to a C source file outside the Apache source tree, for instance `/path/to/mod_foo.c`. The added module is automatically activated and enabled. Use this option to automatically include a simple third-party module to the Apache build process.

Use the `--activate-module=FILE` option to add an entry for an existing module source file into the configuration file on-the-fly. `FILE` has to be a valid path beginning with `src/modules/`, and the file has to have been copied to this location in the Apache source tree before running configure. The module is automatically enabled. Use this option to automatically include a complex third-party module to the Apache build process when, for instance, a module like `mod_perl` or `mod_php3` consists of more than one file which was created by a third-party configuration scheme.

Use the `--enable-module=NAME` and `--disable-module=NAME` options to enable or disable a particular already distributed module from the Apache `src/Configuration.tmpl` file. The correct module names (no `mod_` prefix!) and defaults (yes=enabled, no=disabled) can be seen when running `./configure --help`. There are two special NAME variants: `all` for enabling or disabling all modules and `most` for enabling or disabling only these modules which are useable on all platforms (currently this is `all` minus the modules `auth_db`, `log_agent`, `log_referer`, `example`, `so` and `mmap_static`). For a compact overview of available modules see the following list (remove the `mod_` prefix to get the NAME).

**LIST OF AVAILABLE MODULES**

### Environment Creation

| | | |
|---|---|---|
| + | `mod_env` | Set environment variables for CGI/SSI scripts |
| + | `mod_setenvif` | Set environment variables based on HTTP headers |
| - | `mod_unique_id` | Generate unique identifiers for request |

### Content Type Decisions

| | | |
|---|---|---|
| + | mod_mime | Content type/encoding determination (configured) |
| - | mod_mime_magic | Content type/encoding determination (automatic) |
| + | mod_negotiation | Content selection based on the HTTP Accept* headers |

### Directory Handling

| | | |
|---|---|---|
| + | mod_dir | Directory and directory default file handling |
| + | mod_autoindex | Automated directory index file generation |

### Access Control

| | | |
|---|---|---|
| + | mod_access | Access control (user, host, network) |
| + | mod_auth | HTTP basic authentication (user, passwd) |
| - | mod_auth_dbm | HTTP basic authentication via Unix NDBM files |
| - | mod_auth_db | HTTP basic authentication via Berkeley-DB files |
| - | mod_auth_anon | HTTP basic authentication for anonymous-style users |
| - | mod_digest | HTTP digest authentication |

### HTTP Response

| | | |
|---|---|---|
| - | mod_headers | Arbitrary HTTP response headers (configured) |
| - | mod_cern_meta | Arbitrary HTTP response headers (CERN-style files) |
| - | mod_expires | Expires HTTP responses |
| + | mod_asis | Raw HTTP responses |

### Scripting

| | | |
|---|---|---|
| + | mod_include | Server Side Includes (SSI) support |
| + | mod_cgi | Common Gateway Interface (CGI) support |
| + | mod_actions | Map CGI scripts to act as internal handlers |

### Internal Content Handlers

| | | |
|---|---|---|
| + | `mod_status` | Content handler for server run-time status |
| - | `mod_info` | Content handler for server configuration summary |

### Request Logging

| | | |
|---|---|---|
| + | `mod_log_config` | Customizable logging of requests |
| - | `mod_log_agent` | Specialized HTTP user-agent logging (deprecated) |
| - | `mod_log_refer` | Specialized HTTP referrer logging   (deprecated) |
| - | `mod_usertrack` | Logging of user click-trails via HTTP cookies |

### Miscellaneous

| | | |
|---|---|---|
| + | `mod_imap` | Server-side image map support |
| - | `mod_proxy` | Caching proxy module (HTTP, HTTPS, FTP) |
| - | `mod_so` | Dynamic Shared Object (DSO) bootstrapping |

### Experimental

| | | |
|---|---|---|
| - | `mod_mmap_static` | Caching of frequently served pages via `mmap()` |

### Development

| | | |
|---|---|---|
| - | `mod_example` | Apache API demonstration (developers only) |

| | |
|---|---|
| + | enabled per default (disable with --disable-module) |
| - | disabled per default (enable  with --enable-module) |

Use the `--enable-shared=NAME` and `--disable-shared=NAME` options to enable or disable the shared object support for a particular module from the Apache `src/Configuration.tmpl` file. The defaults (yes=enabled, no=disabled) can be seen when running `./configure --help`. There are two special `NAME` variants: `max` for enabling or disabling DSO on all modules except the bootstrapping `so` module, and `remain` for enabling or disabling DSO for only those modules which are still not enabled (and this way implicitly enables them).

*Note 1:* The `--enable-shared` option does not automatically enable the module, because there are variants like `--enable-shared=max` which should not imply `--enable-module=all`.

*Note 2:* Per default, the DSO mechanism is globally disabled, i.e., no modules are built as shared objects.

*Note 3:* The usage of any `--enable-shared` option automatically implies an `--enable-module=so` option because the bootstrapping module `mod_so` is always needed for DSO support.

*Note 4:* When you later want to extend your Apache installation via third-party modules through the DSO+APXS mechanism, make sure that you at least compile with `mod_so` included, even when no distributed modules are built as shared objects. This can be achieved by explicitly using `--enable-module=so`.

*Note 5:* Some platforms require `--enable-rule=SHARED_CORE` for the DSO mechanism to work, i.e., when you want to use `--enable-shared` for some modules on these platforms you also have to enable the `SHARED_CORE` rule. For more details please read the document `htdocs/manual/dso.html`.

Use the `--permute-module=N1:N2` option to permutate the AddModule lines of modules `mod_N1` and `mod_N2` in the configuration file. This method gives modules different priorities. Two special and important variants are supported for the option argument: first `BEGIN:N` which permutes module `mod_N` with the beginning of the module list, i.e., it moves the module to the beginning of the list (giving it lowest priority). And second, `N:END` which permutes `mod_N` with the end of the module list, i.e., it moves the module to the end of the list (giving it highest priority).

Use the `--with-perl=FILE` option to select a particular Perl interpreter executable to be used with Apache. By default, APACI tries to find it automatically. But if multiple Perl instances exist on your system, you have to select the correct one manually.

Use the `--without-support` option to explicitly disable the build and installation of support tools from the `src/support/` area. This can be useful when you have compilation problems with one or more of these programs on your platform, or if you just don't need them.

Use the `--without-confadjust` option to explicitly disable some built user/situation-dependent adjustments to the `config` files (Group, Port, ServerAdmin, ServerName, etc.). This is usually only interesting for vendor package maintainers who want to force the keeping of defaults.

Use the `--without-execstrip` option to disable the stripping of executables on installation. This can be important on some platforms in combination with `--enable-rule=SHARED_CORE` or if Apache was built with debugging symbols which shouldn't be lost.

Use the `--enable-suexec` option to enable the suEXEC feature by building and installing the `suexec` support program. Use `--suexec-caller=UID` to set the allowed caller user ID; `--suexec-userdir=DIR` to set the user subdirectory, `--suexec-docroot=DIR` to set the `suexec` root directory, `--suexec-uidmin=UID/--suexec-gidmin=GID` to set the minimal allowed UID/GID, `--suexec-logfile=FILE` to set the log-file, and `--suexec-safepath=PATH` to set the safe shell PATH for the suEXEC feature. At least one `--suexec-xxxxx` option has to be provided together with the `--enable-suexec` option to let APACI accept your request for using the suEXEC feature.

*Caution:* For details about the suEXEC feature, we highly recommend that you read the document `htdocs/manual/suexec.html` before using the above options.

Using the suEXEC feature properly can considerably reduce the security risks involved with allowing users to develop and run private CGI or SSI programs. However, if `suexec` is improperly configured, it can cause any number of problems and possibly create new holes in your computer's security. If you aren't familiar with managing `setuid` root programs and the security issues they present, we highly recommend that you not consider using `suexec` and keep away from these options.

Use the `--shadow` option to let APACI create a shadow source tree of the sources for building. This is useful when you want to build for different platforms in parallel (usually through an NFS, AFS, or DFS mounted file system). You may specify a directory to the `--shadow` option into which the shadow tree will be created.

Use the `--quiet` option to disable all configuration verbose messages.

Use the `--verbose` option to enable additional verbose messages.

### Building the Package

Now you can build the various parts which form the Apache package by simply running the command

```
$ make
```

Please be patient here, this takes approximately two minutes to complete under a Pentium-166/FreeBSD-2.2 system, depending on the number of modules you have enabled.

### Installing the Package

Now it's time to install the package under the configured installation PREFIX (see --prefix option above) by running:

```
$ make install
```

For the paranoid hackers among us, the above command really installs under prefix _only_, i.e., no other stuff from your system is touched. Even if you upgrade an existing installation, your configuration files in PREFIX/etc./ are preserved.

*Note for package authors:* To simplify rolling a package tarball from the installed files, APACI provides a way to override the installation root for the install step. Additionally, you can get rid of the user message at the end of the installation process by using the install-quiet target. For example:

```
$ make install-quiet root=/tmp/apache-root
```

**NOTE:** *Please note that for reinstalling Apache on AIX you should use the command* slibclean *before using* make install *to really unload any old versions of the DSO's that might still be cached by the dynamic loader.*

### Testing the Package

Now you can fire up your Apache HTTP server by immediately running

```
$ PREFIX/bin/apachectl start
```

and then you should be able to request your first document via URL http://localhost/ (when you built and installed Apache as root or at least used the --without-confadjust option) or http://localhost:8080/ (when you built and installed Apache as a regular user). Then stop the server again by running:

```
$ PREFIX/bin/apachectl stop
```

### Customizing the Package

Finally, you can customize your Apache HTTP server by editing the configuration files under PREFIX/etc./.

```
$ vi PREFIX/etc./httpd.conf
$ vi PREFIX/etc./access.conf
$ vi PREFIX/etc./srm.conf
```

Have a look at the Apache manual under htdocs/manual/ or http://www.apache.org/docs/ for a complete reference of available configuration directives.

### Preparing the System

Proper operation of a public HTTP server requires at least the following:

1. A correctly working TCP/IP layer, since HTTP is implemented on top of TCP/IP. Although modern UNIX platforms have good networking layers, always make sure you have all official vendor patches referring to the network layer applied.

2. Accurate time keeping, since elements of the HTTP protocol are expressed as the time of day. So, it's time to investigate setting some time-synchronization facility on your system. Usually the ntpdate or xntpd programs are used for this purpose which are based on the Network Time Protocol (NTP). See the USENET newsgroup comp.protocols.time.ntp and the NTP homepage at http://www.eecis.udel.edu/~ntp/ for more details about NTP software and public time servers.

### Contacts

- If you want to be informed about new code releases, bug fixes, security fixes, general news, and information about the Apache servers, subscribe to the Apache-announce mailing list as described under http://www.apache.org/announcelist.html.

- If you want freely available support for running Apache, please join the Apache user community by subscribing at least to the following USENET newsgroup: `comp.infosystems.www.servers.unix`.
- If you want commercial support for running Apache, please contact one of the companies and contractors which are listed at `http://www.apache.org/info/support.cgi`.
- If you have a concrete bug report for Apache, please go to the Apache Group Bug Database and submit your report: `http://www.apache.org/bug_report.html`.
- If you want to participate in actively developing Apache, please subscribe to the `new-httpd` mailing list as described at `http://dev.apache.org/mailing-lists`.

Thanks for running Apache.
The Apache Group
`http://www.apache.org/`

# Apache JServ Installation on UNIX

## Introduction

This file guides you through the installation process for UNIX systems.

**NOTE:** *Win32 users are highly recommended to use the self-installing distribution (the* `exe` *distribution) or read the proper instructions in the* `docs/install/` *directory.*

## Installing the Apache JServ Servlet Engine

### Requirements

The following requirements exist for building Apache JServ:

- Disk Space:
  The complete Apache JServ installation requires less than 2MB of

hard disk space. The compiled, non-compressed jar archive is more or less 100KB.

- Apache HTTP Server:

  Apache JServ 1.0 works only with the Apache HTTP Server (both versions 1.2 and 1.3 are supported).

- Java Runtime Environment:

  A fully compliant Java 1.1 Runtime Environment is required for Apache JServ to execute.

  The official list of compatible ports is found on the Sun Java Web site: <http://java.sun.com/cgi-bin/java-ports.cgi>.

  The list of supported platforms and Java ports may be found in the documentation (docs/support.html).

  *Note:* since Apache JServ uses only standard Java APIs (java.*), please do not submit a bug report if your Java virtual machine fails to execute Apache JServ because of broken compliance. Send it to your Java virtual machine implementors.

- Java Servlet Development Kit 2.0:

  The Sun Java JSDK 2.0 is required by Apache JServ for proper servlet execution. This package is freely available from the Sun Java Web site:

  <http://java.sun.com/products/servlet/index.html>

  *Note:* this version of Apache JServ requires exactly the 2.0 version of the JSDK in order to operate properly. Any other version [past, present, or future and including the version that comes with the Java Server Pages (JSP) jar file] is not supported.

- Java Compiler:

  Since most distributions include the precompiled Java binary archive, compilation of the Java source is optional.

  A list of supported Java compilers may be found in the documentation (docs/support.html).

  *Note:* a Java compiler is needed to build servlets if you plan to write your own.

- ANSI-C Compiler:

  Make sure you have an ANSI-C compiler installed and relative Make tools. The GNU C compiler (GCC version 2.7.2 is fine) and GNU Make (make preferably version 3.75) from the Free Software Foundation (FSF) is recommended. If you don't have GCC then at least make sure your vendor's compiler is ANSI compliant. You can find the homepage of GNU at `<http://www.gnu.org/>` and the GCC distribution under `http://www.gnu.org/order/ftp.html`.

■ Dynamic Shared Object (DSO) support (Optional):

See your Apache documentation for more information on how to add DSO support and if your system is supported.

### Choose How To Add the Apache JServ Module to Apache

There are two choices:

■ Compile it in: This requires that you have a source distribution of the Apache server handy as it adds source to that tree and lets Apache build the Apache JServ module into itself statically.

■ DSO: This requires that you have an installation of Apache 1.3. that was configured to have DSO support when it was built. If you're not sure whether your's does, follow the instructions on configuring Apache JServ for DSO and the configure script will tell you.

### Configure Apache

If you are using a source distribution then you have to configure Apache first (some generated header files are needed for Apache JServ to pass its configure checks). You do not need to worry about specifying the Apache JServ module.

If you are using DSO then you can ignore this step. If you have a source distribution and would like to build it with DSO support and install it for use by Apache JServ, then use the following options when configuring Apache:

```
--enable-rule=SHARED_CORE --enable-module=so
```

### Configure Apache JServ

Now you are ready to configure Apache JServ. To do this you may (or may not) need to specify quite a few arguments to configure. These are:

■ Apache Dir

For DSO use: `--with-apache-install=/path/to/apache/ installation`

*Note:* The configure script will check the default installation `dir` so if you have it there you may leave this argument out.

For a static compile use: `--with-apache-src=/path/to/apache/source`

*Note:* For those using a source distribution Apache JServ will configure Apache for you (taking care to preserve your previous configuration) if you use this option: `--enable-apache-conf`

- Prefix Path

  `make install` will copy the documentation and Apache JServ `.jar` file into the directory that you specify with this option: `--prefix=/usr/local/jserv`

- JDK programs (java, javac, javadoc, and jar)

  By default, `configure` will first look at the `JDK_HOME` and `JAVA_HOME` environment variables, if they aren't set then `configure` will check your PATH environment variable. The results from using the PATH can be overriden by: `--with-jdk-home=/path/to/jdk`.

  If they are not found, `configure` will tell you and default back to whatever is in your PATH.

  *Note:* By default, debugging symbols are left out of the JServ classes, you can put them back in by using this option: `--enable-debugging`

  *Note:* By default, the jar file is not compressed, this can be changed with: `--enable-compressed-jar`

- JSDK classes

  Apache JServ needs to know where your servlet classes are. If they are not in your `CLASSPATH` then you need to specify them with: `--with-jsdk=/path/to/jsdk.jar` or `--with-jsdk=/path/to/unpacked/jsdk`

**Build**

Once you have configured Apache JServ you can run `make`. Run `make install` to make a `.jar` file, and copy it and the `docs` into the directory you specified as `--prefix`.

If you are using an Apache source distribution, then you also have to run `make` in the Apache source directory to build Apache with Apache JServ support in it.

You can see if Apache has loaded the `mod_jserv` module by executing `httpd -l`.

See the HTML `docs` for information on setting up and running servlets.

**Manual Installation**

If you want to install Apache JServ manually, you'll need to compile the Java classes by hand. Make sure you have the JSDK classes in your classpath, and compile `src/java/org/apache/java/*/*.java` and `src/java/org/apache/jserv/*.java`. Make a jar file from these, or copy them into your classpath, or list this directory in your classpath.

Next, you'll need to set up Apache. First, create a subdirectory in `$apache_dir/src/modules` called `jserv`. Then copy `Makefile.tmpl`, `.gif`, and `.[ch]` from `src/c` to `$apache_dir/src/modules/jserv`. Then either edit `Configuration`, adding `AddModule modules/jserv/mod_jserv.o` (if you use `Configure`), or run `Configure` with (in addition to whatever options are appropriate for you) `--activate-module= src/modules/jserv/mod_jserv.c`. Then build Apache as you normally do.

This will create `mod_jserv.o` and link it in (statically); `docs` for creating `mod_jserv.so` (a DSO) will be added later. In the meantime, you can use Apache JServ's `configure` to create this.

Last, you'll need to create a `jserv.properties` file; `example/jserv.properties` provides a sample. You'll also need to add certain directives to your Apache configuration files (or include another file via `Include`); `example/jserv.conf` provides a sample for this.

**Problems**

First read the Frequently Asked Questions and documentation to see if your issues have already been covered. If you think that you have found a bug, please report it to the Apache Bug Database at:

```
<http://bugs.apache.org/>
```

Note that manual mode operation is not supported in this beta release; it will be in a future release.

If you just have a question, please join the Apache JServ Users mailing list and ask there. Please do not mail project group members directly because this is a 100% volunteer project and most members have day jobs.

Enjoy!
The Apache JServ Project

# PostgreSQL Installation

For a fresh install or upgrading from previous releases of PostgreSQL:

**1.** Create the PostgreSQL superuser account. This is the user the server will run as. For production use you should create a separate, unprivileged account (postgres is commonly used). If you do not have root access or just want to play around, your own user account is enough.

Running PostgreSQL as root, bin, or any other account with special access rights is a security risk; don't do it. The postmaster will in fact refuse to start as root.

You need not do the building and installation itself under this account (although you can). You will be told when you need to login as the database superuser.

**2.** Configure the source code for your system. It is this step at which you can specify your actual installation path for the build process and make choices about what gets installed. Change into the `src` subdirectory and type:

```
./configure
```

followed by any options you might want to give it. For a first installation you should be able to do fine without any. For a complete list of options, type:

```
./configure --help
```

Some of the more commonly used ones are:

```
--prefix=BASEDIR
```

Select a different base directory for the installation of PostgreSQL. The default is `/usr/local/pgsql`

```
--enable-locale
```

if you want to use locales.

```
--enable-multibyte
```

allows the use of multibyte character encodings. This is primarily for languages like Japanese, Korean, or Chinese.

```
--with-perl
```

builds the Perl interface and `plperl` extension language. Please note that the Perl interface needs to be installed into the usual place for Perl modules (typically under `/usr/lib/perl`), so you must have root access to perform the installation step. (It is often easiest to leave out `--with-perl` initially, and then build and install the Perl interface after completing the installation of PostgreSQL itself.)

```
--with-odbc
```

builds the ODBC driver package.

```
--with-tcl
```

builds interface libraries and programs requiring Tcl/Tk, including `libpgtcl`, `pgtclsh`, and `pgtksh`.

**3.** Compile the program. Type:

```
gmake
```

The compilation process can take anywhere from 10 minutes to an hour. Your mileage will most certainly vary. Remember to use GNU make.

The last line displayed will hopefully be:

```
All of PostgreSQL is successfully made. Ready to install.
```

**4.** If you want to test the newly built server before you install it, you can run the regression tests at this point. The regression tests are a test suite to verify that PostgreSQL runs on your machine in the way the developers expected it to. For detailed instructions see Regression Test. (Be sure to use the "parallel regress test" method, since the sequential method only works with an already-installed server.)

**5.** If you are not upgrading an existing system then skip to step 7. You now need to back up your existing database. To dump your fairly recent post-6.0 database installation, type

```
pg_dumpall db.out
```

If you wish to preserve object id's (OIDs), then use the -o option when running `pg_dumpall`. However, unless you have a special reason for doing this (such as using OIDs as keys in tables), don't do it.

Make sure to use the `pg_dumpall` command from the version you are currently running. Version 7.0's `pg_dumpall` will not work on older databases. However, if you are still using 6.0, do not use the `pg_dumpall` script from 6.0 or everything will be owned by the PostgreSQL superuser after you reload. In that case you should grab `pg_dumpall` from a later 6.x.x release. If you are upgrading from a version prior to Postgres95 v1.09 then you must back up your database, install Postgres95 v1.09, restore your database, then back it up again.

*Note:* You must make sure that your database is not updated in the middle of your backup. If necessary, bring down postmaster, edit the permissions in file `/usr/local/pgsql/data/pg_hba.conf` to allow only you on, then bring postmaster back up.

**6.** If you are upgrading an existing system then kill the database server now. Type

```
ps ax | grep postmaster
```

or

```
ps -e | grep postmaster
```

(It depends on your system which one of these two works. No harm can be done by typing the wrong one.) This should list the process numbers for a number of processes, similar to this:

```
263   ?   SW    0:00 (postmaster)
777   p1  S     0:00 grep postmaster
```

Type the following line, with pid replaced by the process id for process postmaster (263 in the above case). (Do not use the id for the process "grep postmaster".)

```
kill pid
```

*Note:* On systems which have PostgreSQL started at boot time, there is probably a startup file that will accomplish the same thing. For example, on a Redhat Linux system one might find that the following works:

```
/etc./rc.d/init.d/postgres.init stop
```

Also move the old directories out of the way. Type the following:

```
mv /usr/local/pgsql /usr/local/pgsql.old
```

(substitute your particular paths).

**7.** Install the PostgreSQL executable files and libraries. Type

```
gmake install
```

You should do this step as the user that you want the installed executables to be owned by. This does not have to be the same as the database superuser; some people prefer to have the installed files be owned by root.

**8.** If necessary, tell your system how to find the new shared libraries. How to do this varies between platforms. The most widely usable method is to set the environment variable LD_LIBRARY_PATH:

```
LD_LIBRARY_PATH=/usr/local/pgsql/lib
export LD_LIBRARY_PATH
```

on sh, ksh, bash, zsh or

```
setenv LD_LIBRARY_PATH /usr/local/pgsql/lib
```

on csh or tcsh. You might want to put this into a shell startup file such as /etc./profile.

On some systems the following is the preferred method, but you must have root access. Edit file /etc./ld.so.conf to add a line

```
/usr/local/pgsql/lib
```

Then run command /sbin/ldconfig.

If in doubt, refer to the manual pages of your system. If you later on get a message like

```
psql: error in loading shared libraries libpq.so.2.1: cannot open
  shared object file: No such file or directory
```

then the above was necessary. Simply do this step then.

**9.** Create the database installation (the working data files). To do this you must log in to your PostgreSQL superuser account. It will not work as root.

```
mkdir /usr/local/pgsql/data
chown postgres /usr/local/pgsql/data
su - postgres
/usr/local/pgsql/bin/initdb -D /usr/local/pgsql/data
```

The -D option specifies the location where the data will be stored. You can use any path you want, it does not have to be under the installation directory. Just make sure that the superuser account can write to the directory (or create it, if it doesn't already exist) before starting `initdb`. (If you have already been doing the installation up to now as the PostgreSQL superuser, you may have to log in as root temporarily to create the data directory underneath a root-owned directory.)

**10.** The previous step should have told you how to start up the database server. Do so now. The command should look something like

```
/usr/local/pgsql/bin/postmaster -D /usr/local/pgsql/data
```

This will start the server in the foreground. To make it detach to the background, you can use the -S option, but then you won't see any log messages the server produces. A better way to put the server in the background is

```
nohup /usr/local/pgsql/bin/postmaster -D /usr/local/pgsql/data \
</dev/null >>server.log 2>>1 &
```

**11.** If you are upgrading from an existing installation, dump your data back in:

```
/usr/local/pgsql/bin/psql -d template1 -f db.out
```

You also might want to copy over the old `pg_hba.conf` file and any other files you might have had set up for authentication, such as password files.

This concludes the installation proper. To make your life more productive and enjoyable you should look at the following optional steps and suggestions.

Life will be more convenient if you set up some environment variables. First of all you probably want to include `/usr/local/pgsql/bin` (or equivalent) into your PATH. To do this, add the following to your shell startup file, such as `~/.bash_profile` (or `/etc./profile`, if you want it to affect every user):

```
PATH=$PATH:/usr/local/pgsql/bin
```

Furthermore, if you set **PGDATA** in the environment of the PostgreSQL superuser, you can omit the -D for postmaster and initdb. You probably want to install the man and HTML documentation. Type

```
cd /usr/src/pgsql/postgresql-7.0/doc
gmake install
```

This will install files under /usr/local/pgsql/doc and /usr/local/pgsql/man. To enable your system to find the man documentation, you need to add a line like the following to a shell startup file:

```
MANPATH=$MANPATH:/usr/local/pgsql/man
```

The documentation is also available in PostScript format. If you have a PostScript printer, or have your machine already set up to accept PostScript files using a print filter, then to print the User's Guide simply type

```
cd /usr/local/pgsql/doc
gunzip -c user.ps.tz | lpr
```

Here is how you might do it if you have Ghostscript on your system and are writing to a laserjet printer.

```
gunzip -c user.ps.gz \
| gs -sDEVICE=laserjet -r300 -q -dNOPAUSE -sOutputFile=- \
| lpr
```

Printer setups can vary wildly from system to system. If in doubt, consult your manuals or your local expert.

The Adminstrator's Guide should probably be your first reading if you are completely new to PostgreSQL, as it contains information about how to set up database users and authentication.

Usually, you will want to modify your computer so that it will automatically start the database server whenever it boots. This is not required; the PostgreSQL server can be run successfully from non-privileged accounts without root intervention.

Different systems have different conventions for starting up daemons at boot time, so you are advised to familiarize yourself with them. Most systems have a file /etc./rc.local or /etc./rc.d/rc.local which is almost certainly no bad place to put such a command. Whatever you do, postmaster must be run by the PostgreSQL superuser (postgres) and not by root or any other user. Therefore you probably always want to form your command lines along the lines of su -c '...' postgres.

It might be advisable to keep a log of the server output. To start the server that way try:

```
nohup su -c 'postmaster -D /usr/local/pgsql/data > server.log
 2>&1' postgres &
```

Here are a few more operating system–specific suggestions.

Edit file `rc.local` on NetBSD or file `rc2.d` on SPARC Solaris 2.5.1 to contain the following single line:

```
su postgres -c "/usr/local/pgsql/bin/postmaster -S -D
/usr/local/pgsql/data"
```

In FreeBSD 2.2-RELEASE edit /usr/local/etc/rc.d/pgsql.sh to contain the following lines and make it `chmod 755` and `chown root:bin`.

```
#!/bin/sh
[ -x /usr/local/pgsql/bin/postmaster ] && {
su -l pgsql -c 'exec /usr/local/pgsql/bin/postmaster
-D/usr/local/pgsql/data
-S -o -F > /usr/local/pgsql/errlog' &
echo -n ' pgsql'
}
```

You may put the line breaks as shown above. The shell is smart enough to keep parsing beyond end-of-line if there is an expression unfinished. The exec saves one layer of shell under the postmaster process so the parent is `init`.

In RedHat Linux add a file /etc./rc.d/init.d/postgres.init which is based on the example in contrib/.linux/. Then make a soft-link to this file from /etc./rc.d/rc5.d/S98postgres.init.

Run the regression tests against the installed server (using the sequential test method). If you didn't run the tests before installation, you should definitely do it now. For detailed instructions see Regression Test.

To start playing around, set up the paths as explained above and start the server. To create a database, type

```
createdb testdb
```

Then enter

```
psql testdb
```

to connect to that database. At the prompt you can enter SQL commands and start experimenting.

# APPENDIX B

## Setting Up the PostgreSQL Database

This Appendix discusses installation of PostgreSQL. It also lists all of the databases used by the sample code in the book. For each database, a listing of the tables in that database is presented as well as the SQL code required to create the table. Procedures for loading the databases with data identical to that used in the sample code in the book are discussed.

# Configuring and Running PostgreSQL

Most Linux distributions include PostgreSQL. If yours does not, or if you chose not to include it when you installed Linux, you should install it from the CD. PostgreSQL is also available from postgresql.org.

The document at URL http://www.linuxdoc.org/HOWTO/ PostgreSQL-HOWTO.html contains installation instructions and useful tips. The most important points are:

- Create a user called postgres belonging to the postgres group.

- Log in as user postgres to perform the installation.

- Set the environment variable PG_DATA to the directory in which the databases are located. For host dormouse.instantjsp.com, this is /usr/local/postgres/data.

- Set the environment variable PGLIB to the directory in which the PostgreSQL library is located. For host dormouse.instantjsp.com, this is /usr/local/pgsql/lib.

- Run initdb to initialize the database system.

- Start PostgreSQL by typing postmaster -iS -p 5432. The S parameter is important. It indicates that PostgreSQL is to accept connections from TCP/IP sockets, which is required by JDBC.

# The Databases

To execute the sample code in the book, you need to create five databases. You create a database using the command `createdb dbname`, where `dbname` is the database name. The first column in Table B-1 contains the names of the five databases.

# The Database Tables

For each database, the second column in Table B-1 contains the names of the tables in that database. The procedure for creating a table and loading it with data is as follows:

1. Log in as user `postgres`.
2. Copy all of the files from the `/database` directory on the CD to `mydir`, where `mydir` is a directory of your own choosing.
3. Start the interactive client by typing `psql dbname`, where `dbname` is the name of the database for which you want to create and load tables.
4. At the `psql` prompt, type `\i /mydir/cr_tablename`, where `tablename` is the name of a table found in column 2 of Table B-1. You will see messages displayed as the table is created. When you see EOF displayed, you may continue.
5. If column 3 contains a sequence name, type `\i /mydir/cr_seqname`, where `seqname` is the name of the sequence found in column 3. You will see messages displayed as the sequence is created. When you see EOF displayed, you may continue.
6. Type `\d tablename` to display the table definition.
7. Type `\d seqname` to display the sequence (if applicable).
8. Type `\copy tablename from /mydir/f_tablename`, substituting the appropriate table name. This will load the table from the file `/mydir/f_tablename`.

**TABLE B-1**

Databases and
Tables

| Database Name | Table Name | Sequence Name |
| --- | --- | --- |
| business | customer | seq_cust |
| | feedback | |
| | orderdetail | |
| | orders | seq_ord |
| | prefcust | |
| | prices | |
| | product_categories | seq_cat |
| | product_rating | |
| | product_subcats | seq_subcat |
| | products | seq_sku |
| | satisfaction | |
| | special_offers | |
| | survey | |
| | survey_data | |
| company | faqs | faq_seq |
| | saleslit | |
| empl | empdata | |
| | skills | |
| fun | currentvotes | |
| | fortunes | fortune_seq |
| | messages | |
| | participants | |
| | postcards | postcard_seq |
| | songlist | |
| instantjsp | empdata | |
| | idpassword | |
| | rawpagestats | |
| | sessionstats | |

9. Type `select * from tablename` to display the rows of data in the table.

10. Repeat steps 4 through 9 for each table in the database.

11. Type `vacuum` to clean up.

12. Type `\q` to exit from the interactive client.

13. Repeat steps 3 through 10 for each of the five databases.

*NOTE*:   *Where you see a command of the type* `command` *above, you do not type the quotes.*

# APPENDIX C

## THE JSP API

This Appendix describes each class and interface in the JavaServer Pages API. The classes and interfaces are presented in alphabetical order. For each class or interface, the hierarchy is given as well as a description, a method summary, inherited methods, and a detailed description of each method.

# javax.servlet.jsp
# Interface HttpJspPage

```
public abstract interface HttpJspPage
    extends JspPage
```

This is the interface that a JSP processor-generated class for the HTTP protocol must satisfy.

## Method Summary

| _jspService | Corresponds to the body of the JSP page. |
|---|---|

## Methods Inherited from javax.servlet.jsp.JspPage

jspDestroy, jspInit

## Methods Inherited from Interface javax.servlet.Servlet

destroy, getServletConfig, getServletInfo, init, service

## Method Detail

### _jspService

```
void _jspService(javax.servlet.http.HttpServletRequest request,
                 javax.servlet.http.HttpServletResponse response)
        throws javax.servlet.servletException, java.io.IOException
```

_jspService corresponds to the body of the JSP page. This method is defined automatically by the JSP processor and should *never be defined by the JSP author.*

# javax.servlet.jsp
# JspEngineInfo

```
public abstract class JspEngineInfo
    extends java.lang.Object
```

JspEngineInfo is an abstract class that provides information on the current JSP engine.

## Method Summary

| getImplementationVersion | Returns implementation version. |
| --- | --- |

## Methods Inherited from `java.lang.Object`

```
clone, equals, finalize, getClass, hashCode, notify, notifyAll,
toString, wait, wait, wait
```

## Method Detail

### getImplementationVersion

```
public java.lang.String getImplementationVersion()
```

Specification version numbers use a "Dewey Decimal" syntax that consists of positive decimal integers separated by periods "." (for example, "2.0" or "1.2.3.4.5.6.7"). This allows an extensible number to be used to represent major, minor, micro (and so forth) versions. The version number must begin with a number.

*Returns:*

The specification version; null is returned if it is not known

# javax.servlet.jsp
# Class JspFactory

```
public abstract class JspFactory
    extends java.lang.Object
```

JspFactory is an abstract class that defines a number of factory methods available to a JSP page at runtime for the purposes of creating instances of various interfaces and classes used to support the JSP implementation.

During its initialization, a conformant JSP engine implementation will instantiate an implementation-dependent subclass of this class and make it globally available for use by JSP implementation classes by registering the instance created with this class via the static setDefaultFactory() method.

The JspFactory is *not* intended for use by the JSP page author.

## Method Summary

| | |
|---|---|
| getDefaultFactory | Returns the default factory for this implementation. |
| getEngineInfo | Gets implementation-specific information on the current JSP engine. |
| getPageContext | Obtains an instance of an implementation-dependent javax.servlet.jsp.PageContext abstract class for the calling Servlet and currently pending request and response. |
| releasePageContext | Releases a previously allocated PageContext object. |
| setDefaultFactory | Sets the default factory for this implementation. |

## Methods Inherited from java.lang.object

```
clone, equals, finalize, getClass, hashCode, notify, notifyAll,
  toString, wait, wait, wait
```

## Method Detail

### getDefaultFactory

```
public static jspFactory getDefaultFactory()
```

*Returns:*

The default factory for this implementation

### getEngineInfo

```
public abstract JspEngineInfo getEngineInfo()
```

Called to get implementation-specific information on the current JSP engine.

*Returns:*

A JspEngineInfo object describing the current JSP engine

### getPageContext

```
public abstract PageContext getPageContext(
                javax.servlet.Servlet servlet,
                javax.servlet.ServletRequest request,
                javax.servlet.ServletResponse response,
                java.lang.String errorPageURL,
                boolean needSession,
                int buffer,
                boolean autoflush)
```

Obtains an instance of an implementation-dependent javax.servlet.jsp.PageContext abstract class for the calling Servlet and currently pending request and response.

This method is typically called early in the processing of the _jspService() method of a JSP implementation class to obtain a PageContext object for the request being processed.

Invoking this method results in the PageContext.initialize() method being invoked. The PageContext returned is properly initialized.

All PageContext objects obtained via this method shall be released by invoking releasePageContext().

*Parameters:*

| | |
|---|---|
| servlet | The requesting Servlet |
| config | The ServletConfig for the requesting Servlet |
| request | The current request pending on the Servlet |

| | |
|---|---|
| response | The current response pending on the Servlet |
| errorPageURL | The URL of the errorpage for the requesting JSP, or null |
| needsSession | True, if the JSP participates in a session |
| buffer | Size of buffer in bytes, PageContext.-NO_BUFFER if no buffer, PageContext.-DEFAULT_BUFFER if implementation default |
| autoflush | True, if the buffer should autoflush to the output stream on buffer overflow; false, if it should throw an IOException |

*Returns:*

The page context

*See also:*

PageContext

### releasePageContext

```
public static void releasePageContext(PageContext pc)
```

Called to release a previously allocated PageContext object. Results in PageContext.release() being invoked. This method should be invoked prior to returning from the _jspService() method of a JSP implementation class.

*Parameters:*

pc A PageContext previously obtained by getPageContext()

### setDefaultFactory

```
public static void setDefaultFactory(JspFactory default)
```

Set the default factory for this implementation. It is illegal for any principal entity other than the JSP Engine runtime to call this method.

*Parameters:*

default The default factory implementation

# javax.servlet.jsp
# Interface JspPage

```
public abstract interface JspPage
    extends javax.servlet.Servlet
```

This is the interface that a JSP processor-generated class must satisfy.

This interface defines two methods: jspInit() and jspDestroy(). A service method, jspService() is defined in protocol-specific subinterfaces. The only current subinterface is HttpJspPage.

A class implementing this interface is responsible for invoking the preceding methods at the appropriate time based on the corresponding Servlet-based method invocations.

The jspInit() and jspDestroy() methods can be defined by a JSP author.

## Method Summary

| | |
|---|---|
| jspInit | Invoked when JSP page is initialized. |
| jspDestroy | Invoked before JSP page is destroyed. |

## Methods Inherited from Interface javax.servlet.Servlet

| |
|---|
| destroy, getServletConfig, getServletInfo, init, service |

## Method Detail

### jspInit

```
public void jspInit()
```

jspInit() is invoked when the JspPage is initialized. At this point getServletConfig() will return the desired value.

**jspDestroy**

```
public void jspDestroy()
```

jspDestroy() is invoked when the JspPage is about to be destroyed.

# javax.servlet.jsp JspWriter

```
public abstract class JspWriter
    extends java.io.Writer
```

This abstract class emulates some of the functionality found in the java.io.BufferedWriter and java.io.PrintWriter classes; however, it differs in that it throws java.io.IOException from the print methods, whereas PrintWriter does not.

The out implicit variable of a JSP implementation class is of this type. If the page directive selects autoflush="true", then all the I/O operations on this class will automatically flush the contents of the buffer if an overflow condition would result if the current operation were performed without a flush. If autoflush="false", then all the I/O operations on this class will throw an IOException if performing the current operation would result in a buffer overflow condition.

*See also:*

Writer, java.io.BufferedWriter, PrintWriter

## Variables

**autoFlush**

```
protected boolean autoflush
```

When true, the buffer will be flushed if an overflow condition would result if the current operation were performed without a flush.

When false, an IOException will be thrown if performing the current operation would result in a buffer overflow condition.

## bufferSize

```
protected int bufferSize
```

The current size of the buffer. The initial value is implementation dependent but not less than 8K.

## DEFAULT_BUFFER

```
public static final int DEFAULT_BUFFER
```

Constant indicating that the Writer is buffered and is using the implementation default buffer size.

## NO_BUFFER

```
public static final int NO_BUFFER
```

Constant indicating that the Writer is not buffering output.

# Method Summary

| | |
|---|---|
| clear | Clears the contents of the buffer. |
| clearBuffer | Clears the currents of the buffer. |
| close | Closes the stream, flushing it first. |
| flush | Flushes the stream. |
| getBufferSize | Gets the buffer size. |
| getRemaining | Gets the number of unused bytes in the buffer. |
| isAutoFlush | Gets current value of autoFlush. |
| newLine | Writes a line separator. |
| print | Prints a boolean value. |
| print | Prints a character. |
| print | Prints an array of characters. |
| print | Prints a double-precision floating-point number. |
| print | Prints a floating-point number. |

| print | Prints an integer. |
|---|---|
| print | Prints a long integer. |
| print | Prints an object. |
| print | Prints a string. |
| println | Terminates the current line by writing the line separator string. |
| println | Prints a boolean value and then terminates the line. |
| println | Prints a character and then terminates the line. |
| println | Prints an array of characters and then terminates the line. |
| println | Prints a double-precision floating-point number and then terminates the line. |
| println | Prints a floating-point number and then terminates the line. |
| println | Prints an integer and then terminates the line. |
| println | Prints a long integer and then terminates the line. |
| println | Prints an object and then terminates the line. |
| println | Prints a string and then terminates the line. |

# Method Detail

### clear

```
public abstract void clear()
    throws java.io.IOException
```

Clears the contents of the buffer. If the buffer has already been flushed, then the clear operation throws an IOException to signal the fact that some data have already been irrevocably written to the client response stream.

*Throws:*

java.io.IOException    If an I/O error occurs

### clearBuffer

```
public abstract void clearBuffer()
    throws java.io.IOException
```

Clears the current contents of the buffer. Unlike clear(), this method does not throw an IOException if the buffer has already been flushed; it merely clears the current content of the buffer and returns.

*Throws:*

    java.io.IOException    If an I/O error occurs

### close

```
public abstract void close()
    throws java.io.IOException
```

Closes the stream, flushing it first. Once a stream has been closed, further write() or flush() invocations will cause an IOException to be thrown. Closing a previously closed stream, however, has no effect.

*Throws:*

    java.io.IOException    If an I/On I/O error occurs

*Overrides:*

    Close in class java.io.Writer

### flush

```
public abstract void flush()
    throws java.io.IOException
```

Flushes the stream. If the stream has saved any characters from the various write() methods in a buffer, it writes them immediately to their intended destination; then, if that destination is another character or byte stream the method flushes it. Thus one flush() invocation will flush all the buffers in a chain of Writers and OutputStreams.

*Throws:*

    java.io.IOException    If an I/On I/O error occurs

*Overrides:*

    Flush in class java.io.Writer

### getBufferSize

```
public int getBufferSize()
```

*Returns:*

The size of the buffer in bytes, or 0 if unbuffered

## getRemaining

```
public abstract int getRemaining()
```

*Returns:*

The number of bytes unused in the buffer

## isAutoFlush

```
public boolean isAutoFlush()
```

*Returns:*

True    If this `JspWriter` is auto flushing

False   If this `JspWriter` is throwing IOExceptions on buffer overflow conditions

## newLine

```
public abstract void newLine()
  throws java.io.IOException
```

Writes a line separator. The line separator string is defined by the system property line separator and is not necessarily a single newline ($\n$) character.

*Throws:*

`java.io.IOException`    If an I/On I/O error occurs

## print

```
public abstract void print(boolean b)
  throws java.io.IOException
```

Prints a boolean value. The string produced by `String.-valueOf(boolean)` is translated into bytes according to the platform's default character encoding, and these bytes are written in exactly the manner of the `Writer.write(int)` method.

*Parameters:*

b   The boolean to be printed

*Throws:*

`java.io.IOException`   If an I/On I/O error occurs

## print

```
public abstract void print(char c)
    throws java.io.IOException
```

Prints a character. The character is translated into one or more bytes according to the platform's default character encoding, and these bytes are written in exactly the manner of the `Writer.write(int)` method.

*Parameters:*

c   The char to be printed

*Throws:*

`java.io.IOException`   If an I/On I/O error occurs

## print

```
public abstract void print(char[] ca)
    throws java.io.IOException
```

Prints an array of characters. The characters are converted into bytes according to the platform's default character encoding, and these bytes are written in exactly the manner of the `Writer.write(int)` method.

*Parameters:*

ca   The array of chars to be printed

*Throws:*

`NullPointerException`   If s is null
`java.io.IOException`   If an I/On I/O error occurs

## print

```
public abstract void print(double d)
    throws java.io.IOException
```

Prints a double-precision floating-point number. The string produced by `String.valueOf(double)` is translated into bytes according to the platform's default character encoding, and these bytes are written in exactly the manner of the `Writer.write(int)` method.

*Parameters:*

    d   The double to be printed

*Throws:*

    `java.io.IOException`   If an I/On I/O error occurs

*See also:*

    `java.lang.Double.toString(double)`

### print

```
public abstract void print(float f)
    throws java.io.IOException
```

Prints a floating-point number. The string produced by `String.valueOf(float)` is translated into bytes according to the platform's default character encoding, and these bytes are written in exactly the manner of the `Writer.write(int)` method.

*Parameters:*

    f   The float to be printed

*Throws:*

    `java.io.IOException`   If an I/On I/O error occurs

*See also:*

    `java.lang.Float.toString(float)`

### print

```
public abstract void print(int i)
    throws java.io.IOException
```

Prints an integer. The string produced by `String.valueOf(int)` is translated into bytes according to the platform's default character encoding, and these bytes are written in exactly the manner of the `Writer.write(int)` method.

*Parameters:*

i  The int to be printed

*Throws:*

java.io.IOException  If an I/On I/O error occurs

*See also:*

java.lang.Integer.toString(int)

## print

```
public abstract void print(long l)
    throws java.io.IOException
```

Prints a long integer. The string produced by String.valueOf(long) is translated into bytes according to the platform's default character encoding, and these bytes are written in exactly the manner of the Writer.write(int) method.

*Parameters:*

l  The long to be printed

*Throws:*

java.io.IOException  If an I/On I/O error occurs

*See also:*

java.lang.Long.toString(long)

## print

```
public abstract void print(java.lang.Object obj)
    throws java.io.IOException
```

Prints an object. The string produced by the String.valueOf(Object) method is translated into bytes according to the platform's default character encoding, and these bytes are written in exactly the manner of the Writer.write(int) method.

*Parameters:*

obj  The object to be printed

*Throws:*

java.io.IOException  If an I/On I/O error occurs

*See also:*

```
Object.toString()
```

## print

```
public abstract void print(java.lang.String s)
    throws java.io.IOException
```

Prints a string. If the argument is null then the string null is printed; otherwise, the string's characters are converted into bytes according to the platform's default character encoding, and these bytes are written in exactly the manner of the Writer.write(int) method.

*Parameters:*

 s The string to be printed

*Throws:*

 java.io.IOException If an I/On I/O error occurs

## println

```
public abstract void println()
    throws java.io.IOException
```

Terminates the current line by writing the line separator string. The line separator string is defined by the system property line.separator and is not necessarily a single newline character (\n).

*Throws:*

 java.io.IOException If an I/On I/O error occurs

## println

```
public abstract void println(boolean x)
    throws java.io.IOException
```

Prints a boolean value and then terminates the line. This method behaves as though it invokes print(boolean) and then println().

*Parameters:*

 b The boolean to be printed

*Throws:*

 java.io.IOException If an I/On I/O error occurs

## println

```
public abstract void println(char c)
    throws java.io.IOException
```

Prints a character and then terminates the line. This method behaves as though it invokes print(char) and then println().

*Parameters:*

   c  The char to be printed

*Throws:*

   java.io.IOException  If an I/On I/O error occurs

## println

```
public abstract void println(char[] x)
    throws java.io.IOException
```

Prints an array of characters and then terminates the line. This method behaves as though it invokes print(char[]) and then println().

*Parameters:*

   ca  The array of chars to be printed

*Throws:*

   java.io.IOException  If an I/On I/O error occurs

## println

```
public abstract void println(double d)
    throws java.io.IOException
```

Prints a double-precision floating-point number and then terminates the line. This method behaves as though it invokes print(double) and then println().

*Parameters:*

   d  The double to be printed

*Throws:*

   java.io.IOException  If an I/On I/O error occurs

### println

```
public abstract void println(float f)
    throws java.io.IOException
```

Prints a floating-point number and then terminates the line. This method behaves as though it invokes print(float) and then println().

*Parameters:*

   f   The float to be printed

*Throws:*

   java.io.IOException   If an I/On I/O error occurs

### println

```
public abstract void println(int i)
    throws java.io.IOException
```

Prints a long integer and then terminates the line. This method behaves as though it invokes print(int) and then println().

*Parameters:*

   i   The integer to be printed

*Throws:*

   java.io.IOException   If an I/On I/O error occurs

### println

```
public abstract void println(long l)
    throws java.io.IOException
```

Prints a long integer and then terminates the line. This method behaves as though it invokes print(long) and then println().

*Parameters:*

   l   The long to be printed

*Throws:*

   java.io.IOException   If an I/On I/O error occurs

### println

```
public abstract void println(java.lang.Object o)
    throws java.io.IOException
```

Prints an object and then terminates the line. This method behaves as though it invokes print(Object) and then println().

*Parameters:*
    o   The object to be printed

*Throws:*
    java.io.IOException   If an I/On I/O error occurs

### println

```
public abstract void println(java.lang.String s)
    throws java.io.IOException
```

Prints a string and then terminates the line. This method behaves as though it invokes print(String) and then println().

*Parameters:*
    s   The string to be printed

*Throws:*
    java.io.IOException   If an I/On I/O error occurs

# javax.servlet.jsp PageContext

```
public abstract class PageContext
    extends java.lang.Object
```

PageContext is an abstract class, designed to be extended by conformant JSP engine runtime environments to provide an object that encapsulates implementation-dependent features and provides convenience methods.

A PageContext instance is obtained by a JSP implementation class by calling the JspFactory.getPageContext() method, and is released by calling JspFactory.releasePageContext().

The facilities provided by PageContext for the page/component author and page implementor, include:

- a single API to manage the various scoped namespaces
- a number of convenience APIs to access various public objects
- a mechanism to obtain the `JspWriter` for output
- a mechanism to manage session usage by the page
- a mechanism to expose page directive attributes to the scripting environment
- mechanisms to forward or include the current request to other active components in the application
- a mechanism to handle `errorpage` exception processing

# Variables

### APPLICATION

```
public static final java.lang.String APPLICATION
```

Name used to store `ServletContext` in `PageContext` name table.

### APPLICATION_SCOPE

```
public static final int APPLICATION_SCOPE
```

Application scope: named reference remains available in the `ServletContext` until it is reclaimed.

### CONFIG

```
public static final java.lang.String CONFIG
```

Name used to store `ServletConfig` in `PageContext` name table.

### EXCEPTION

```
public static final java.lang.String EXCEPTION
```

Name used to store uncaught exception in `ServletRequest` attribute list and `PageContext` name table.

## OUT

```
public static final java.lang.String OUT
```

Name used to store current `JspWriter` in `PageContext` name table.

## PAGE

```
public static final java.lang.String PAGE
```

Name used to store current `JspWriter` in `PageContext` name table.

## PAGE_SCOPE

```
public static final java.lang.String PAGE_SCOPE
```

Page scope (this is the default): the named reference remains available in this `PageContext` until the return from the current `Servlet.service()` invocation.

## PAGECONTEXT

```
public static final java.lang.String PAGECONTEXT
```

Name used to store this `PageContext` in its own name tables.

## REQUEST

```
public static final java.lang.String REQUEST
```

Name used to store `ServletRequest` in `PageContext` name table.

## REQUEST_SCOPE

```
public static final java.lang.String REQUEST_SCOPE
```

Request scope: the named reference remains available from the `ServletRequest` associated with the Servlet until the current request is completed.

## RESPONSE

```
public static final java.lang.String RESPONSE
```

Name used to store `ServletResponse` in `PageContext` name table.

## SESSION

```
public static final java.lang.String SESSION
```

Name used to store `HttpSession` in `PageContext` name table.

## SESSION_SCOPE

```
public static final java.lang.String SESSION_SCOPE
```

Session scope (valid only if this page participates in a session): the named reference remains available from the `HttpSession` (if any) associated with the Servlet until the `HttpSession` is invalidated.

# Method Summary

| | |
|---|---|
| findAttribute | Searches for the named attribute in page, request, session (if valid), and application scope(s) in order and returns the value associated or null. |
| forward | Redirects, or "forwards" the current `ServletRequest` and `ServletResponse` to another active component in the application. |
| getAttribute | Returns the object associated with the name in the page scope or null. |
| getAttribute | Returns the object associated with the name in the page scope or null. |
| getAttributeNamesInScope | Returns an enumeration of names of all the attributes the specified scope. |
| getAttributesScope | Returns the scope of the object associated with a name. |
| getException | Returns an exception passed to this as an errorpage. |
| getOut | Returns the current `JspWriter` stream being used for client response. |
| getPage | Returns the Page implementation class instance (Servlet) associated with this `PageContext`. |
| getRequest | Returns the `ServletRequest` for this `PageContext`. |
| getResponse | Returns the `ServletResponse` for this `PageContext`. |

| | |
|---|---|
| getServletConfig | Returns the `ServletConfig` for this `PageContext`. |
| getServletContext | Returns the `ServletContext` for this `PageContext`. |
| getSession | Returns the `HttpSession` for this `PageContext` or null. |
| handlePageException | Processes an unhandled "page" level exception by redirecting the exception to either the specified error page for this JSP, or if none was specified, to perform some implementation-dependent action. |
| include | Causes the resource specified to be processed as part of the current `ServletRequest` and `ServletResponse` being processed by the calling Thread. |
| initialize | Called to initialize an uninitialized `PageContext` so that it may be used by a JSP implementation class to service an incoming request and response within it's `_jspService()` method. |
| release | This method shall "reset" the internal state of a `PageContext`, releasing all internal references, and preparing the `PageContext` for potential reuse by a later invocation of `initialize()`. |
| removeAttribute | Removes the object reference associated with the specified name. |
| removeAttribute | Removes the object reference associated with the specified name. |
| setAttribute | Registers the name and object specified with page scope semantics. |
| setAttribute | Registers the name and object specified with page scope semantics. |

# Method Detail

### findAttribute

```
public abstract java.lang.Object findAttribute(java.lang.String name)
```

Searches for the named attribute in page, request, session (if valid), and application scope(s) in order and returns the value associated or null.

*Returns:*
    The value associated or null

## forward

```
public abstract void forward(java.lang.string relativeUrlPath)
    throws javax.servlet.ServletException,
        java.io.IOException
```

This method is used to redirect, or "forward" the current `ServletRequest` and `ServletResponse` to another active component in the application.

If the `relativeUrlPath` begins with a / then the URL specified is calculated relative to the DOCROOT of the `ServletContext` for this JSP. If the path does not begin with a / then the URL specified is calculated relative to the URL of the request that was mapped to the calling JSP.

It is valid to call this method only from a Thread executing within a `_jspService(...)` method of a JSP.

Once this method has been called successfully, it is illegal for the calling Thread to attempt to modify the `ServletResponse` object. Any such attempt to do so, shall result in undefined behavior. Typically, callers immediately return from `_jspService(...)` after calling this method.

*Parameters:*

| | |
|---|---|
| `relativeUrlPath` | Specifies the relative URL path to the target resource as described earlier |

*Throws:*

| | |
|---|---|
| `javax.servlet.ServletException` | |
| `java.io.IOException` | |
| `java.lang.Illegal-ArgumentException` | If target resource URL is unresolvable |
| `java.lang.Illegal-StateException` | If `ServletResponse` is not in a state where a forward can be performed |
| `java.lang.Security-Exception` | If target resource cannot be accessed by caller |

## getAttribute

```
public abstract java.lang.Object getAttribute(java.lang.String name)
```

*Returns:*

The object associated with the name in the page scope or null

*Parameters:*

name    The name of the attribute to get

*Throws:*

NullPointerException    If the name is null
java.lang.Illegal-         If the scope is invalid
  ArgumentException

### getAttribute

```
public abstract java.lang.Object getAttribute(java.lang.String name,
                                              int scope)
```

*Returns:*

The object associated with the name in the specified scope or null

*Parameters:*

name    The name of the attribute to set
scope   The scope with which to associate the name/object

*Throws:*

NullPointerException    If the name is null
java.lang.Illegal-         If the scope is invalid
  ArgumentException

### getAttributeNamesInScope

```
public abstract java.util.Enumeration getAttributeNamesInScope-
  (int scope)
```

*Returns:*

An enumeration of names (java.lang.String) of all the attributes of the specified scope

### getAttributesScope

```
public abstract int getAttributesScope(java.lang.String name)
```

*Returns:*

The scope of the object associated with the name specified or 0

### getException

```
public abstract java.lang.Exception getException()
```

*Returns:*
> Any exception passed to this as an errorpage

### getOut

```
public abstract JspWriter getOut()
```

*Returns:*
> The current JspWriter stream being used for client response

### getPage

```
public abstract java.lang.Object getPage()
```

*Returns:*
> The Page implementation class instance (Servlet) associated with this PageContext

### getRequest

```
public abstract javax.servlet.ServletRequest getRequest()
```

*Returns:*
> The ServletRequest for this PageContext

### getResponse

```
public abstract javax.servlet.ServletResponse getResponse()
```

*Returns:*
> The ServletResponse for this PageContext

### getServletConfig

```
public abstract javax.servlet.ServletConfig getServletConfig()
```

*Returns:*

The `ServletConfig` for this `PageContext`

## getServletContext

```
public abstract javax.servlet.ServletContext getServletContext()
```

*Returns:*

The `ServletContext` for this `PageContext`

## getSession

```
public abstract javax.servlet.http.HttpSession getSession()
```

*Returns:*

The `HttpSession` for this `PageContext` or null

## handlePageException

```
public abstract void handlePageException(java.lang.Exception e)
    throws javax.servlet.ServletException,
        java.io.IOException
```

This method is intended to process an unhandled "page"-level exception by redirecting the exception to either the specified `errorpage` for this JSP, or if none was specified, to perform some implementation-dependent action.

A JSP implementation class will typically clean up any local state prior to invoking this and will return immediately thereafter. It is illegal to generate any output to the client or to modify any `ServletResponse` state after invoking this call.

*Parameters:*

e    The exception to be handled

*Throws:*

```
javax.servlet.ServletException
java.io.IOException
NullPointerException          If the exception is null
java.lang.Security-           If target resource cannot be
    Exception                 accessed by caller
```

## include

```
public abstract void include(java.lang.String relativeUrlPath)
    throws javax.servlet.ServletException,
        java.io.IOException
```

Causes the resource specified to be processed as part of the current `ServletRequest` and `ServletResponse` being processed by the calling Thread. The output of the target resources processing of the request is written directly to the `ServletResponse` output stream.

The current `JspWriter` out for this JSP is flushed as a side effect of this call, prior to processing the `include`.

If the `relativeUrlPath` begins with a /, then the URL specified is calculated relative to the DOCROOT of the `ServletContext` for this JSP. If the path does not begin with a /, then the URL specified is calculated relative to the URL of the request that was mapped to the calling JSP.

It is valid to call this method only from a Thread executing within a `_jspService(...)` method of a JSP.

*Parameters:*

    `relativeUrlPath`    Specifies the relative URL path to the target resource to be included

*Throws:*

    `javax.servlet.ServletException`

    `java.io.IOException`

    `java.lang.IllegalArgument-`    If the target resource URL
      `Exception`    is unresolvable

    `java.lang.SecurityException`    If target resource cannot be accessed by caller

## initialize

```
public abstract void initialize(javax.servlet.Servlet servlet,
                                javax.servlet.ServletRequest request,
                                javax.servlet.ServletResponse
                                    response,
                                java.lang.String errorPageURL,
                                boolean needsSession,
                                int bufferSize,
                                boolean autoFlush)
    throws java.io.IOException,
                                java.lang.IllegalStateException,
                                java.lang.IllegalArgumentException
```

The `initialize` method is called to initialize an uninitialized `PageContext` so that it may be used by a JSP implementation class to service an incoming request and response within its `_jspService()` method.

This method is typically called from `JspFactory.getPageContext()` to initialize state.

*Parameters:*

| | |
|---|---|
| `servlet` | The Servlet that is associated with this `PageContext` |
| `request` | The currently pending request for this Servlet |
| `response` | The currently pending response for this Servlet |
| `errorPageURL` | The value of the `errorpage` attribute from the `page` directive or null |
| `needsSession` | The value of the `session` attribute from the `page` directive |
| `bufferSize` | The value of the `buffer` attribute from the `page` directive |
| `autoFlush` | The value of the `autoflush` attribute from the `page` directive |

*Throws:*

| | |
|---|---|
| `java.io.IOException` | During creation of `JspWriter` |
| `java.lang.IllegalState-`<br>`Exception` | If out not correctly initialized |

### release

```
public abstract void release()
```

This method resets the internal state of a `PageContext`, releasing all internal references and preparing the `PageContext` for potential reuse by a later invocation of `initialize()`. This method is typically called from `JspFactory.releasePageContext()`.

Subclasses will envelope this method.

### removeAttribute

```
public abstract void removeAttribute(java.lang.String name)
```

*Remove:*

The object reference associated with the specified name

## removeAttribute

```
public abstract void removeAttribute(java.lang.String name,
                                     int scope)
```

*Remove:*

The object reference associated with the specified name

## setAttribute

```
public abstract void setAttribute(java.lang.String name,
                                  java.lang.Object attribute)
```

*Register:*

The name and object specified with page scope semantics

*Throws:*

NullPointerException    If the name or object is null

## setAttribute

```
public abstract void setAttribute(java.lang.String name,
                                  java.lang.Object o,
                                  int scope)
```

*Register:*

The name and object specified with appropriate scope semantics

*Parameters:*

| | |
|---|---|
| name | The name of the attribute to set |
| o | The object to associate with the name |
| scope | The scope with which to associate the name/object |

*Throws:*

| | |
|---|---|
| NullPointerException | If the name or object is null |
| java.lang.Illegal-<br>ArgumentException | If the scope is invalid |

## SERVLET API

Throughout the book, many of the examples use the Servlet API. This Appendix contains the documentation for those Servlet classes and interfaces used in this sample code. The classes and interfaces are presented in alphabetical order. For each class or interface, the hierarchy is given as well as a description, a method summary, and a detailed description of each method.

# `javax.servlet.http.Cookie`
# Cookie

## `javax.servlet.http.Cookie`

```
public class Cookie
extends Object
implements Cloneable
```

This class represents a "Cookie," as used for session management with HTTP and HTTPS protocols. Cookies are used to get user agents (Web browsers, etc.) to hold small amounts of data associated with a user's Web browsing. Common applications for cookies include storing user references, automating low security user sign-on facilities, and helping collect data used for "Shopping Cart" style applications.

Cookies are named, and have a single value. They may have optional attributes, including a comment presented to the user, path and domain qualifiers for which hosts see the cookie, a maximum age, and a version. Current Web browsers often have bugs in how they treat those attributes, so interoperability can be improved by not relying on them heavily.

Cookies are assigned by servers, using fields added to HTTP response headers. In this API, cookies are saved one at a time into such HTTP response headers, using the `javax.servlet.http.HttpServlet-Response.addCookie` method. User agents are expected to support twenty cookies per host, of at least four kilobytes each; use of large numbers of cookies is discouraged.

Cookies are passed back to those servers using fields added to HTTP request headers. In this API, HTTP request fields are retrieved using the cookie module's `javax.servlet.http.HttpServletRequest.` `getCookies` method. This returns all of the cookies found in the request. Several cookies with the same name can be returned; they have different path attributes, but those attributes will not be visible when using "old format" cookies.

Cookies affect the caching of the Web pages used to set their values. At this time, none of the sophisticated HTTP/1.1 cache control models are supported by this class. Standard HTTP/1.0 caches will not cache pages which contain cookies created by this class.

Cookies are being standardized by the IETF. This class supports the original Cookie specification (from Netscape Communications Corp.), as well as the updated RFC 2109 specification. By default, cookies are stored using the original specification. This promotes maximal interoperability; an updated RFC will provide better interoperability by defining a new HTTP header field for setting cookies.

## Summary

| | |
|---|---|
| `clone` | Returns a copy of this object |
| `getComment` | Returns comment describing purpose of cookie |
| `getDomain` | Returns the domain of the cookie |
| `getMaxAge` | Returns the maximum specified age of the cookie |
| `getName` | Returns the name of the cookie |
| `getPath` | Returns the prefix of all URLs for which the cookie has been targeted |
| `getSecure` | Returns the value of the 'secure' flag |
| `getValue` | Returns the value of the cookie |
| `getVersion` | Returns the version of the cookie |
| `setComment` | Sets comment describing purpose of cookie |
| `setDomain` | Sets domain pattern of hosts to whom cookie may be presented |
| `setMaxAge` | Sets the maximum age of the cookie |
| `setPath` | Sets beginning portion of URLs to whom cookie may be presented |
| `setSecure` | Sets HTTPS indicator |
| `setValue` | Sets the value of the cookie |
| `setVersion` | Sets the version of the cookie protocol |

# Constructor

```
public Cookie(String name, String value)
```

Defines a cookie with an initial name/value pair. The name must be an HTTP/1.1 "token" value; alphanumeric ASCII strings work. Names starting with a $ character are reserved by RFC 2109.

*Parameters*:

name   name of the cookie

value   value of the cookie

# Methods

**clone**

```
public Object clone()
```

Returns a copy of this object.

*Overrides*:

clone in class Object

**getComment**

```
public String getComment()
```

Returns the comment describing the purpose of this cookie, or null if no such comment has been defined.

*See also*:

setComment

**getDomain**

```
public String getDomain()
```

Returns the domain of this cookie.

*See also*:

setDomain

### getMaxAge

```
public int getMaxAge()
```

Returns the maximum specified age of the cookie. If none was specified, a negative value is returned, indicating the default behavior described with setMaxAge.

*See also*:
    setMaxAge

### getName

```
public String getName()
```

Returns the name of the cookie. This name may not be changed after the cookie is created.

### getPath

```
public String getPath()
```

Returns the prefix of all URLs for which this cookie is targeted.

*See also*:
    setPath

### getSecure

```
public boolean getSecure()
```

Returns the value of the 'secure' flag.

*See also*:
    setSecure

### getValue

```
public String getValue()
```

Returns the value of the cookie.

*See also*:
    setValue

### getVersion

```
public int getVersion()
```

Returns the version of the cookie. Version 1 complies with RFC 2109; version 0 indicates the original version, as specified by Netscape. Newly constructed cookies use version 0 by default to maximize interoperability. Cookies provided by a user agent will identify the cookie version used by the browser.

*See also*:
```
setVersion
```

### setComment

```
public void setComment(String purpose)
```

If a user agent (Web browser) presents this cookie to a user, the cookie's purpose will be described using this comment. This is not supported by version 0 cookies.

*See also*:
```
getComment
```

### setDomain

```
public void setDomain(String pattern)
```

This cookie should be presented only to hosts satisfying this domain name pattern. Read RFC 2109 for specific details of the syntax. Briefly, a domain name begins with a dot (".foo.com") and means that hosts in that DNS zone ("www.foo.com," but not "a.b.foo.com") should see the cookie. By default, cookies are only returned to the host who saved them.

*See also*:
```
getDomain
```

### setMaxAge

```
public void setMaxAge(int expiry)
```

Sets the maximum age of the cookie. The cookie will expire after this established number of seconds have passed. Negative values indicate the default behavior: the cookie is not stored persistently, and will be deleted when the user agent (Web browser) exits. A zero value causes the cookie to be deleted.

*See also*:

    getMaxAge

### setPath

```
public void setPath(String uri)
```

This cookie should be presented with requests only beginning with this URL. Read RFC 2109 for a specification of the default behavior. Basically, URLs in the same "directory" as the one which set the cookie, and in subdirectories, can all see the cookie unless a different path is set.

*See also*:

    getPath

### setSecure

```
public void setSecure(boolean flag)
```

Indicates to the user agent that the cookie should only be sent using a secure protocol (https). This should only be set when the cookie's originating server used a secure protocol to set the cookie's value.

*See also*:

    getSecure

### setValue

```
public void setValue(String newValue)
```

Sets the value of the cookie. BASE64 encoding is suggested for use with binary values.

With version 0 cookies, you need to be careful about the kinds of values you use. Values with special characters (whitespace, brackets and parentheses, the equals sign, comma, double quote, slashes, question marks, the "at" sign, colon, and semicolon) should be avoided. Empty values may not behave the same way on all browsers.

*See also*:

    `getValue`

## setVersion

```
public void setVersion(int v)
```

Sets the version of the cookie protocol used when this cookie saves itself. Since the IETF standards are still being finalized, consider version 1 as experimental; do not use it (yet) on production sites.

*See also*:

    `getVersion`

# javax.servlet.http.HttpServlet Request HttpServletRequest

### javax.servlet.http.HttpServletRequest

```
public interface HttpServletRequest
extends ServletRequest
```

An HTTP servlet request. This interface gets data from the client to the servlet for use in the `HttpServlet.service` method. It allows the HTTP-protocol specified header information to be accessed from the service method. This interface is implemented by network-service developers for use within servlets.

## Summary

| | |
|---|---|
| getAuthType | Gets authentication scheme of request |
| getCookies | Gets array of cookies in request |
| getDateHeader | Gets value of requested date header field for request |
| getHeader | Gets value of requested header field for request |
| getHeaderNames | Gets header names for request |

| | |
|---|---|
| `getIntHeader` | Gets the value of the specified integer header for request |
| `getMethod` | Gets the HTTP method |
| `getPathInfo` | Gets optional extra path info following request URI |
| `getPathTranslated` | Gets optional extra path info following request URI and translates to real path |
| `getQueryString` | Gets any query string that is part of request URI |
| `getRemoteUser` | Gets name of user making request |
| `getRequestedSessionId` | Gets session ID specified with request |
| `getRequestURI` | Gets the part of the request URI to the left of query string |
| `getServletPath` | Gets part of URI referring to servlet being executed |
| `getSession` | Gets current valid session or optionally creates session |
| `isRequestedSessionIdFromCookie` | Checks if session ID is from cookie |
| `isRequestedSessionIdFromUrl` | Checks if session ID is part of URL |
| `isRequestedSessionIdValid` | Checks if request is associated with a session valid in current context |

# Methods

### getAuthType

```
public abstract String getAuthType()
```

Gets the authentication scheme of this request. Same as the CGI variable AUTH_TYPE.

*Returns*:

This request's authentication scheme, or null if none

### getCookies

```
public abstract Cookie[] getCookies()
```

Gets the array of cookies found in this request.

*Returns*:

The array of cookies found in this request

### getDateHeader

```
public abstract long getDateHeader(String name)
```

Gets the value of the requested date header field of this request. If the header can't be converted to a date, the method throws an IllegalArgumentException. The case of the header field name is ignored.

*Parameters*:

name   the string containing the name of the requested header field
*Returns*:

The value the requested date header field, or -1 if not found

### getHeader

```
public abstract String getHeader(String name)
```

Gets the value of the requested header field of this request. The case of the header field name is ignored.

*Parameters*:

name   the string containing the name of the requested header
field
*Returns*:

The value of the requested header field, or null if not known

### getHeaderNames

```
public abstract Enumeration getHeaderNames()
```

Gets the header names for this request.

*Returns*:

An enumeration of strings representing the header names for this request. Some server implementations do not allow headers to be accessed in this way, in which case this method will return null.

### getIntHeader

```
public abstract int getIntHeader(String name)
```

Gets the value of the specified integer header field of this request. The case of the header field name is ignored. If the header can't be converted to an integer, the method throws a NumberFormatException.

*Parameters*:

name   the string containing the name of the requested header field

*Returns*:

The value of the requested header field, or -1 if not found

### getMethod

```
public abstract String getMethod()
```

Gets the HTTP method (for example, GET, POST, PUT) with which this request was made. Same as the CGI variable REQUEST_METHOD.

*Returns*:

The HTTP method with which this request was made

### getPathInfo

```
public abstract String getPathInfo()
```

Gets any optional extra path information following the servlet path of this request's URI, but immediately preceding its query string. Same as the CGI variable PATH_INFO.

*Returns*:

The optional path information following the servlet path, but before the query string, in this request's URI; null if this request's URI contains no extra path information

### getPathTranslated

```
public abstract String getPathTranslated()
```

Gets any optional extra path information following the servlet path of this request's URI, but immediately preceding its query string, and translates into a real path. Similar to the CGI variable PATH_TRANS-LATED.

*Returns*:

Extra path information translated to a real path or null if no extra path information is in the request's URI

### getQueryString

```
public abstract String getQueryString()
```

Gets any query string that is part of the HTTP request's URI. Same as the CGI variable QUERY_STRING.

*Returns*:

Query string that is part of this request's URI, or null if it contains no query string

### getRemoteUser

```
public abstract String getRemoteUser()
```

Gets the name of the user making this request. The user name is set with HTTP authentication. Whether the user name will continue to be sent with each subsequent communication is browser-dependent. Same as the CGI variable REMOTE_USER.

*Returns*:

The name of the user making this request, or null if not known.

### getRequestedSessionId

```
public abstract String getRequestedSessionId()
```

Gets the session ID specified with this request. This may differ from the actual session ID. For example, if the request specified an ID for an invalid session, then this will get a new session with a new ID.

*Returns*:

The session ID specified by this request, or null if the request did not specify a session ID

**getRequestURI**

```
public abstract String getRequestURI()
```

Gets, from the first line of the HTTP request, the part of this request's URI that is to the left of any query string. For example:

| First line of HTTP request | Return from getRequestURI |
|---|---|
| POST /some/path.html HTTP/1.1 | some/path.html |
| GET http://foo.bar/a.html HTTP/1.0 | http://foo.bar/a.html |
| HEAD /xyz?a=b HTTP/1.1 | /xyz |

To reconstruct a URL with a URL scheme and host, use the method `javax.servlet.http.HttpUtils.getRequestURL`, which returns a `StringBuffer`.

*Returns*:

This request's URI

**getServletPath**

```
public abstract String getServletPath()
```

Gets the part of this request's URI that refers to the servlet being invoked. Analogous to the CGI variable SCRIPT_NAME.

*Returns*:

The servlet being invoked, as contained in this request's URI

**getSession**

```
public abstract HttpSession getSession(boolean create)
```

Gets the current valid session associated with this request, if create is false or, if necessary, creates a new session for the request, if create is true.

▬ ▬ ▬ ▬ ▬ ▬ ▬ ▬ ▬ ▬ ▬ ▬ ▬ ▬ ▬ ▬ ▬ ▬ ▬ ▬ ▬
**NOTE**:  *To ensure the session is properly maintained, the servlet developer must call this method (at least once) before any output is written to the response.*

Additionally, developers need to be aware that newly created sessions (that is, sessions for which `HttpSession.isNew` returns `true`) do not have any application-specific state.

*Returns*:

The session associated with this request or `null` if `create` was `false`, and no valid session is associated with this request

### isRequestedSessionIdFromCookie

```
public abstract boolean isRequestedSessionIdFromCookie()
```

Checks whether the session ID specified by this request came in as a cookie. (The requested session may not be one returned by the `getSession` method.)

*Returns*:

`true` if the session ID specified by this request came in as a cookie; otherwise returns `false`

### isRequestedSessionIdFromUrl

```
public abstract boolean isRequestedSessionIdFromUrl()
```

Checks whether the session ID specified by this request came in as part of the URL. (The requested session may not be the one returned by the `getSession` method.)

*Returns*:

`true` if the session ID specified by the request for this session came in as part of the URL; otherwise returns `false`

### isRequestedSessionIdValid

```
public abstract boolean isRequestedSessionIdValid()
```

Checks whether this request is associated with a session that is valid in the current session context. If it is not valid, the requested session will never be returned from the `getSession` method.

*Returns*:

`true` if this request is associated with a session that is valid in the current session context

# javax.servlet.http.HttpServlet Response HttpServletResponse

`javax.servlet.http.HttpServletResponse`

```
public interface HttpServletResponse
extends ServletResponse
```

An HTTP servlet response. This interface allows a servlet's service method to manipulate HTTP-protocol specified header information and return data to its client. It is implemented by network service developers for use within servlets.

## Variables

### SC_ACCEPTED

Status code (202) indicating that a request was accepted for processing, but was not completed.

### SC_BAD_GATEWAY

Status code (502) indicating that the HTTP server received an invalid response from a server it consulted when acting as a proxy or gateway.

### SC_BAD_REQUEST

Status code (400) indicating the request sent by the client was syntactically incorrect.

### SC_CONFLICT

Status code (409) indicating that the request could not be completed due to a conflict with the current state of the resource.

### SC_CONTINUE

Status code (100) indicating the client can continue.

### SC_CREATED

Status code (201) indicating the request succeeded and created a new resource on the server.

### SC_FORBIDDEN

Status code (403) indicating the server understood the request but refused to fulfill it.

### SC_GATEWAY_TIMEOUT

Status code (504) indicating that the server did not receive a timely response from the upstream server while acting as a gateway or proxy.

### SC_GONE

Status code (410) indicating that the resource is no longer available at the server, and no forwarding address is known.

### SC_HTTP_VERSION_NOT_SUPPORTED

Status code (505) indicating that the server does not support, or refuses to support, the HTTP protocol version that was used in the request message.

### SC_INTERNAL_SERVER_ERROR

Status code (500) indicating an error inside the HTTP server which prevented it from fulfilling the request.

### SC_LENGTH_REQUIRED

Status code (411) indicating that the request cannot be handled without a defined Content-Length.

### SC_METHOD_NOT_ALLOWED

Status code (405) indicating that the method specified in the Request-Line is not allowed for the resource identified by the Request-URI.

### SC_MOVED_PERMANENTLY

Status code (301) indicating that the resource has permanently moved to a new location, and that future references should use a new URI with their requests.

### SC_MOVED_TEMPORARILY

Status code (302) indicating that the resource has temporarily moved to another location, but that future references should still use the original URI to access the resource.

`SC_MULTIPLE_CHOICES`

Status code (300) indicating that the requested resource corresponds to any one of a set of representations, each with its own specific location.

`SC_NO_CONTENT`

Status code (204) indicating that the request succeeded but that there was no new information to return.

`SC_NON_AUTHORITATIVE_INFORMATION`

Status code (203) indicating that the meta information presented by the client did not originate from the server.

`SC_NOT_ACCEPTABLE`

Status code (406) indicating that the resource identified by the request is only capable of generating response entities which have content characteristics not acceptable according to the accept headers sent in the request.

`SC_NOT_FOUND`

Status code (404) indicating that the requested resource is not available.

`SC_NOT_IMPLEMENTED`

Status code (501) indicating the HTTP server does not support the functionality needed to fulfill the request.

`SC_NOT_MODIFIED`

Status code (304) indicating that a conditional GET operation found that the resource was available and not modified.

`SC_OK`

Status code (200) indicating the request succeeded normally.

`SC_PARTIAL_CONTENT`

Status code (206) indicating that the server has fulfilled the partial GET request for the resource.

**SC_PAYMENT_REQUIRED**

Status code (402) reserved for future use.

**SC_PRECONDITION_FAILED**

Status code (412) indicating that the precondition given in one or more of the request-header fields evaluated to `false` when it was tested on the server.

**SC_PROXY_AUTHENTICATION_REQUIRED**

Status code (407) indicating that the client MUST first authenticate itself with the proxy.

**SC_REQUEST_ENTITY_TOO_LARGE**

Status code (413) indicating that the server is refusing to process the request because the request entity is larger than the server is willing or able to process.

**SC_REQUEST_TIMEOUT**

Status code (408) indicating that the client did not produce a request within the time that the server was prepared to wait.

**SC_REQUEST_URI_TOO_LONG**

Status code (414) indicating that the server is refusing to service the request because the Request-URI is longer than the server is willing to interpret.

**SC_RESET_CONTENT**

Status code (205) indicating that the agent SHOULD reset the document view which caused the request to be sent.

**SC_SEE_OTHER**

Status code (303) indicating that the response to the request can be found under a different URI.

**SC_SERVICE_UNAVAILABLE**

Status code (503) indicating that the HTTP server is temporarily over-loaded and unable to handle the request.

### SC_SWITCHING_PROTOCOLS

Status code (101) indicating the server is switching protocols according to Upgrade header.

### SC_UNAUTHORIZED

Status code (401) indicating that the request requires HTTP authentication.

### SC_UNSUPPORTED_MEDIA_TYPE

Status code (415) indicating that the server is refusing to service the request because the entity of the request is in a format not supported by the requested resource for the requested method.

### SC_USE_PROXY

Status code (305) indicating that the requested resource MUST be accessed through the proxy given by the Location field.

## Summary

| | |
|---|---|
| addCookie | Adds specified cookie to response |
| containsHeader | Checks whether response message header has filed with specified name |
| encodeRedirectUrl | Encodes specified URL for use in sendRedirect |
| encodeUrl | Encodes URL to include session ID |
| sendError | Sends error response to client using specified status code and default message |
| sendError | Sends error response to client using specified status code and specified message |
| sendRedirect | Sends temporary redirect response to client using specified URL |
| setDateHeader | Adds field to response header with specified name and date value |
| setHeader | Adds field to response header with specified name and value |
| setIntHeader | Adds field to response header with specified integer value |
| setStatus | Sets status code for response |
| setStatus | Sets status code and message for response |

# Methods

### addCookie

```
public abstract void addCookie(Cookie cookie)
```

Adds the specified cookie to the response. It can be called multiple times to set more than one cookie.

*Parameters*:

cookie   the cookie to return to the client

### containsHeader

```
public abstract boolean containsHeader(String name)
```

Checks whether the response message header has a field with the specified name.

*Parameters*:

name   the header field name

*Returns*:

true if the response message header has a field with the specified name; otherwise returns false

### encodeRedirectUrl

```
public abstract String encodeRedirectUrl(String url)
```

Encodes the specified URL for use in the sendRedirect method or, if encoding is not needed, returns the URL unchanged. The implementation of this method should include the logic to determine whether the session ID needs to be encoded in the URL. Because the rules for making this determination differ from those used to decide whether to encode a normal link, this method is separate from the encodeUrl method.

All URLs sent to the HttpServletResponse.sendRedirect method should be run through this method. Otherwise, URL rewriting cannot be used with browsers which do not support cookies.

*Parameters*:

URL   the URL to be encoded

*Returns*:

> The encoded URL if encoding is needed; otherwise returns the
> unchanged URL

### encodeUrl

```
public abstract String encodeUrl(String url)
```

Encodes the specified URL by including the session ID in it, or, if encoding is not needed, returns the URL unchanged. The implementation of this method should include the logic to determine whether the session ID needs to be encoded in the URL. For example, if the browser supports cookies, or session tracking is turned off, URL encoding is unnecessary.

All URLs emitted by a servlet should be run through this method. Otherwise, URL rewriting cannot be used with browsers which do not support cookies.

*Parameters*:

> URL   the URL to be encoded

*Returns*:

> The encoded URL if encoding is needed; otherwise returns the
> unchanged URL

### sendError

```
public abstract void sendError(int sc) throws IOException
```

Sends an error response to the client using the specified status code and a default message.

*Parameters*:

> sc   the status code

*Throws*:

> IOException   If an I/O error has occurred

### sendError

```
public abstract void sendError(int sc, String msg)
   throws IOException
```

Sends an error response to the client using the specified status code and descriptive message. If setStatus has previously been called, it is reset to the error status code. The message is sent as the body of an HTML page, which is returned to the user to describe the problem. The page is sent with a default HTML header; the message is enclosed in simple body tags (<body></body>).

*Parameters*:
    sc   the status code
    msg   the detail message
*Throws*:
    IOException   If an I/O error has occurred

### sendRedirect

```
public abstract void sendRedirect(String location) throws IOException
```

Sends a temporary redirect response to the client using the specified redirect location URL. The URL must be absolute (for example, https://hostname/path/file.html). Relative URLs are not permitted here.

*Parameters*:
    location   the redirect location URL
*Throws*:
    IOException   If an I/O error has occurred

### setDateHeader

```
public abstract void setDateHeader(String name, long date)
```

Adds a field to the response header with the given name and date-valued field. The date is specified in terms of milliseconds since the epoch. If the date field had already been set, the new value overwrites the previous one. The containsHeader method can be used to test for the presence of a header before setting its value.

*Parameters*:
    name   the name of the header field
    value   the header field's date value

### setIntHeader

```
public abstract void setIntHeader(String name, int value)
```

Adds a field to the response header with the given name and integer value. If the field had already been set, the new value overwrites the previous one. The `containsHeader` method can be used to test for the presence of a header before setting its value.

*Parameters*:

    `name`   the name of the header field

    `value`   the header field's integer value

**setStatus**

```
public abstract void setStatus(int sc)
```

Sets the status code for this response. This method is used to set the return status code when there is no error (for example, for the status codes `SC_OK` or `SC_MOVED_TEMPORARILY`). If there is an error, the `sendError` method should be used instead.

*Parameters*:

    `sc`   the status code

**setStatus**

```
public abstract void setStatus(int sc, String sm)
```

Sets the status code and message for this response. If the field had already been set, the new value overwrites the previous one. The message is sent as the body of an HTML page, which is returned to the user to describe the problem. The page is sent with a default HTML header; the message is enclosed in simple body tags (`<body></body>`).

*Parameters*:

    `sc`   the status code

    `sm`   the status message

# `javax.servlet.http.Session HttpSession`

**`javax.servlet.http.Session`**

```
public interface HttpSession
```

The HttpSession interface is implemented by services to provide an association between an HTTP client and HTTP server. This association, or session, persists over multiple connections and/or requests during a given time period. Sessions are used to maintain state and user identity across multiple page requests.

A session can be maintained either by using cookies or by URL rewriting. To expose whether the client supports cookies, HttpSession defines an isCookieSupportDetermined method and an isUsingCookies method.

HttpSession defines methods which store these types of data:

- Standard session properties, such as an identifier for the session and the context for the session.

- Application layer data, accessed using this interface and stored using a dictionary-like interface.

The following code snippet illustrates getting and setting the session data value.

```
//Get the session object - "request" represents the HTTP servlet
request
HttpSession session = request.getSession(true);

//Get the session data value - an Integer object is read from
//the session, incremented, then written back to the session.
//sessiontest.counter identifies values in the session
Integer ival = (Integer) session.getValue("sessiontest.counter");
if (ival==null)
    ival = new Integer(1);
else
    ival = new Integer(ival.intValue() + 1);
session.putValue("sessiontest.counter", ival);
```

When an application layer stores or removes data from the session, the session layer checks whether the object implements HttpSessionBindingListener. If it does, then the object is notified that it has been bound or unbound from the session.

An implementation of HttpSession represents the server's view of the session. The server considers a session to be new until it has been joined by the client. Until the client joins the session, the isNew method returns true. A value of true can indicate one of these three cases:

1. the client does not yet know about the session,

2. the session has not yet begun,

3. or the client chooses not to join the session. This case will occur if the client supports only cookies and chooses to reject any cookies

sent by the server. If the server supports URL rewriting, this case will not commonly occur.

It is the responsibility of developers to design their applications to account for situations where a client has not joined a session. For example, in the following code snippet isNew is called to determine whether a session is new. If it is, the server will require the client to start a session by directing the client to a welcome page welcomeURL where a user might be required to enter some information and send it to the server before gaining access to subsequent pages.

```
//Get the session object - "request" represents the HTTP servlet request
HttpSession session = request.getSession(true);

//insist that the client starts a session
//before access to data is allowed
//"response" represents the HTTP servlet response
if (session.isNew()) {
    response.sendRedirect (welcomeURL);
}
```

## Summary

| | |
|---|---|
| getCreationTime | Returns time at which session was created |
| getId | Returns session identifier |
| getLastAccessTime | Returns last time client sent request carrying ID of the session |
| getSessionContext | Returns context in which session is bound |
| getValue | Returns object bound to specified name in application-layer data |
| getValueNames | Returns names of application-layer data objects bound to session |
| invalidate | Causes session to be invalidated and removed from its context |
| isNew | Checks if client has joined session |
| putValue | Binds specified object to session's application-layer data using specified name |
| removeValue | Removes object bound to specified name in session's application-layer data |

# Methods

### getCreationTime

```
public abstract long getCreationTime()
```

Returns the time at which this session representation was created, in milliseconds since midnight, January 1, 1970 UTC.

*Returns*:

The time when the session was created

*Throws*:

IllegalStateException   If an attempt is made to access session data after the session has been invalidated

### getId

```
public abstract String getId()
```

Returns the identifier assigned to this session. An HttpSession identifier is a unique string that is created and maintained by HttpSessionContext.

*Returns*:

The identifier assigned to this session

*Throws*:

IllegalStateException   If an attempt is made to access session data after the session has been invalidated

### getLastAccessedTime

```
public abstract long getLastAccessedTime()
```

Returns the last time the client sent a request carrying the identifier assigned to the session. Time is expressed as milliseconds since midnight, January 1, 1970 UTC. Application-level operations, such as getting or setting a value associated with the session, do not affect the access time.

This information is particularly useful in session-management policies. For example, a session manager could leave all sessions which have not been used in a long time in a given context. The sessions can be sorted according to age to optimize some task.

*Returns*:

The last time the client sent a request carrying the identifier assigned to the session

*Throws*:

IllegalStateException   If an attempt is made to access session data after the session has been invalidated

### getSessionContext

```
public abstract HttpSessionContext getSessionContext()
```

Returns the context in which this session is bound.

*Returns*:

The name of the context in which this session is bound

*Throws*:

IllegalStateException   If an attempt is made to access session data after the session has been invalidated

### getValue

```
public abstract Object getValue(String name)
```

Returns the object bound to the given name in the session's application-layer data. Returns null if there is no such binding.

*Parameters*:

name   the name of the binding to find

*Returns*:

The value bound to that name, or null if the binding does not exist

*Throws*:

IllegalStateException   If an attempt is made to access HttpSession's session data after it has been invalidated

### getValueNames

```
public abstract String[] getValueNames()
```

Returns an array of the names of all the application-layer data objects bound into the session. For example, if you want to delete all of the data objects bound into the session, use this method to obtain their names.

> *Returns*:
>> An array containing the names of all of the application-layer data objects bound into the session
>
> *Throws*:
>> IllegalStateException   If an attempt is made to access session data after the session has been invalidated

## invalidate

```
public abstract void invalidate()
```

Causes this representation of the session to be invalidated and removed from its context.

> *Throws*:
>> IllegalStateException   If an attempt is made to access session data after the session has been invalidated

## isNew

```
public abstract boolean isNew()
```

A session is considered to be new if it has been created by the server, but the client has not yet acknowledged joining the session. For example, if the server supported only cookie-based sessions and the client had completely disabled the use of cookies, then calls to HttpServletRequest. getSession() would always return new sessions.

> *Returns*:
>> true if the session has been created by the server, but the client has not yet acknowledged joining the session; otherwise returns false
>
> *Throws*:
>> IllegalStateException   If an attempt is made to access session data after the session has been invalidated

## putValue

```
public abstract void putValue(String name, Object value)
```

Binds the specified object into the session's application-layer data with the given name. Any existing binding with the same name is replaced. New (or existing) values that implement the `HttpSessionBindingListener` interface will call its `valueBound()` method.

*Parameters*:

name the name to which the data object will be bound. This parameter cannot be null.

value the data object to be bound. This parameter cannot be null.

*Throws*:

IllegalStateException If an attempt is made to access session data after the session has been invalidated

**removeValue**

```
public abstract void removeValue(String name)
```

Removes the object bound to the given name in the session's application-layer data. Does nothing if there is no object bound to the given name. The value that implements the `HttpSessionBindingListener` interface will call its `valueUnbound()` method.

*Parameters*:

name the name of the object to remove

*Throws*:

IllegalStateException If an attempt is made to access session data after the session has been invalidated

# javax.servlet.http.HttpUtils
# HttpUtils

## javax.servlet.http.HttpUtils

```
public class HttpUtils
   extends Object
```

A collection of static utility methods useful to HTTP servlets.

## Summary

| | |
|---|---|
| getRequestURL | Reconstructs URL used by client to make request |
| parsePostData | Parses FORM data |
| ParseQueryString | Parses query string |

## Methods

### getRequestURL

```
public static StringBuffer getRequestURL(HttpServletRequest req)
```

Reconstructs the URL used by the client to make the request. This accounts for differences such as addressing scheme (http, https) and default ports, but does not attempt to include query parameters. Since it returns a StringBuffer, not a String, the URL can be modified efficiently (for example, by appending query parameters).

This method is useful for creating redirect messages and for reporting errors.

### parsePostData

```
public static Hashtable parsePostData(int len, ServletInputStream in)
```

Parses FORM data that is posted to the server using the HTTP POST method and the application/x-www-form-urlencoded mime type.

*Parameters*:
> len   the length of the data in the input stream
> in   the input stream

*Returns*:
> A hashtable of the parsed key, value pairs. Keys with multiple values have their values stored as an array of strings.

*Throws*:
> IllegalArgumentException   If the POST data is invalid

### parseQueryString

```
public static Hashtable parseQueryString(String s)
```

Parses a query string and builds a hashtable of key-value pairs, where the values are arrays of strings. The query string should have the form of a string packaged by the GET or POST method. [For example, it should have its key-value pairs delimited by ampersands (&), and its keys separated from its values by equal signs (=).]

A key can appear one or more times in the query string. Each time a key appears, its corresponding value is inserted into its string array in the hashtable. (So keys that appear once in the query string have, in the hashtable, a string array of length one as their value; keys that appear twice have a string array of length two, etc.)

When the keys and values are moved into the hashtable, any plus signs (+) are returned to spaces and characters sent in hexadecimal notation (%xx) are converted back to characters.

*Parameters*:
   s   query string to be parsed
*Returns*:
   A hashtable built from the parsed key-value pairs; the hashtable's
      values are arrays of strings
*Throws*:
   IllegalArgumentException   If the query string is invalid

# javax.servlet.ServletRequest
# ServletRequest

`javax.servlet.ServletRequest`

```
public interface ServletRequest
```

This interface is for getting data from the client to the servlet for a service request. Network service developers implement the ServletRequest interface. The methods are then used by servlets when the service method is executed; the ServletRequest object is passed as an argument to the service method.

Some of the data provided by the ServletRequest object includes parameter names and values, attributes, and an input stream.

Subclasses of `ServletRequest` can provide additional protocol-specific data. For example, HTTP data is provided by the interface `HttpServletRequest`, which extends `ServletRequest`. This framework provides the servlet's only access to this data.

MIME bodies are either text or binary data. Use `getReader` to handle text, including the character encodings. The `getInputStream` call should be used to handle binary data. Multipart MIME bodies are treated as binary data, since the headers are US-ASCII data.

## Summary

| | |
|---|---|
| `getAttribute` | Returns value of named attribute of request |
| `getCharacterEncoding` | Returns character set encoding for input of request |
| `getContentLength` | Returns size of request entity data |
| `getContentType` | Returns Internet Media Type of request entity data |
| `getInputStream` | Returns input stream for reading binary data in request body |
| `getParameter` | Returns string containing lone value of specified parameter |
| `getParameterNames` | Returns parameter names for this request |
| `getParameterValues` | Returns values of specified parameter as enumeration of strings |
| `getProtocol` | Returns protocol and version for request |
| `getReader` | Returns buffered reader for reading text in request body |
| `getRealPath` | Returns real path derived from applying aliasing rules to virtual path |
| `getRemoteAddr` | Returns IP address of agent that sent request |
| `getRemoteHost` | Returns fully qualified host name of agent that sent request |
| `getScheme` | Returns scheme of URL making request |
| `getServerName` | Returns host name of server that received request |
| `getServerPort` | Returns port on which request was received |

# Methods

### getAttribute

```
public abstract Object getAttribute(String name)
```

Returns the value of the named attribute of the request, or null if the attribute does not exist. This method allows access to request information not already provided by the other methods in this interface. Attribute names should follow the same convention as package names. The following predefined attributes are provided:

| Attribute Name | Attribute Type | Description |
| --- | --- | --- |
| javax.net.ssl. cipher_suite | string | The string name of the SSL cipher suite in use, if the request was made using SSL. |
| javax.net.ssl. peer_certificates | array of javax.security.cert. X509Certificate | The chain of X.509 certificates which authenticates the client. This is only available when SSL is used with client authentication. |
| javax.net.ssl. session | javax.net.ssl. SSLSession | An SSL session object, if the request was made using SSL. |

The package (and therefore attribute) names beginning with java.* and javax.* are reserved for use by JavaSoft. Similarly, com.sun.* is reserved for use by Sun Microsystems, Inc.

*Parameters*:

name   the name of the attribute whose value is required

### getCharacterEncoding

```
public abstract String getCharacterEncoding()
```

Returns the character set encoding for the input of this request.

### getContentLength

```
public abstract int getContentLength()
```

Returns the size of the request entity data, or -1 if not known. Same as the CGI variable CONTENT_LENGTH.

### getContentType

```
public abstract String getContentType()
```

Returns the Internet Media Type of the request entity data, or null if not known. Same as the CGI variable CONTENT_TYPE.

### getInputStream

```
public abstract ServletInputStream getInputStream()
    throws IOException
```

Returns an input stream for reading binary data in the request body.

*Throws*:

IllegalStateException   If getReader has been called on this same request

*Throws*:

IOException   On other I/O-related errors

### getParameter

```
public abstract String getParameter(String name)
```

Returns a string containing the lone value of the specified parameter, or null if the parameter does not exist. For example, in an HTTP servlet this method would return the value of the specified query string parameter. Servlet writers should use this method only when they are sure that there is only one value for the parameter. If the parameter has (or could have) multiple values, servlet writers should use getParameterValues. If a multiple-valued parameter name is passed as an argument, the return value is implementation dependent.

*Parameters*:

name   the name of the parameter whose value is required

### getParameterNames

```
public abstract Enumeration getParameterNames()
```

Returns the parameter names for this request as an enumeration of strings, or an empty enumeration if there are no parameters or the input stream is empty. The input stream would be empty if all the data had been read from the stream returned by the method `getInputStream`.

### getParameterValues

```
public abstract String[] getParameterValues(String name)
```

Returns the values of the specified parameter for the request as an array of strings, or `null` if the named parameter does not exist. For example, in an HTTP servlet this method would return the values of the specified query string or posted form as an array of strings.

*Parameters*:

> name   the name of the parameter whose value is required

### getProtocol

```
public abstract String getProtocol()
```

Returns the protocol and version of the request as a string of the form `<protocol>/<major version>.<minor version>`. Same as the CGI variable `SERVER_PROTOCOL`.

### getReader

```
public abstract BufferedReader getReader()
  throws IOException
```

Returns a buffered reader for reading text in the request body. This translates character set codings as appropriate.

*Throws*:

> UnsupportedEncodingException   If the character set encoding is unsupported, so the text can't be correctly decoded

*Throws*:

> IllegalStateException   If `getInputStream` has been called on this same request

*Throws*:

> IOException   On other I/O-related errors

### getRealPath

```
public abstract String getRealPath(String path)
```

Applies alias rules to the specified virtual path and returns the corresponding real path, or null if the translation cannot be performed for any reason. For example, an HTTP servlet would resolve the path using the virtual docroot, if virtual hosting is enabled, and with the default docroot otherwise. Calling this method with the string "/" as an argument returns the document root.

*Parameters*:

path   the virtual path to be translated to a real path

### getRemoteAddr

```
public abstract String getRemoteAddr()
```

Returns the IP address of the agent that sent the request. Same as the CGI variable REMOTE_ADDR.

### getRemoteHost

```
public abstract String getRemoteHost()
```

Returns the fully qualified host name of the agent that sent the request. Same as the CGI variable REMOTE_HOST.

### getScheme

```
public abstract String getScheme()
```

Returns the scheme of the URL used in this request, for example "http", "https", or "ftp". Different schemes have different rules for constructing URLs, as noted in RFC 1738. The URL used to create a request may be reconstructed using this scheme, the server name and port, and additional information such as URIs.

### getServerName

```
public abstract String getServerName()
```

Returns the host name of the server that received the request. Same as the CGI variable SERVER_NAME.

### getServerPort

```
public abstract int getServerPort()
```

Returns the port number on which this request was received. Same as the CGI variable SERVER_PORT.

# javax.servlet.ServletResponse
# ServletResponse

## javax.servlet.ServletResponse

```
public interface ServletResponse
```

Interface for sending MIME data from the servlet's service method to the client. Network service developers implement this interface; its methods are then used by servlets to return data to clients when the service method is run. The ServletResponse object is passed as an argument to the service method.

To write MIME bodies which consist of binary data, use the output stream returned by getOutputStream. To write MIME bodies consisting of text data, use the writer returned by getWriter. If you need to mix binary and text data, for example, because you're creating a multipart response, use the output stream to write the multipart headers, and use that to build your own text bodies.

If you don't explicitly set the character set in your MIME Media Type, with setContentType, one will be selected and the content type will be modified accordingly. If you will be using a writer, and want to call the setContentType method, you must do so before calling the getWriter method. If you will be using the output stream, and want to call setContentType, you must do so before using the output stream to write the MIME body.

For more information about MIME, see the Internet RFCs such as RFC 2045, the first in a series which defines MIME. Note that protocols such as SMTP and HTTP define application-specific profiles of MIME, and that standards in this area are evolving.

# Summary

| | |
|---|---|
| getCharacterEncoding | Returns character set encoding used for this MIME body |
| getOutputStream | Returns output stream used for writing binary response data |
| getWriter | Returns print writer used for formatting text responses |
| setContentLength | Sets content length for response |
| setContentType | Sets content type for response |

# Methods

### getCharacterEncoding

```
public abstract String getCharacterEncoding()
```

Returns the character set encoding used for this MIME body. The character encoding is either the one specified in the assigned content type, or one which the client understands. If no content type has yet been assigned, it is implicitly set to *text/plain*.

### getOutputStream

```
public abstract ServletOutputStream getOutputStream()
    throws IOException
```

Returns an output stream for writing binary response data.

*Throws*:

   IllegalStateException   If getWriter has been called on this same request

*Throws*:

   IOException   If an I/O exception has occurred

### getWriter

```
public abstract PrintWriter getWriter()
    throws IOException
```

Returns a print writer for writing formatted text responses. The MIME type of the response will be modified, if necessary, to reflect the character encoding used, through the charset=... property. This means that the content type must be set before calling this method.

*Throws*:

UnsupportedEncodingException If no such encoding can be provided

*Throws*:

IllegalStateException if getOutputStream has been called on this same request

*Throws*:

IOException On other errors

### setContentLength

```
public abstract void setContentLength(int len)
```

Sets the content length for this response.

*Parameters*:

len the content length

### setContentType

```
public abstract void setContentType(String type)
```

Sets the content type for this response. This type may later be implicitly modified by addition of properties such as the MIME charset=<value> if the service finds it necessary, and the appropriate media type property has not been set.

This response property may only be assigned one time. If a writer is to be used to write a text response, this method must be called before the method getWriter. If an output stream will be used to write a response, this method must be called before the output stream is used to write response data.

*Parameters*:

type the content's MIME type.

# APPENDIX E

## The Contents of the CD

The files that were already mentioned in Appendices A (Apache, JServ, and PostgreSQL) are in directory /contrib. If you already have a working JSP environment, you will not need the files in this directory. If you need to create a JSP environment, use the files in the /contrib directory as outlined in Appendix A.

Directory /javaservlets/jdbc contains the ConnectionPool class mentioned in Chapter 3 and used in subsequent chapters. You should copy the entire contents of /javaservlets and the full contents of all its sub-directories to a directory known to the JSP container. If you are using the same directory structure as that used by dormouse.instantjsp.com (the host used to develop the sample code) and your configuration files contain the same information as those presented in Appendix A, you should copy the /javaservlets directory to /usr/local/apache/classes.

The /database directory contains the files discussed in Appendix B. You should install these according to the instructions presented in that Appendix.

The directories into which you copy the remainder of the files contained on the CD depend on your system configuration. The placement of the files discussed in this Appendix assumes that Apache has been installed in /usr/local/apache. If this is the case, you can simply copy the /usr directory and all of its subdirectories directly under your root directory and skip the remainder of this Appendix. If you have installed Apache elsewhere, you should copy the files from each of the directories listed below, substituting your directory structure wherever you see /user/local/apache.

The directory /htdocs contains one subdirectory for each of the chapters in the book. The subdirectories contain the JSP files and HTML files presented in each chapter. You should copy the /htdocs directory and all its subdirectories to /usr/local/apache.

The /images directory contains the JPEG and GIF files used in Chapter 9. You should copy them to /usr/local/apache/htdocs/images.

The /beans directory contains a subdirectory /com that, in turn, contains a subdirectory /instantjsp, which contains the Beans used throughout the book. You should copy the /beans directory and all of its subdirectories to /usr/local/apache.

The /common directory contains JSP pages that are used by more than one chapter. The files in this directory should be copied to /usr/local/apache/htdocs/common.

  If you wish, you can place all of the .class files found in /beans/com/instantjsp in a .jar file and add the .jar file to your CLASS-PATH. If you do this, make sure you include the subdirectory /Chapter2.

***NOTE***:   *With the exception of the* readme *file, all files on the CD use the UNIX end-of-line convention. The files are usable under NT, but will be more easily read if they are passed through a filter that converts them to DOS-style end of line.*

# INDEX

# W

# X

# ABOUT THE AUTHOR

Paul Tremblett is a Distinguished Member of the Technical Staff at Cap Gemini Telecommunications where he works in the Research and Development department. He has been programming in Java since the first Java Development Kit was released. He has written articles for *Dr. Dobb's Journal* and is a frequent presenter at technical conferences.

## SOFTWARE AND INFORMATION LICENSE

The software and information on this diskette (collectively referred to as the "Product") are the property of The McGraw-Hill Companies, Inc. ("McGraw-Hill") and are protected by both United States copyright law and international copyright treaty provision. You must treat this Product just like a book, except that you may copy it into a computer to be used and you may make archival copies of the Products for the sole purpose of backing up our software and protecting your investment from loss.

By saying "just like a book," McGraw-Hill means, for example, that the Product may be used by any number of people and may be freely moved from one computer location to another, so long as there is no possibility of the Product (or any part of the Product) being used at one location or on one computer while it is being used at another. Just as a book cannot be read by two different people in two different places at the same time, neither can the Product be used by two different people in two different places at the same time (unless, of course, McGraw-Hill's rights are being violated).

McGraw-Hill reserves the right to alter or modify the contents of the Product at any time.

This agreement is effective until terminated. The Agreement will terminate automatically without notice if you fail to comply with any provisions of this Agreement. In the event of termination by reason of your breach, you will destroy or erase all copies of the Product installed on any computer system or made for backup purposes and shall expunge the Product from your data storage facilities.

## LIMITED WARRANTY

McGraw-Hill warrants the physical diskette(s) enclosed herein to be free of defects in materials and workmanship for a period of sixty days from the purchase date. If McGraw-Hill receives written notification within the warranty period of defects in materials or workmanship, and such notification is determined by McGraw-Hill to be correct, McGraw-Hill will replace the defective diskette(s). Send request to:

Customer Service
McGraw-Hill
Gahanna Industrial Park
860 Taylor Station Road
Blacklick, OH 43004-9615

The entire and exclusive liability and remedy for breach of this Limited Warranty shall be limited to replacement of defective diskette(s) and shall not include or extend to any claim for or right to cover any other damages, including but not limited to, loss of profit, data, or use of the software, or special, incidental, or consequential damages or other similar claims, even if McGraw-Hill has been specifically advised as to the possibility of such damages. In no event will McGraw-Hill's liability for any damages to you or any other person ever exceed the lower of suggested list price or actual price paid for the license to use the Product, regardless of any form of the claim.

**THE McGRAW-HILL COMPANIES, INC. SPECIFICALLY DISCLAIMS ALL OTHER WARRANTIES, EXPRESSED OR IMPLIED, INCLUDING BUT NOT LIMITED TO, ANY IMPLIED WARRANTY OF MERCHANTABILITY OR FITNESS FOR A PARTICULAR PURPOSE.** Specifically, McGraw-Hill makes no representation or warranty that the Product is fit for any particular purpose and any implied warranty of merchantability is limited to the sixty day duration of the Limited Warranty covering the physical diskette(s) only (and not the software or information) and is otherwise expressly and specifically disclaimed.

This Limited Warranty gives you specific legal rights; you may have others which may vary from state to state. Some states do not allow the exclusion of incidental or consequential damages, or the limitation on how long an implied warranty lasts, so some of the above may not apply to you.

This Agreement constitutes the entire agreement between the parties relating to use of the Product. The terms of any purchase order shall have no effect on the terms of this Agreement. Failure of McGraw-Hill to insist at any time on strict compliance with this Agreement shall not constitute a waiver of any rights under this Agreement. This Agreement shall be construed and governed in accordance with the laws of New York. If any provision of this Agreement is held to be contrary to law, that provision will be enforced to the maximum extent permissible and the remaining provisions will remain in force and effect.